NAPOLEON BONAPARTE AND THE LEGACY OF THE FRENCH REVOLUTION

D1500230

Napoleon Bonaparte and the Legacy of the French Revolution

MARTYN LYONS

St. Martin's Press   New York

First published in the United States of America in 1994

ISBN 0–312–12122–9 (cloth)
ISBN 0–312–12123–7 (paper)

Library of Congress Cataloging-in-Publication Data
Lyons, Martyn.
Napoleon Bonaparte and the Legacy of the French Revolution /
Martyn Lyons.
p. cm.
Includes bibliographical references and index.
ISBN 0–312–12122–9 (cloth) — ISBN 0–312–12123–7 (paper)
1. Napoleon I, Emperor of the French, 1769–1821. 2. France–
–History—Revolution, 1789–1799—Influence. 3. France—History-
–Consulate and Empire, 1799–1815. 4. Napoleonic Wars, 1800–1815.
I. Title.
DC201.L96 1994
944.05'092—dc20   93–44280
                                                                      CIP

Printed in Hong Kong

Without power, ideals cannot be realised;
with power, they rarely survive

Fidel Castro

My wife and I, we have the Emperor in our guts

A distillery worker in Provence, 1822

Contents

List of Plates

List of Maps

List of Figures and Tables

Figures

Tables

List of Documents

Abbreviations

AmHistRev	*American Historical Review*
AM	*Annales du Midi*
AESC	*Annales – économies, sociétés, civilisations*
AhRf	*Annales historiques de la Révolution française*
DN	Tulard, Jean, *Dictionnaire Napoléon* (Paris: Fayard 1987)
FHS	*French Historical Studies*
JMH	*Journal of Modern History*
P&P	*Past and Present*
PSDF	Soboul, A. *et al.*, *Les Pays sous Domination française, 1799–1814* (Paris: Centre de documentation universitaire, 1968)
PCRE	*Proceedings of the Consortium on Revolutionary Europe, 1770–1850*
RE	*Revue économique*
RH	*Revue historique*
Rhmc	*Revue d'histoire moderne et contemporaine*

The Revolutionary Calendar

The revolutionary calendar was introduced by decree in October 1793, and remained officially in operation untion 1806. Every month had thirty days, and the new months were named as follows:

Vendémaire	=	22 September–21 October
Brumaire	=	22 October–20 November
Frimaire	=	21 November–20 December
Nivôse	=	21 December–19 January
Pluviôse	=	20 January–18 February
Ventôse	=	19 February–20 March
Germinal	=	21 March–19 April
Floréal	=	20 April–19 May
Prairial	=	20 May–18 June
Messidor	=	19 June–18 July
Thermidor	=	19 July–17 August
Fructidor	=	18 August–16 September

Year 1 of the Republic began retrospectively on 21 September 1792, in the Gregorian calendar, and

Year 2 was the equivalent of	22 September 1793–21 September 1794
Year 3	22 Sepember 1794–21 September 1795
Year 4	22 Sepember 1795–21 September 1796
Year 5	22 Sepember 1796–21 September 1797
Year 6	22 Sepember 1797–21 September 1798
Year 7	22 Sepember 1798–21 September 1799
Year 8	22 Sepember 1799–21 September 1800
Year 9	22 Sepember 1800–21 September 1801
Year 10	22 Sepember 1801–21 September 1802
Year 11	22 Sepember 1802–21 September 1803
Year 12	22 Sepember 1803–21 September 1804
Year 13	22 Sepember 1804–21 September 1805
Year 14	22 Sepember 1805–21 September 1806

Acknowledgements

The author and publishers are grateful for permission to reproduce copyright material for the following:

Armand Colin Éditeur for diagrams from "Mariages et Naissances sous le Consulat et l'Empire" by A. Armengaud in the journal *Revue d'histoire moderne et contemporaine* (vol. 17, 1970).

Constable Publishers for a map from *Pasquale Paoli: An Enlightened Hero* by Peter Adam Thrasher.

Cambridge University Press for maps from *France under the Directory* by Martyn Lyons.

Hachette for maps copied from *La Révolution, 1770–1880*, by François Furet, © Hachette, 1988.

HarperCollins Publishers, Inc. for a table from *The Napoleonic Revolution* by Robert B. Holtman. Text Copyright © 1967 by Robert B. Holtman. Maps and charts copyright © 1967 by J.P. Lippincott Company. Reprinted by permission.

Librairie Droz SA for a map from *Le Plebiscite des Cent-Jours, 1815* by F. Bluche.

Oxford University Press for a diagram from *Family Breakdown in late 18th Century France: Divorces in Rouen, 1792–1803* (1980) by Roderick Phillips.

Every effort has been made to contact all the copyright-holders, but if any have been inadvertently omitted the publishers will be pleased to make the necessary arrangement at the earliest opportunity.

1   Introduction

Napoleon Bonaparte, for his enemies and admirers, was the "Ogre", the Corsican brigand, the man of destiny, a new Attila, a latter-day Nero, a Prometheus chained to his rock by the mean-spirited British. It has apparently been impossible to discuss Bonaparte without squandering superlatives or attributing diabolical or mythical dimensions to the man. British cartoonists knew him more candidly as "Boney", although later in the Empire, when older and more corpulent, he became "Fleshy".[1] For most commentators, traditional historians and novelists, the personality of Bonaparte dominates a twenty-year period of European and even world history.

In the light of the mass of histories, biographies and Bonapartiana in print since 1815, it seems slightly ridiculous to claim that the Napoleonic era has suffered from neglect. The trouble is that so much writing about the Napoleonic era has focused solely on Bonaparte himself, and sometimes solely on the trivial details of his life and death. This tradition, which the French call "la petite histoire", usually fails to illuminate Bonaparte's historical context and overall historical significance. This is a historical tradition obsessed with such items as his sexual life (did he really love Joséphine? was he impotent? did he have an incestuous relationship with his sister Pauline?[2]), or the contents of his stomach (did the British poison him with arsenic on St Helena?).

To satisfy the curious and clear the decks, let me attempt to dispel a few myths. Napoleon was indeed in love with Joséphine, although he later regarded this as a youthful aberration, and it is very doubtful whether his passion was reciprocated. He was *not* impotent, judging by the son he had with his mistress Eléonore Denuelle, and the son he had with Marie Walewska in 1810, not to mention the unfortunate King of Rome, born to the Empress Marie-Louise in 1811 (Plate 1). He *was* a short man, even by the standards of the day, measuring 5 ft 2 in. in his later years.[3] He was born under the sign of Leo, and his favourite foods were beans and lentils. He was not left-handed. He was not an epileptic. His stomach did contain arsenic, although it had most probably been taken deliberately for medicinal purposes. He died of a stomach cancer, which was probably linked to an ulcer.[4]

My intention in this book is not to retell Bonaparte's life, or to rehearse the battles he fought, which have been thoroughly analysed by military historians far more competent than I am in the matter. The aim of this book is to examine the importance of the Napoleonic period for the social, economic, political and cultural history of France. Since French conquests made the period a formative one for Italy and Germany, too, its impact on Europe as a whole will be assessed in later chapters. The reader should therefore expect neither an exercise in hagiography nor a treatise on the history of warfare. My subject is rather the transformation of post-revolutionary French society and of the French state.

The Napoleonic era straddles two centuries. It must be understood in the context of what went before it and also with reference to what followed. Thus the main theme of this study is Bonaparte's connection with the French Revolution. How far Bonaparte squandered his revolutionary inheritance and how far he strengthened the legacy of the Revolution, are questions which historians will continue to debate. This book will emphasise Napoleon's role as the heir and executor of the French Revolution rather than his role as the liquidator of revolutionary ideals. Napoleon will be discussed as a part of the Revolution, preserving its social gains and consecrating the triumph of the bourgeoisie.

Historians will also continue to argue about the question: when did the French Revolution end? It went on for another hundred years, some respond, although I am not sure if this answer is a genuine attempt to illuminate the history of the nineteenth century, or just a way of avoiding the question. The French Revolution ended for some in 1794 when the revolutionary terror effectively ended, which implies a Robespierrist interpretation of events (when Robespierre fell, it assumes, the Revolution was over). For others, the Revolution ended when Bonaparte seized power in the Coup of Brumaire Year 8 – an interpretation which sees the Napoleonic period as totally reactionary. Perhaps it ended in 1815, when the Bourbon monarchy was definitively restored – an interpretation which locates the entire Napoleonic saga firmly within the history of the French Revolution. Perhaps, this book will suggest, a case can be made for a closing date somewhere in between, such as 1804, when Napoleon was crowned hereditary Emperor, or 1808, when he created the new imperial nobility, or 1812, when the absurd logic of the war pushed the French army to its destruction in the depths of Russia. Every date implies a particular interpretation of the Revolution and of Napoleon. Every attempt at periodisation makes a statement about Napoleon Bonaparte's relationship with his revolutionary legacy.

The nineteenth century must also be kept in mind, to assess how much of Napoleon's work in France and Europe endured after his fall from power. Napoleon's regime must ultimately be contrasted with the Bourbon Restoration, and not only with the First French Republic, if we are to see it in perspective against the backdrop of the revolutionary years. Bonapartism and not just Bonaparte must be considered as a political tradition with a long life ahead of it. Bonaparte was more than an individual, he also represented a political system based on a strong executive, seeking legitimacy in direct consultation with the electorate rather than in cooperation with its elected representatives.

On the whole, then, I intend to steer away from a personal and heroic interpretation of the period. Great individuals only achieve historical significance within the broad historical movements and profound social changes of which they are the unconscious expression. This study will explore developments in French society, taking account of recent research into the social, demographic and economic life of the period.

From this angle the Napoleonic period has perhaps suffered from neglect, particularly in Britain. With the exception of Geoffrey Ellis's excellent monograph on the Continental Blockade in Alsace, very little attention had been paid to the Consulate and Empire by British historians until the very recent work of Forrest and Broers.[5] French historical studies in Britain have deflected attention away from the Napoleonic era – the influence of Richard Cobb has much to answer for in this respect. There are several reasons for this neglect. The attractions of the anarchic tendencies of the French Revolution have little competition during a régime of order and stability. The historian of popular movements, moreover, has little scope for his or her talents in a period of relative prosperity and efficient political repression. Historians who, like some *sans-culottes*, have a visceral hatred of bureaucracy put themselves at a disadvantage when trying to come to terms with the workings of the Consular or Imperial administration.

I do have a debt, however, to a multitude of researchers in the field. This is fully acknowledged in my footnotes but I must express my gratitude to a few colleagues in particular. First, any work like this which tries to incorporate the findings of research in the social history of the Empire is indebted to the work of Louis Bergeron. His work on the notables, economic life and social hierarchies have sparked a new interest in the period. Second, I am grateful to Jean Tulard, whose encyclopaedic *Dictionnaire Napoléon* is a fundamental tool of reference. Third, Stuart Woolf's recently published work and personal interest have greatly encouraged this enterprise. My linguistic range cannot match that of Professor Woolf. It will be clear that my knowledge of sources in English and French is supplemented only by occasional forays into the secondary literature in Italian and Spanish.

Lastly, I should like to thank all past and present students of early modern Europe at the University of New South Wales. The difficult and unexpected questions they have posed over the years have shaped much of what follows; for the answers offered, however, I accept full responsibility.

2 Bonaparte the Jacobin

Eighteenth-century Corsica was a wild, mountainous island inhabited by feuding clans, illiterate shepherds, and a succession of foreign garrisons. Its sparse population of about 120 000 lived mainly on what was produced by its own coastal farmers. Except for a few olives and chestnuts, and a little wine, Corsica's main exports were soldiers and sailors. Like Bonaparte, they sought their fortune outside the island in the armed forces of France, Genoa or Naples. There were few roads and no industry but an abundance of clerics. According to the English traveller Boswell, mid-century Corsica had no less than sixty-five convents of friars.[1] Kinship networks dominated social and political life. They demanded absolute loyalty from relatives and clients, for whom they operated as sources of patronage and huge mutual aid societies. Although occupying forces might control the ports, real power in the interior tended to lie with local groups of brothers or cousins. In the hereditary *vendetta*, they exacted a brutal vengeance against their enemies, the sons of their enemies, and the sons of their enemies' sons.

There was, however, another side of eighteenth-century Corsica – an enlightened and progressive side. For a short period in the 1750s and 1760s, Corsica was hailed as an exciting laboratory of enlightened legislation. The Genoese Republic had ruled Corsica for 400 years, exploiting the *vendetta* to turn clan against clan, in a classic divide-and-rule strategy.[2] In 1756, however, an insurrection led by Pasquale Paoli drove the Genoese from all their strongholds, except for that of the capital, Bastia. From his headquarters in Corte, in the interior, Paoli began to introduce a series of enlightened reforms. He reduced taxation, planned to build a fleet and inaugurated a university. He encouraged trade and agriculture. He tried to end the *vendetta* and even established a Constitution, but in deference to Corsica's clan structure Paoli only gave the vote to heads of families.[3] In all this, he kept the support of Corsica's fiercely patriotic clergy. For Jean-Jacques Rousseau, and other enthusiasts of enlightened reforms, Paoli's Corsica seemed an ideal arena in which to test the powers of reason. It was an old world, but a simple and an unspoilt one, where virtue was still theoretically attainable. Corsica appeared uncontaminated by the sophistication and corruption of modernity. These two contradictory faces of Corsica were to reappear later in the career of Napoleon Bonaparte. On the one hand, there was his youthful advocacy of Rousseauism and of egalitarian ideas, followed by the enlightened and moderate rationalism of the Consulate. On the other hand, blood ties were strong in the Bonaparte family. Their influence was to envelop all Europe as, at the height of Empire, the clan and its clients appropriated all the foreign thrones within their grasp.

Napoleon Bonaparte was a member of a large family from Ajaccio, on the west coast. He was the second surviving son of a family of eleven children, of whom three died in infancy. A large family, which could establish multiple connections and alliances by marriage, was a sign of wealth and power (Figure 2.1). Napoleon's father was a lawyer, comfortably well-off, at least by Corsican standards.[4]

Bonaparte came to personify the idea of careers open to talent and the new prospects for social advancement available in post-revolutionary society. Bonaparte himself, however, did not rise to fame from the humblest of social origins. His family belonged to the Corsican nobility, owning three houses, a mill, a small estate and some vineyards. The family warmly supported Paoli's defence of Corsican independence and Napoleon's father Carlo acted as Paoli's secretary in Corte.

The demise of Genoa created a problem for the European powers. In the age of sail, Corsica had some strategic significance and the island was too important and too vulnerable to be left to its own devices (Map 2.1). In 1768, France reacted to Genoese impotence by invading Corsica and annexing it to the Bourbon crown. Paoli was forced into exile, where he was welcomed as the darling and the martyr of the enlightenment. Bonaparte, born in Ajaccio in 1769, was therefore born on French soil and was not a foreigner to France as has sometimes been alleged.

The fortunes of the Bonaparte family now depended on Corsica's new French masters. For the ambitious and talented Corsica offered little scope and Carlo made plans to send his sons to the mainland. He followed a tradition in poorer noble families by sending Joseph, his eldest son, into the Church, and Napoleon, his second son, into the army. Both began their French education at the Oratorian college at Autun (Joseph was to go on to study law in Pisa), but

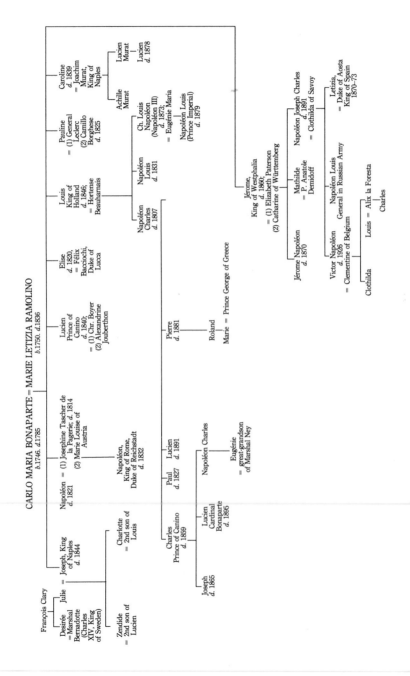

Figure 2.1 The Bonaparte Family Tree

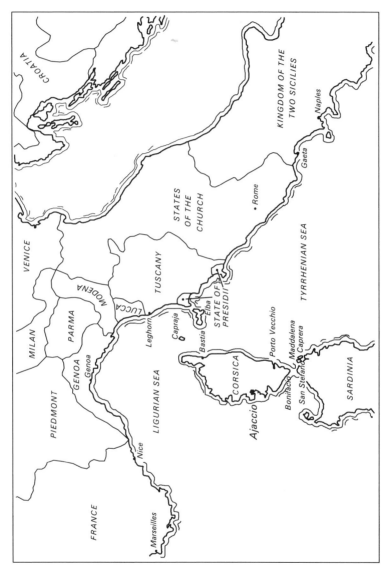

Map 2.1   Corsica and its Neighbours in the Eighteenth Century

Napoleon soon moved on to military school, supported by a royal scholarship. His claims to nobility were officially verified, in order to qualify for bursaries offered to impoverished aristocrats. He was an expensive investment; like many other junior officers whose resources were limited, he was to take long periods of leave to return home and look after the family's affairs.

His Corsican background and accent perhaps made him an outsider. Southerners were in a minority in the ranks of the French army, which drew most recruits from the northern and eastern provinces.[5] Men from the Midi, for one thing, tended to be too short for the height requirements – Bonaparte stood about 1.48 metres (4 ft 10 in.) in 1784, when he was 15 years old.[6] His chosen branch was the artillery, where promotion prospects were good. In the technical branches of the army, where mathematical and engineering skills were essential, professionalism could be rewarded, even in the Old Régime army, where aristocratic birth and connections were very important. In 1784, Bonaparte became the first Corsican to pass through the Ecole Militaire.[7]

At military school in Brienne, Bonaparte filled his free time studying and writing the history of Corsica. Increasingly, however, his career was directed towards France. At some point, the family gave itself French names: Buonaparte became Bonaparte, Giuseppe became Joseph, and their younger sister Maria-Annonciata was to be known more fashionably as Caroline. The beginnings of the Revolution in France opened up new opportunities both for Corsica and the Bonapartes, and brought to an end three tedious years spent by Napoleon in French garrisons.

Corsican patriots saw that a change of government in Paris created a favourable situation for the return of the Corsican exiles, led by the elder statesman of the independence struggle, Pasquale Paoli. The campaign for the return of Paoli was led by Saliceti, a lawyer and future Jacobin, who had been elected to represent the Third Estate of Corsica at the meeting of Estates-General in Versailles. In 1790, Saliceti prompted the National Constituent Assembly to make Corsica an integral part of the French state – the island was to be no longer a colony with a special governor. Before long, Paoli returned in triumph, and was welcomed in Ajaccio by Joseph Bonaparte representing the town's new revolutionary administration. Since his father's death in 1788 Joseph was the head of the family and played an important role in Corsican politics along with Saliceti, until 1793.

In 1792, Napoleon was on leave from France. He was elected lieutenant-colonel of a battalion of Ajaccio volunteers – but only after he had surrounded the church of San Francesco, where the voting took place, with his supporters, armed with pistols and daggers. He was to show an equally military contempt for the electoral process, when he seized power in France in Brumaire Year 8 (November 1799). His battalion quickly became notorious, being engaged in a series of skirmishes against local supporters of the non-juring priests, who refused to accept the new revolutionary Civil Constitution of the Clergy.[8] Bonaparte won few friends in this Ajaccio affair. He demonstrated not only his anticlericalism but also his inexperience, and a high-handed attitude towards the civilian authorities. Paoli called him a *ragazzone inesperto* – a big inexperienced boy.[9] On Joseph's advice, he soon sailed for France.

The Bonapartes maintained their political base and source of influence when their ally, Saliceti, was elected for what was now the French department of Corsica to the National Convention. The rise of the Jacobins in Paris, however, had serious repercussions in Corsica. Pasquale Paoli's reputation as a statesman and his credentials as a patriot made his authority supreme. Saliceti and the Bonapartes were his sincere supporters. This common front could be maintained as long as Paoli's cause coincided with their support for revolutionary France.

Events in France created tensions within this coalition of Corsicans. Food shortages, inflation and the dismal progress of the war undermined support for moderate leaders. Support grew for the ideas of the Mountain, a group of left-wing members of the National Convention, who urged stronger measures to control the economy and repress sedition. At the beginning of June 1793, the Montagnards expelled the Girondin deputies from the National Convention and seized power. This sudden change of government in Paris provoked a howl of outrage in provincial centres. The Revolution appeared to have fallen into the hands of the unruly Parisian crowd, who had intimidated the legal representatives of the nation into expelling the Girondins. The Revolution, it was argued, was no longer "free"; it had been confiscated by the *sans-culotte* agitators of the capital. Local interests prepared to resist the Montagnard coup. A series of local power struggles divided Jacobins and "federalists" in cities like Bordeaux, Lyon, Marseilles and Toulon which now went over to the anti-Jacobin rebellion.

These developments had repercussions in Corsica. Divisions began to appear within the patriot camp. Some Paolists did not appreciate the eagerness with which Corsican Jacobins, like Saliceti and the Bonapartes, purchased *biens nationaux*, ecclesiastical property which was nationalised and auctioned by the Revolution.[10] The relationship between Paoli, Corsica's revered hero and patriot, and the younger generation of ambitious politicians came under increasing strain. As the course of the French Revolution brought more radical policies in its wake, Paoli appeared to be out of sympathy with these new directions. If the Bonapartes ever had to choose between Paoli and France, their historic loyalty to Paoli could be compromised. The events of 1793 forced them to make just such a choice. Paoli was a moderate in the terms of 1793 – he was more sympathetic to the Catholic clergy than many of his younger supporters and he opposed Parisian Jacobinism.

As a result, Saliceti and the Bonapartes broke with him in 1793. His leadership was under attack. Lucien Bonaparte spoke against Paoli in the Jacobin clubs of the Midi, accusing him of harbouring pro-English sympathies and aspirations to a personal dictatorship in Corsica.[11] Joseph and Napoleon were prepared to organise a rising in Ajaccio against him. These challenges, however, were unsuccessful: Paoli still had plenty of support in the interior and he took control in Ajaccio. The Bonapartes paid for this defeat. The family was forced to leave for Marseilles, their property was attacked and their house ransacked.[12] Soon, in 1794, Paoli was to collaborate with the Royal Navy to set up an Anglo-Corsican kingdom. Hundreds more francophile Republicans from Corsica's port cities then left the island.

In the summer of 1793, the French Republic was threatened on all sides. In the west, resistance against conscription had generated a widespread peasant revolt. In the Vendée and surrounding departments, a brutal guerrilla war was to drain the strength of the republican army for years to come. France was invaded in the north by the combined forces of the allied coalition. She was threatened in the east by the army of the kingdom of Savoy, and in the Pyrenees the armies of the "tyrant of Castile" stood on French soil. In the south, the federalist revolt controlled Bordeaux, Lyon and Marseilles. An army under General Carteaux was entrusted with the task of crushing the rebellion in the Midi. The Revolution was fighting for its life. Suppression of the revolts was vital, not only to the Montagnards in the Convention but also to the unity of the country as a whole, and to the government's ability to defend the Revolution against foreign invasion. The repression of the federalist revolts was fierce, but it provided Napoleon Bonaparte with a chance for promotion.

In Marseilles, the mercantile élite saw Jacobin extremism as a danger to international trade. They feared the imposition of forced loans and the introduction of maximum price controls, which would discourage foreign cargo ships from entering French ports. The rebels arrested leading local Jacobins and forced the Convention's representatives, Bayle and Boisset, to flee to Montélimar. Carteaux's army, however, cut off the rebels' supply routes and at the end of August 1793 he entered Marseilles to end the revolt. A total of 289 death sentences were issued, but the rank and file of the federalist revolt were largely spared. The repression fell most heavily on the wealthier merchants, the city's traditionally moderate leaders.[13] Many federalists escaped to Toulon.

The Republic's next task in the Midi was to win the siege of Toulon. Toulon was the arsenal and chief naval base for the Mediterranean fleet – the "Kronstadt of the French Revolution". In July, the opponents of Jacobinism in Toulon had closed the Jacobin club and hanged twenty-four local Jacobins.[14] In defiance of Paris and the Revolution, Toulon proclaimed its allegiance to Louis XVIII. The full consequences of the revolt now became apparent. Toulon was caught in a dilemma. Opposed by an advancing Republican army on one side, and a British naval blockade on the other, the city faced possible starvation. On 27–28 August 1793, Toulon went over to the English – a major blow for the French Republic.

A three-month siege followed, during which Carteaux was replaced by General Dugommier and Saliceti gave Bonaparte command of the artillery. By mid-December, Bonaparte had been instrumental in ending the siege. The English evacuated the city and thousands tried to escape the forces of the National Convention. Many drowned in the port, in their desperate flight from the vengeance of the Republic. Toulon was renamed Port-la-Montagne and 800 federalist rebels were shot. As for Bonaparte, his success in finishing the siege earned him promotion to brigadier-general. Bonaparte was at this stage a strong partisan of the revolutionary government. In 1793, he published a pamphlet, *Le Souper de Beaucaire*, in support of the Mountain.[15]

Bonaparte had now allied himself closely with local Jacobins who included the Conventionnel Saliceti and also Augustin Robespierre, younger brother of Maximilien. In Nice, they planned a further offensive against the Piedmontese which resulted in the capture of the town of Oneglia. In Germinal, Augustin Robespierre mentioned Bonaparte favourably in a despatch from Nice to his brother Maximilien:

I add to the names of patriots I have already mentioned citizen Buonaparte, general in command of artillery, a man of transcendent merit. He is Corsican, and brings me the simple guarantee of a man of that country who resisted the blandishments of Paoli, and whose property has been destroyed by that traitor.[16]

These Jacobin associations were omitted in later versions of the Napoleonic myth. Bonaparte was subsequently represented as a young romantic hero, but his political connections during the Jacobin period were carefully obscured. Any association with Robespierre could discredit him – it led in fact to his brief arrest in the fort of Antibes after the Robespierrists were overthrown on 9 Thermidor Year 2.

Bonaparte was now posted to an infantry regiment in the Vendée, in the west, where an atrocious guerrilla war was raging between the republican forces and the local peasantry, fighting under royalist and clerical banners. Bonaparte preferred to take leave rather than obey. He had no intention of abandoning the artillery for the infantry, and perhaps he also feared that the Vendean war was a graveyard of military reputations. He stayed on leave in Paris, short of money, seeking a breakthrough which would allow the government to give him a better position.

In Vendémiaire Year 4, the Republic called on him again. The National Convention was no more. It had dismantled the economic controls of the Jacobin Terror, which led to astronomic price rises during famine conditions. It had crushed the last spasms of the *sans-culotte* movement in Paris. It had tried to restore parliamentary procedures, had drawn up a new Constitution which terminated its own existence, and handed power to a new régime, the Directory. The Directory thus inherited galloping inflation, frightening levels of mortality and completely untried political machinery.[17]

The members of the thermidorean Convention, however, had not bowed out completely. They introduced a law which preserved two-thirds of the seats in the new legislature for members of the old Convention. Continuity, they believed, would be preserved, but many saw the law of the two-thirds as a selfish attempt by the Conventionnels to perpetuate themselves in power for as long as possible. The greatest danger came from the Right; in Vendémiaire, the constitutional royalists, angered by the law of the two-thirds, organised an unsuccessful rising in Paris.[18]

Bonaparte played a contributing role to the defeat of the insurrection which was limited to the residential areas of the right bank, especially near the Stock Exchange. It was here, in the bourgeois sections of Paris, that support for constitutional royalism was strongest, and where the anti-Jacobin street gangs, known as the *jeunesse dorée*, had their bases. The government's artillery successfully beat off attacks from the dissident sections. Bonaparte's personal role in the affair has often been exaggerated. Barras, in charge of the Convention's forces, welcomed Bonaparte's assistance, but Bonaparte was never in command or even second-in-command of them. The cliché that Bonaparte dispersed the royalists with the legendary "whiff of grapeshot" is also misleading. There was bloody fighting around the rue St Honoré and the church of St Roch, and there were hundreds of casualties on both sides.

Bonaparte was now a full general at the age of 26 and a grateful protégé of Barras, the Director who had organised the defeat of the Vendémiaire rising. When Barras relinquished his military responsibilities, Bonaparte became commander of the Army of the Interior. Barras did much more than this for Bonaparte. He introduced him to his own ex-mistress, Joséphine de Beauharnais, whom Bonaparte married in 1796. Then Barras launched Bonaparte on his political and at the same time on his European career: he appointed him to command the army of Italy. Before considering the impact of the Italian campaign, however, we must pause to examine the problems of the Directory and its relations with its own generals.

3 Bonaparte the Republican

The French Revolution had always been wary of its generals. Ever since the emigration of many royalist army officers between 1789 and 1791, the political loyalties of France's military leadership were closely scrutinised. The Republic attempted to make the army subservient to the politicians but during the régime of the Directory (1795–9), Bonaparte established a wide sphere of independence for himself. He commanded the army of Italy as a loyal republican but his success enhanced his own reputation rather than that of the ailing Directory. The Italian campaign did not only make Bonaparte an illustrious commander, it also transformed him into a figure of political importance in European affairs.

There were very good reasons why the Revolution had tried to keep its generals under close surveillance. Their personal ambitions had frequently threatened to undermine political stability. Lafayette had defected to the Prussians after the Revolution of 10 August 1792, taking twenty-two members of his general staff with him. Then, in 1793, General Dumouriez had defected to the Austrians after failing to launch a military coup against Paris. Generals who failed to deliver the victories the Republic needed were dismissed and could be accused of treason.

The best guarantee against military dictatorship was to politicise the troops themselves. *Sans-culotte* recruits were not blindly obedient foot soldiers; they were quick to criticise and denounce the deficiencies of their commanders. General Dillon had even been shot by his own troops during a retreat near Lille in 1792. Another method of maintaining civilian control over the army was to appoint civilian *commissaires des guerres* (war commissars) to the armies, who could report disloyalty and incompetence to Paris. In Italy, however, Bonaparte's *commissaires* were his allies. They included his Corsican colleague, Saliceti.

The Republican army offered rapid promotion to talented and ambitious individuals. Deaths, emigration and dismissals opened up new avenues for social advancement. Many soldiers, besides Bonaparte himself, rose to high positions at a comparatively young age, in a sphere where the principle of the career open to talent seemed to be a spectacular reality. Hoche, for example, son of an ostler, was a general at the age of 26, and Augereau, the son of a fruiterer, emerged from humble origins to become a general in his thirties.[1] The Directory tried to keep its generals at arm's length. Augereau, for example, was twice a candidate for election as a Director, but was twice unsuccessful. In the Year 5, however, the army made a decisive intervention in domestic politics. The elections of Fructidor Year 5 (1797) produced the result that the republican government most feared: a royalist majority was returned. Afraid for the stability of the regime, the Directory annulled the elections in forty-nine departments and called in Augereau's forces to disperse the deputies. On the night of 17 Fructidor, troops of the 17th division occupied the legislative chambers and arrested royalist sympathisers. Fifty-three deputies became victims of the "dry guillotine" – in other words, they were deported. The survival of the Republic was guaranteed, but at a huge price. The Constitution of the Year 3 had been violated, the electoral process devalued, and the régime was now indebted to the army.[2] Bonaparte was to be the ultimate beneficiary of the process of change set in motion by the coup of Fructidor. The constitution was increasingly discredited and the Directory was becoming dangerously dependent on its generals. This dependency was exploited by Bonaparte in the brilliant Italian campaign of 1796–7.

Italy was a patchwork of tiny states, divided by long-standing municipal rivalries and exploited for centuries as a battleground for the great European powers (Map 3.1). The Kingdom of Sardinia, which ruled over Piedmont from its capital in Turin, guarded the Alpine passes. The Milanais was a dominion of the Austrian Habsburgs and fossilised oligarchies ruled the ancient republics of Genoa and Venice. Genoa had lost its control over Corsica; Venice held on to its possessions along the Dalmatian coast and the Ionian Islands. Austria was the dominant power in the Italian peninsula which it defended from the northern system of fortresses, known as the Quadrilateral, and consisting of Mantua, Verona, Peschiera and Legnago. Austrian influence was strong south of the river Po in the miniature duchies of Parma, Piacenza and Modena, as well as in Tuscany. The Papal States straddled the peninsula from Rome in the west to the port of Ancona in the east, including the Papal Legations of Bologna, Ferrara, Ravenna and Forlì. In the south, the Neapolitan Bourbons gave the British fleet access to the harbours of the Kingdom of the Two Sicilies.

In Italy, therefore, France could strike at the power of its arch enemy, Austria, as well as limiting British Mediterranean sea power.

Map 3.1 Italy on the Eve of the Revolutionary Wars

The valuables and art treasures stored in the churches and courts of
Italy also attracted a régime which still faced acute financial difficulties. Bonaparte urged the government to authorise an advance on
Turin and then the Milanais, to separate the Sardinian and Austrian
forces. The Directory, he argued in a note of 29 Nivose Year 4, should
give its commander (himself, he hoped) plenty of scope (*une grande
latitude*), because speed was of the essence, and because a general
who sent a despatch to Paris from Savona, on the Genoese coast,
would have to wait a month to receive a reply.[3]

Bonaparte was persuasive, and in March 1796 he was appointed to lead the army of Italy, only 50 000 strong. The Directory's efforts, however, were focused principally on the Rhine and the government did not envisage the degree of commitment to the Italian sphere which followed. Bonaparte married Joséphine and arrived in Nice. According to Masséna, his generals found him a very unimposing figure, and did not know what to make of the clumsy new arrival who insisted on showing everybody his wife's portrait.[4] He was a Corsican and had been an associate of terrorists. He had helped to clear the streets of Paris of royalists in Vendémiaire, but that was hardly comparable to the experience of real warfare. Doubters were soon to be disabused. On 27 March, he made a proclamation to his ill-fed troops, which was later glamorised on St Helena when the memoirs and the myth of Napoleon were carefully constructed. "Soldiers, you are naked and hungry", he later claimed to have said to them continuing:

> The government owes you much, but can give you nothing. I am about to lead you into the world's most fertile plains. Rich provinces and great cities will be in your power, and in them you will find honour, glory, and riches. Soldiers of Italy, why should you want for courage and steadfastness?[5]

The plains of Lombardy beckoned, like a promised land offering milk and honey to every French soldier who would follow him. What Bonaparte actually told his troops, however, and what he "remembered" having told them more than twenty years later were not necessarily the same thing. He may have regretted this invitation to indiscriminate pillage, if he ever actually uttered it. For he was soon executing looters and enforcing his own monopoly of Italian plunder.

Bonaparte fulfilled his promise. He divided the forces of his enemies and defeated the Sardinians in the series of engagements known as the Battle of Mondovi. The confrontation at Lodi produced a propaganda painting which fuelled the Napoleonic legend (see Chapter 13). An armistice was signed with Sardinia at Cherasco and the French pressed on to Milan, which they occupied in May 1796. French success in both Piedmont and Lombardy was aided by the activities of Italian Jacobins, who saw in the French a hope for liberal government and progress towards a unified Italy. Their hopes, as we shall see, were to be disappointed, but for a time it suited the French to encourage them. In Milan, Bonaparte sponsored the production of a republican newspaper, the *Courier of the Army of Italy*, edited by Jullien, the son of a deputy in the National Convention.[6] The Austrians, however, were not defeated; they had withdrawn to their defences in the Quadrilateral. The Directory ordered Bonaparte to advance no further against Austria, but to concentrate on the subordination and plunder of central Italy. But Bonaparte was soon in a position to determine his own policy.

The mere threat of a French advance was usually enough to force the Italian states into submission. They were compelled to pay dearly for their neutrality. Parma paid an indemnity of 2 million lire, and Modena 7.5 million lire. The Papal Legations were occupied by the French and according to the Treaty of Tolentino, signed in Ventôse Year 5, the Pope paid a "tribute" to France of 21 million lire and 100 works of art. In addition, he agreed to abandon his claims to Avignon and to exclude British shipping from his harbours. Lucca paid a ransom to keep French forces from entering its territory, and Tuscany did not escape either. The French took the port of Livorno, which deprived Britain of a naval base, and opened up the possibility of the French reconquest of Corsica.[7]

Bonaparte paid his troops in cash instead of in *assignats*, the discredited paper currency of the Revolution, which helped to establish his personal control over the army of Italy. Otherwise, the conduct of the campaign thus far was entirely consistent with the aims of the Directory in Paris. He was careful to behave as a loyal servant of the Republic. After Cherasco, he laid the captured flags of the enemy before the Republican government. He willingly complied with the government's explicit directives to seek out valuable art treasures. The transport of such works to Paris would "repair the ravages of vandalism" during the Revolution, and ensure France's rightful "supremacy in art". He sent Correggios from Piacenza, and booty from Our Lady of Loretto, which the Directory had particularly coveted.[8] By the end of 1796, 46 million francs had been mulcted from Italy, not to mention priceless art works. Bonaparte himself pocketed 3 million francs, much of which was distributed to members of his large and needy family network.[9]

Paris approved of all this, but the creation of an independent Cispadane Republic (= south of the river Po), comprising Modena and the Legations, was not on the government's agenda. Formed in Reggio (Emilia) in January 1797, the Cispadane adopted the Italian version of the tricolour, the red, white and green which were to become the national colours. The Directory, however, was reluctant to enter into the long-term commitment of supporting sister or satellite Republics. Italy, in the Directory's thinking, could help to finance the war and provide bargaining counters when the Rhine frontier was to be negotiated. An independent Bonapartist policy, however, was emerging, over which Paris had little control.[10] The French became even more deeply embroiled in Italy when the Cisalpine Republic was created, uniting the Cispadane with Lombardy and Bergamo, with its capital in Milan.

The French *biennio* of 1796–7 was a formative period in Italian history. It raised hopes of liberalism and moves towards unification, only to disillusion the Jacobins of northern Italy. At the same time, it gave a foretaste of what French administration was to mean for the rest of Europe in the fifteen years to come. The Cisalpine Republic's constitution was modelled on that of the French Republic, with a bicameral legislature and a limited franchise, although Bonaparte retained supreme power. It had its own army, the Italian legion. The Republic united $3\frac{1}{2}$ million Italians under a single government which, although it was not truly independent, was far preferable in the eyes of Italian patriots to Austrian rule. It seemed an advance on the municipal rivalries which had eternally confused and divided the Italian political scene. A progressive intellectual élite gathered in Milan, strengthened by the arrival of patriotic exiles from Venice or Turin.[11]

Civil marriage was introduced and religious orders were secularised. Church lands were nationalised and sold, in the manner in which the *biens nationaux* had been exploited in France. In Bologna, the property of thirty-one religious corporations was sold.[12] In Rome, property of the hospitals, the Jesuits and of vacant benefices was taken by the French or sold to meet immediate financial needs. Many rich properties were quickly swallowed up by army contractors to whom the French Republic was heavily indebted for the war effort. Others were bought by speculators, administrators, professional men and members of the lower clergy. In the Papal States, there were no artisans or peasants among land purchasers, but many members of the landowning or commercial bourgeoisie were able to buy outright the property they had leased from the Church.[13] Bonaparte thus exported the legislation of the French Revolution to pay the army's debts and to enlist the support of middle-class Italian landowners.

French support for Italian Jacobins, however, was mitigated by strategic imperatives. The Jacobins had been useful as thorns in the side of Austrian rule in Lombardy, but once in power Bonaparte relied on conservative rather than radical interests. He reported to the Directory that there were three political parties in Lombardy, the first pro-French, the second impatient for freedom and the third pro-Austrian. "The first," he explained, "I support and encourage, the second I restrain, the third I suppress."[14] He was more responsive to the wealthy aristocratic senators of Bologna than to the democratically minded patriots of Milan. Denis Richet has argued that Bonaparte identified in these enlightened patricians the future collaborators of his Empire. He saw in them the instruments of a French-led reform movement which would isolate the Jacobins and "anarchists".[15]

The French made themselves the focus of Jacobin aspirations in Italy, only in order to subordinate those aspirations to French needs. The armistice of Cherasco with the Sardinians, for example, effectively abandoned the Piedmontese Jacobins to the Turin government. The cynical treatment of Venice was to alienate Jacobin sympathies further. The conquerors, in their turn, tended to treat Italian Jacobins with condescension. Chauvinistic French administrators placed little faith in the capacity of priest-ridden Italians to benefit from *liberté* and the Rights of Man. Bonaparte's aide-de-camp Sulkowski found the Italians cunning, surly and brainwashed by their papist clergy. When he saw people in Bologna wearing tricolour rosettes, he assumed the Pope must have given them a secret order to appear friendly to the French.[16] For such writers, there seemed no point in extending the benefits of the French Revolution to those who were not ready to appreciate them. Bonaparte offered fraternal assistance to fellow republicans but French military interests remained paramount, and the French sense of superiority in all things revolutionary was undiminished.

There was little time for peaceful progress under French rule during the *biennio* of 1796–7. Italy was always a land under military occupation. French exactions and secularising policies met resistance. Some anti-French resistance came from extreme republicans, some from the endemic banditry of the *mezzogiorno*, while elsewhere it was clerically inspired. There was a rising in Pavia in 1797, to which Bonaparte responded by allowing French troops free rein there for twenty-four hours, as a lesson to all Italians.[17] In Rome, the flight of the Pope and his court removed the city's principal employer and source of income. Requisitioning, the sale of ecclesiastical property and a reduction in the number of religious holidays did not endear the populace to the

French occupation. When Jews were seen sporting the tricolour in the Trastevere suburb, anti-French revolts ensued.[18] In the Papal States, Cardinal Fabrizio Ruffo led guerrilla bands of *sanfedisti* (defenders of the holy faith) against the French. After the French were driven out in 1799, Jacobins and Jews would be massacred when reaction again seized hold of the peninsula. Many areas of Italy were too disturbed for French administration land sales to come into effect. Enough had been attempted, however, to sketch some of the advantages and problems of French rule, and thoroughly to antagonise the chief long-term victim of Bonaparte's advance: the Habsburg Empire.

The Austrians had retreated to the Quadrilateral and the French army, weakened by exhaustion and casualties, took months to beat them back. Bonaparte's short interlude with Joséphine in Brescia did not help to speed up military operations. Eventually, French victories at Arcole and Rivoli in the winter of 1796–7 forced the Austrians to abandon the fortress of Mantua (Plate 3). Having dislodged the Austrians from their stronghold, Bonaparte marched into the Tyrol, disobeying instructions once again, and forced an armistice at Leoben, only eighty miles from Vienna, on 29 Germinal Year 5. The terms of the armistice were to be consolidated in the Treaty of Campoformio in the Year 6.

In these diplomatic negotiations, Bonaparte asserted his own version of French foreign policy and presented the outcome to the Directory as a *fait accompli*. He forced the Austrians to accept his Cisalpine Republic, offering them compensation in Venice. In Paris, the Director Reubell was appalled. Bonaparte had committed France too deeply in Italy and the all-important problem of the Rhineland had been shelved, pending a projected Congress at Rastadt. Many interpreted the French failure to insist on territorial security in Germany as a feeble surrender to Austria.

This was hardly the view that the Austrians themselves took of Campoformio. Vienna had lost Belgium, Lombardy, the Papal Legations and Mantua. These severe losses left the Habsburgs powerless to prevent the spread of Republicanism in the Italian peninsula. On the one hand, the partition of Venice provided some consolation for these disasters. It could satisfy the longing of the eighteenth-century Habsburgs to develop their sea power. On the other hand, Austria could not accept the loss of Lombardy and of her dominant influence in Italy as a permanent solution. Bonaparte's orientation of French policy towards a new Mediterranean dimension condemned the whole of Europe to a continuation of the war.

Campoformio could not be consummated without first annexing the Most Serene Republic of Venice. Minor skirmishes against the French near Verona were now used as a pretext for invasion and punitive looting. The Venetian fleet was commandeered to send an expedition to occupy Corfu, and its impressive arsenal could prove an asset in projected conquests of Malta or Egypt. Italian Jacobins felt betrayed by the partition of Venice between France and Austria. In 1793, the French Constitution had offered help for the liberation of the oppressed peoples of Europe. Now, the Milanese Jacobins realised that Venice was not to be absorbed into a great Italian Republic. Instead, it was sacrificed to French greed and diplomatic security.

Campoformio was a triumph for Bonaparte. The Directory, divided within itself, could not argue with a general who delivered such spectacular victories and war booty. They reluctantly accepted his decisions: the bronze horses of San Marco were exhibited in Paris, and Vernet's painting dramatising the engagement at Arcole was copied for an eager public. The Directory had failed to secure peace with England or an alliance with Prussia, and peace on Bonaparte's terms was popular in France. It was a fragile and a transient peace but it brought the First Coalition against France to an end. It made Bonaparte a continental statesman as well as a military commander and, for him, this constituted a double victory: that of the French over the Austrians, and that of Bonaparte over the civilian government.

The Directory's attempts to weaken or defeat Britain had proved abortive. An expedition had left Brest in 1796 to invade Ireland, but bad weather and indifferent navigation had prevented it from reaching its destination. A further plan to send a fleet across the English Channel was judged too risky. Attention shifted to Egypt, where France could inhibit British trade and sea power, and cut the route to India. Egypt could also perhaps provide France with cotton, rice and coffee in compensation for her lost Caribbean possessions. Egypt was dominated by the warrior élite of Mamelukes, 50 000-strong, originally imported by the Turks from the Caucasus. If the expedition could turn the population against the Mamelukes, the Ottoman Empire might be enticed into an alliance.[19]

The Egyptian expedition offered Bonaparte further scope for his talents and inevitably revived the coalition against France. The Directory, it is often thought, was happy to get rid of Bonaparte, whose success and personal ambitions were a political embarrassment. But this was hardly a good reason for risking an experienced army so far afield, across seas patrolled by the Royal Navy. It is more likely that Bonaparte wanted to put distance between himself and the Directory. In Egypt he would be free of political supervision and the attention of civilian war commissars. There he could pose as a modern Alexander and become a statesman on a grand intercontinental scale.

The Egypt expedition was a vast intellectual enterprise as well as a military adventure. In order to further France's civilising mission, the army was accompanied by a throng of distinguished *savants*. They included Monge and Berthollet the chemists, Fourier the geometrician, students from the new Ecole Polytechnique, naturalists, antiquarians, historians and geologists. All in all, a contingent of 167 intellectuals landed in Alexandria.[20] They were to set up the Institute of Cairo and spread science and enlightenment amongst the native population. Ironically enough, the Institute met in the premises of the *bey*'s former harem, to ponder ways to clarify the waters of the Nile, to manufacture gunpowder in Egypt, and begin the development of viticulture.[21] Some scientists had refused to join the party: Laplace and Cuvier, for example, foresaw no benefit to themselves in the enterprise. This did not deter the the scientific commission. Egypt was a laboratory where a new partnership between goverment and science was to be tested. Monge studied the optics of the mirage and Berthollet investigated the possibilities of indigo production. They took printing presses with Greek and Arabic characters. Their scientific mission was both to collect knowledge of the east and disseminate the benefits of French civilisation. Here in the deserts of Egypt, they glimpsed the mirage of what *Le Clef des Cabinets des Souverains* called "the imposing alliance of philosophy and bayonets".

The Egypt expedition has been seen as the first example of modern orientalism, a European encounter with the Islamic east, in which the abilities of scholars and intellectuals were harnessed for an imperialist purpose (Document 3.1).[22] To "know" Egypt, to record it, draw its pyramids, study its agriculture and social arrangements were as much expressions of colonial domination as the presence of the French army. To chart the land and define its resources were synonymous with subordinating it and making it into an extension of French learning. The twenty-three volumes of the *Description de l'Egypte*, published between 1809–1828, were perhaps the most lasting result of the Egypt expedition, and an important contribution to the subjugation of the east by western imperialism.

DOCUMENT 3.1   BONAPARTE'S POLICY IN EGYPT

Proclamation to the army of Egypt issued on board L'Orient, *4 Messidor Year 6 (22 June 1798):*

Soldiers!

You are about to undertake a conquest which will have incalculable consequences for civilisation and world trade.

You will strike the most direct and painful blow possible against England, a foretaste of the death-blow which awaits her.

The Mameluke *beys*, who give English commerce their exclusive protection, who have poured insults on our merchants and who tyrannise the unfortunate inhabitants of the Nile, will soon exist no more.

The peoples with whom we are going to live are Mahometans; the first article of their faith is this: "There is no other God but God, and Mahomet is his prophet."

Do not contradict them. Behave towards them as we dealt with the Jews, or with the Italians. Respect their *muftis* and their *imams*, as you have respected rabbis and bishops.

Be tolerant towards the ceremonies prescribed by the Koran, as you were tolerant to the convents, the synagogues, the religion of Moses and of Jesus Christ.

The Roman legions protected all religions. Here you will encounter ways which are different from those of Europe. You must get accustomed to them.

The peoples whose land we are entering treat women differently from us; but in all countries, one thing is universal: rape is a monstrosity.

Only very few men ever get rich by looting. It dishonours us, destroys our resources and makes us the enemies of people we need to keep as our friends.

The first town where we shall arrive was built by Alexander. At every step, we will find memories worthy of emulation by Frenchmen.

Bonaparte

(Napoleon, *Correspondance*, vol.4, no.2710, pp.256–7)

The Battle of the Nile, on 1 August 1798, in which Nelson's fleet finally located the French at anchor in Aboukir Bay, and destroyed it, made lasting success in Egypt impossible. Nevertheless, Bonaparte set about defeating the Mamelukes and attempting, by his benevolent administration, to win Moslem cooperation. "We are the friends of true Moslems" he told the people of Alexandria and he insisted that the French should respect Islamic conventions.[23] Bonaparte discussed the Koran with Islamic leaders, and General Menou even converted to Islam.[24] Bonaparte's declarations were translated, Moslem feast days were respected, and native leaders were given a role in local government. He ruled Egypt with characteristic pragmatism, but there were limits to his wish to placate local leaders. The French could not be accepted as "true Moslems" unless they accepted both circumcision and the religious ban on the consumption of alcohol. Not even a Bonaparte could demand such sacrifices from a French army. The French levied taxes, which were collected by the Coptic minority, and confiscated the property of the defeated Mamelukes. Windmills were introduced to grind flour and the irrigation system was improved. French coinage was introduced and a hospital founded.[25]

From a western liberal point of view, the consultative Divan which Bonaparte established in Cairo was a huge advance on the feudal domination of the Mamelukes. For many Moslems, however, the French remained infidels whose very presence profaned the holy places of Islam. As a result, and also in response to the property tax imposed by the conquerors, there were anti-French disturbances. But French authority would tolerate no challenge. The tricolour fluttered from the minarets, *muftis* were ordered to wear a tricolour shawl, and protests in Cairo were crushed in Vendémiaire Year 7 (October 1798).[26] In June 1800, however, General Kléber was assassinated by a Moslem.

In Egypt, Bonaparte filled the gap left by Joséphine's absence and her continued infidelities with an affair with Pauline Fourès. Madame Fourès had recently married a sub-lieutenant of cavalry and made the passage to Egypt disguised as a man to complete the honeymoon. Fourès was soon sent on a mission to Malta and Pauline became Bonaparte's mistress, known to his subordinates as "Cleopatra", until a new campaign brought the interlude to an end.[27]

Without naval support Bonaparte's options were limited. In 1799, he marched on Syria, hoping to force Turkey out of the coalition against France. He took Jaffa, where 2 000 were slaughtered by the

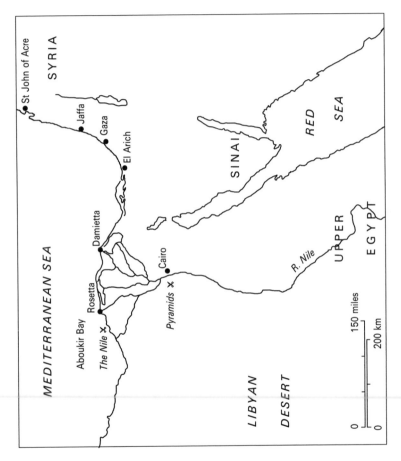

Map 3.2 The Egyptian Campaign

French. Many prisoners were killed because the French did not have enough supplies to feed them. Bonaparte was then held up for two months at St John of Acre by Djezzar Pasha, whose *jihad* (holy war) against the French was supported by a squadron of the Royal Navy. Plague began to reduce French forces, and in May 1798 Bonaparte was compelled to retreat. Yet another contrived propaganda painting (Plate 4) shows him visiting plague-stricken soldiers in hospital in Jaffa (the compassionate and caring commander was an essential feature of the Napoleonic myth). But it has been claimed that before he retreated he ordered that the sick be given a fatal dose of opium.[28] Perhaps less than one half of the 10 000 troops who invaded Syria returned alive.

By now news had reached Bonaparte of French military defeats in Europe and a developing political crisis in Paris. These events called him back to France, and a new political role. On 6 Fructidor (24 August 1799), Bonaparte abandoned his army, evaded the British naval blockade and sailed for home.

4 The Coup of Brumaire

The Directory lasted for four years and was the longest survivor of all the régimes of the First French Republic. Thanks to Bonaparte and its generals, it had pursued the war against the First Coalition with some success. It had defeated royalist threats and was beginning to pull the Republic out of financial chaos. Yet the Republic had paid a high price for the Directory's survival. The government's manipulation of election results had discredited Republican politics and destroyed credibility in the Constitution of the Year 3. By 1799, the Directory looked increasingly like a temporary solution which was already out of date. The military defeats and internal insurrections of that year made constitutional revision even more imperative.

The Directory's record was consistently blackened by subsequent Bonapartist propaganda which sought to portray Bonaparte as a saviour, rescuing France from the paralysis into which corrupt and incompetent politicians had led the Revolution. One hundred and sixty years later, Gaullists tried to write off the incompetence of the Fourth Republic in similar terms, just as Napoleon III had posed as the man of order and progress, saving the country from the inflation and social revolution which the Second Republic had inflicted on France. The myth of the saviour, however, always obscured the persistence of features inherited from previous parliamentary régimes. The Gaullist emphasis on France's independent nuclear deterrent was a policy which had its roots in the Fourth Republic; just as Bonaparte's successes had their foundations in the reforms of the Directory.

The Directory had inherited a rate of inflation comparable to that of a heavily indebted "banana republic". The Revolution's paper currency, the *assignats*, were very unpopular and almost worthless. The Republic could not guarantee the salary of government employees; both they and the army contractors had to be paid in kind, through grants of land or grain rations. The Directory, to its credit, had eventually been uncharacteristically decisive in dealing with the problem. It had written off a portion of France's debt, abandoned any further experiments with paper currency and set the budget on the road to solvency. In addition, the much maligned Directory had reformed and rationalised the fiscal system. The land tax, the tax on commercial patents, a tax on moveable property and taxes on selected items of luxury consumption formed the basis of tax revenue, not only under Bonaparte but until the early twentieth century.[1] The decimal currency, too, was a product of the Directory period.

The civil service, which was becoming part of a smoothly operating bureaucratic machine, qualifies as another Directorial success. It combined the survivors of Ancien Régime cadres with new revolutionary personnel. In this way, the civil service was becoming a very professional branch of administration, ready to serve the government of the day, whatever its political hue. One-third of those employed in the central bureaucracy had entered government service before 1788; another 46 per cent had been recruited by the Directory itself, at a time of economic upheaval when a secure job was especially attractive, even if the pay was somewhat irregular.[2] The public service was a successful amalgamation of Old Régime experience and revolutionary youth.

After the Vendémiaire rising, attempts to purge the bureaucracy of subversive royalist sympathisers failed, as Clive Church has shown, because very few royalists were found in its ranks. A total of 131 were dismissed for absence during the uprising, and another twenty-six lost their posts for avoiding conscription. In the end, however, only 9 per cent of the 11 000 personnel employed in Paris were officially suspect, but the government refused to act on many of the recommendations for dismissal laid before it.[3] The Directory developed the nucleus of a permanent civil service, which was to prove a valuable instrument of the Napoleonic imperial administration.

It had produced men like Charles Cochon, the dedicated but completely unimaginative Minister of Police, who never flinched at the numerous and inevitable puns on his surname.[4] Cochon was an undistinguished provincial lawyer from the Vendée, thrust into national politics in 1789 when he had to replace a dead colleague in the Estates-General. He was a Conventionnel and a protégé of Carnot, and he became an efficient and inscrutable administrator in the suppression of the Babeuf conspiracy in 1796. After the coup of Fructidor Year 5, he fell briefly into disgrace for unproven royalist sympathies and was sentenced to deportation. In fact, he was never taken further than the Ile d'Oléron, off the Atlantic coast. He was the ideal candidate for the prefectures of the Empire, where loyalty and conservatism were rewarded. Cochon served first in Poitiers, before his promotion to the prefecture at Antwerp.

For all these administrative successes, the Directory had failed to find a lasting solution to France's political problems. It had been unable to mobilise sufficient moderate support to protect it against threats from the right and the left. The Directory was quite capable, on occasion, of repulsing extremists on both sides. The attempted landing by the *émigré* army in the west, for instance, at Quiberon Bay in 1795, had been another fiasco for the royalists. The government had infiltrated left-wing conspiracies, neutralised the Babouvists in 1796, and rounded up the neo-Jacobin raid on the Grenelle camp in the same year. Nevertheless, the broad consensus of support for moderate republicanism did not materialise.

By 1799, there appeared to be five main sources of political instability. The first lay in the Directory's *politique de bascule* itself, in other words, in the way the government swung first towards the right and then to the left, using illegal means to preserve equilibrium. In Fructidor Year 5, the pro-royalist deputies had been "purged" from the legislature. Then, in Floréal Year 6, it was the turn of pro-Jacobin deputies to find their electoral mandates annulled by the government. Unsure of an overall majority, the Directory eliminated 127 deputies in the Year 6 to prevent the formation of a constitutional opposition. Isser Woloch and Lynn Hunt have both argued that the Directory was stifling a promising development towards the growth of a party system – something for which Napoleon has often been exclusively condemned.[5] Political "parties" are probably a misleading description of political groups in this period, when they were often united by no more than a local personality and perhaps a newspaper. These were "parties" with no electoral programme, no permanent organisation for mobilising voters, and in many regions a very weak sense of a common national purpose. For revolutionaries, moreover, the very notion of a political party was implicitly seditious. It had connotations of factional politics, of the pursuit of selfish or sectional interests at the expense of the common good. Politics were still too bitter, and the outcome of the war too uncertain, to allow the peaceful evolution of anything resembling a party system.

Parties or no parties, however, the Directory unwittingly prepared the way for Bonaparte by eliminating some of the fundamental principles of democratic politics, such as respect for the ballot. The governmental *coup d'état* was becoming an annual event. In Prairial Year 7, the scenario was slightly different. In this "coup", the Council of the 500 ejected two of the five Directors (La Revellière and Moulin de Douai). For a moment, the drive to "revise" the Constitution of the Year 3 united both anti-Jacobins like Sieyès and the neo-Jacobins themselves. The coup of Prairial temporarily disguised the contradictions inherent within this odd alliance of the Directory's opponents. Nevertheless, with the appointment of Roger-Ducos as Director, and of Fouché as Minister of Police, the future brumairiens already had a foothold on power.

The *politique de bascule* undermined credibility in the electoral process and showed contempt for constitutional legality – two crimes for which, once again, Bonaparte has often been exclusively blamed. It had serious repercussions, too, in the field of religious policy. Every swing to the left brought in its wake an intensification of measures against the clergy. A more energetic policy of deportation for refractory priests was adopted, and suggestions appeared for new and stricter oaths of loyalty by the clergy to the republican régime. When the political pendulum swung to the right, however, Catholic worship flourished, the *émigrés* felt confident enough to return, and the deportation of priests was halted. The religious schism caused by the revolutionary legislation of 1790 was not healed by the Directory: the official separation of Church and State, decreed in 1795, had not resolved the problems of division and uncertainty.

The second great political weakness of the Directory was an institutional flaw and it lay in the feebleness of executive authority. The Directory was an executive of five men, elected by the legislature, which drew straws every year to decide which member would be replaced. This bizarre method of renewing its membership left the stability of the government at the mercy of fortune and intrigue. The group of five was also prone to internal divisions, although a few personalities could exert a strong influence – Barras and Carnot in the early years, then La Revellière and Reubell, and finally Sieyès. After the period of Jacobin government, the republicans had been determined to restore parliamentary life and forestall any aspirations towards dictatorship. Their efforts had spawned a fragile and vulnerable executive which had few channels of communication with the legislature, except for the "Directorial messages" it periodically issued in an attempt to assert its authority. Under Napoleon, the problem was resolved by the installation of a central executive fortified with all the new power available to the post-revolutionary state.

In addition to these fatal shortcomings, the republican régime of 1795–99 faced a more or less continual law and order problem. In the Year 3, the murder gangs of the White Terror had operated with impunity in the Midi, taking their savage revenge against ex-Jacobins and purchasers of the *biens nationaux*. Well over 1000 Jacobin sympathisers had been hung, shot, stabbed or massacred openly in their prison cells in Lyon and Marseilles, their bodies thrown into the river Rhône. The Mediterranean Midi was a particularly dangerous part of the Republic in which to travel. None of the roads leading out of Toulon, home of the convict hulks, was safe. According to François de Nantes in the Year 9, passengers between Avignon and Aix had to carry at least 4 louis in cash to avoid being shot by robbers. In the Vaucluse department, seventy-nine murders were reported during the last six months of the Year 8.[6] In the west of the France, too, the sporadic peasant resistance known as the *chouannerie* had never been completely eradicated. By 18 Brumaire, half of the western department of the Sarthe was in the hands of *chouan* rebels. On the plains of the Beauce and elsewhere, bandit gangs raided farmsteads and committed highway robbery for years in defiance of the authorities.[7]

The problem was exacerbated by the famine conditions of 1795–6, and also by desertion and draft dodging, which added to the number of fugitives trying to survive on the margins of the law. Peasant insurgency was rife: an insurrection briefly seized the town of Sancerre (Cher) in Germinal Year 4, and several hundred peasant rebels attacked Montbrison (Loire) in Floréal of the same year. Liberty trees would be cut down, purchasers of *biens nationaux* might be threatened, ex-Jacobins or Protestants would have their heads shaved. The Directory had not found an answer to these problems. In some parts of the country, it was dangerous to volunteer for responsibility in local government. Attempts to collect taxes, enforce order or execute unpopular religious legislation could provoke a violent response, or even a stiletto in the back. Private obscurity was preferable, especially for those who had already held office during the revolutionary years.[8] Hence crime and disorder continued with local connivance. Witnesses to murder would fail to come forward, refractory priests, protected by local residents, could not be found, local justices would prove obstructive, and impartial juries could not be assembled. Colin Lucas has argued that, at least in the department of the Loire, the Directory had lost its struggle to impose an impartial and effective system of justice as early as the Year 4.[9]

One way to bring about change would have been to organise the election of reforming candidates to the Directory itself. Bonaparte found, however, like General Hoche before him, that this was impossible. Bonaparte and Hoche were too young for election: according to the Constitution, Directors had to be over the age of 40. Unfortunately, it was very hard to alter the political framework in a legal and constitutional fashion. A fourth problem can therefore be isolated in the rigidity of the Constitution of the Year 3, which put insuperable barriers in the path of constitutional revision. Constitutional revision had to be ratified by both chambers three times, at intervals of three years. Even if, after this nine-year period, there was still a majority in favour of constitutional revision, this had to be ratified by a special assembly, called especially for the purpose, and also by the primary electoral assemblies. This forced the constitutional revisionists to look for a quick and direct route to change: a military *coup d'état*.

The sister republics of the Directory had already shown one way ahead. A stronger executive had been canvassed for the Cisalpine Republic. In the Helvetic Republic, prefects had been appointed. In the Roman Republic of 1798, there were consuls, senators, tribunes and prefects: all ephemeral prototypes of the Bonapartism of the future.[10]

The bourgeoisie, fifthly and finally, was still searching for the best institutional framework to satisfy its aspirations, and secure the gains it had made in the Revolution. The Directory was no longer a convincing response to these needs. It had tried to restore constitutional government, but had violated its own constitution. It had attempted to make a limited form of representative government a reality, in circumstances which made this impossible. War, religious schism and political conflict were not conducive to the peaceful development of the Republic's experiment in parliamentary democracy. The professional, administrative and commercial classes which had made the Revolution needed security for their new social position, and their land purchases. Yet these were still threatened by war, invasion, royalist revolts and a resurgence of neo-Jacobinism. Any new form of government would be judged on its ability to dispel these threats.

The crisis of 1799 frightened the bourgeoisie further, and made revision an urgent necessity. The military defeats in Germany and Italy brought the Austrian and Russian armies closer to France's borders, and were so serious as to compel Bonaparte to return to France. The French forces were too divided and overstretched; they could not hold a broad front against the huge allied armies which now closed on France.[11] Jourdan was defeated in Germany, the Russians entered Milan, and Masséna abandoned Zurich. Relief came in

September, when Masséna split the armies of Austria and Russia and re-entered Zurich. Until then, France faced a serious invasion threat for the first time since 1793.

This emergency provoked a resurgence of Jacobinism, demands that France declare *La patrie en danger* once again, and impose a state of emergency similar to that of the Year 2. A forced loan was introduced to pay for conscription, and on 24 Messidor Year 7 the law of hostages permitted the arrest of relatives of *émigrés* and ex-nobles in the emergency. This seemed to many like a return to the Law of Suspects of 1793 and the nightmarish extremism of the Terror. Property owners were frightened by the return to "revolutionary" methods of taxation. Their fear of Jacobinism was an important ingredient in their acceptance of the Bonapartist seizure of power in Brumaire.

At the same time, armies of *chouans* materialised again in the west; in Vendémiaire Year 8 (October 1799), they held the Norman town of Le Mans for three days. A peasant insurrection broke out in the south-west, poorly armed and badly led, but assisted by the presence of bands of deserters from the Toulousain and the Pyrenees. The insurrection of the Year 7 still awaits its modern historian; but it is clear that it gave local officials, Protestants and the Republicans of Toulouse a very nasty shock. In St Gaudens, the Directory's *commissaire* fled for his life to the woods and hid there for a week, taking the town council with him.[12] Of course, these were temporary setbacks: Masséna's victory at Zurich in September 1799 gave the Republic some breathing space; and the royalist insurrection was defeated at Montréjeau, leaving 4000 dead in the south-western departments. Plans for a coup had been laid, however, and the moment for its execution had come. The Directory was unpopular, and with Sieyès as Director since May 1799 it had been undermined from within. Little pressure was needed to send it toppling. Would the coup be difficult? Bonaparte asked Roederer. No, was the reply, because it was already three-quarters complete.[13]

The *brumairiens* responsible for the coup of that month were a mixture of revolutionary veterans from the Estates-General of 1789, intellectuals and soldiers. The group included ex-nobles, ex-clergymen, constitutional royalists and ex-members of the National Convention. Sieyès himself had become spearhead of the anti-Jacobins in 1799 and played a prominent rôle in the conspiracy. He had the Jacobins' club in the rue du Bac closed down, and it was rumoured (falsely) that he had been bribed by Bonaparte to prepare a royalist coup.[14] Sieyès had a reputation as the constitutional wizard of the Revolution, a one-man "think-tank" always ready to produce a new constitution from his pocket. He was proud, irascible, but a highly respected political thinker. Robespierre had called Sieyès the "mole" of the Revolution, suggesting that his main effort was always out of sight, below the surface of revolutionary politics. There was also something prophetic about the phrase, given Sieyès's attempts to undermine the Directory's Constitution which he hated.

Within the Directory, he had the support of Roger-Ducos and he rallied other *brumairiens*, some of whom had been his associates since 1789. These included Cambacérès, Talleyrand and Roederer, moderate royalists who joined with ex-Conventionnels to support the revisionist cause. Talleyrand, as Bishop of Autun, had celebrated Mass on the Champ de Mars on 14 July 1790 at the great national festival of Federation. He had discreetly left France after the September massacres in 1792 but returned from his travels in England and America in 1796. In the following year, he had become Foreign Minister and was valued by the Directory for his diplomatic skills. In the crisis of 1799, he made a timely resignation from the government. Cambacérès, like Sieyès, was a regicide, but unlike Sieyès, he had given his support to the thermidorean constitution. He was a lawyer from Montpellier, whose experience as a drafter of constitutions was to be useful to the conspirators. His support was rewarded by nomination as second consul and he was entrusted with an important role in the reform of the civil code. Boulay de la Meurthe, a lawyer from Nancy, was a member of the Council of 500, and helped to draft Bonaparte's Constitution of the Year 8. Fouché, too, once a dechristianiser and now Minister of Police, had an important role. "I am handing the royalists over to you," Sieyès is supposed to have confided to Fouché, "but the anarchists come with them; pound them all to pulp for me in the same mortar, and you will have done your duty".[15]

At first sight, the leaders of Brumaire appear an unlikely combination. Talleyrand was club-footed but remained an agile diplomat with a taste for women and the luxuries of the Old Régime. Sieyès was a celibate dogmatist, and Fouché an expert policeman and a model *père de famille*. All three had been men of the Church, and all three were among the great survivors of the Revolution. Some *brumairiens*, like Talleyrand and Cambacérès, were of noble origin. They had embraced the Revolution fully, in 1789 in the case of Sieyès, in 1790 in the case of Talleyrand, far more dangerously in 1793 in Fouché's case, and then withdrawn to safety. They had not sacrificed their career to principles, but waited for the favourable moment when political passions cooled, and their skills as managers, administrators or diplomats could come into their own.

The *brumairiens* also included a group of intellectuals, or Idéologues, who had a great admiration for Bonaparte, especially since the Egypt expedition.[16] Bonaparte had made the invasion an important intellectual enterprise and had established the Institut in Cairo. In so doing, he had attracted the attention of an élite of intellectuals and scientists. Daunou, like his fellow-*brumairiens* Sieyès and Talleyrand, had been a member of the pro-revolutionary clergy. He had sat in the Convention, but his sympathy for the expelled Girondin deputies earned him a term of imprisonment during the Terror. After Thermidor, he had worked on educational reform, and the establishment of the Institut National. Perhaps men like Daunou and the mathematician Monge imagined themselves playing Voltaire to a new enlightened despot: Bonaparte was the personal key to their support for the Brumaire coup.

The expanding Bonaparte clan completed this improbable team. The success of Brumaire was to require the presence not only of Napoleon Bonaparte, but also of his younger brother Lucien. Lucien had conveniently been elected president of the Council of 500 and, as we shall see, his cool head saved the day for his brother on 19 Brumaire. Historians have come to think of the coup as the 18 Brumaire of Napoleon Bonaparte, but the seizure of power might well be renamed the 19 Brumaire of Lucien Bonaparte. Other Bonapartes waited in the wings to lay their claims to the spoils of power: Joseph, and brothers-in-law Murat and Leclerc, who had married Caroline and Pauline respectively. Even Joséphine played her part: she was to neutralise the Director Gohier, by inviting him and his wife to breakfast at 8 a.m. on the 18 Brumaire.[17] (Gohier was not fooled – he sent his wife to see Joséphine alone.)

The *brumairiens* needed a popular general. At first, Bonaparte was not conspicuous on the short list. Sieyès looked to Joubert, who met his death at Novi. Both Jourdan and Augereau seemed too committed to the republican left.[18] Then Moreau was approached, but he stood aside for Bonaparte whose successes in Italy and in Egypt made him a popular choice. Behind Bonaparte stood a whole group of generals, the "military–revolutionary complex" which the ailing Directory had been powerless fully to control. There had been repeated quarrels between the generals in the field and the Directory's army commissars.[19] In Lombardy, for example, Joubert could not tolerate the presence of *commissaire* Amelot and both of them resigned. In Naples, the conflict was even more serious. General Championnet resented the attempts by *commissaire* Faipoult to call him to account for the army's financial exactions. Apart from the question of accountability, there was also a political problem. The government did not approve of the republican-isation of conquered territories. Championnet had proclaimed the Neapolitan Republic and his requisitions of money and supplies were illegal. The government had two objections to this: first, it wanted to minimise the risk of a revolt against the French, and second, it wanted the profits of conquest to return to Paris, instead of being appropri-ated by the generals personally. The Directory ordered Championnet's arrest, but the coup of Prairial Year 7 exonerated him. The civilian gov-ernment backed down to the *parti militaire*, and abolished the civil commissars who had encroached upon the independence of the gen-erals. The military leaders lobbied the Paris politicians, forming a powerful group around Barras and Lucien Bonaparte.

The conspiratorial duet of Bonaparte and Sieyès was full of ironies. Both were ambitious men with impatient and implacable tempera-ments. Neither was made for the niceties and intrigue of party pol-itics, but they had little else in common. Sieyès is usually described as the theorist, a man who dealt in political abstractions, but lacked the means to realise his constitutional schemes. Bonaparte, in contrast, was a realist with a pragmatic approach to power who needed Sieyès's authority in the Directory and the upper house (the Conseil des Anciens) to reach it. The nineteenth-century historian Edgar Quinet was to call Brumaire the alliance of fear and glory, and Sieyès's most recent biographer, Bredin, sees it as the meeting of the ideologue and the adventurer.[20]

Perhaps there was a little more to Sieyès than is implied by this con-ventional portrait of the difficult and eccentric intellectual. He was also an effective propagandist. His whole revolutionary reputation rested on his authorship of the most famous pamphlet of the Revolu-tion, *Qu'est-ce-que c'est que le Tiers Etat?*, which had mobilised opinion in support of the Third Estate at Versailles. The pamphlet had sold 30 000 copies in the early months of 1789, and it was significantly reprinted in Messidor Year 7, with its language slightly modified, and "le peuple" replacing "le Tiers Etat".[21] Sieyès was thus identified with the end of noble privilege, and with the motion he proposed in June 1789 to rename the Third Estate as the National Assembly. For many republicans, Sieyès would always remain the incarnation of that early resistance to the monarchy and the privileged orders. In forging a

link with Sieyès, therefore, Bonaparte was harnessing the coup of
Brumaire to the great revolutionary ideals of 1789.

The *brumairiens* had found their general; and his brother presided
over the Council of 500. The neutrality of Directors Barras and
Gohier also seemed assured (it is not clear what bribes had been
offered to Barras). It was time to act. On 18 Brumaire Year 8
(10 October 1799), plans were put into effect to remove both legislative chambers to a safe distance, far from the unpredictable Parisian
crowd. In his capacity as Director, Sieyès drew up a decree which
ordered the emergency transfer of the legislature away from the capital, where it was allegedly in danger, to the safety of St Cloud, to the
west. Special meetings of the Conseil des Anciens and the Council of
500 were called at short notice to announce the move, and in the
Council of 500 Lucien Bonaparte stifled any discussion by ordering a
prompt adjournment. General Bonaparte was entrusted with the task
of "ensuring the protection" of the deputies, who were summoned to
reassemble on the following day.

The Director Gohier, alarmed at the implications of these measures, tried desperately to assemble the Directory. Barras, however,
had already been given his part in the murky plot. He protested that
it was too early in the morning, that he was taking his bath, and could
not respond to Gohier's call.[22] Gohier could only find General
Moulin, because their colleagues Sieyès and his acolyte Roger-Ducos
had resigned their position as Directors. Gohier could do nothing;
he and Moulin were escorted to the Luxembourg Palace, with a
guard for their own "protection".

There was now a delay until the meeting of the deputies at
St Cloud on 19 Brumaire, which might have proved fatal to the
brumairiens. The conspirators lost an opportunity to arrest their leading Jacobin opponents before the meeting of the Council of 500.[23] It
was clear the next day in the Council of 500 that there was a majority
hostile to the intended coup. Cries of "A bas les dictateurs!" (Down
with the dictators!) emanating from the meeting place incensed
Bonaparte, but the deputies defiantly voted to swear their loyalty to
the Constitution, one by one. Bonaparte became increasingly impatient. At four in the afternoon, he entered the Conseil des Anciens,
surrounded by a group of officers and demanded action. One deputy
invited him to respect the Constitution. "The Constitution?" he
retorted. "Do you claim the right to invoke it? Can it still offer any
guarantee to the French people? You violated it on 18 Fructidor, you

violated it on 22 Floréal, you violated it on 30 Prairial. The Constitution has been invoked and then violated by every single faction!"[24]

Bonaparte and his officers then marched into the Council of 500, with swords drawn, where the deputies exploded with anger. They physically challenged the intruders, although the story that the deputies had brandished daggers and pistols was a subsequent Bonapartist fabrication.[25] There were calls to outlaw Bonaparte, who withdrew in a fury. This was a critical moment. Lucien tried to assert control of the meeting but was unable to silence the uproar. He then took the most important decision of the day. In a Roman gesture, he laid down the robe of presidential office and left the chamber. He harangued the troops, told them that an attack had been made on General Bonaparte, and then led his brother Napoleon and his troops into the Council of 500. The deputies were evicted, several escaping through the windows, just as, in 1792, the voters of Ajaccio had been brutally treated by the young Napoleon Bonaparte and his clan. Murat betrayed the true tone of the military takeover, as he ordered amid the confusion: "Clear this fucking crowd out of here!" (*Foutez-moi tout ce monde dehors!*).[26] In ten minutes, the assembly was empty.

For the interim, executive power was entrusted to three consuls, Bonaparte, Sieyès and Roger-Ducos. Since the main pretext for the coup had been the existence of a Jacobin plot, the deportation of thirty-four Jacobins to Guyana was ordered. The Law of Hostages and the forced loan were abrogated. Bonaparte, however, did not wish to align himself clearly with any one faction and the deportations were later repealed. The meaning of the coup was ambiguous. Paris remained quiet, to the relief of the *brumairiens*, and the value of government bonds rose on the Stock Exchange, which enabled Talleyrand to make a substantial profit on the day's events.[27] Lucien presented the events as the continuation of the fraternal resolve encapsulated in the Tennis Court Oath of June 1789. Most of France seemed resigned or apathetic towards the change. After four years of the Directory's twists and turns, a republican *coup d'état* was hardly a novelty.

With hindsight, the coup of 18–19 Brumaire appears as both a momentous and destructive event. At the time, however, it seemed nothing of the sort. It did not immediately usher in a personal dictatorship and was merely another in a long line of Directorial coups, brought about with military support, just like the coup of Fructidor Year 5. The Consulate of three was simply a smaller version of its predecessor, and to ensure continuity it even included two former

Directors. In 1800, the Consulate had no more legitimacy or popularity than the régime it replaced.

Bonaparte was sometimes reluctant to acknowledge his debt to the legacy of the Revolution, but in fact there were many elements of continuity between the Directory and the Consulate. The administrative and fiscal reforms of the Directory laid essential foundations for the later success of Bonaparte. The Republic survived, and so did the revolutionary calendar, at least officially. Brumaire may be seen as one step along the road towards the personal power of Napoleon Bonaparte, but that was not fully accomplished until the inauguration of the Empire in 1804. That date was a turning-point in revolutionary history which was just as significant as 18 Brumaire, if not more so.

We should not therefore rush to condemn Brumaire as the liquidation of the French Revolution. Troops had unceremoniously scattered the legal representatives of the nation, but the electoral process had already been considerably devalued under the Directory itself. Repeated manipulation and cancellation of election results encouraged popular apathy. By the elections of the Year 7, only about 10 per cent of the electorate bothered to vote. If Bonaparte was the gravedigger of political liberty, the Directory had already presented him with the corpse.

Continuities between Brumaire and the revolutionary past are therefore worth stressing on more grounds than one. Bonaparte built on the Directory's achievements; but, at the same time, Brumaire also signified the continuing depoliticisation of revolutionary France. Reaction to the coup itself was tepid. In the Pyrénées-Orientales, the administration refused to promulgate the decrees of 19 Brumaire. The department of the Jura declared them an attack on popular sovereignty. There was an isolated royalist demonstration in Bordeaux.[28] But that was all. The fact that there was so little resistance to the coup of Brumaire signifies how far the process of depoliticisation had already gone since the fiercely contested elections of 1797. There were very few messages of congratulations to the victors, either, in comparison to the quick response from the provinces which had followed the news of the overthrow of the Robespierrists in Thermidor Year 2. Apathy, rather than a rush to find a saviour, was the secret of Brumaire's success.

Brumaire, then, did not announce the end of the principles of the French Revolution. It signified rather that one particular institutional form of those revolutionary ideals had served out its usefulness, and succumbed to history. The revolutionary bourgeois of France had spent four years navigating a dangerous passage between the perils of a royalist restoration and Jacobin-led economic controls. They needed to defend their gains, the abolition of the monarchy and of aristocratic privilege, and they needed an assurance that the end of seigneurialism and the sale of the *biens nationaux* were definitive. The Directory no longer provided a sufficient guarantee; they turned to a new set of institutions to protect the legacy of the French Revolution. The coup of Brumaire may best be interpreted not as a rupture with the immediate revolutionary past, but as a new attempt to secure and prolong the hegemony of the revolutionary bourgeoisie. It was ironic that the French bourgeoisie, usually so timid, concerned with stability and wary of risk, had entrusted the Revolution to a diminutive Corsican soldier and his creole wife from Martinique, who had offered herself to the Directorial elite as one of the spoils of power.

5 *France in 1800*

The first two decades of the nineteenth century witnessed the last and most spectacular flowering of French hegemony in Europe. France had dominated the rest of Europe to such an extent that, by 1813, the first item on the agenda of European diplomacy had become the need to defeat and contain French aggression. French domination was not to endure for very much longer; the long general peace after 1815 probably disguised France's relative decline, but in 1870 the French defeat at Sedan in the Franco-Prussian War provided dramatic evidence that the period of French European supremacy was definitively closed.

The power of the French state and the successes of French expansionism were not the product of accidental factors, nor can they be solely attributed to the ambitions and talents of Napoleon Bonaparte. They reflected the powerful energies released by the French Revolution, and they were made possible by France's superior resources, both of manpower and of agricultural wealth. France was still an agricultural country but a well-populated, rich and fertile one. Anglo-Saxon historians who focus on the industrial revolution which was developing in Britain have often wondered why the French economy was backward or retarded in the nineteenth century. This reflects an insular view of French society; from a continental perspective, French power was based on her leading position as a producer of wealth and people. Jacques Godechot began his book *La Grande Nation* in 1956 by analysing the conditions of French expansion. His conclusion was that a primary precondition was France's large population, whose surplus had not yet been absorbed by industry.[1] The size and nature of this population need to be appreciated, in an overview of the France which Bonaparte inherited in 1800.

France had a large population by European standards, numbering over 29 million in 1800.[2] This was more than the population of the Habsburg Empire (about 20 million), more than double the population of England (about 12 million), and more than four times the population of Prussia (6 million). Seventeen per cent of Europeans were French in 1789; today, the percentage is closer to 7 per cent.

Napoleon was thus able to call upon enormous reserves of man-power. As the Emperor surveyed the corpse-strewn battlefield of Eylau in 1807 (Plate 5), he is reported to have made the cynical comment: "I have an annual income of 100,000 men; one night in Paris will replace this."

France's rapid population expansion in the second half of the eighteenth century had also altered the age structure of the population. As a result, a higher proportion of the population was young. In 1801, 63 per cent of France's population were aged 19 or younger.[3] In fact, the high proportion of young men everywhere in Europe was conducive to a period of generalised warfare.

Although the French hexagon was therefore bulging at the seams with youthful endeavour, there were signs that the population's expansionist trends would not continue. Demographic historians argue that important transformations occurred in the revolutionary years which halted expansion, and stabilised the growth of population. These transformations must be put into perspective by considering in turn the contemporary patterns of deaths, marriages and births. The old European pattern of high death rates, accompanied by high birth rates was giving way to the pattern of much lower death rates and birth rates with which we are familiar. France offers a precocious example of this change.

The death rate was certainly declining. In 1792, it had stood at 31.5 deaths per thousand inhabitants; by 1806–10, it was only 26.3 per thousand.[4] The periodic subsistence crises of early modern Europe were still likely to occur, when bad harvests carried off thousands, leaving malnutrition and fatal vulnerability to disease in their wake. The poor diet of many regions, dependent almost exclusively on the consumption of bread (often adulterated) and alcohol (always adulterated) gave the population little resistance to traditional scourges like typhus and dysentery. Nevertheless, the subsistence crises of this period (1816–17 apart) were less fatal than their predecessors. The evidence from the years of dearth in 1802–3 and again in 1812–13 suggests that food shortages did not necessarily lead to a demographic holocaust.[5] Epidemics of pleurisy and what contemporaries classified as "catarrhal fever" were still regular visitors, but their impact on mortality was diminishing.

Epidemics such as these always tended to carry off the frailest members of the population – the very old and very young. Infant mortality, however, was declining all over Europe at the end of the eighteenth century, long before the generalisation of smallpox vaccinations

began to take effect. Consider the population of the French town of
Meulan, in the Paris region, in this period. For every 1000 new-born
inhabitants between 1765 and 1789

197 died in their first year,
249 died between their first and fifth birthdays,
51 died between their fifth and tenth birthdays, and
503 therefore survived.

But for the period of the Revolution and the Empire, 1790–1814

109 died in their first year,
186 died between their first and fifth birthdays,
39 died between their fifth and tenth birthdays, and
666 therefore survived.[6]

The infant survival rate had thus improved from one half to two-
thirds over half a century. Smallpox, responsible for about 30 per
cent of infant deaths up to the age of 4 during the Old Régime, was
disappearing.

There was only a gradual decline, however, in the persistent practice of wet-nursing, whereby urban mothers "farmed out" their
infants to peasant women who, for a fee, nursed and breast-fed them.
There was a strong demand for country wet-nurses, especially from
working mothers of the labouring and artisan classes, as well as from
public authorities responsible for foundlings and orphans. During
the Empire, the Paris Bureau of Wet-nurses (*Nourrices*) placed
between 4–5000 babies with country women annually.[7] Unfortunately, the standard of care provided by such surrogate breast-feeders
left plenty to be desired by modern standards. Their profits
depended on minimising expenses and the infants were often
neglected, especially at harvest-time. Some parents, meanwhile,
could not afford to maintain payments to wet-nurses and simply
abandoned their children. The mortality rate for infants in this situation remained somewhere between 25–33 per cent.

Nevertheless, the broad picture is one of decline in the rate of
infant mortality. Midwifery techniques had not changed, but perhaps
the diminishing risk of famine and improving nutrition were significant factors. Better fed parents meant that both mother and child
were more likely to survive the rigours of childbirth and enjoy good
health. Ordinary people still lived principally on bread, but potatoes
were becoming commoner and meat consumption was gradually
reducing the dependence on cereal foods. The food ration of a

soldier in the imperial army, for instance, included 1 $\frac{1}{2}$ kilograms of beef per week.[8]

The war losses of the revolutionary and Napoleonic era were not as devastating as once was supposed. Jacques Houdaille, using a sampling technique and concentrating on selected regiments, has calculated French war losses over this whole period at 916 000, a figure which includes soldiers who died of disease as well as those who fell in battle.[9] Perhaps half this figure are known to have died of their wounds or in one of the period's primitive military hospitals; the rest were reported missing. Napoleon is supposed to have remarked to the Austrian Chancellor Metternich: "A man like me is not concerned about a million dead."[10] This was an unwittingly accurate estimate of what Napoleon and the Revolution had cost France in terms of manpower. This constituted a substantial haemorrhage of human resources, and of male reproductive power, which had repercussions in future generations. The losses, however, were sustained over a long period of fifteen years, with the climax falling in the years after 1812.

While the death rate was declining, the marriage rate was soaring. The Revolution had made marriage much easier. Parental consent was no longer necessary for the marriage of spouses over the age of majority. Marriage had been secularised, and the ceremony at the local *mairie* was not subject to Catholic restrictions at certain times of year, such as during Lent. Although the Catholic Church tried to maintain Lenten observance in the face of widespread indifference during the Revolution and Empire, it gave up attempts to ban marriages in the Advent period.[11] In 1792, divorce was legalised. Furthermore, the conscription laws gave a new incentive for young men to marry because this could exempt them from the call-up. In the 1780s, about 5100 marriages were celebrated every year in Paris; in the Year 2, there were 9300 marriages in the capital.[12] The marriage rate tended to fluctuate, and at the beginning of the Consulate it was probably lower than in the last years of the Old Régime. By the end of the Empire, the rate had risen considerably, and the national average was close to a quarter of a million marriages annually.[13] The conscription of 1813, from which the newly-wed were exempted, provoked a rush to the town hall (Figure 5.1). In Toulouse, there were 21.8 new spouses for every 1000 inhabitants in 1813, but the marriage rate fell back to only 13.5 in the following year.[14] The Church's proscriptions on Lenten marriage were absolutely powerless in Toulouse in 1813, when fear of the call-up outweighed traditional religious taboos.

A declining death rate and rising marriage rate appear at first sight to be obvious symptoms of the late eighteenth-century population explosion. The figures, however, mask a long-term trend towards a much slower rate of population growth. Historians in the 1960s used to refer to France as the "China of Europe", attempting to conjure up a picture of a land pullulating with people. But as in contemporary China, forces were at work to check this growth.

Couples married earlier in the revolutionary period than in the Old Régime, when the average age at marriage had been relatively late by modern standards: between 27 and 29 years for men and between 24 and 27 for women.[15] At the end of the Old Régime, the bride's average age at marriage was about 26 ½, but in the decade between 1810 and 1819, it fell to an average of 25.6.[16] The earlier average age of married couples, however, did not produce the baby boom which one might have expected. Although the marriage rate soared during the French Revolution, the birth rate failed to match it. Before the Revolution, the French birth rate had stood at thirty-seven births annually per thousand inhabitants. By 1810, according to André Armengaud, the birth rate had declined to 31.8 per thousand.[17] For the first time, France produced fewer than a million births annually.[18] Clearly, the fertility of France's millions of new married couples was lower than before. In the parts of Languedoc studied by LeRoy Ladurie, the birth rate fell from about thirty-eight per thousand in 1787, to only thirty-two per thousand in 1813: a remarkable drop which was turning the province from a late developer into an area with a lower birth rate than that of the rest of the country (Figure 5.2).[19] There seems little doubt that fertility was being deliberately controlled, and that it was increasingly common for French couples to limit the size of their families. The 1790s were a turning point, giving France its unique character as a society which adopted widespread family limitation practices at a very early stage.

In the space of a single French generation, a decisive change had occurred in conjugal behaviour. This was a generation which had experienced an unprecedented attack on Catholic teaching, and a Revolution which had even deprived many parishes of the services of a priest for several years. Perhaps this undermined respect for traditional Catholic teaching on sex and matrimony, and helped to generalise knowledge of the "terrible secrets" of contraceptive techniques, as LeRoy Ladurie called them. Strictly speaking, family limitation is a more accurate description than contraception, since the commonest

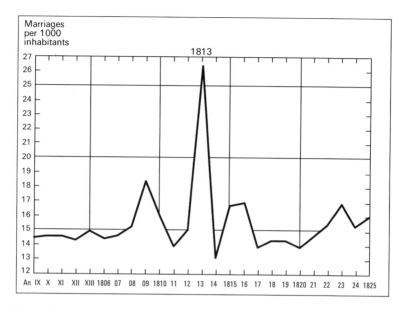

Figure 5.1   Marriage Rate in France, 1801–25

Source: A. Armengaud: "Mariages et Naissances sous le Consulat et l'Empire", *Rhmc*, 17, 1970.

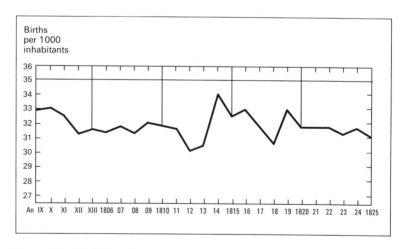

Figure 5.2   Birth Rate in France, 1801–25

Source: As Figure 5.1.

techniques used were still either *coitus interruptus* (the withdrawal method) or deliberate abstinence from sexual relations. The break with Catholic teaching on conception was probably more complete for men than for women, judging by the strength of female religiosity in the nineteenth century.

There were social and economic reasons behind these new practices adopted by French couples. Revolutionary legislation had ended primogeniture, the inheritance system by which the eldest son became the sole heir of the family estate. Instead, revolutionary and Napoleonic legislation favoured shared inheritances, which may have encouraged smaller families. If peasant families had to divide their estates equally amongst all male descendants, then there was an incentive to reduce the number of heirs in order to prevent a division of the property into tiny, uneconomic lots.

There were more intangible reasons, too. The Revolution had encouraged individualism and opened up new possibilities for social promotion for young men. Professional advancement was no longer blocked by one's low birth, aristocratic monopolies, cliques and exclusive kinship connections. There was more scope and greater reason in post-revolutionary France to look forward to social promotion in the future, if not for oneself, then for one's sons and daughters. Those with ambitions for their children needed to save and to plan. They needed to focus their resources on a smaller number of children, in order to provide the resources and education required to give them a sound footing on the ladder of success. These considerations may have persuaded those who were upwardly mobile to limit the size of their families.

A new kind of family structure was emerging as the expectations of French couples changed, and the lives of women in particular were radically modified. Marriage had not lost its reproductive function, for the proportion of childless couples remained steady at about 11 per cent, but women were waiting longer than before between pregnancies.[20] After the 1790s, a gap of four years between births was increasingly common, where the arrival of a baby every eighteen months had once been the norm. In the town of Meulan, 40 per cent of families had only one or two children in the Revolution and the Empire, while families with ten children or more had disappeared from the statisticians' view. The average number of births per marriage in France as a whole fell from about six in the middle of the eighteenth century to four by 1815.[21]

Much of what we "know" about family life in the past will always remain speculative. The historian cannot penetrate the secret of the confessional or eavesdrop on the intimate life of the couple. Conclusions drawn from well-studied communities like Meulan may not necessarily apply to the rest of France. The records of the revolutionary period present special problems since so many of them were destroyed, or remain incomplete, as a result of the administrative confusion inevitable during great upheaval and conflict. The *état-civil*, or register of births, marriages and deaths, may not be completely reliable. In the revolutionary decade, some Catholic families may have shunned the civil authorities, in the belief that only marriages and baptisms sanctified by traditional priests were valid in the sight of God. So the existence of clandestine records of these sacraments may mean that we have slightly underestimated the birth rate between 1793 and 1800.[22]

In spite of these difficulties, the historian of the Napoleonic period is better informed than ever before about a wide range of topics. This was a régime which policed more aspects of life more systematically and more efficiently than any of its predecessors. It made the collection of information into an important instrument of government, enlisting its employees in a vast statistic-gathering enterprise. The prefects described and classified the characteristics of local citizens in their charge with the enthusiasm of a naturalist discovering new and eccentric species of butterflies. They reported on their physique, diet and temperament, and on the climatic and environmental influences which made them energetic or lazy, rational or superstitious, muscular or enervated.[23] The government requested details on typography, population fluctuations, the price of grain, the state of the hospitals, the incidence of begging and local customs, in a burst of anthropological curiosity which had ulterior motives: to demonstrate French achievements and French enlightenment, as well as to equip the central government with more powerful means of control. For example, a population census seemed a necessary prerequisite for an efficient system of conscription. Statistical inquiries proliferated, forming a new science in the service of the state.[24]

The newly established Bureau de Statistique supervised three population censuses in 1801, 1806 and 1811. By present-day standards, they were crude affairs which did not systematically record ages or the size of families. Demographic historians only regard the first two of these censuses as worthy of consideration.[25] Although technically immature, they were milestones demonstrating the link between detailed knowledge of one's subjects and firm political control over their lives.

The geographical distribution of France's large population had not been substantially changed by the Revolution. Compared to Britain, France had a relatively low level of urbanisation. In 1806, Paris and Lyon were still the only two cities in the country with a population of over 100 000. Ten years later, Marseilles had become the third. Only about one French person in six (or 17.5 per cent) lived in an urban agglomeration with more than 2000 inhabitants.[26] Even by the time of the July Monarchy, there were still fifteen French departments which did not have a town with more than 10 000 inhabitants.[27] France was predominantly a country of small towns and villages. Provence, for example, had a particularly dense network of small market-towns (*bourgs*) or "urbanised villages", with the administrative and commercial functions of any town but no more than 2000 inhabitants.[28] Most Frenchmen had never seen a town with a population of more than a few thousand – but Napoleon showed them Rome, Cairo and the gates of Moscow.

Eighteenth-century towns were insanitary and overcrowded places. They retained close links with the surrounding countryside so that it was not unusual to see livestock in the streets, even in an important provincial capital like Toulouse. Narrow streets collected private garbage and could rapidly become an open sewer. Meanwhile, Alain Corbin suggests, the smell of recently butchered animals must have pervaded many urban centres.[29] The centre of Paris was a melting pot of migrants, but the principal focus of urban social life was still the local neighbourhood.[30] The church and the wine shop were important hubs of urban social and political life, and the neighbourhood was often the place of work for residents, too. Paris was still largely a preindustrial city dominated by small craftsmen and workshops, rather than by large-scale factories which were still very rare.

Many urban centres had in fact shrunk during the revolutionary years. The effects of war and conscription, together with associated economic difficulties, were partly responsible for this "de-urbanisation." Emigration had also reduced urban populations, and on the Atlantic coast the collapse of international commerce introduced a long period of stagnation. Nancy had lost 8 per cent of its population, for example, and Caen 10 per cent.[31] Revolutionary legislation had other indirect consequences for urban populations. Provincial centres like Toulouse had depended on their Parlement as a source of income and employment for artisans and hoteliers, who had catered for the law courts and the visiting litigants they attracted. Toulouse's population had declined in the Revolution because the abolition of the Parlements had deprived the city of one of its main economic functions and poles of attraction.[32] The reorganisation of France's administrative map reproduced this pattern on a smaller scale in many other centres which lost their *bailliage* court, or saw their bishopric reduced in status. This meant they were deprived of a major employer and generator of income. For many French towns, the Napoleonic period was one spent in "catching up" with the level of population and of economic activity they had enjoyed during the Old Régime.

This was true even of Paris, although the population of the capital climbed over the half million mark during the Empire. Much of this increase was made up of new arrivals from the provinces. Paris regularly attracted thousands of migrants from all corners of France, but especially from its overpopulated and economically underdeveloped regions like Brittany, the Massif Central and the Alps. Some came for a season every year, but the regular annual migration often lengthened into quasi-permanent settlement in the capital.

Many regions provided migrants who specialised in particular trades. The Limousin, for example, was renowned for its stonemasons seeking seasonal work on Parisian building sites. Savoy was traditionally a supplier of chimney sweeps, to the extent that the term *savoyard* became synonymous with chimney sweep. Paris was not the only destination for France's many temporary migrants. From the Pyrenees and the Cantal pedlars of all sorts tramped the roads of France – ropemakers, scissor-sharpeners, vendors of rabbit skins, chapbooks, combs, pins and ribbons. The Drômois were sheep-shearers, while Parisian gardeners were often recruited from Normandy's migrant contingent.

All over France, migrants left home for part of the year to find work at harvest-time. They found it in the Paris region, in Aquitaine, Languedoc and Poitou. Scything lasted only three weeks and the grape harvest could be completed in a fortnight. In the south-west, however, the grain, chestnut and olive harvests kept itinerants employed for two or three months, if they were prepared to move in the direction of the ripening crops. In the Pyrenean departments, up to 20 per cent of the total population joined the annual exodus in search of seasonal work.[33]

Seasonal migration like this was not an exclusively male responsibility. Some migrants took their whole family to work with them, and the women and children would be employed tying up the corn or gleaning in the fields after harvesting.[34] They followed traditional patterns and well-known routes in order to supplement a meagre family income. The wages they collected represented a rare injection of cash into rural economies which were still primarily subsistence based. The money earned might allow an heir to pay off his brothers in order to keep the family property intact. The price of these advantages was sometimes short-term penury. The prefect of the Cantal reported that in one small community near Aurillac the heads of eleven households had left, leaving the population in misery.[35] Seasonal migration was also an example of geographical mobility in a society where the movement of people was unusual. Travel, it is often said, broadens our horizons, and temporary migration may have contributed to the dissemination of new ideas and practices within traditional French society.

France remained a predominantly agricultural country until well into the twentieth century. It was a rich and immense peasant economy. Agriculture accounted for the majority of total production and employed well over half of the working population. Most agricultural production depended on peasant households, owning small family plots, rather than on large estates, run according to either paternalistic or capitalist methods. In Picardy and Artois, large commercial estates existed and it was no coincidence that this northern area was also densely urbanised. A large urban population was everywhere an incentive to develop intensive and profitable farming methods. The Beauce was another area of *grande propriété*, producing grain for Paris. This commercial orientation did not mean that the local peasants lived comfortably; while the best wheat was exported to Paris, the peasants ate black bread and very little meat.

The peasants already owned about one-third of France before the Revolution, but the land was very unevenly distributed between them. The majority of peasants had very small holdings which did not always provide for their subsistence. The peasantry as a whole was never a unified class: it included various strata, from the wealthy landowner with a surplus of goods to sell to the poor day-labourer, with no security or regularity of employment. The various terms used to describe the peasants – *laboureur, ménager, cultivateur, brassier, journalier* – suggest different nuances of status, but they also had different connotations in different regions of France, making generalisations difficult.

The Revolution had a very uneven impact on the peasantry. The end of seigneurialism helped those who were already landowners; their property was no longer subject to feudal burdens and obligations. The new system of revolutionary taxation, reorganised by the Directory, is estimated to have been no more burdensome on the whole than that of the Old Régime.[36] For the landless labourer, however, the Revolution changed little. And there was a third category of peasant, besides the small landowner and the landless labourer, who had also benefited little: – the share-cropper or *métayer*. Especially numerous in the centre and the south-west of France, the share-croppers rented a farm and basic equipment for a share of the produce, but the landlord's share might be as much as one-half. In the Garonne valley, the size of a normal *métairie* was about 15 hectares.[37] Sometimes, the share-croppers' clerical landlords had been replaced by aristocrats or bourgeois, but this was no guarantee that the terms of their lease would be more lenient.

More than half of the land of France was devoted to cereal production which demanded a large labour supply and a rotation of crops. A system of three-field rotation, in which one field grew cereals while another grew animal fodder or beans and a third lay fallow, was popular in the north of the country, and this was increasingly the case elsewhere.

France's grain often travelled south, from the wheat fields of Picardy or the Beauce towards Mediterranean consumers; but her wine was sent north, from the Midi, the Bordelais or Alsace, towards the capital and towards export markets like Britain. Vines took up little space but prospered wherever there was a concentration of rich urban consumers in the vicinity. Viticulture could also be the resort of peasants who could no longer maintain livestock after the enclosure of common pasture land.

Besides the production of bread and wine, there were also many other agricultural activities which helped to supplement rural incomes. Monoculture was a risk and peasants needed other resources to fall back on in difficult times. In Normandy, peasants produced cider and cheese, and in the south-east there was an active silk industry. The Rhine departments grew tobacco. On the south-western fringes of the Massif Central, Roquefort cheese production quadrupled between 1800 and 1830.[38] In the south-west, maize frequently saved the population from famine when the harvest of other grains failed; and in good years it could be consumed locally to enable the best wheat to be exported. Near every large city, market gardens produced vegetables and fruit, although little of this produce would be consumed by the growers because the cash income they earned made them too valuable to eat. The north coast of

France looked to English consumers; by 1830, 4 million eggs crossed the Channel every month, but trade in this direction was only possible in peacetime.[39] The countryside was also the site of many industrial activities. In spite of the richness of France's natural agricultural resources, peasants needed to supplement their incomes by making (for example) lace, ribbons or woollen stockings. The textile industry was largely based on rural manufacturing and its labour force included many unskilled or partially skilled female workers. Cotton spinning, for instance, was an industry in which adult male workers were probably outnumbered by women and children.[40]

When goods did travel they went by sea or by river rather than by road, since this was cheaper and faster, and because the risk of shipwreck or running aground was no greater than the risk of highway robbery. The communications network was still very poor, in spite of the improvements brought about by the monarchy at the end of the eighteenth century. This made France a very fragmented country. There was, as yet, no national economy in which it was normal and easy to produce where it was cheapest and sell where the demand was high. Instead, there were several regional economies which tended to be isolated from each other. In spite of France's rich resources, therefore, local shortages were common.

Regionalism, however, was not simply a matter of the failure to market local surpluses on a national scale. It had important cultural, as well as economic manifestations. France was an impressively diverse society, to the extent that historians such as Richard Cobb have abandoned hope of ever generalising about it fruitfully. Fernand Braudel described France as a country of *micro-pays* or micro-regions, an archipelago of separate economic units, each with distinctive cultural and linguistic characteristics.[41] The south had its olives, vines, maize, mulberries and chestnuts. Brittany had its slate roofs, and the Alps their thatched cottages. The legacy of Rome still left its traces in the south, in its languages, legal traditions and inheritance customs. Conscripts from northern and north-eastern France were taller and better educated than their counterparts from Brittany or the rural south, and they came from a wider range of economic activities which reflected a faster and more complex process of urbanisation in northern France.[42] Even family structures betrayed France's great regional diversity. French families were a mixture of nuclear couples, stem-families with a link between two or three generations, and the distinctive southern pattern of the horizontal or multiple family structure with traditionally close ties between brothers. Family life was altogether different in the south-west, argue Le Bras and Todd;[43] couples divorced less often than they did in the north and east, women became pregnant before marriage less often, and people got drunk less frequently. France was still large enough to accommodate a wide variety of cultures.

The most striking feature of this diversity was France's linguistic patchwork. Over 6 million inhabitants of France knew no French at all, according to the Abbé Grégoire, who presented the findings of his survey on this question to the National Convention in 1793. Another 6 million, he reported, were unable to sustain a conversation in French.[44] According to the government's statistics collected in 1806, to which we have already referred, there were about a million Breton speakers in the French Empire and about 100 000 Basque speakers. Even before the imperial conquests, France also incorporated about a million German speakers and smaller numbers of Flemish and Italian speakers. These figures do not include the many patois speakers of the centre, the south and the south-west, described by Pierre Chaunu as the "deep south, impervious to French".[45]

For millions of French citizens the Revolution had been conducted in a foreign language, as indeed the business of all political authorities was, including the Bourbon monarchy and the Napoleonic Empire. They perceived the events and the legislation of what we call the "history" of the period through intermediaries, like the clergy, local notables, professional men, or occasionally a workmate who could read a newspaper aloud in a café or a tavern. They were forced to use the French language whenever they had formal dealings with the authorities, in order to write a will, draw up a bill of sale or a marriage contract, but for everyday purposes they used the familiar dialect or patois. Patois-speaking France was itself a collection of microcosms exhibiting bewildering linguistic variety. There were occitan-based dialects in the south-west, provençal-based dialects in the Midi, and various mixtures of French and provençal further north. In isolated and mountainous regions, a traveller might encounter a different language in every valley.

This was the diversity which first the revolutionaries and then the Empire tried to weld into a nation. They were aided in this task by intellectuals like the Abbé Grégoire, and by elements of the French bourgeoisie.[46] For Grégoire, patois had to be eliminated. They were corrupt languages, full of vulgarities and swear words. They expressed the rustic ignorance and prejudices which the enlightened

Revolution aimed to eliminate. National unity dictated the deliberate spread of the use of French. The Revolution had opened the professions to "talent", and asserted the principle of equality of opportunity. But equal access to jobs could not become a reality unless all French citizens acquired a knowledge of the same language – French. Literacy in French was vital for the formation of the citizen and the acculturation of the masses. The educational reforms of the revolutionary years were unable to achieve the instant linguistic homogeneity of which Grégoire dreamed. Few of them were put into practice, for lack of funds. However, the armies of the Revolution and the Empire were to demand a comprehension of French from illiterate peasant conscripts; in so doing, they played an influential nation-building role.

While labourers and artisans spoke patois, the educated clergy and bourgeoisie were francophone. In the south, the bourgeoisie were already bilingual, using French for business and official purposes, but perhaps still reverting to their local language in daily conversation or in familiar surroundings. Ambitious artisans, Grégoire was told, tried to learn French in Bordeaux, because this would distinguish them from the rest of the Gascon-speaking populace. In the Aveyron, Grégoire was informed that French speakers consisted of retired soldiers, doctors, priests, nobles and businessmen – a social élite either with education or a broad experience of life. In Catalonia, Peter McPhee also found a bourgeoisie ready to play the rôle of cultural intermediary, adapting to the structures of the French state with more enthusiasm than either the local nobility or the more xenophobic Catalan peasantry.[47]

Out of this diverse but mainly agricultural society, then, a national bourgeoisie was emerging. The Revolution had accelerated its promotion, and its support was vital for the success of the Empire, and of every subsequent nineteenth-century régime. It formed about 20 per cent of the population, as defined by Daumard,[48] and its presence must loom large in any history of post-revolutionary French society.

It was a bourgeoisie which was slow to shed its Old Régime habits of subservience, respect for certain aspects of the aristocratic way of life, and its attachment to the land. Indeed, the more traditional features of the revolutionary bourgeoisie have led some to question whether it existed at all as a separate, fully self-conscious social class. The French bourgeois was a *rentier* or *rentière*, a *propriétaire*, or he was a professional man, a lawyer, doctor or administrator, or perhaps a merchant, rather than a manufacturer. The revolutionary bourgeoisie, Alfred Cobban reminded us, was a bourgeoisie of royal officials and professionals, not of capitalistic industrial entrepreneurs.[49] His or her wealth lay in stocks or in land, not in factories.

Cobban's description of the bourgeoisie, however, has probably been too persuasive. It was supported, after all, only by a head count of the professional status of the deputies in the National Assembly, which was certainly dominated by lawyers and officials. This was a very narrow basis, in numerical terms, on which to build a theoretical attack on the notion of a link between the French Revolution and the progress of capitalism. Cobban's "method" did not take into account the broader sources of support for the revolutionary ideology in the country as a whole. In Marseilles, for example, there was a self-conscious mercantile élite, accustomed to dominating the life of the great port-city, and interested in promoting its own special interests at Versailles and in the revolutionary assemblies which succeeded the Estates-General.[50] Other provincial perspectives may also suggest that perhaps the role of the capitalist bourgeoisie has been too easily dismissed by historians, and on the basis of too little evidence.

No doubt, the French bourgeois did not match the caricature presented for political purposes by Marx in the Communist Manifesto of 1846. Here we are introduced to a bourgeoisie which, in Marx's terms, has already ruled for a century, and has become the owner of the modern, industrial means of production. This certainly represented an exaggerated view of France's industrial development in the nineteenth century.

Nevertheless, the French bourgeois was no longer exclusively a town-dweller, and he was no longer necessarily a member of an urban corporation, although these had once been defining characteristics. The traditional face of the French bourgeoisie should not obscure the evolution which had occurred since the middle of the eighteenth century. The French bourgeoisie of the Napoleonic period is best envisaged in a state of transition: it was no longer confined within the structures of the Old Régime, and it had established a firm grip on the machinery of state; but it had not yet become the dominating manufacturing class of Marx's prophecy.

The Périer family is a symbolic illustration of the ambiguities of the French bourgeoisie and of its evolution.[51] The family's wealth was founded both on land and industry. Claude Périer was a manufacturer of printed cottons in Grenoble, as well as being a great land-owner. He owned plantations in St Domingo (today Haiti) and aspired to the status of nobility, which he purchased in 1779. The purchase of nobility and of *seigneuries*, however, was by no means incompatible with Périer's continuing industrial activities. Landed property was a form of security and a way of authenticating his family's social ascension. One of the properties Périer acquired was the château of Vizille, just outside Grenoble, where Périer installed his manufacture. It was in Périer's château that the Estates of the province of Dauphiné gathered in July 1788, in a brief display of unity between clergy, nobles and commoners. It was typical of the contradictions of the revolutionary bourgeoisie that the bourgeois Revolution of 1789 should have begun here, in a once-aristocratic château, which was at the same time a textile factory. Vizille may be seen as a symbolic site in the rise of the revolutionary bourgeoisie; appropriately enough, it now houses the Museum of the French Revolution.

6   Republic of Notables: the Constitution of the Year 8

All French revolutionary régimes had begun by overhauling the electoral system and remodelling their institutional structure. In 1799, accordingly, the first task of Bonaparte and the *brumairiens* was to give France a new Constitution. This necessary political ritual had several precedents. The French Revolution had generated three different constitutions: the 1791 Constitution, defining the constitutional monarchy based on limited suffrage; the Jacobin Constitution of 1793, never put into effect; and then the ill-fated Thermidorean Constitution of the Year 3. On each occasion, the purpose had been similar. Each Constitution had first formulated a new statement of universal rights and general principles, dealing with the duties of citizenship, the sanctity of property and inviolable freedoms. At the same time, the Constitution created a political framework which was designed to empower the new régime's bases of support and to exclude its enemies. Every Constitution, therefore, aspired to be definitive, but in spite of its long-term ambitions it also served more immediate needs. Political debts had to be paid, rivals outflanked and critics placated. The Constitution of the Year 8 was no exception.

The Constitution of the Year 8 (1800) departed from precedent in one respect: it was not prefaced by a definition of the rights of citizenship, nor by any grand declaration in defence of liberty, equality and the *patrie*. This exemplified the pragmatism which Bonaparte brought to a Republic weary of paper utopias. Like preceding régimes, however, that of the Year 8 sought to reassure the revolutionary bourgeoisie as well as to reward its supporters, the Bonapartists. There was an overriding need for reconciliation between the revolutionary élites and the forces of the Old Régime. The mistakes of the past had to be avoided: like the Directory before it, the Consulate had to protect the Republic from the twin dangers of a royalist restoration, and a Jacobin, social-democratic revolution. Institutions had to be designed to make both the return of the monarchy and a repeat of the Terror impossible. At the same time, the lessons of the

Directory showed there was now yet another hazard to be avoided – the fatal paralysis of central institutions themselves.

These problems were to be resolved by introducing a greater degree of centralisation than ever before. The increasing concentration of authority in Bonaparte's hands was an important consequence, although this was by no means inevitable in 1799. The Constitution which emerged bore the unmistakable traces of a compromise between Bonaparte's personal ambitions, and the demands of the *brumairiens* who had helped him into power. The leader of this group was Sieyès, who played a central role in the preliminary negotiations. Unfortunately, the precise opinions of Sieyès are not easy to judge. In spite of his reputation as a master-drafter of Constitutions, he himself protested that he did not have a ready-made scheme to offer in Brumaire. We know of his ideas only from second-hand sources, like his collaborators Roederer, Daunou and Boulay de la Meurthe, who claimed to have written down exactly what the "Oracle" (Sieyès) dictated.[1] Much of the Constitution was the work of Sieyès but he was compelled to compromise with Bonaparte, as we shall see, over the role of the head of state.

The principle of popular sovereignty, so vigorously defended by Sieyès in 1789, was recognised in the right of adult male suffrage for all those with a one-year residence qualification. But the principle was immediately curtailed in practice by an elaborate system of indirect elections (see Figure 6.1). An electorate of about 6 million at the base would nominate a tenth of its number to form lists of notables at the municipal level (*listes communales*). From these 600 000 notables would be appointed all local officials, municipal councillors, mayors and sub-prefects. They were also to be responsible for choosing the next tier of the electoral system, namely, the *listes départementales* of 60 000 men, from whom officials would be chosen at the level of every department, including departmental councillors and prefects. The notables on the departmental lists would then elect a *liste nationale*, whose 6000 members would be eligible for membership of the national legislature. This electoral pyramid envisaged by Sieyès was designed to neutralise popular democratic forces, and to ensure that elections would produce a conservative result. Elections were not even to be held until the Year 11 (1801–2), and once established, the lists would stand unchanged, except for elections every three years to fill vacancies.

Sieyès' plan created a legislature in three separate parts. The Tribunate and the Legislative Chamber (Corps Législatif) were both

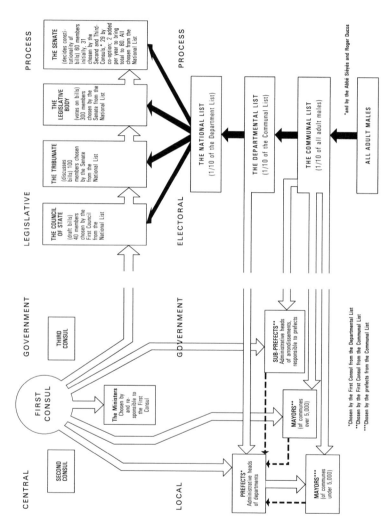

Figure 6.1 The French Government under the Constitution of the Year 8

to be chosen by the Senate from the *liste nationale*. The Tribunate was composed of 100 members, all over 25; while the Legislative Chamber had 300 members with a minimum age of 30. Every department had to be represented in the Legislative Chamber, but the functions of these two houses were rigidly defined and took the idea of the separation of powers to extremes. The Tribunate could discuss new legislation but not vote on it; the Legislative Chamber voted laws without the right to discuss them. The *Ami de la Paix* commented cynically on this bizarre segregation of roles: "The Tribunes are getting 15 000 francs for talking – it is too much. The legislators have 10 000 francs for keeping quiet, which is really not enough."[2] What is more, the Tribunate could not introduce new legislation, for this could only originate from the Senate or the Consuls. In other words, the legislature had little legislative power in its own right, and the authority to discuss, amend and make final decisions was carefully dispersed throughout the system. In this way, Sieyès hoped to prevent the concentration of power in the hands of one parliamentary body, which had occurred in the Convention under the revolutionary government of the Year 2. The Tribunate, which did have the right to discuss legislative proposals, was to be a focus for the early opposition to Bonaparte. But within two years the Tribunate was purged and it became clear that the real sources of power lay elsewhere.

The Senate was allotted an influential role in the new structure of government, which thoroughly incorporated the nomenclature of ancient Rome. The Senate was an élite of eighty men, with a minimum age of 40, who were to be chosen by the Consuls or coopted by the legislature. Senators included generals like Kellermann, bankers like Perregaux (who had to be rewarded for financing the coup of Brumaire) bishops, high-ranking magistrates and public servants, and a sprinkling of intellectuals, like Monge and Volney. Bonaparte made subsequent nominations of notables in conquered territories, so that by the end of the Empire there were over 140 Senators all told. They held office for life, drew a comfortable salary, and the institution was collectively endowed by Bonaparte with estates in Tuscany. Senators were thus rewarded with substantial "fiefs". The senatorship of the mathematician Berthollet, for example, came with 25 000 francs per year and the palace of the Bishop of Narbonne.[3] This was to make a seat in the Senate an ideal and secure retirement opportunity for revolutionary veterans like Sieyès himself. Sieyès may have been disgruntled about some aspects of the Constitution of the Year 8, but any resentment was neutralised by the handsome present he received from a grateful nation. It included the farm of the Ménagerie near Versailles, the customs building in the rue de Choiseul and, for good measure, a residence (*hôtel*) in the Faubourg St Germain which housed the Turkish ambassador. Sieyès was buried, as a popular song put it, in this generous and luxurious portion of the national patrimony.[4]

Sieyès and his supporter Roger-Ducos were foundation members of the Senate and, as part of the compromise forged between Bonaparte and the *brumairiens,* Sieyès nominated twenty-nine of the original Senators. The Senate officially elected the three Consuls, appointed appeal court judges and was supposed to act as a watchdog of the Constitution, condemning any legislation which seemed unconstitutional. As Bonaparte became increasingly confident that the Senators would comply with his wishes (which was not at all guaranteed at the start), he used its power to nullify the parliamentary opposition. The Senate had the power to issue decrees in the form of *senatus consulta,* which bypassed the legislature altogether. Such decrees were used, for example, to deport Jacobins in 1801.

Sieyès had constructed a complex apparatus of institutions, in which checks and balances and indirect elections would tame the democratic forces which had erupted between 1792 and 1794. Bonaparte, more concerned with the realities of power than with theoretical politics, broadly accepted these aims and the methods designed to achieve them. The régime was new and insecure and needed the support of the *brumairiens.* Sieyès had helped to rally his supporters in Brumaire, and he could still deliver the votes Bonaparte needed. Bonaparte, however, also had his own ideas, and when it came to discussion of the Consuls themselves he was ready to impose them.

Sieyès had envisaged an executive with relatively limited powers. He named his ideal head of state the Great Elector, in incongruously Prussian fashion, but his notional executive had few of the powers of the mighty Hohenzollerns. It was impossible to imagine an executive head in the abstract because Bonaparte alone was in a position to fill the post. Sieyès, it appears, originally wished to give Bonaparte wide powers of appointment but make him accountable to the Senate, which would have the right to withdraw the mandate of the three Consuls.[5] The possibility of the Senate "demoting" Bonaparte from his rank of Consul was sheer fantasy on the part of Sieyès. Battle was joined here between the protagonists of different conceptions of the "republican monarchy" Sieyès had outlined. An elected monarch who appointed ministers and received ambassadors in style, but who could be recalled by the veteran politicans in the Senate, was not a role likely to appeal to Bonaparte. He had not carried out the coup of Brumaire in order to play a figurehead Doge to Sieyès' Venetian oligarchy.

In theory, the three Consuls were to act as President in daily rotation, and Bonaparte only presided over the first meeting by virtue of alphabetical order. Neither Bonaparte nor anyone else, however, intended simply to replace the defunct Directory of five with a slightly more streamlined Consulate of three. Bonaparte defended a much more "presidential" view of the Consulate, and he prevailed. The other two Consuls were not to have equal votes, but merely "consultative votes", which left Bonaparte much greater freedom as First Consul. Payment of the Consuls reflected Bonaparte's pre-eminence. Bonaparte's salary was set at 500 000 francs annually, while his two colleagues would each receive 125 000 francs per year. He was to appoint and dismiss ministers, who had no collective responsibility and were not united by anything resembling a ministerial cabinet. In fact the appointment of all officers of state was in his power for a period of office of ten years, and the First Consul could initiate legislation through the Conseil d'État (Council of State). After 1802, when Bonaparte became Consul for Life, he also assumed the power to appoint the other two consuls and to designate his own successor.

Sieyès, unwilling (as he put it) to be Bonaparte's aide-de-camp, refused nomination for the post of Second Consul. Instead, Bonaparte's fellow-consuls were Cambacérès, who had sat in the Convention as a moderate member of "the Plain", and Lebrun, who had been a secretary of chancellor Maupeou in the 1770s, and was probably still a royalist.[6] The choice of Consuls thus demonstrated the desire for conciliation between the Revolution and the Old Régime. France's new body of legislators were also from diverse backgrounds, but out of the 400 members of the Tribunate and Legislative Chamber 149 (or 37.25 per cent) had been members of revolutionary assemblies before 1796, and no fewer than 340 (or 85 per cent) had sat in the councils of the Directory. Forty-seven (or 11.75 per cent) were new men. There were eleven regicides in the Legislative Chamber and nine in the Tribunate.[7] The Consulate therefore ensured a considerable continuity of personnel who had served under its republican predecessors.

THE SECOND CONSUL

Jean-Jacques-Régis de Cambacérès belonged to the robe nobility. He was the son of a Montpellier magistrate and followed a legal career in his home department of the Hérault, until he was elected to the National Convention in 1792. He worked long hours in the Committee on Legislation and was very careful not to commit himself too far to any political programme. He had voted for the death of Louis XVI but was in favour of suspending the death sentence. After the fall of Robespierre, he joined the thermidorean Committee of Public Safety and was elected to the Council of the Ancients under the Directory, becoming Minister of Justice in the Year 7. He was a prudent, moderate jurist and followed an illustrious career as a trusted deputy to Bonaparte. He presided over the Senate, helped to prepare the codification of the law, and took charge of routine administration while Bonaparte was away from Paris. He wrote daily to Napoleon during these absences but never took an independent initiative. He amassed huge wealth as Napoleon's Arch-Chancellor and Duke of Parma, which he invested in land, private companies and government bonds. He was a model second-in-command, and a shrewd *notable*. He was a homosexual.[8]

Bonaparte was impatient for the political theorists to finish their discussions and put the new institutions into effect. He had little respect for what he called Sieyès's "metaphysical claptrap" (*niaiseries métaphysiques*), and it was typical of his methods that he made the drafting committee work and negotiate repeatedly into the early hours of the morning, to complete the constitution as quickly as possible.[9] As far as Bonaparte was concerned, everything had to be finished yesterday, and when destiny called there was no time for erudite discourse on the finer points of jurisprudence. At a meeting on 22 Frimaire Year 8, he forcefully persuaded the deputies drafting the Constitution to elect the three Consuls, although decisions like this were supposed to be submitted to the full legislature for formal discussion. A plebiscite was designed to present the Constitution for popular ratification but, again, Bonaparte could not wait for the results to come in. A law voted the inauguration of the Constitution from Christmas Day 1799 (4 Nivôse Year 8) before the results of the plebiscite were known. This was unbridled arrogance, and Georges Lefebvre argued that it was just one of the illegalities marking the birth of what he called the "dictatorship of the notables".[10] On 19 February 1800, Bonaparte moved from his rooms in the Luxembourg palace which had been the headquarters of the Directory. He took up official residence instead in part of the royal palace of the Tuileries, a move symbolic of the political rupture he wanted to emphasise, and an omen perhaps of his personal aspirations. The régime had not devoted its attention solely to the drawing up of a Constitution. Restrictions which had been imposed on the relatives of *émigrés* were lifted, and as another conciliatory gesture full funeral honours were ordered for Pope Pius VI, who had died in Valence. Since the pretext for the seizure of power in Brumaire had been a Jacobin conspiracy, a consular decree of 20 Brumaire sentenced thirty-four Jacobins to deportation to Guyana. The decree, however, was never carried out and two weeks later it was rescinded. Pacification was better than further provocation.

The Law of Hostages and the Forced Loan of 1799, which had so alarmed conservative republicans, were quickly repealed by Bonaparte to reassure the banks and the commercial bourgeoisie. Bonaparte visited the Temple prison personally to liberate the detainees.[11] The new régime's finances, however, were an urgent problem. General Tax Collectors (*Receveurs-Généraux*) were appointed in every department, but they were expected to lend the government money in anticipation of collected revenue, just as the tax farmers had done for the Old Régime monarchy. The Bank of France was established to underwrite the bonds and promissory notes issued by the government.

Centralisation of authority was exemplified by the Conseil d'Etat, a hand-picked committee of experts who advised the First Consul on administrative and legal business, and were responsible for drafting legislation. Here, in secret discussions, Bonaparte listened to criticism and expert advice offered by the wisest heads in political and public administration. The Conseil d'Etat had a consultative function but it also trained the administrative cadres of the Napoleonic state. Most of the Ministers subsequently appointed emerged from its ranks, and by 1813 thirty-one prefects had also trained as *auditeurs* of the Conseil d'Etat.[12] It was thus the ancestor of today's nursery of French administrators and technocrats, the Ecole Nationale d'Administration. Only the diplomatic service, which still preferred to recruit from the military, was an exception to this pattern.[13] The

fact that Roederer chose membership of the Conseil d'Etat in preference to a seat in the Senate spoke volumes for its real power. As a
young man, the novelist Stendhal's great ambition was to train as an
auditeur of the Conseil d'Etat. To him this meant a salary, an entrance
to high society and access to attractive women. His appointment in
1810 was "un jour remarquable in my life".[14]

Members of the Conseil d'État were selected not for their political
loyalties, but for the expertise they could bring to the management of
public affairs. The Conseil brought together royalists like Portalis
and Barbé-Marbois with Jacobin sympathisers like Treilhard, and one
ex-regicide, Berlier. They were paid a secure salary of 25 000 francs
per year and many of them enjoyed a long uninterrupted career.
Seven of the original twenty-nine were still members at the end of the
Empire. They were administrative experts, an essential part of the
non-political apparatus of the Napoleonic state.

The creation of such a bureaucracy was not Napoleon's doing; the
Directory had already laid the basis for a successful combination of
pre-revolutionary and republican personnel. In Clive Church's
phrase, the arrival of Bonaparte did not immediately create an
"administrative nirvana".[15] One persistent problem was the continuing rivalry between the Conseil d'Etat and the ministries, of
which the Ministry of War was by far the largest and most demanding
of resources. Under Napoleon, however, the service became more
centralised and subordinate to the Bonapartist élite, as well as being
less responsive to public pressure.

A few of Bonaparte's ministers were also trusted advisers, like
Charles Gaudin, a technocrat and a friend of Sieyès, who held the
Finance ministry from 1799 until 1814. The Ministry of the Interior
was a particularly important post, held first by Lucien Bonaparte
and then by Chaptal (1800–4). The Minister of the Interior was
directly in touch with the prefect in every department, and was
responsible for education, prisons, agriculture and public works.
One or two other ministerial choices were almost inevitable –
Talleyrand held the Ministry of Foreign Affairs until 1807, and
Fouché could not be overlooked at the Ministry of Police, which he
held until 1810. Once again, these power-brokers of Brumaire had
to be offered their share of the spoils. Bonaparte's ministers, however, had little decision-making power of their own. The régime
gathered together the most enlightened advisers and the most
efficient executives, but real power was increasingly centralised in
the hands of the First Consul.

In every department of the Republic, a prefect now represented the central government. Appointed by the First Consul, as were his subordinate sub-prefects, the prefect became an essential agent of central control and information gathering. The creation of the prefects in Pluviôse Year 8 resolved a series of experiments which had explored in turn the merits of decentralisation (as in the 1791 Constitution) and centralisation (as in the Jacobin Constitution). The Bonapartist régime, however, went further than its centralising ancestors. The Old Régime Intendants had tried to administer entire provinces; under the Jacobin government, the *agent national* had been appointed over the much smaller unit of the district. In his department, however, the prefect enjoyed wider powers of administration and appointment, which could be exercised with more freedom than those of any of his predecessors. Unlike the Intendant before him, the prefect did not have to deal with local opposition from the now defunct Parlements. Unlike the deputies *en mission* in 1793–4, he was not subjected to constant scrutiny and criticism by influential Parisian deputies. Distance from Paris gave prefects some freedom of action. It still took eight days for messages to reach Toulouse from Paris. Napoleon half jokingly told Castellane, Prefect of the distant Basses-Pyrénées, "Castellane, you are a pasha here. Once they get more than 100 miles from the capital, prefects have more power than I do."[16] So successful did the prefectoral system prove, and so valuable was it to all succeeding governments, that restored Bourbons and Republicans alike never contemplated changing it. The system only underwent minor modifications until the presidency of François Mitterrand.

The instructions given by Lucien Bonaparte to the new prefects explained their mission as an apolitical one: they were the agents of the government, not the supporters of any individual revolutionary faction (Document 6.1). They stood above parties, and their first loyalty was always to the state. They had wide responsibilities for public order, trade and manufactures, and conscription.

Local independence was to be strictly curbed, especially in Paris itself. Local departmental councils were to meet for only two weeks annually, simply in order to sub-allocate the department's tax load. Municipal and departmental councils were to be chosen by the government or the prefect, who would also appoint the mayor in small communes with fewer than 5000 inhabitants. Paris had its twelve municipalities, but was subservient not only to the Prefect of the Seine but also to the new Prefecture of Police established in 1800.

---

*DOCUMENT 6.1   LUCIEN BONAPARTE, MINISTER OF THE
INTERIOR, EXPLAINS THE MISSION OF THE PREFECTS IN 1800*

This post demands a wide range of duties, but it offers you great
rewards in the future: you have been summoned to assist the government in its noble design to restore France to her ancient
splendour, to revive in her all that is great and generous, and to
establish this magnificent edifice on the unshakeable foundations
of liberty and equality ... You will not be called upon to carry out
the whims or passing desires of a fickle government, unstable in its
operation, and anxious about its future. Your first task is to destroy
irrevocably, in your department, the influence of those events
which for too long have dominated our minds. Do your utmost to
bring hatred and passion to an end, to extinguish rancour, to blot
out the painful memories of the past ... In your public decisions,
and even in your private lives, be always the first magistrate of your
department, never the man of the revolution. Do not tolerate any
public reference to the labels which still cling to the diverse political parties of the revolution; merely consign them to that most
deplorable chapter in the history of human folly ... You will receive
from the War Minister all the instructions necessary for the administrative responsibilities within his jurisdiction. I will simply limit
myself to a reminder to apply yourself immediately to the conscription draft ... I give special priority to the collection of taxes: their
prompt payment is now a sacred duty. Agriculture, trade, the
industries and professions must resume their honoured status.
Respect and honour our farmers ... Protect our trade, whose freedom can never have any limit except the public interest ... Visit
our manufactures; bestow your highest compliments on those distinguished citizens engaged in them ... Encourage the new generations; fix your attention on public education, and the formation
of Men, Citizens and Frenchmen.
(Translated from Archives Nationales F[1] A 23)

The mayors of the Consulate were often drawn from the ranks of
the notables, or in other words they were landowners, *rentiers* or lawyers, although in 1811 9 per cent of mayors were noblemen. An
increasing number of mayors were of peasant origin – about 40 per

cent in the Empire – and they were young for the job. The average age of Napoleonic mayors was about 50, which made them a younger group than at any other moment of the nineteenth or twentieth centuries.[17] In the judicial hierarchy, the practice of electing local officials was almost completely eradicated. Only justices of the peace, the arbiters of petty disputes at the neighbourhood level, were still to be elected. The judges of the appeal courts which were set up – one for every group of four departments – were appointed by the Senate. Under the Bonapartist system, initiative came from above rather than from below. The changes gave a superficial impression of a return to Bourbon centralisation. The Prefect of Police resembled the Old Régime's Lieutenant de Police, while the appeal courts recalled the defunct Parlements. The power of Paris was strengthened and there was not even a pretence of democratic consultation. With the benefit of hindsight, the parliamentary system can be dismissed as a façade which masked the personal power of the First Consul. The right of universal male suffrage was recognised, provided that it was rarely, if ever, actually used.

The Bonapartist régime, however, was not a revival of the monarchy, and it was too early in 1800 to conclude that a dictatorship was inevitable. The Consulate was a régime of technocrats; Bonaparte would only consult the people when he was sure of their answer, but he readily referred to the experts, the group of moderate administrators who had survived the Revolution, and showed a competence in administration and the law, which the French state found indispensable. In the Conseil d'État, in the prefectures and in the Senate, they were the notables, the cream of the revolutionary bourgeoisie united with Old Régime personnel, now well ensconced in the governing machinery of Bonaparte's Republic.

A plebiscite was organised to solicit public approval for the Constitution of the Year 8. As is normally the case in such plebiscites, the electorate was not presented with a set of options but simply asked to ratify a *fait accompli*. Voters had little alternative to supporting the régime in power; but the whole aim was to legitimise the coup of Brumaire, rather than to advertise the government's non-existent commitment to pluralism. Registers were opened in every commune, where voters had three days to sign their acceptance or rejection of the Constitution. Illiterate voters could, in theory, vote by proxy, but in practice the method of voting tended to exclude the illiterate. For the first time, the vote could be registered in a notary's office – an innovation which effectively allowed the bourgeois and the land-owner to vote secretly and discreetly. On the 18 Pluviôse, the government announced that over 3 million had voted *oui*, approving the Constitution, while only 1562 had the audacity to reject it openly.[18] The figures had been carefully and systematically "massaged" in Lucien Bonaparte's Ministry of the Interior, as Langlois has shown.[19] The number of signatures in favour of the Constitution was "increased" by about 8000 votes per department. In Paris, the falsification was less blatant, but when the votes for the south-eastern departments were added up, a round figure of 13 000 was added on for each department. In addition, half a million votes of approval were "counted" for the army, although its members never in fact had the opportunity to vote. The falsification of the results, amounting to what Langlois called a new *coup d'état*, created almost a million and a half fictitious Bonapartist supporters. Far from assembling 3 million supporters, the Consulate's real friends probably numbered only 1 550 000. This was fewer than those who had officially supported the Jacobin Constitution of 1793 (Table 6.1).

Table 6.1   Votes in Approval of Revolutionary Constitutions

Year	No. in favour	No. against
1793 Constitution	1 801 918	11 610
1795 Constitution	1 057 390	49 938
Year 8 (official)	3 011 007	1562
Year 8 (revised)	1 550 000	1562

The government manufactured the electorate of 3 million voters it required, in order to claim the support of a clear majority and to measure its success against previous revolutionary constitutions. The high abstention rate, however, which had plagued the last years of the Directory, remained a worrying feature of the plebiscite of the Year 8. Paris had been reluctant to vote. In Marseilles, a city with more than 100 000 inhabitants, only 1200 voted in the Year 8.[20] The electorate as a whole still witheld its approval from the Consulate, which failed, at least until 1802, to convince voters of its credibility and legitimacy.

Bonaparte would never again risk a public consultation in winter, when adverse weather conditions deterred thousands of voters in rural and mountainous areas. In future, he would be much better prepared. In 1800, the new government was trying to win a plebiscite with the machinery of local government it had inherited from the Directory. Reluctant or hostile departmental administrations could obstruct the Consulate's plans. Some local authorites preferred to wait for the outcome before committing signatures to an official list, which they feared might one day be used against the signatories. Not until the prefectoral system was operational, and could exert the kinds of electoral pressure which were the prefect's speciality, would the government be fully confident about preparing new plebiscites.

The victory at Marengo in 1800 consolidated Bonaparte's position, but the immediate future of the Consulate was still uncertain. The attempted assassination of Bonaparte on 3 Nivôse Year 9 helped to focus attention on the problem of long-term stability. A huge explosive device, known as the "infernal machine", was disguised as a water-barrel and planted on a cart in the rue Niçaise, a narrow street near the Tuileries, as Bonaparte was on his way to the Opera.[21] The explosion was poorly timed. Thirteen people were killed, several houses gutted, and windows in the Tuileries palace were blown out 400 metres away. But the First Consul and his party were unscathed.

Bonaparte used this opportunity to force the Senate and the Council of State to grant him emergency powers. He blamed the conspiracy on the Jacobins, although Fouché proved to Bonaparte that royalists were responsible. Two of them were eventually executed for their part in the "Opera Plot", but 130 Jacobin suspects had already been deported. The plot had exposed the fragility of the new régime. If Bonaparte was killed on the battlefield, or murdered by an assassin, what would become of the Consulate's attempts to stabilise the French Revolution? The shock of this narrow escape from death initially provoked Bonaparte's rage. Once his fury had subsided, his mind turned to thoughts of securing his succession. Perhaps, too, the event encouraged greater ruthlessness in his pursuit of power.

The Bonapartist Constitution of the Year 8 established the framework for cementing in place the main social changes brought about by the French Revolution. The new régime pursued three main aims – greater centralisation of power, the reconciliation of the Old Régime with the new, and the cultivation of the support of the notables.

The prefectoral system proved a lasting solution to the problem of centralisation. The 1791 Constitution had favoured decentralisation, reacting against the abuses of royal absolutism and the arbitrary powers of despotic royal ministers. The 1795 Constitution had similarly reacted against the concentration of emergency wartime powers, including powers of political police, in the hands of the committees of the National Convention. But neither had provided stability, and the Directory had not found an enduring solution either. The Bonapartist remedy, which gave supreme authority to the First Consul, operating through the Council of State and hand-picked prefects, was more Jacobin in spirit, furthering the French tradition of strengthening centralised state authority at the expense of the regions. According to Chaptal at the Ministry of the Interior, under the new system, policy could be transmitted into action "with the speed of magnetic fluid".[22]

The task of reconciliation was promoted by an amalgamation of old and new élites within the new parliamentary institutions set up by Bonaparte. In the Senate, the Tribunate and the prefectoral body, moderates from the right and left were brought together and invited to find common ground. The bureaucracy already inherited from the Directory was preserved and expanded, while the principle of devotion to the state took preference over previous factional loyalties. In the Council of State, ex-royalists cooperated with ex-Conventionnels, following the example set by the second and third consuls, Lebrun the administrator of the Old Régime, and Cambacérès, a regicide from a southern robe family.

The electoral system (which became a formality) rested on the selection of local "notables", whom Bonaparte strove to rally and to reassure. They formed an élite of educated property owners, who had rendered or who could in future render service to the state. They were men of "merit" – in other words, they belonged to a class which had most to gain from the careers and opportunities opened up by the Revolution. Roederer explained to Bonaparte his view of the social foundations of the Consulate:

> There are four principal circumstances which confer the respect of public opinion and *notabilité*: high birth, wealth, merit and age. We cannot and do not wish to establish *notabilité* on birth. But we can and do want to establish it on the basis of property, merit and age; and that is what the Constitution has in mind.[23]

The lists of notables also had the function of excluding the undesirable from positions of influence, those whose political sympathies were suspect or who were otherwise considered incompetent or unworthy. They illustrate the Bonapartist attempt to incorporate and consolidate the new élite of talent and property thrown up by the revolutionary decade into a Republic of Notables. Several urgent problems still awaited a solution. The first was the religious schism initiated by the oath to the Civil Constitution of the Clergy in 1790, which remained the most divisive long-term issue in French revolutionary politics. The second was royalist activity, known as the *chouannerie*, in Brittany, and the seething revolt against the Republic in the Vendée, where fear of reprisals had reduced voters to a paltry number in the Year 8 plebiscite. The educational system functioned only intermittently and the economy was stagnant. Above all, France needed peace (Document 6.2). Bonaparte offered peace to Austria, and despatched a Christmas letter to the King of England, which was given maximum publicity, in these terms: "Must this war which for eight years has ravaged the four corners of the globe continue until eternity? Is there no way of reaching an understanding? How can the two most enlightened nations of Europe … forget that peace is the first of our needs and our chief glory?"[24] Peace and glory, however, were to prove strangely incompatible.

DOCUMENT 6.2   THE RESTORATION OF ORDER, 1800–1

Toulouse had a reputation for Jacobinism under the Directory, but the surrounding countryside had been the scene of a royalist uprising in 1799. The Prefect of Toulouse reported with usual exaggeration and smugness on the miraculous transformation of his department from a state of Directorial violence into one of exemplary Bonapartist order.

Prefect of the Haute-Garonne to the Minister of the Interior, Toulouse, 3 Germinal Year 9

A year has now passed, Citizen Minister, since I was given the honour of administering the department of the Haute-Garonne. It is not without a certain satisfaction that I consider the situation in this region when I arrived, and compare it to its present condition. In Germinal Year 8, the department of the Haute-Garonne was beset by troubles and disorder. Toulouse was in open revolt … a seditious crowd had forced the sale of grain at a low price; authority was flouted, property was violated with the consent of local government, trade was destroyed, and the troops had been disarmed by the multitude … there were garrisons everywhere, and two half-brigades of infantry and a regiment of cavalry did not suffice to contain the rebels and troublemakers ...

A great number of factious subjects dominated the countryside and tyrannised citizens. They defied every law with impunity; they attacked and beat in broad daylight those whose clothing or manners did not meet with their approval ...

Today the department enjoys the greatest tranquillity, although it is completely without troops, and supplies, especially bread, are excessively expensive. Anxiety and troubles have given way to the most complete security. Each citizen is calmly enjoying his property and his industry, blessing the government which protects him, and provides him with the benefits of order ... Administrative matters are despatched with speed and impartiality. Crime is rare and the guilty are promptly apprehended and punished. The spirit of faction is nowhere in evidence, and the brawls which used to occur daily are not repeated. In a word, I dare to suggest, there is not a calmer department in the Republic.

(Translated from Archives nationales F^1cIII.Garonne (Hte-) 8)

7 *The Concordat*

The plebiscite of the Year 8 had not given the Consulate the legitimacy or the security it was seeking. The future still looked uncertain: one military defeat, one successful assassination attempt could end Bonaparte's career. Royalists could still hold out some hope of a restoration, and veterans of the Revolution like Talleyrand and Fouché were inclined to hedge their bets against unpredictable developments. The French victory at Marengo in Piedmont in 1800 resolved these doubts and encouraged the waverers to throw in their lot with Bonaparte. The risky but successful campaign in Italy secured Bonaparte's personal authority in France. He could now deal from a position of strength not only with the Austrians, but also with the domestic opposition and troublesome *brumairiens*.

The allied advances of 1799 had effectively driven the French from Italy and threatened the Rhine frontier. The French, however, held the stronghold of Switzerland and Bonaparte assembled a reserve army near Lyon, which gave him the option of attacking the Austrians either in Italy or southern Germany. Since 1796 Bonaparte had committed French foreign policy to a new Mediterranean dimension. His preference was for another invasion of Italy, especially as Masséna's army was cut off and blockaded in Genoa. In May 1800, Bonaparte crossed the Great St Bernard pass over the Alps, not quite as heroically as David depicted the occasion, on a white charger, following in the footsteps of Hannibal and Charlemagne (Plate 6). In fact he rode a mule, which was a far more sensible way of negotiating the difficult mountain paths.

Once across the Alps, Bonaparte did not hurry to relieve Masséna in Genoa. Instead he moved towards Milan and secured both sides of the Po valley. While the Austrians besieged Masséna, he would block their retreat. The French, however, hardly had a secure line of retreat themselves, which made an early victory desirable. This gamble nearly failed when the Austrians launched a surprise attack near Alessandria, but the French victory was secured by Desaix, who was killed in battle, and by Kellermann's cavalry.

The battle of Marengo, trumpeted as a victory for Bonaparte, did not in itself guarantee peace. Events in St Petersburg, for instance, worked against France. In 1796, Catherine the Great's successor, Tsar Paul, had led a reaction against all his mother's works and adopted an attitude hostile to Britain. In March 1801, however, Paul was assassinated and his successor Alexander I once again reversed the trend of Russian policy, in favour of the coalition. Meanwhile, Moreau had led a decisive attack on the Rhine, occupied Munich, and in December 1800 defeated the Austrians at Hohenlinden.

At Lunéville, in 1801, France secured Venice and the Dalmatian coast, while Austria was forced to recognise the Swiss, Dutch, Cisalpine and Ligurian Republics. The Cisalpine in particular was expanded to include Verona and the Papal legations. Piedmont was divided into departments, to be ruled from Paris. Lucca became a Republic, with Bonaparte's old Corsican colleague Saliceti as resident French representative. France was now in control of the left bank of the Rhine, as well as northern and central Italy. Bonaparte's generals had given France a commanding position in Europe, and he could now turn to domestic problems with a new authority and confidence in the future.

The religious pacification of France was one of the most urgent of these problems, and Bonaparte had already made overtures to the Pope before the battle of Marengo. The French Revolution had reorganised the Church in France, sold much of its property, and turned the clergy into salaried public servants. In so doing, the revolutionaries had responded to a genuine desire for reform within the Church of the Ancien Régime, and satisfied the democratic aspirations of an impoverished lower clergy. Unfortunately, the Revolution had also created a religious schism which poisoned relations between the Republic and the Catholic Church for more than a century to come.

The Civil Constitution of the Clergy had been introduced unilaterally by the National Assembly in 1790, without reference to the Pope or any other representative ecclesiastical body. Bonaparte, in contrast, required the Pope himself to ratify the religious policies of the Revolution. Most divisive of all, the Revolution had demanded an oath of loyalty from the clergy, which forced them into an unequivocal decision either to support or reject the Revolution. For the parish priest, taking the oath ensured a better salary and a pension, but many could not reconcile their consciences with the new legislation. In many villages, the local congregation helped the priest to solve his dilemma, intimidating him either into a pro-revolutionary or a traditionalist position.

Those who accepted the oath (the jurors, or constitutional clergy) only barely outnumbered those who refused it (the non-jurors, or refractory clergy). The clergy and the country were split in two, and the enemies of the Revolution were immediately presented with millions of potential new recruits. Bonaparte's negotiations with the Pope intended to heal this schism, and to reconcile both sides of the cultural divide which had been growing wider since 1790. His task was to do this without jettisoning the essentials of the Revolution's religious policies – namely, the nationalisation of church property, religious toleration and full government control over the French clergy. Since 1790, the situation of the clergy and of traditional Catholicism within France had worsened. Divorce had been introduced, and the registration of births, deaths and marriages had been secularised. Jews and Protestants were emancipated. Priests had been subject to deportation and the guillotine for subversive activities. Both refractories and constitutional clergy had been victims of the repression of the Terror in the Year 2. A campaign of dechristianisation, spearheaded in the provinces by a handful of deputies *en mission* at the head of *sans-culotte* militia (the *armées révolutionnaires*) had offended rural susceptibilities, by disrupting public worship and traditional religious practices. The iconoclastic activities of the dechristianisers have been dubbed the French "cultural revolution" by Serge Bianchi, making a comparison with the violent propaganda of the Red Guards in China during the 1960s.[1] Priests were encouraged to marry or abjure the priesthood in order to demonstrate their loyalty to the Republic. Many were happy to do so, making a public *autocritique*, welcoming the opportunity for liberation, and repudiating religious bigotry and Catholic "fanaticism". Others succumbed unwillingly to the political or local pressures of the moment to conform to the anticlerical fury of the dechristianisation campaign.[2]

Dechristianisation, in its most aggressive and aggravated form, was a transient phenomenon and it is tempting to interpret it as an episode with no tangible consequences. When the whirlwind visit of the *représentant en mission* was over, and the local contingent of the *armée révolutionnaire* moved on, villagers breathed a sigh of relief and attempted to recover the threads of continuity. Although the dechristianisation campaign was shortlived, however, it was no mere accident. It reflected a growing feeling of anticlericalism in French society, and particularly in urban French society, which could not be easily dismissed as a passing phase. It was part of a long process visible during the Ancien Régime in the decline in masses for the dead, the fall in religious vocations, the declining number of books on theological subjects emanating from Parisian presses, and the beginnings of more generalised techniques of family limitation.[3] Dechristianisation was a brief convulsion which betrayed the presence of deeper, long-term secularising tendencies. Any settlement with the Catholic Church could not alter this underlying reality.

Longstanding regional differences, too, would always help to determine the effect of an agreement between the Republic and the Catholic Church. The oath of 1790 had revealed a geography of French religious practice which has remained surprisingly constant ever since. It reflected wide variations in regional culture, and between urban and rural patterns of religious allegiance. Catholic practice remained stong in western France, Brittany, Alsace, Lorraine and most of the Massif Central. On the other hand, indifference to traditional Catholicism was very marked in the Limousin, and in the group of departments forming the Parisian basin. Traditional religious practice was also weak in parts of the Mediterranean littoral, where the department of the Var recorded a massive acceptance of the oath to the Civil Constitution of the Clergy, and Marseilles was likened by Vovelle to one of the cities of the plain for its rejection of traditional Catholic observance.[4] In many parts of France, the French Revolution broke the habit of universal religious practice once and for all, and no Concordat could repair it. The Church's prohibition on marriage during Lent, for instance, was increasingly ignored in the revolutionary and Napoleonic years, especially in the Paris region.[5] Attendance at Easter Communion during the First Empire remained nearly unanimous in the diocese of Clermont-Ferrand, but in the diocese of Soissons it had already dropped to only 40 per cent of the population aged over 14.[6]

During the Directory, the government's religious policies had oscillated to the right and left as regularly as its periodical *coups d'état*, but in 1795, Church and state had been officially separated. The constitutional church, denied consistent government support, declined, and all Republican alternatives to traditional Catholicism tended to have only limited appeal. The clandestine Church grew more daring, holding baptisms and secret masses, while nuns, monks and *curés* were allowed to return to their functions in schools and hospitals. Indeed, they were sometimes invited to do so by local authorities or by the Minister of the Interior. The Christian Brothers (Frères des Ecoles Chrétiennes) had resumed their teaching activities in many parts of France. By 1800, therefore, a religious revival was under way, and there was a need to recognise the true place of Catholicism in French culture and popular beliefs. Religious peace depended on the full restoration of public worship.

This semi-clandestine revival was, as Olwen Hufton has argued, largely the product of female devotion and militancy.[7] Women were often intimately involved in sheltering proscribed priests, attending secret ceremonies, and putting pressure on the local authorities to make the parish church available again. They organised local boycotts of unpopular constitutional priests. The Abbé Grégoire indeed lamented that his church had been undermined by "debauched and seditious women" (*les femmes crapuleuses et séditieuses*). The restoration of public religious services was demanded, and sometimes enforced, by vociferous female worshippers.

The prospects for this religious revival were not good, considering the long-term decline of the Catholic Church in France. For instance, there was a severe shortage of priests, just as there had been at the end of the Ancien Régime, and Bonaparte's Concordat could do little to solve this crisis of recruitment. In the diocese of Grenoble, between 1801 and 1809, the population grew by 15 per cent, while the number of priests fell by 18.6 per cent.[8] The Revolution had interrupted ordinations in many parts of the country and, except in the Catholic west, they did not resume their old rhythm until after the Empire. There were only eleven ordinations in the Grenoble diocese between 1803 and 1809, but meanwhile 122 clergymen had died. Others had become too old to work and some had abdicated in the Revolution and taken other jobs. In the diocese of Grenoble, only 30 per cent of the clerical personnel of 1789 resumed their functions after the Concordat. Between 1802 and 1814, there were about 6000 ordinations in France – as many as took place in one average year at the end of the Ancien Régime. The clergy, drawn increasingly from rural areas, were not numerous enough to serve every parish. Old age removed priests faster then they could be replaced. In 1814, 42 per cent of active priests were over 60 years' old.[9]

The post-revolutionary Church thus had great difficulty in staging a recovery. Its numbers were depleted and its buildings had fallen out of use. In 1811, a Mâcon dealer bought the famous monastery of Cluny simply to sell the stone.[10] Although there were signs of revival, they were limited to the west and to the countryside. Unfortunately for the Church, the poor rural areas where the revival was strongest became important sources of migration in the nineteenth century. In urban areas, middle-class anticlericalism was a persistent legacy of the

Enlightenment. A generation had grown up in the Revolution ignor-
ant of traditional Catholic teaching, including men like Victor Hugo,
born in 1802, and never baptised by his anticlerical mother who,
although a believer, refused to set foot inside a church.[11] Popular religious practices continued with or without the clergy's approval. In
Brittany, for example, the cult of the saints (to whom powers of heal-
ing were attributed), the blessing of the fleet and other ceremonies
tended to escape clerical control. The *pardon*, a local breton pilgrim-
age in which the whole village participated, marked by drinking and
other festivities, was one manifestation of an old peasant culture
which was only superficially Christianised.[12]

The assumption, therefore, that Bonaparte's reconciliation with
the Catholic Church reflected an irresistible traditionalist groundswell needs to be viewed cautiously. The Catholic revival is often associated with the publication, in 1802, and popularity of one book:
Châteaubriand's *Génie du Christianisme*, interpreted as a timely sign of
the rejection of the rationalist spirit of the eighteenth-century
enlightenment. Châteaubriand's work, however, may be put alongside a thriving, less erudite, less reverent tradition of popular fiction,
exploited by anticlerical novelists like Pigault-Lebrun, who frequently
found his work banned by ecclesiastical authorities. Pigault's popular
novel *L'Enfant du Carnaval*, for instance, featured a greedy and lecherous Capucin, who fathered the hero, and a villainous priest who
forced the heroine to sleep with him. This brand of salacious tale
touched an anticlerical vein of popular culture which had not dried
up. The church's difficulties in a secularising age proved more permanent than this temporary revival of Catholic devotion.

Bonaparte's motives were political and pragmatic, and his methods
opportunist. His policy, as recorded by Roederer, was

> to govern people as the majority desires to be governed. That is, I
> believe, the best way to recognise the sovereignty of the people. By
> turning Catholic I ended the war in the Vendée, by becoming a
> Moslem I established myself in Egypt, by becoming an ultra-
> montane I won over the Italians. If I was governing a people of
> Jews, I would rebuild the temple of Solomon.[13]

In these terms, Bonaparte expounded his realist philosophy.
Unfettered by dogma, he persistently saw his relations with the Papacy
in military terms. He negotiated as a soldier who could occupy the
Papal port of Ancona with impunity, as he did in 1805, overrun the
Papal States if need be, and even arrest the Pope himself, as he did in

1809. The means of physical intimidation were always available to him. When he grew impatient in May 1801 about the pace of negotiations, he sent the Pope an ultimatum: he must agree to terms in five days or French troops would march on Rome (the Papal delegate Consalvi saved the situation by rushing to Paris). When the French representative Cacault asked him how he should treat Pius VII, Bonaparte replied, "as if he had 200,000 men". The Pope was a minor power who could be brushed aside if necessary. Pius, too, negotiated from a position of strength. His power did not lie in generals and armies, but in the humble conviction of the certainty of his beliefs. Bonaparte's military aggression came up against Pius's doctrinaire temperament and unshakeable spiritual faith. He protested against the introduction of the Civil Code and the legalisation of divorce in Napoleonic Italy. After Napoleon seized Rome in 1809, Pius excommunicated him. Only once did he waver: on one tired evening in Savona in 1811, the sick and harassed pontiff agreed to invest Napoleon's bishops – a decision which, refreshed and fortified, he immediately rescinded the following morning.[14] "Your majesty," he announced defiantly on 8 April 1808, "you cover the earth with your armies and your powers, but you cannot give marching orders to our consciences."

Both Napoleon and Pius were to some extent isolated in their capitals, and the Concordat was a personal triumph for both men. Bonaparte's ministers were not enthusiastic about the idea of a compromise with Rome. Fouché had been a dechristianiser during the Terror of 1793–4, while Talleyrand was a married bishop and a founding father of the constitutional church in 1790.

In Rome, Pius was regarded with suspicion as something of a "Jacobin" because he had been prepared to cooperate with the Cisalpine Republic. In addition, Vienna had opposed his candidature, which probably enhanced his credentials from Paris's point of view. His cardinals, however, were divided in their support.[15] The opportunist in Paris thus faced the dogmatist in Rome. Pius VII could not retrieve Avignon, lost to the French Republic at the Treaty of Tolentino in 1797, but he could, later on, stubbornly refuse to consecrate Napoleon's bishops.

For Bonaparte, a religious pacification promised substantial political advantages. At one stroke, it would remove one of the main pillars of the counter-revolution. The seething revolts in the Vendée and in Brittany (the *chouannerie*) could then be effectively suppressed. One of the French negotiators was in fact the Abbé Bernier, a priest from Angers and a Vendean leader who rallied to Bonaparte in the hope of religious peace and personal promotion. The war against the peasant rebels in the Vendée had been a thorn in the side of the Republic since 1793, tying down troops, destroying villages and depopulating the countryside. Vendean casualties have been estimated at about 117 000 dead, or 14 per cent of the area's population. The losses on the Republican side were probably much greater than this, in the region of 200 000 dead.[16] After an agreement between the French state and the Pope, the priests themselves could become local agents of pacification. Conscription had originally sparked off the revolt; but Catholics could now be forced to obey draft orders issued from the mouths of the bishops themselves. In 1801, the *chouans* too were faced with the determined opposition of the First Consul. Special military tribunals, which dispensed with local juries sympathetic to the *chouans*, stifled the rebellion and the royalist leader Cadoudal fled to England.

Bonaparte also needed the Pope's authority to eliminate the opposition of the counter-revolutionary bishops, many of whom had supported anti-republican activities from the safety of exile. "Fifty *émigré* bishops in the pay of England," he claimed, "are now directing the French clergy. Their influence must be destroyed, and for this I require the authority of the Pope." These royalist extremists had made life difficult for moderates within the church, who argued that Catholics could accept any form of political authority, even including a Republic, provided that it guaranteed certain minimum freedoms. Bonaparte could not afford to leave the French Church under their uncompromising influence, but to break it he needed a higher authority, that of Rome itself.

Neutralising the counter-revolution inside and outside France was not Bonaparte's only objective in the negotiations which led to the Concordat. An agreement with Rome, he hoped, would also make the assimilation of conquered territories easier in future. The expansion of French power would be greatly assisted by the acquiescence of the clergy in strongly Catholic parts of Europe like Belgium and northern Italy. In 1803, for instance, a form of the Concordat was introduced into the Italian Republics. For Bonaparte, there was a European as well as merely a French dimension to the problem.

Above all, Bonaparte wanted to reaffirm state control over the Church in France. He sought to heal the divisions of 1790, and at the same time to bring to an end the régime of separation of Church and state inaugurated in 1795. He recognised that religion was too important to be left in the hands of supporters of the refractory church, who would not recognise the sale of the *biens nationaux*, the abolition of the tithe or the secularisation of births and marriages. Fuller government control over salaries and clerical appointments would make the Church subservient to the state and produce clerics who worked to strengthen, rather than to sabotage, the régime. The priesthood could become a kind of moral police in support of the Consulate. "People need a religion," Bonaparte declared, "this religion must be in the hands of the government." "In religion," he also said, "I see not the mystery of the incarnation, but the mystery of social order." France's strong position in Italy, after Marengo and the Treaty of Lunéville, gave him an excellent opportunity to force the Pope into negotiations.

He succeeded because the Catholic Church, for its part, stood to gain enormously from the rechristianisation of France. The authority of the Papacy in revolutionary Europe was at a low ebb. The Jesuits had come under attack from the critics of the Enlightenment, and Clement XIV had officially dissolved the order in 1774. (It was restored in 1814.) In the Habsburg Empire, the most loyally Catholic power in Europe, the reforms of Joseph II had restricted the influence of Rome. The blows dealt by the enlightened absolutists, however, were kind compared to the devastating consequences of French revolutionary expansion. The ecclesiastical principalities of the Rhineland disappeared, the Bourbons of Naples gave way to Murat. The Church found itself deprived of revenue, and disorganised by these upheavals. The papal nuncio at Cologne saw such disasters as the just punishment of heaven for the indifference and corruption of the clergy. But now the population of Europe's largest Catholic state was returning to the bosom of the Church. Freedom of Catholic worship was to be restored in France, and the Pope could not afford to let slip such an opportunity.

The terms of the Concordat forced him to pay a high and sometimes humiliating price. In order to reassure the purchasers of church property auctioned by the Revolution (*biens nationaux*), Pius VII recognised the permanency of these land transfers. He did so reluctantly, demanding compensation (in vain), and refusing to accept the legal rights of new proprietors. This, however, was simply a face-saving phrase. Bonaparte was to decide what level of compensation was appropriate, and he made it clear that the state of government finances prevented the release of anything more than a trivial sum. The French bourgeoisie received an essential guarantee that the land sales were "immutable", and without this the Concordat would have been worthless.

Catholicism was restored as "the religion of the great majority of citizens" – a formula which recognised the literal truth, without violating the idea that in religious terms France was a pluralistic society. In a society which recognised the rights of Protestants and Jews, Catholicism could not claim to be the established or even the dominant religion. The Concordat therefore accepted the limitations of revolutionary anticlericalism; but the state retained its secular character, and Bonaparte preserved the principle of religious toleration which the Revolution had established.

The clergy themselves became salaried employees of the state, as the Civil Constitution of the Clergy of 1790 had intended. The state agreed to pay the bishops and about 3500 parish priests. Cathedral chapters and seminaries could be re-established, but there was no guarantee that the state would subsidise them. All clergy were obliged to take an oath of loyalty to the government, but the mistake of 1790 was not repeated. The oath was a sensitive issue and Bonaparte agreed that a declaration of loyalty to the government would suffice. This did not necessarily mean a promise of submission to its laws: an incongruous nuance which satisfied the Pope, but which seems a travesty of Napoleonic logic. At the end of mass, prayers were to be offered for the state and for the Consuls: *domine salvam fac rempublicam, salvos fac consules.* The clergy could once more be regarded as allies of political order and obedience. Their status had changed but they could again become an important part of the ideological apparatus of the state.

The fate of the bishops, both *émigré* and constitutional, proved the most difficult issue of all. Bonaparte demanded the complete renewal of the episcopate. He was determined to compel the Pope to dismiss the uncompromising counter-revolutionary bishops who had opposed the Civil Constitution of the Clergy since 1790. In return, he would push the constitutional clergy within France to accept the Concordat. For Pius VII, this was the most humiliating sacrifice of all those he made in the interests of the restoration of Catholic worship. He agreed to dismiss those bishops who had been most loyal to the traditional Church. He was being forced to abandon his strongest and most orthodox supporters; their decade of exile was rewarded by outright rejection by Rome. Of the ninety-three survivors of the Ancien Régime episcopate, thirty-eight refused to accept the Concordat, and the Pope himself deprived them of their jurisdiction.

This threatened to revive an old quarrel between those who supported the independence and autonomy of the French Church (Gallicans), and those who defended the prerogatives of Papal power (ultramontanes). The rights of the French Church *vis-à-vis* Rome had usually been defended, of course, by the absolute monarchs, but they sometimes found allies in the French bishops, jealous of papal encroachments on their powers. There was a theoretical and theological justification for this episcopal Gallicanism; the bishops argued that their authority, like that of Christ's apostles, came directly from God. The Pope, therefore, they insisted, had no right to dismiss them. But the dismissal of refractory bishops by the Pope was exactly what Bonaparte secured.

Only in the question of the nomination of new bishops could Pius VII claim a victory. The Concordat stipulated that Bonaparte should nominate the bishops, while the Pope invested them with their spiritual authority. Before long, however, the "honeymoon period" of the negotiations was over, and the Pope and the First Consul were at loggerheads over this question. The Pope made special difficulties over the canonical investiture of twelve of Bonaparte's appointees who had accepted the oath to the Civil Constitution of the Clergy in 1790, ten of whom defied papal instructions to retract. Bonaparte's aim was to liquidate the past without recrimination, in a spirit of reconciliation. He told his bishops that it was illegal to make the ex-constitutional clergy recant their errors, and when he appointed his uncle Fesch as Archbishop of Lyon in 1802, he urged reconciliation between ex-constitutionals and ex-refractories. He did not allow the Pope to veto the appointment of constitutional bishops to the episcopacy of the Concordat.

Personal exchanges between Rome and Paris were to end altogether in 1806 when the Pope refused to recognise Joseph Bonaparte as King of Naples, and the Archbishop of Naples fled to seek refuge in Rome. But Napoleon's arrogance and Pius's calm inflexibility had long since proved incompatible. In captivity, Pius refused to accept Napoleon's nominations to vacant bishoprics. When Napoleon finally ordered the bishops to resume their posts without official inauguration, they were frequently rejected by their own chapters. This recrudescence of internal clerical strife demonstrated how much Napoleon relied on the Pope's blessing as a guarantee of domestic order.

Bonaparte's aim, as ever, was to reunite the moderates on both sides; but the Concordat had opponents both in Rome and on the

French left. The cardinals were divided, the die-hards (*zelanti*) being reluctant to ratify what they saw as craven submission to the demands of a usurper. Thirty-six of the non-juring bishops also refused to accept the Concordat. The counter-revolution, in the person of Louis XVIII's representative Cardinal Maury, consistently argued against an agreement which would consolidate the Consulate.

There was opposition from Catholics in France, too. "La Petite Eglise" rallied a small number of clergy who refused to accept the Concordat. The war against Catholic Spain and the imprisonment of the Pope were to strengthen these rebels. Opposition was predictably strong in the breton west. In 1806, one group kidnapped and ransomed Bishop Pancemont of Morbihan because he was considered too pro-Bonapartist.[17]

Some Jacobins were also thrown into despair by the Concordat. On 28 Germinal Year 10 (Easter Day, 1802), the government and diplomatic corps attended mass in Notre Dame for the first time after the Concordat was signed. General Delmas was heard to object on this occasion that "all we need is the 100 000 men who got themselves killed to be rid of all this".[18] There was opposition from Grégoire, the leader of the constitutional Church. There was criticism in the Conseil d'État and amongst the republican opposition in the Tribunate. In 1802, Bonaparte purged the Tribunate of these opponents, and two years later the popular verdict seemed clear when Pius VII was greeted by enthusiastic crowds on his visit to France, in 1804–5.

Perhaps Bonaparte took note of the opposition, because he realised that the Concordat needed strengthening. The Concordat had explicitly foreseen the need for executive measures to spell out the details of its implementation. Bonaparte took advantage of this to issue, unilaterally and without regard for the Pope, a series of Organic Articles to strengthen secular authority over the clergy. No papal Bull was to be published without government permission, and papal representatives in France required government authority to carry out their missions. Bishops would in future require the permission of a Minister to leave their dioceses or establish cathedral chapters. Organic Articles providing for the payment of salaries to Protestant clergy were also added to these decrees. They amounted to a strengthening of centralised authority at the expense of the helpless Papacy.

Within their dioceses, however, the power of the bishops was enhanced by the Organic Articles. For the bishops had the power to appoint parish priests – a function which the Civil Constitution of the

Clergy had entrusted to election by "active" citizens. The bishop was thus empowered to overrule the private patrons who had controlled benefices in the Ancien Régime, as well as to ignore, if necessary, the wishes of local congregations. The democratic and Richerist agitation of the lower clergy at the end of the Ancien Régime was forgotten, and the sense of hierarchy was reinforced.

The confrontation between the First Consul and Pius VII was rich in historical resonances. The struggle over the appointment and investiture of bishops resembled the conflicts of the seventeenth century between the Pope and Louis XIV. Napoleon's request that the Pope should crown him Emperor deliberately suggested the precedent of Charlemagne. Pius could hardly refuse, since the French Empire seemed to control the fate of so many European Catholics. But he insisted that Napoleon and Joséphine should go through a secret religious marriage ceremony beforehand. In 1805, the ceremony was performed in Milan, with Napoleon symbolically putting the crown on his own head (this was planned: he did not seize it from the Pope at the last moment, as is sometimes believed).[19] This rite, however, was only a superficial attempt at the "resacralisation" of monarchy, whose religious aura had been shattered in 1793 by the decapitation of Louis XVI (Plate 7). (A much more serious attempt to reunite throne and altar was to be made after 1815 by the restored Bourbons, and it ended in disaster in the 1830 Revolution.) Difficult years lay ahead for the Papacy, severely weakened and struggling to resist the demands of French imperialism all over the continent. Pius and Bonaparte had nevertheless brought about a much needed reconciliation to heal the disastrous schism of 1790.

It was not easy to make this reconciliation effective. A series of bitter conflicts erupted between refractories and constitutional priests, resonant with echoes of 1790–1 (Document 7.1). Some priests refused the sacrament to purchasers of *biens nationaux* of ecclesiastical origin, and to married priests. In the west, *chouans* were even prepared to murder the wives of ex-clergymen, if it was clear that their marriage had been consummated.[20] Some congregations, on the other hand, were determined to defy the authorities in order to hang on to their constitutional priests. According to Bonaparte's guidelines, about one-third of the post-Concordat priesthood was to be drawn from the ranks of the constitutional priests of 1790–1. This was achieveable in a diocese like Grenoble, but not in Vannes, where there were far too few juring priests.

*DOCUMENT 7.1   RELIGIOUS CONFLICTS AFTER THE
CONCORDAT*

*In an unsigned report probably written in 1803, a police inspector
summarised a wide range of recent incidents for the Minister of Police. The
emphatic underlinings are those of the angry inspector.*

I have already on more than one occasion drawn to your
Excellency's attention the conduct of a few turbulent priests,
whose incorrigible obstinacy gives rise every day to fresh <u>scenes
of scandal</u>.

Perhaps the most revolting incidents are those provoked by
the refusal of <u>church burial</u>. These are also the most frequent.

In Fructidor the justice of the peace of the canton of Braine
(Aisne) denounced the *curé* of that commune for refusing burial
to Fouquet and Carguet, deceased, because, he said, they had
died <u>without the benefit of sacrament</u>, and that besides, the
former was a <u>married priest</u> ...

Even more recently, Plochon, *curé* of St Gervais (Vienne)
refused to conduct a religious funeral for the mayor's assistant.
He alleged that the deceased <u>had never made his Easter confes-
sion</u>, and that he did not attend Church services regularly.

The police commissar of Nevers denounces several priests ...
accusing them of preaching disorder and anathematising purchasers of national properties ...

The assistant mayor of Boisguillaume (Seine-Inférieure)
denounces the priest Autin ... for having refused the sacraments
to two men on their deathbed, because they had been married
by a <u>constitutional priest</u>. He has written to the prefect and the
Minister of Religion.

Fontelaye, curate of Rasnes (Orne) was denounced for recommending <u>the King, the Queen and the Royal Family</u> to his congregation from the pulpit at high mass ... A prosecution was
initiated. The facts were clearly proved, and were not even
denied by Fontelaye, but he excused himself claiming it was an
accident which he calls a <u>lapsus linguae</u>. Several witnesses supported this allegation, the prefect himself seemed to enjoy it,
and ordered that the matter <u>be dropped</u>.

(Translated from Archives Nationales F[7].8058, Affaires
religieuses-Aisne)

The application of the agreement over the next few years was entrusted to Portalis, the lawyer and firm Catholic to whom Bonaparte awarded the religious portfolio. Bonaparte advised Portalis in 1802: "Mix the constitutional priests with the others in such a way that no party seems to be triumphing at the expense of the other."[21] Portalis's administration was, if anything, benevolent to the Catholic Church. His interpretation of disputes often protected the clergy from anticlerical prefects, and gave the Church considerable freedom over its own affairs. For example, he allowed the Church to refuse the sacraments as it pleased, denying remarriage to divorcees, and determining its own qualifications for receiving first communion.[22] From an expanding budget, the government also helped the Church with its recruitment problems, providing scholarships for seminarians in 1807, and exempting theology students from the call-up in 1809.

In 1808, Napoleon made secondary education for boys a state monopoly; but primary education and the education of girls were effectively turned over to the Catholic Church. Portalis therefore initiated a policy favourable to the re-emergence of female religious orders, who could play a vital teaching role. The Ursulines and the Visitandines were provisionally re-established in 1807, and a spate of authorisations for female teaching congregations followed. This growth of the female orders provided a career for women which was compatible with prevailing stereotypes of the feminine character as caring, passive and vulnerable to religious sentiment. The Church was also attractive as an important focus for female sociability. The expansion of female religious orders seemed a social necessity and thus received some official assistance, although it was boosted even further after the Empire until, at some point in the 1850s, women became a majority of the French clergy as a whole.[23]

What were the consequences of the Concordat? It helped to achieve the internal pacification of France and the conclusion of the civil war in the Vendée. The rebels were now forced to pray for the Republic, and the bishops encouraged obedience to the government. The forces of royalism and counter-revolution were weakened by the agreement, and many of their supporters disarmed by it.

The formation of a new episcopate illustrated the idea of reconciliation of the old France and the new. The extremists on both sides were isolated, as the distinctions between jurors and non-jurors gradually became redundant. There were many immediate problems to resolve. Priests who had married wished to know their status in the eyes of the Church. Others who had burned their ordination papers during the Revolution applied for reinstatement. The authority of both Bonaparte and Pius VII, however, was now united in favour of softening tension and satisfying the demand for a resumption of Catholic worship.

In spite of the grumblings of Delmas on the steps of Notre Dame, the Concordat had preserved many important gains of the Revolution. There was no going back on religious toleration, and the Pope had to accept that Catholicism was one of several religions existing side by side in France. The interests of property-owners were guaranteed by the protection of their purchases of *biens nationaux* from the Church. A secular state had emerged from the Revolution in which the clergy enjoyed no special privileges. The Church was no longer an independent corporation within the state, but a body of salaried state servants dependent on the government, just as the National Assembly had intended.

Diocesan boundaries were reorganised. Instead of making every department into a bishopric, which had been the policy in 1790, the number of bishops was reduced to fifty. In the Ancien Régime, a few very rich bishoprics contrasted with a multitude of small and poorer ones, mainly in the south. These inequalities had definitively disappeared, and the notion that the secular government could redraw the ecclesiastical map was not weakened.

Perhaps the most important repudiation of the Civil Constitution was the rejection of the principle of the lay election of the clergy. Instead, there was a return to authoritarian, hierarchical arrangements, in which the bishops ruled the dioceses, and the Ministry of Religion restrained the bishops.

The consequences for the Church were the end of a debilitating schism and the restoration of Catholic worship. The Concordat, in the short term at least, appeared as a victory for Gallicanism. The bishops were all powerful within their dioceses, and the Organic Articles greatly limited the scope for papal interference in French ecclesiastical affairs.

In the long run, however, the Concordat ensured the success of ultramontanism. Episcopal Gallicanism had argued that the Catholic Church was not an absolute monarchy, but a monarchy tempered by an aristocracy of bishops. The Pope's dismissal of the *émigré* bishops, however, effectively torpedoed this concept. Events seemed to bear out the ultramontane argument that Christ had given the keys of authority to St Peter alone, and the Papacy had inherited them.

Lamennais, pioneer of liberal catholicism in the 1830s, went further. All the bishops had collaborated with Napoleon, he argued, except for one: the Pope, implying that his authority alone was untainted by French imperial influence. Thus the Concordat paved the way for the ultramontane crescendo of the nineteenth century. Pius VII had shown that the principles of 1789 could be baptised; he was the first liberal Catholic.

8   Law Codes and Lycées

The codification of the law, and the construction of a new educational system were the most permanent achievements of the Napoleonic period. The French Revolution had shattered ancient assumptions about education, property rights, family law and individual freedoms: to Bonaparte fell the task of making a final pronouncement. His Civil Code provided a clear statement of the citizen's rights and duties, in marriage and divorce, dowries, adoption and illegitimacy, wills and inheritances.

Napoleon, looking back from exile and defeat, claimed the Civil Code as a greater victory than any he had won on the battlefield. It may seem strange that a man so devoted to speedy action and incisive conquest should be closely associated with the work of dry and meticulous legists. The Civil Code, however, known after 1807 as the Code Napoléon, bears the stamp of Bonaparte. Stendhal was to claim he read it and reread it as a model of prose clarity.[1] Its provisions on property, family and inheritance law consolidated the Revolution, and the gains of the propertied bourgeoisie. The Code became an instrument of French rule in Europe and an object of emulation all over the globe. Together with the system of secular secondary education put in place by Bonaparte, it also became an important foundation stone of national unification.

Bonaparte himself was only sporadically involved in the discussions on the draft Civil Code, which he initiated in 1800. He chose his legal experts carefully, and with an eye to the spirit of reconciliation which was the hallmark of his most creative reforms. One of them was Tronchet, the lawyer who had defended Louis XVI before the National Convention. Like his colleague, Bigot de Préameneu, he represented the common law tradition of northern France. They were joined by two ex-*parlementaires* from the Midi, Maleville, from Bordeaux, and Portalis from Aix, who had presided over the Council of the Ancients during the Directory period, before being deported after the left-wing coup of Fructidor Year 5. Portalis was nearly blind, but he had a phenomenal memory and an unparalleled knowledge of the law.[2]

When the outline of the Civil Code was under examination by the Council of State, Bonaparte presided personally over about half of the meetings, intervening especially when the legal rights of women were under review. Was the Civil Code influenced by Bonaparte's own experience of marriage to an unfaithful and probably infertile wife? It is impossible to judge. He certainly used his influence to defend patriarchal values in the family law provisions, enhancing the authority of the *paterfamilias* and reducing the rights of illegitimate children. His energetic supervision was chiefly responsible for the lightning speed at which a few guiding principles were effectively transformed into a complete code of civil law, remarkable for its brevity, compactness and accessibility (it could be carried in a convenient pocket-sized volume). The first draft was finished in 1801, but in the Tribunate the Republican opposition rejected parts of the Civil Code which were found to be not revolutionary enough in spirit. But Bonaparte eliminated this opposition by purging the Tribunate in 1802. The Civil Code was promulgated in 1804.

The Revolution had introduced new decrees, about 15 000 of them, which dramatically altered existing law. It freed property of all feudal burdens, for example, it introduced divorce and changed the rights of testators. It abolished seigneurial justice altogether. Revolutionary law was likely to change as rapidly as the republican régime itself, leaving a mass of edicts which were not always consistent with each other. The purpose of the Civil Code was to make order out of these confused legacies of the past. It was to give France, and then Europe, a social charter which would combine Ancien Régime custom with revolutionary innovations. In so doing, the Civil Code ratified the irrevocable end of seigneurialism and feudal privilege. The same laws would now apply equally to all citizens, whatever their social status. Unlike the legal patchwork of Ancien Régime France, the Civil Code would also apply nationally, in every corner of the Republic without exception.

Local custom, interacting with Roman, feudal and then revolutionary law made France a country of great juridical diversity. In the eighteenth century, Montesquieu had seen local diversity and provincial power as essential protection against the encroachments of a centralising monarchy. The monarchy, on the other hand, and then the eighteenth century Enlightenment, had long dreamed of the kind of legal uniformity which Bonaparte was to create, giving all subjects equal rights and duties under laws which were universal, rational and secular.

Regional differences were particularly marked in the law of inheritance. In the Midi, this tended to favour the eldest son at the expense

of other children (the principle of primogeniture), in order to preserve the family estate intact. Northern customs, in contrast, were
inclined to be more egalitarian in their treatment of descendants.
Given provincial diversity, however, it is rash to generalise even this
far: even in parts of the north, such as Flanders, complete equality of
all descendants was not recognised by custom, since all heirs were
considered equal only after the exclusion of offspring already provided with dowries.[3] The Revolution's attempt to abolish feudal primogeniture and make complete equality between heirs compulsory
came into conflict with habits deeply ingrained in half of France.
In the Midi, too, there was a strong dowry system which southern
lawyers did not want to abandon.

There was agreement on the fundamental principles of the Civil
Code, which confirmed a decisive break with the pre-revolutionary
world. The abolition of privilege, equality before the law, and the
notion of careers open to talent were enshrined in this and every subsequent legal code designed for a democratic society. In preventing
any return to the Ancien Régime in these areas, Napoleonic law
developed the legacy of the liberal revolutionaries of 1789–91. The
gains of the revolutionary bourgeoisie were preserved, since individual property rights were recognised within limits defined by the
state. The unregulated economic liberalism of the Code also gave
employers distinct advantages over their workers. Finally, the Civil
Code demonstrated the secularisation of the law, most vividly illustrated by the Revolution's introduction of civil marriage and divorce.
These ideas and their implications can be briefly examined in the
fields of property law, inheritance law, and in the Code's interpretation of marriage and divorce.

The Civil Code embodied the modern conception of property
ownership. It began with the premise that the individual had absolute
rights of ownership. In practice, of course, the right to dispose of
one's property was to be limited by inheritance law. Article 544 still
stands today, defining property as "the right to enjoy and to dispose
of one's property in the most absolute fashion, provided that it is not
used in a manner prohibited by law". New legal constraints have from
time to time eroded the absolute nature of individual property ownership: for example, in the form of laws which today protect the
rights of tenants and control rents.

Property was seen as landed property, rather than commercial or
industrial wealth – an assumption which, as we have seen, reflected
the agricultural basis of the national economy at this time. In a spirit

of bourgeois individualism, land was freed of feudal obligations and ancient servitudes. The principles of the Code were those suited to a mainly pre-industrial society of peasant and bourgeois landowners. Those principles, however, basic to a liberal and capitalist society, remain intact.

The Code's provisions in the field of family law were conservative in the sense that the authority of fathers and husbands was strengthened. Fathers had the right to imprison their children for a month up to the age of 16, and for six months thereafter, and they controlled all their children's property until they reached the age of 18. A father could veto his son's marriage until he was 26, and his daughter's until she was 21. Even after the age of 25, "children" needed to obtain the formal advice of their parents before marrying. The husband could also administer the couple's joint property. Marriage itself, previously considered only as a sacrament, was completely secularised. The Revolution had abolished church courts and made marriage illegal unless a civil ceremony took place.

Dowry customs were a legal nightmare. In some areas of France, the couple's property was held in common; in others, any property brought to the marriage as a dowry remained the wife's property. The Civil Code solved the problem by allowing couples to decide on whichever arrangement they preferred in their marriage contract. In this area at least, the Code recognised the diversity of customary law while upholding patriarchal authority.

Patriarchy was not to have things all its own way. Individual children could not be disinherited, and children born outside the marriage could not inherit unless they had been officially legitimised. (This provision was a reversal of revolutionary law, which had given bastards full rights as heirs.) The Revolution had also tried to regulate the testator's freedom, by compelling him or her to give the heirs equal shares of the inheritance. This measure reflected the Revolution's new recognition of individual rights, which here overshadowed the rights of the family as a collective unit anxious to avoid a partition of its assets. The Civil Code was more moderate, seeking an equilibrium between the family and the individual, and between different practices in various parts of France: it allowed the testator to dispose of a quarter of the estate as he or she pleased (or more than a quarter, if there were fewer than three children), leaving the rest to be shared equally between heirs. A surviving spouse, however, had no automatic right to receive any portion of the estate. This régime recognised the egalitarianism of customary law, but still left some room to promote a principal heir, the favoured strategy of many peasant families.

The idea of equal shares for inheritors had important repercussions, which opponents of the Civil Code were not slow to point out. Some feared that it would lead to the excessive fragmentation of rural properties, reinforcing existing trends towards a society of small but struggling peasant proprietors. By the late nineteenth century, conservatives alleged that peasant families had responded by limiting the number of their offspring, to reduce fragmentation of the estate. A "natalist" argument emerged, accusing the Civil Code of contributing to the depopulation of the country.

The laws on divorce provide an excellent example of the revolutionary attempt to secularise marriage and protect the rights of the individual. They illustrate, too, the direction of the Bonapartist compromise between the old and the revolutionary. The right to divorce was preserved in the Civil Code, but Bonapartist policy was socially conservative and it explicitly recognised the "supremacy of the husband" as part of the "natural order".

In the Ancien Régime, divorce had been completely illegal. Although spouses had been allowed to apply to the courts for a judicial separation, this was expensive and rarely successful. In 1792 the French Revolution introduced the most liberal divorce provisions anywhere in the world, making divorce relatively easy, inexpensive and moreover, equally available to both men and women. The Civil Code repealed the remarkable legislation of 1792 but continued to allow divorce on more restricted grounds. The moderation of the Napoleonic divorce laws was clearly retrograde in comparison with the régime of 1792 and damaging to the status of women; but it should also be seen in the light of subsequent events. In 1816, the Bourbon Restoration abolished divorce altogether. Divorce was not legal again in France until the Naquet Law of 1884 revived the Napoleonic legislation.

The most startling innovation of the 1792 law was to allow divorce by mutual consent. In addition, divorce could be requested unilaterally on grounds of incompatibility, and also for other specified reasons. These included insanity, cruelty, desertion and emigration, criminal conviction, absence without news for five years and "dissolute morals". The immediate result was a flood of applications for divorce by couples who wanted to regularise separations and legitimise existing *de facto* relationships. This rush to divorce has given rise to unfair accusations that the Revolution encouraged immorality and a cynical attitude towards marriage. Such comments deserve to be dismissed as mere clerical propaganda, blind to the liberating effect of the revolutionary legislation. Even the constitutional Church had accepted divorce, although it was not so generous about remarriage. The introduction of divorce had simply opened up a tap through which poured the frustrations and miseries of thousands of couples, some deprived of legal separation, others cohabiting but forced to do so illegally. In Paris, between 1792 and 1803, there was one divorce for every four marriages. Abandonment, emigration or desertion constituted the most frequently cited reasons for divorce under the 1792 law. In Rouen there were 953 divorces, or one for every eight marriages – a relatively high number for a provincial city.[4] Twenty-four per cent of divorces in Rouen during this period were on the grounds of mutual consent, and women appear as the main beneficiaries of the new legislation. In divorce proceedings in both Rouen and Metz initiated by one or the other spouse, women petitioned for divorce two-and-a-half times more frequently than did men.

The Civil Code permitted divorce – and before very long Napoleon himself was to divorce Joséphine – but it ended the liberality of the previous régime. Although Napoleonic legislation did not deny the right to divorce by mutual consent, it nevertheless made it much more difficult than in the past. Both spouses were obliged to provide written consent to their divorce from their parents, and this written parental statement had to be submitted four times within a year before divorce could be decreed. Even then, a judge had to examine the chances of reconciliation. This was divorce by consent of a sort – but it seems more accurately described as divorce by *parental* consent.

The Civil Code permitted divorce on only three other grounds: ill-treatment (*excès, injures graves*), criminal conviction or adultery. "Ill-treatment" was a legal euphemism for wife-beating, which was a common enough reason for divorce petitions. Society tolerated a limited degree of domestic violence, seen as part of the husband's natural right to administer "correction" to wayward spouses. But if the neighbours were kept awake by domestic disputes, or if one violent party resorted to a knife or a blunt instrument, the neighbourhood would intervene to restore peace, chastise the offender and shelter the victim. This was sometimes necessary after a drinking session or a religious festival (which might amount to the same thing). Insanity was no longer a basis for divorce under the Civil Code; families were expected to care for their own in time of ill-health.

The law on adultery discriminated against the woman. A man could petition for divorce on the grounds of his wife's infidelity, but a woman could only petition for divorce on the grounds of her husband's infidelity if he had an adulterous relationship with another woman in the conjugal dwelling itself. Women convicted of adultery were also liable to a two-year prison sentence, which was not the case for men. The law thus applied a double standard to sexual conduct, apparently condoning extra-marital affairs involving the husband but witholding the same tolerance from the wife. In many ways the Civil Code was ahead of its time, but its misogyny was an exception.

It is no wonder that divorces were rarer during the Napoleonic Empire. In Lyon, the annual divorce rate fell from eighty-seven before the Civil Code to seven after 1805. In Rouen, the average rate of divorce between 1803 and 1816 fell to only six per year. Only 7 per cent of these were divorces by mutual consent.[5] Phillips' study of Rouen divorcees in the revolutionary and Napoleonic period suggests that divorce was most likely to occur when the woman had married between the ages of 15 and 20, when the marriage was less than five years old, or when the couple was childless (Figure 8.1). In fact, custody arrangements seem rarely to have been contentious, which suggests that the fate of children, if there were any, was not regarded as an important issue.

Divorce was overwhelmingly an urban option. In the department of the Haute-Garonne, for example, the number of divorces diminished in direct proportion to distance from the city of Toulouse. The city provided a multitude of jobs and refuges for women fleeing an unsatisfactory marriage, which were not available in small rural communities. The main beneficiaries of divorce legislation were young working women of the cities, where wage-earning opportunities for women in workshops and factories gave them a small but independent income. In the countryside, perhaps, the impact of Catholic teaching was stronger, and the traditional family economy was not so readily undermined by independent female wage-earners. Participation in the job market, however exploitative and poorly paid, may be considered here as a factor in female emancipation.[6] In Rouen, 69 per cent of men who divorced and 72 per cent of women were workers and artisans, many of them employed in the city's textile industry. Divorce did not involve expensive litigation and it was not a rich person's prerogative. It involved appearance at a family court, but it was genuinely available to the urban lower and lower middle classes.

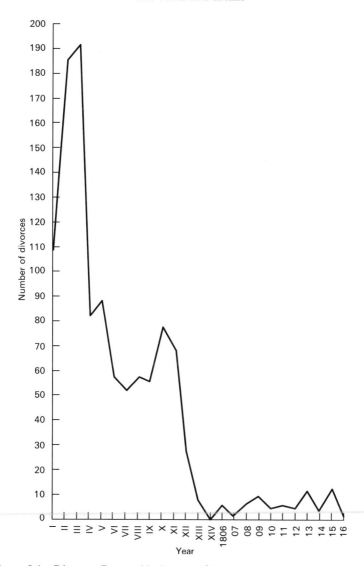

Figure 8.1   Divorces Decreed in Rouen, 1792–1816

Source: R. Phillips, *Family Breakdown in Late 18th Century France* (Oxford, 1980).

The legal status of women had therefore been dramatically improved by the French Revolution, but Bonapartist legislation put a brake on the advances achieved. Divorce was still possible, but the law conceived it rather as a punishment for misconduct (usually by the

woman), rather than as the humane recognition of an irretrievable
marital breakdown. The Revolution had recognised women's civil
rights, as equal access to divorce clearly demonstrated. There was,
however, no corresponding recognition of women's *political* rights. In
practice, no one had stopped women taking part in revolutionary
politics. They attended political clubs and even if they were segreg-
ated in a special gallery, this did not prevent them from intervening
and participating vigorously in debates. Women played a leading
role, too, in the food and grocery riots of the Revolution, although in
these cases their militancy reflected their important domestic role as
supervisers of household consumption. Women, however, were still
denied a political existence. They were not permitted to vote, and
this was never on the political agenda of the Revolution, let alone the
Consulate and Empire.

Bonaparte's régime continued to exclude women from the sphere
of politics and public affairs, and it also made explicit several of the
legal disabilities affecting women. Under the Civil Code, the wife
owed obedience to the husband and she could not enter any legal
contract without his permission. As we have seen, her infidelity was
penalised much more severely than her partner's. The husband controlled his wife's domicile and could legally evict her and her children. If she was unmarried, a woman could not even witness a legal
document. Patriarchal authority, buttressed by assumptions about
innate female frailty and lack of seriousness, was underlined.[7]

The Civil Code was not the only effort at legal reform made in this
period. A Commercial Code was introduced in 1807, and in 1808 the
Code of Criminal Procedure confirmed the principle of trial by jury.

The Penal Code of 1810 was conceived in a spirit of utilitarianism,
valuing public order above the need for retribution against the criminal. Nevertheless, it contained some clauses reminiscent of the
harshness of the Ancien Régime. The death penalty was retained for
murder, arson and forgery. Parricide could be punished by amputation of the offending hand, and some criminals were still liable to be
sentenced to forced labour for life (*peines perpétuelles*). Judges had
more scope for leniency than the Constituent Assembly of 1791 had
given them: they could use their discretion to award prison sentences
whose length varied within a statutory range (for example, one to five
years for theft).

The Napoleonic Codes, especially the Civil Code, had a European
and even global significance. The Code was an integral part of the
spread of French Revolutionary ideas all over the world. It became

an instrument of French conquest and a weapon in the war against the coalition. It promised to liberate Europe from clericalism and feudalism. It was introduced in Belgium and the Netherlands, the Rhineland, Bavaria, Switzerland and parts of Italy. The Code helped to win the support of the local bourgeoisie for French rule. Its influence in these areas of Europe is still present today. It was translated for the benefit of the Spanish and Portuguese, and it inspired law codes in Egypt and South America, Louisiana, Japan, Rumania and Yugoslavia.[8]

The Civil Code inspired European intellectuals: in Dresden, the playwright Kleist had a burning ambition to translate it into German.[9] At the same time, it antagonised conservatives. It was accused of peddling philosophical abstraction, and of spreading the dogma of individualism which would dissolve the social fabric of the European Ancien Régime. Above all, it upheld divorce, and threatened to destroy the family, a sacred institution and one which was fundamental to social stability. This is perhaps what Castlereagh meant, when he is reported to have remarked at the Congress of Vienna: "There is no point in destroying France, the Civil Code will do it for us."

In France itself, the Civil Code has had a long life. It has survived the upheavals and many changes of constitution which punctuated French history in the following century and a half. As a result, it has been claimed that the Civil Code itself should be considered the "real" Constitution of France.[10] The Codes have been adapted to recognise new ideas, such as modern notions of equality between men and women, but their basic structure is still intact. The Code was an instrument in the spread of revolutionary ideas; it preserved the essential social gains of the Revolution, abolishing privilege, recognising equality and individualism, and completely extracting the legal system from its old religious framework. By reconciling different legal traditions within France, and striking a compromise between a wide variety of regional customs, the Code helped to establish a unified nation. It endured because it was a body of secular law which applied to all citizens without exemption, no matter where in France they lived.

National unity, centralisation, the needs of the secular state, the ambitions of the revolutionary bourgeois: all these considerations lay behind the law codes. They also informed the preparation of Bonaparte's educational reforms, especially the creation of the *lycées* (secondary schools). He could not regard his régime as secure unless the youth of France was taught at an early age to respect its laws and

NAPOLEON BONAPARTE

institutions. Schools could implant in their students the values of hard work, respect for property, obedience to the social hierarchy and loyalty to the nation, as a guarantee of social and political stability. The Revolution had long since appreciated the importance of education in fostering a new revolutionary and republican culture. The revolutionary years had been extremely fertile in schemes for educational reform. Unfortunately, there had been little time and very few resources to put any of them into effect. As a result, the Revolution had weakened the clerical monopoly of education by nationalising church property, but had not replaced it with a solidly based network of state schools. Catholic schools could not be replaced overnight. Buildings had to be found, teachers had to be trained and properly paid, and even if experts managed to agree on a republican curriculum, they then had to persuade Catholic Frenchmen and women that it was more desirable than the teaching of the Jesuits, the Oratorians or the Christian Brothers. The soaring ambitions of revolutionary educators had far outrun their capacity to realise them.

Only the Central Schools established under the Directory provided a precedent for Bonaparte. They offered a republican and scientific curriculum to middle-class students between the ages of 11 and 18. They taught history, political economy, grammar and ancient languages, but technical drawing and mathematics were usually the most popular subjects. They recruited qualified professors and often took over the libraries of the seminaries and convents. The Ecoles Centrales had problems: there was still no professional training for teachers, and students were not always adequately prepared for the demanding lectures they sometimes attended. In spite of their shortcomings, however, the Ecoles Centrales constituted the Republic's best attempt at secondary education along national and secular lines.[11]

As far as Bonaparte was concerned, the Ecoles Centrales had one enormous disadvantage – their relative autonomy. They were organised locally, by notables and departmental administrators, who appointed their own teaching staff, determined their own syllabus and carried out their own inspections. Teachers enjoyed considerable independence, and students could choose exactly what they wanted to study. This degree of local initiative was incompatible with Bonaparte's vision of a uniform system of state secondary education, with a well-defined role in a national hierarchy of schools, all supervised centrally by a Ministry of Education. Schooling had an integrating, nation-forming function, which it could not fulfil unless the government took firm control over it. The Ecoles Centrales were therefore replaced by the *lycées*, in which government-appointed teachers would eventually all teach a similar syllabus from identical textbooks. Bonaparte aimed at a situation so regimented that, as he boasted, he could look at the clock at any time of the day and know exactly what every pupil in France was studying.

The *lycées* were one of Bonaparte's permanent legacies, but the centralisation of the French educational system became notorious. Its continuing rigidity was at least partly responsible for the student revolt of May 1968. The spirit of standardisation produced a brand of cultural imperialism which did not always adapt well to local needs. Until recently, even Melanesian schoolchildren in French New Caledonia were made familiar with the history text that told them: "The first inhabitants of our land, the Gauls, lived in round huts of dried earth and straw" (a passable description, incidentally, of their own housing).

The educational law of 1802 revealed the Consulate's priorities. These lay in the education of a middle-class élite at secondary level, with a view to the training of military and administrative personnel for state service. To achieve this, Bonaparte was effectively prepared to leave the education of women and younger children to the care of the Catholic Church. He later had to deal with clerical competition in boys' secondary education, but he was quite prepared to allow the clergy to operate freely in the spheres of primary and of girls' education. The poor needed only the most elementary instruction, which would reinforce their docility and conservatism, and the Church had successfully achieved this for centuries; and the First Consul did not regard the formal education of women as important enough to warrant the attention he devoted to the *lycées*. "Girls," Bonaparte believed, "cannot be brought up better than by their mothers. Public education does not suit them, as they are not called into public life; manners are everything for them; marriage is their whole destination."[12] These areas, then, could be safely entrusted to municipal government, the clergy and the family, and Bonaparte put no obstacles in the way of the Christian Brothers or of female teaching orders.

The law of 1802 provided for forty-five *lycées*; each one was to have eight *professeurs*, of which two were to teach mathematics. The Republic undertook to pay the boarding fees for a large number of students (180 for each school), in order to make them viable from the start, and rescue them from the fate of some of the languishing Ecoles Centrales. Applicants were to qualify for the scholarships by competitive examination. The government reserved 2400 scholarships for sons of soldiers and civil servants. The educated bourgeoisie were being offered a helping hand up this new ladder of advancement, raising them to positions of leadership and power.

The government regulated the uniform and military discipline which was to prevail in the *lycées*. At first, students wore a dark blue uniform with a two-pointed hat. When colonial dyes became rarer, iron grey became the stipulated uniform colour for *lycéens*. They were divided into companies and given ranks as though they were part of an infantry regiment. The réveillé and other turning-points in the school day were signalled by a military drum roll.

The curriculum of the *lycée* was not excessively scientific or dictated purely by the needs of professional training. Instead, it reflected the classical culture in which all educated Frenchmen of the eighteenth century had been raised. Those who had criticised the technical bias of the Ecoles Centrales were comforted by the renewed emphasis on literature, Latin and Greek in the *lycées*. The syllabus was divided into two parallel streams, the first based on Latin and literature, and the other based on mathematics, and including geography, technical drawing, natural history and chemistry. History was a controversial discipline and was given limited space in the syllabus, and philosophy was at first entirely absent from the curriculum – a concession to Catholic sensitivities. (Philosophy was restored in 1809.) The curriculum was structured over six years. Every student began with two years' study of humanities and the classics. The scientific stream did not begin until the third year of study, but it culminated in a special class of "transcendental mathematics" which prepared candidates for entrance to the Ecole Polytechnique. Modern languages, music, dancing and fencing were optional for students who wished to pay for instruction.

All *lycées* were intended to have a library whose contents were determined by the government. The policing of library resources would ensure that all government schools used identical texts. The texts prescribed for secondary and higher education in the government's list of 1802 showed the importance the state now gave to the study of the classics. Out of 526 titles listed, 142 were works of classical antiquity, and 54 were works of French literature. Above all, this official canon consecrated the authors of the classical seventeenth century, like Corneille, Pascal, Boileau, Fénélon and Molière, together with Rousseau and Voltaire from the eighteenth century.[13] This official conception of the classical text framed the literary culture of French schoolchildren for generations to come.

In 1809, Napoleon introduced the *baccalauréat*, the national examination which was the culmination of secondary study and which determined admission to institutions of higher education. The *baccalauréat* was a state monopoly, which became the essential qualification for any professional career. By 1813, 1700 students sat for their "bac" every year.[14] At the same time, *lycée* teachers qualified by passing another competitive examination which became a permanent French institution, the *agrégation*.

Paris was to have four *lycées*. Perhaps the most prestigious of all, Louis-le-Grand, became the Lycée Impérial, Henri IV was renamed the Lycée Napoléon, alongside the Lycée Charlemagne and the Lycée Bonaparte (previously the Lycée Condorcet). *Lycées* were planned in provincial centres, and in annexed departments, in Belgium, Piedmont, Mainz and Bonn. Their distribution was extremely rational: most of them were created in cities with a population of more than 20 000. Designed to educate an administrative élite, they were established in France's most prominent administrative centres. In many cases, it took some time before they were ready to open. In Toulouse, the *lycée* did not open until 1806, and the Avignon *lycée* did not function until 1810. In the provinces, the *lycées* struggled against early difficulties, and not all the scholarships originally offered by the government were taken up. The Bordeaux *lycée* had only 180 students in 1809, and in Lyon there were no more than 150. In Toulouse, only the support of military personnel kept the local *lycée* alive. In Paris, it was a very different story. The Lycée Imperial taught a thousand students, and the Lycée Bonaparte had 800.[15]

The *lycées* were the élite schools of the public secondary education system. Beneath them was a dense network of municipal secondary schools, or *collèges*, which took over from the Ecoles Centrales. The *lycées* also had to compete with private Catholic schools. In Rennes, for example, more students attended the town's private secondary school than went to the *lycée*. The military discipline of the *lycées* did not always appeal to the bourgeoisie, and many were happier with traditional Catholic schooling. In 1809, however, students in *lycées* and other public secondary schools combined just outnumbered those taught in private schools.[16]

Napoleon's response to this competition was to bring all schools, whether private or public, under the umbrella of the Imperial

University. The University, set up between 1806 and 1808, created a state monopoly of teacher training and established a clear hierarchy of primary, secondary and tertiary education, supervised by the government. The University was to constitute a secular corporation of teachers devoted to national and dynastic interests. The whole educational structure was divided regionally into twenty-six academies, each with its Rector and academic council. Only the University could award degrees, and it alone could authorise the establishment of new schools and the promotion and appointment of teachers. Private schools were thus drawn into a unified administrative structure, and in addition, they were subjected to a special levy for each student they taught. This helped to attract students away from private schools into the *lycées*.

The Imperial University, however, was never as monolithic as its original plan might have suggested. The first Grand Master of the University, as its supreme chief was entitled, was Fontanes, who was happy to admit the clergy to teaching posts in *lycées* and other public secondary schools. Of the administrators of France's 45 *lycées* throughout the Napoleonic period, 31 had taught in the Ecoles Centrales of the Directory, 12 had been Oratorians, 5 Benedictines, 6 Doctrinaires, 6 came from other religious congregations and one had even been a Jesuit. Thirty-seven other *lycée* administrators were or had been members of the secular clergy.[17] Ordinations of priests were very slow but clerical teachers were still vital to the educational system, and the Imperial University did not overlook their expertise. The University expected celibacy from *lycée* personnel above the level of simple *professeur*, which gave clerics an advantage. A survey of the personnel of *lycées* and *collèges* in 1812 divided them as follows:[18]

Priests	692 or 28.3 per cent
Ex-priests	38 or 1.5 per cent
Unmarried laymen	954 or 39.0 per cent
Married laymen	764 or 31.2 per cent

Like other Napoleonic institutions, the University practised ideological toleration.

At the summit of the educational system stood the specialist schools like the Ecole Polytechnique, established in 1794, which Bonaparte inherited. The Ecole Polytechnique was, and still is, a training school for engineers, but during the Empire the school had a predominantly military orientation and sent its best students into the artillery. Military needs also dictated the transformation of St Cyr into an academy for army officers in 1802. The Ecole Normale, whose creation was decreed in 1808, was to become another vital part of the educational system at its highest level. The Ecole Normale was a boarding school which planned to train 300 teachers annually. Before graduation, *normaliens* were subject to the kind of military discipline they would encounter in their *lycées*. They rose at 5 a.m. and their day included long periods of silent study. After graduation, they were bound to at least ten years of service to the state. The special schools were residential and developed a strong *esprit de corps*. Graduates of the Ecole Normale or the Polytechnique were aware that they formed an important grouping within the French ruling élite.

Science had an important role in special schools like the Ecole Polytechnique, the Ecole des Mines and the Muséum d'Histoire Naturelle. Not only did this demonstrate the determination of the Napoleonic state to exploit scientific knowledge for its own ends, but it also represented an important change in the professional careers of French scientists. These institutions of learning gave scientists new career opportunities as teachers and administrators. Through the Ecole Polytechnique, scientists like Monge, Ampère, Gay-Lussac and Berthollet trained the state's technical experts of the future, and influenced the whole structure of scientific education. No discipline was more highly respected than mathematics, which became firmly entrenched in the school curriculum in this period. In the Institut, and the new Napoleonic University, specialists could now envisage the possibility of making a living out of science.[19]

Scientists could therefore look forward to new links with government, and new professional rewards. They became senators, or ministers (like Chaptal, the chemist and industrialist), or members of the Conseil d'Etat (like Fourcroy and Cuvier). They formed a professional scientific community which enjoyed official recognition and a firm base in the educational system. The Emperor, of course, was the ultimate judge of their utility. As a former artillery officer, he appreciated experts in geometry and engineering; but had little time for Lamarck, who first put forward his controversial theories on biological evolution at the Muséum d'Histoire Naturelle in the Year 9.

During the nineteenth century, education was to be the principal battleground in the struggle between secular Republicanism and the influence of the Catholic Church. The University was to lose its monopoly in 1850, when the Catholic Church was allowed greater control over secondary education. Only in the 1880s did the educational reforms of Jules Ferry establish a system of universal, free and secular education at the primary level. A new phase in the arguments between anticlericals and the religious congregations was then launched. Napoleon's main aim was to train the bourgeoisie for specialist careers in state service. The *lycées* and the Ecole Polytechnique survived educational controversies because they served this purpose well. In pursuing this objective, he was prepared to compromise with the Church, bringing theology faculties under the control of the University, fighting the Church as a rival in secondary education, allowing it to work unchallenged in primary schools. He left in place a national system of state secondary education which survives today.

On the night of 14 March 1804, just a week before the Civil Code was officially introduced, a French military detachment entered the small town of Ettenheim, not far from Strasbourg, but actually on foreign soil, in the territory of Baden. There they seized an important prisoner and spirited him over the border into the fortress of Strasbourg. The kidnapped prisoner was the young Duke of Enghien, grandson of Condé, who was himself cousin to Louis XVI, and until 1801 organiser of the *émigré* army at Koblenz on the Rhine.

French intelligence had managed to unravel what appeared to be a vast network of royalist conspirators. Its leaders, Cadoudal and General Pichegru, had already been arrested. Information received from Mehée de la Touche, a French spy and *agent provocateur,* indicated an imminent invasion of France led by a royal prince – assumed to be D'Enghien.

D'Enghien was taken to Paris. On the night of 20 March, he was summarily court martialled, and at about 3 a.m. was shot by firing squad in the moat of Vincennes. On the following morning, the Civil Code was enacted. No evidence linked D'Enghien with the plotters, although he was no friend of the Republic and was on the payroll of the British secret service.

Bonaparte had acted with his usual speed and cynicism. He had violated international law to carry out a political assassination. He did so as a warning to royalist Europe and to the French *émigrés,* and to satisfy Republicans. Like the regicides of the National Convention, Bonaparte too had shed Bourbon blood. Unlike the Conventionnels, he provided no defence lawyer, no democratic vote and no public execution. Instead, D'Enghien was liquidated in a ditch under cover of darkness, and his corpse was certainly not exhibited to the people. But in liquidating the Duke of Enghien, as in his Civil Code and educational reforms, Bonaparte renewed his attachment to the legacy of the French Revolution.

9 Dictatorship by Plebiscite

The Bonapartist dictatorship did not spring fully grown from the *coup d'état* of Brumaire; it took four years to develop. At first, as we have seen, Bonaparte was compelled to negotiate, first with the *brumairiens* who had helped him into power, and then with the Pope to secure religious peace. In introducing the Concordat and the Civil Code, he had to find ways of silencing grumblings and criticisms in the legislature and the Conseil d'État. Not until 1804 did his personal rule achieve its maximum freedom of action.

There were several clear stages in this process towards personal rule and authoritarian government. The first was the Constitution of the Year 8, which had made Bonaparte First Consul. The second came in 1802, when Bonaparte became Consul for Life, with wide powers enabling him to rule by *senatus consulta*, in other words to issue his own decrees with the approval of his hand-picked Senate. The last stage was the establishment of the Napoleonic dynasty in 1804. The creation of the hereditary Empire then superseded the Republic which had survived since 1792. In supplanting the Republic and crowning himself Emperor, Bonaparte made a symbolic but significant departure from his revolutionary legacy.

The process towards authoritarian rule was punctuated at every stage by a plebiscite, in which Bonaparte invited the French people to approve or reject the institutions he proposed. This was one of the distinguishing characteristics of Bonapartism, which was a set of ideas and institutions transcending the man himself, to become an important tradition within French political culture in the nineteenth and twentieth centuries. Bonapartism was not a military dictatorship, in the sense that Napoleon derived his power chiefly from the support of the army. His was rather a civilian dictatorship because it drew its legitimacy from direct consultation with the people, in the form of a plebiscite.

The implications of Bonapartism for representative institutions were severe. Bonapartism rested on the assumption that the leader (the Emperor) himself embodied the nation and was the living incarnation of popular sovereignty in action. His nephew, Napoleon

III, inherited this claim in 1852, and General Charles de Gaulle also seemed to believe himself personally responsible for the French state, when he returned to power in 1958. Parliaments, and other elected representatives of the people, were of limited importance in such a system. It was a "presidential" system in the sense that it created a strong executive power, which bypassed parliamentary institutions regularly and unscrupulously. The legislative system put in place after Brumaire was not a vigorous one to start with; but between 1800 and 1804, it was further emasculated until it became irrelevant. Meanwhile, the coercive apparatus of the state was strengthened and refined, to police and censor the press, the theatre and the production of literature. The workforce, too, was strictly policed in an attempt to restrict movement and ensure docility. Plebiscites, anti-parliamentarianism and the extension of police powers to control what we would now call "the media" were all features of the emerging dictatorship.

The idea of direct consultation with the people had a Roman ancestry, and it had been tried before in the French Revolution itself. The Jacobin Constitution, for example, had been submitted for ratification by the primary electoral assemblies in 1793. Bonaparte's plebiscites, however, asked the voter one very simple question, and they identified the political issues involved with Bonaparte personally. Thus in 1802, voters were asked "Should Napoleon Bonaparte be consul for life?" No details were provided about what changes in France's political institutions were implied by this. There was no possibility of accepting part of the package offered, but rejecting the rest, because no political parties existed to represent such a response, and because the voter could only respond either *oui* or *non*. No alternative to the Life Consulate was provided and it was very difficult to refuse the only option on offer. In 1802, Bonaparte showed his successors exactly how a plebiscite or a referendum could be exploited to strengthen a régime in power. The question put to the electorate could always be phrased in such a way as to compel the answer "yes". The Bonapartist tradition was usually to present French voters with a false choice between either Bonaparte or chaos. The result was hardly in doubt.

There was no secret ballot in 1802. This made it very hard for voters to defy the régime by voting *non*. The voting system relied on registers of votes, opened in town halls and local notaries' chambers. Eligible voters (adult males) recorded their vote by signing their name in the "yes" column or the "no" column in one of these public registers. It was possible for illiterate voters to record their response, too, but this was a system which clearly favoured those who could sign. As a con-

Table 9.1 Plebiscites of the Consulate and Empire[1]

Year	Voting oui	Voting non	Change in oui vote
An 8/1800	1.55m	1562	–
An 10/1802	3 653 600	8272	+ 2.103m = +136%
An 12/1804	3 572 329	2569	– 0.081m = – 2%
1815	1 552 942	5740	– 2.019m = – 57%

sequence, anyone who rejected Bonaparte was forced to identify himself. The signatures of the opposition could be used by the police and were known to the local authorities. It is reasonable to assume that this publicity deterred a large number of "no" voters, who prefered silence to possible police harassment in the future.

In 1800, as we have seen, Lucien Bonaparte falsified the returns to show a large majority in support of Bonaparte. Since contemporaries assumed that the size of the French electorate was about 5 million, a vote of 3 million became the official target, representing about 60 per cent of all possible voters, and a clear majority. In 1802, Bonaparte had no difficulty in achieving this figure. This time there was no need to massage the statistics. The reforms, and the stability of 1800–2 produced a resounding vote in his favour. The plebiscite on the Life Consulate thus gave the régime the legitimacy it had not secured in the immediate aftermath of the Brumaire coup. There were more than 3.6 million oui votes, and only 8272 had dared to vote non. The 80 per cent abstention rate of 1800 was not repeated, and since 1800 Bonaparte's popular vote had doubled.

The results of Bonapartist plebiscites may be compared in Table 9.1. The statistics apply to the population living within French frontiers as they existed in 1815.

Bonaparte was free to introduce the Constitution of the Year 10, which is a rather deceptive title for a series of senatus consulta which extended his personal powers and further weakened the legislature. Bonaparte remained First Consul, but he now had the power to appoint the other two Consuls. He could also select his own successor, conclude peace treaties, and use the prerogative of mercy to reprieve convicted criminals. Strictly speaking, he needed the Senate's approval but he now strengthened his grip on the Senate itself. Bonaparte assumed the right to appoint up to forty new Senators, on condition that they were all over the age of 40, and were members of

the electoral college of their local department. Republican sympathisers in the Senate had originally tried to forestall the Life Consulate
by "offering" Bonaparte re-election for ten years. They were pushed
aside as Bonaparte secured the complete obedience of the Senate.
Bonaparte had the right to dissolve the Corps Législatif and the
Tribunat, and to overrule their decisions. He could bypass the legislature completely, by issuing *senatus consulta*, which might "interpret"
the Constitution, and even suspend it. The Corps Législatif could no
longer elect its president, and the Tribunat was reduced to a rump of
only fifty members. In the Year 12, it was paralysed further by a
decree dividing it into three separate sections.

The plebiscite on the hereditary Empire in 1804 made the Bonapartist dictatorship complete, which is why no further consultation with the
people was necessary. This time, Bonaparte did not increase his support. In fact, the results suggest that support for the régime had actually
fallen, in spite of an increase in the size of the electorate, which now
included several annexed departments. There were massive abstentions
in the Italian departments, and in some departments the voting figures
were officially rounded upwards. This was true, for instance, in the
departments of the Seine and Seine-et-Oise, which included the Paris
region (Figure 9.1). Statistical manipulation was blatant in the Belgian
department of the Dyle, where official results suggested that more than
100 per cent of the electorate had recorded a vote.[2]

If the voting figures are examined at a local level, they show that
support for the government had fallen back to the level recorded for
the Jacobin Constitution of 1793. Table 9.2 shows the approximate
numbers of votes cast in the *arrondissement* of the southern city of
Toulouse, with the number of "no" votes in brackets. Apart from the
facts that the records are almost certainly incomplete for 1815, and
that only a tiny number of Toulousain voters were bold enough to say
non, these figures reflect the national pattern. The drop in support
for the régime in 1804, however, appears more marked here than
nationally. Bonaparte's support had "peaked" in 1802, perhaps
because he still retained the backing of many Republicans. This was
the most creative period of his ascendancy, and the one in which he
most clearly appeared as the executor of the French Revolution.

Bonaparte the Consul now became the Emperor Napoleon, and so
he should be designated in the period after 1804. As hereditary
Emperor, Napoleon's right to nominate his successor took on a new
significance. Until Napoleon produced a son, his dynasty was a mere
genetic fantasy. Meanwhile, he excluded women from the imperial

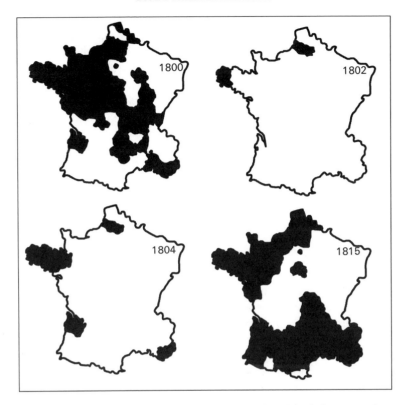

Map 9.1   Abstention Rate in Napoleonic Plebiscites (shaded areas = those where the abstention rate exceeded 80 per cent)

Source: F. Bluche, *Le Plébiscite des Cent-Jours, 1815* (Geneva, Droz) p.97.

succession, and he further disqualified both Lucien and Jérôme Bonaparte who had fallen out of favour. Next in line were his elder brother Joseph, and Louis Bonaparte.

Table 9.2   Voting in Toulouse, 1793–1815

1793	Jacobin Constitution	8,500[3]
1795	Constitution of the Year 3	5,180[4]
1800	Constitution of the Year 8	6,600[5]
1802	Plebiscite on Life Consulate	12,452 (2 *non*)[6]
1804	Plebiscite on Empire	8,888 (1 *non*)[7]
1815	Plebiscite on *Acte Additionnel*	609 (11 *non*)[8]

The Conseil d'État was divided into sections, and so was the Tribunat, to nullify its authority. The Tribunat was eventually abolished by *senatus consulta* in 1807. The fate of the Tribunat is instructive: it illustrates Bonaparte's methods in dealing with a parliamentary opposition which threatened to obstruct his personal authority.

The Tribunat included many experienced parliamentarians from the period of the Directory. They included intellectuals and republicans, and philosophers associated with the group of republican theorists known as the Idéologues. They discussed their ideas at social gatherings, like those in the salon of Madame de Staël, whom Bonaparte found especially irritating as a writer and a woman. Although it was not acceptable for women to appear in the forefront of political affairs, they none the less exerted an indirect influence as salon hostesses, where they could be the organisers and animators of a caucus. Other salons which attracted intellectuals, and around which gravitated a republican opposition, were presided over by Madame Condorcet, widow of the guillotined Girondin, and Madame Helvétius, widow of the enlightenment philosopher who had made no secret of his atheism.

The strength of opposition in the Tribunat has probably been exaggerated both by Bonaparte and by historians.[9] Between 1800 and 1802, the Tribunes took eighty-seven decisions favourable to the Consulate, and only seven hostile to it. Nevertheless, under the presidency of Daunou, they had considerable power to obstruct legislation, and Bonaparte was always impatient to see his projects realised. Some deputies were prepared to express their reservations about the régime's dictatorial pretensions. One Tribune, Riouffe, had gone so far as to compare Bonaparte unflatteringly to Hannibal. The Tribunat had rejected several clauses of the draft Civil Code, and in 1802 the draft on criminal court procedure was the subject of a discussion which lasted ten days. The First Consul detested such long delays and could not tolerate the publicity they provided for the government's critics. Boulay de la Meurthe described the Tribunat as "une pièce inutile, déplacée et discordante" (a useless item, out of place and out of tune).[10] In 1803, the Bonapartist dictatorship made sure that all political debate would continue in secret.

The First Consul was determined to eliminate this breeding ground of opposition. "There are," he declared in 1800, "two dozen metaphysicians who should be thrown overboard. They are vermin on my clothing; ... do they think I can be outwitted, like Louis XVI?"[11] In 1802, he had an opportunity to deal with the obstructionists and ineffectual logic-choppers (as he saw them) who stood in his way. According to the Constitution, one-fifth of the membership of the legislature was due for replacement. Bonaparte made sure that the Senate selected the retiring deputies (*sortants*). Not surprisingly, those designated as *sortants* included troublemakers like Benjamin Constant (Madame de Staël's lover), Chénier, Isnard the ex-Conventionnel, Daunou the political philosopher and Ginguené the literary critic. In their place arrived more reliable supporters, including Lucien Bonaparte, Carnot the ex-Conventionnel and ex-Director, and Boissy d'Anglas. Madame de Staël left for her Swiss property at Coppet. When she returned to France in 1803, Bonaparte had her expelled from the country.

The plebiscite on the Life Consulate signalled the divorce between Bonaparte and the republicans of Brumaire. By 1803, the Tribunat was a docile instrument of government. Between 1805 and its demise in 1807, it expressed no hostile opinions whatsoever. Like the Conseil d'État, it worked in secret and in specialised sections. Legislation could thus be ratified when necessary by small groups of faithful supporters. Napoleon needed the advice of experts, but he refused to allow public debate or the emergence of an organised opposition. His style of government tended to become "technocratic", in that it increasingly depended on direct consultation between the Emperor and qualified specialists in law and administration who had no public mandate and were responsible only to Napoleon. But the lack of public discussion and the lack of accountability on the part of the administration prevented the development of an informed and critical public opinion.

The "purge" of the Tribunat in 1802 seemed to leave the public quite indifferent (although some republican voters may have deserted the régime as a result in 1804). The victims were well treated. Fourteen Tribunes moved on to the new Cour des Comptes in 1807. Twenty of them became prefects. Daunou himself was given a comfortable job as imperial archivist. By the end of its brief life, however, the Tribunat was no longer a parliamentary institution with any real legislative function. It ended its days as a training-ground for Napoleonic administrators.

The Bonapartist dictatorship maintained its control of public opinion through careful policing and censorship of the printed word. The apparatus of control was not fully developed until well after the establishment of the Empire – the policing of the book trade, for example, was only systematised in 1810–11 – but the extension of police powers was a characteristic feature of Bonapartism.

The administration of political police depended heavily on one man – Fouché, the ex-Conventionnel and dechristianiser of 1793, conspirator of Thermidor and of Brumaire. Fouché reorganised the Police Ministry with the help of his associate Desmaret who, like Fouché himself, was a cleric who had renounced the Church. Together they established a network of informers, paid by the government, and a team of agents who intercepted and copied suspicious mail.

Fouché's private situation made him an unlikely candidate for the sinister role of a police chief. He led an apparently dull and peaceful family life with his wife and four children in the rue du Bac. Contemporaries found him charming and humane, always a faithful husband. Yet he was responsible for accumulating secret information on any potential enemy of the régime. Long before the computerisation of police records, Fouché's filing system methodically recorded confidential items on spies, dissidents, writers, ministers, generals, and even the Emperor himself.[12] His biographical dossiers on royalist spies were used to blackmail them and "turn" them into double agents working for France.[13] Fouché knew the traps of collecting police intelligence as well as anyone. Informers tended to multiply information, however trivial, simply to justify their own existence. In their efforts to impress their employer, police agents could magnify a few critical remarks uttered during a casual conversation into evidence of a dangerous anti-imperial conspiracy. Fouché never trusted them. A police agent, he once remarked, "is like a stagecoach which must leave every day, full or empty; if the agent knows nothing, he invents".[14]

Fouché gathered the threads of political intelligence into his own hands, for the Directory, the Consulate, the Empire and then briefly for the restored Bourbons. At police headquarters in the Quai Malaquais, he came to preside over a network of agents and police directors which covered the Empire, from Boulogne to Italy, and from Amsterdam to the chouan-infested west. The income he derived from licensing brothels and gambling-houses gave him some independence and cushioned him against budget cuts. He was an indispensable, but at the same time dangerous, supporter of all these régimes. He knew too much. He had at his fingertips the secret past of France's entire political and intellectual élite. The Emperor was determined to curb his power.

He attempted this by using methods adopted by many authoritarian régimes before and since: he allowed rival police forces to break

Fouché's monopoly of intelligence. In Ventôse Year 8, a Prefect of Police was appointed for Paris, in a move which appeared to resurrect the Old Régime post of Lieutenant de Police. His responsibilities included the issuing of passports, the search for deserters, the surveillance of prisons, workers' associations and the book trade. Fouché had no control over the military police, the *gendarmerie*, or the security service of the imperial household under Duroc. By allowing and encouraging competition between these different police organs, the central government prevented any one of them from becoming too powerful.

Twice Fouché was dismissed: in 1802, because he had not supported the Concordat, and again in 1810, when Napoleon's own informers got wind of his secret negotiations with the British. On each occasion, his absence was disastrous. During his first absence from the Police Ministry, the royalist conspiracy of Georges Cadoudal developed. During his second dismissal, while Napoleon was absent in Russia, the Malet conspiracy broke out. The royalists announced that Napoleon was dead and hoped to seize power in the resulting confusion. Without Fouché at the helm, security seemed bound to lapse.

The policing of the labour force was an important task of the repressive apparatus. The Revolution had liberated the labour market, and established the principle that every individual should have the freedom to pursue the profession of his or her choice. The abolition of the guilds, however, had removed an important mechanism of the social control of the workforce. The Le Chapelier Law of 1791 made associations of workers (and employers) illegal, which effectively banned strikes and workers' combinations. These prohibitions remained in force in France until 1864. The Bonapartist dictatorship tightened control of the workforce, in the interest of employers. In so doing, it revealed the class interests of the Bonapartist state.

In 1803, the *livret*, the worker's passbook, was re-established. The Consulate thus revived an Old Régime technique for controlling the movement of workers from one job to another.[15] The *livret* was not merely a record of employment and good behaviour: it now became an identity card, with a physical description of the holder and his profession (female workers were exempt from the *livret*). On commencing employment, the worker surrendered his *livret* to the employer. In theory, he could not get another job without his *livret*, and a clear indication that his past employers had released him and had no further claim on him. The *livret* was also a passport which authorised and recorded the worker's movements within France. A wage-earner, therefore, could not travel in search of work without the necessary visas from the local authorities along his route. In these ways, the subordination of the worker to the employer was enforced, and the worker's mobility was extremely restricted.

In spite of these police measures, French workers continued to maintain their own networks, like the *compagnonnages*, which had traditionally supported the unemployed and skilled workers "on the tramp". There were known houses and rendezvous in every town where workers belonging to the same trade found shelter, passed on information, and helped each other to find employment. Professional solidarity was also cemented by drinking sessions, initiation rituals, and rivalry with other *metiers* which sometimes erupted into violent brawls. The police tried to set up their own employment agencies, but they could not eradicate working-class organisations like the *compagnonnages*, which remained an integral part of French labouring culture until well into the nineteenth century.

This was especially true because, during the Empire, the balance of forces tilted in favour of the workers. The demands of war and conscription meant that male labour was relatively scarce. This enhanced the workers' bargaining power, and in some areas like the construction industry many employers readily took on workers without a *livret*. This did not mean that the workers' demands were always met. Several strikes ended with their leaders under arrest, and little or no advantage to the workforce, which was the case for the miners of the Maine-et-Loire in 1806, the workers in the abattoirs of Grenelle in 1812, and the Bordeaux tobacco workers in 1813. But it is clear even from these few examples that official attempts to discipline the workforce and to criminalise industrial action had only limited success. Occasionally, strikes *did* succeed. A week-long strike by Parisian stonemasons in 1807 won them the right to a half-hour afternoon meal break.[16]

The censorship of literature, the theatre and the newspaper press was not completely effective either, but it remained an important instrument of Bonapartism. The Bonapartist régime was extremely sensitive to public criticism and had a great respect for the power of the press. It believed, however, that opinion could be moulded into an attitude of conformity and obedience.

Bonapartism did not, of course, invent press censorship. The French Revolution had swept away the restrictions of the Old Régime and inaugurated one of the most liberal press régimes of all time. Literally hundreds of journals and occasional pamphlets appeared in a sudden explosion of print. According to the collections of the Bibliothèque Nationale in Paris, 335 journals appeared in the capital in 1790.[17] Republican régimes, however, all imposed restrictions to protect themselves against the dissemination of royalist propaganda, which threatened to undermine the Revolution. The press was a powerful and influential medium. It had launched the ill-fated political careers of Camille Desmoulins, Jean-Paul Marat and Hébert. For Bonaparte, however, this merely demonstrated the risks of a free press. He came to insist that literature should serve the interests of the state. He told the Conseil d'État in 1809: "Printing is an arsenal which it is essential not to place at everybody's disposal."[18]

He tried to bully editors into subservience, even when military affairs took him far from Paris. He told Fouché in 1805: "Tell the editors that although I may be far away, I read the newspapers; that, if they continue in this tone, I will settle their account."[19] His notion of "settling their account" was to appoint an official censor to each journal, like the *Journal des Débats*, the *Gazette de France* and the *Mercure*, and to make the journal in question pay the censor's salary. Every evening the censors read the proofs, and a few with aspirations managed to insert their own articles for publication. In 1811, legislation restricted Parisian journals to four only, and the departments were only permitted one political journal each (but at least thirteen departments did not even enjoy the luxury of a local journal).[20] The fewer the journals printed, the easier it was for the government to control the content of the press.

Bonapartist censorship of the press, as well as of other printed matter, was primarily aimed at establishing political conformity. Accordingly, there was relatively little official concern with literature which appeared blasphemous, morally offensive or obscene. These moral concerns loomed far greater in the minds of the censors of the Bourbon monarchy after 1815. Table 9.3 illustrates the importance of political concerns.[21]

There were clearly a few exceptions to this rule, and one of them was the popular novelist Pigault-Lebrun. In 1805, the censors refused his *Jérôme* because of its "foul obscenities", its "*libertinage*", and satires on the Church. Two years later, another Pigault novel was condemned by the censor for "vulgar licentiousness" and its "pronounced atheism". The authorities went out of their way to warn the publisher Barba that any further offences would result in the seizure of Pigault-Lebrun's entire output. This was part of a

Table 9.3   Official Reasons for Prohibition or Modification of
Sampled Censorship Cases, 1799–1830 (percentages)

Régime	Challenges to political and social authority	Challenges to moral order	Other reasons
Consulate	92	0	8
Empire	84	8	8
Restoration	66	34	0

broader official attack on popular taste and culture, as the censor
explained: "what could make it especially dangerous, is that the
characters are often taken from the lowest class, and that the work
is written to be read by artisans and workers, rather than by people
of taste and sensitivity".[22]

On the whole, however, literary censorship had three overriding concerns: to protect the reputation of the régime; to dampen any inflam-
matory references to the revolutionary past; and to silence material
which could offend France's international allies (Document 9.1).

Censors would ask for the deletion or modification of historical
references which were controversial or embarrassing. The D'Enghien
affair, for instance, was not to be mentioned. Writers were equally
wise to avoid any reference to the coup of Brumaire. The tragedy
Rienzi, written by the ex-Conventionnel Laignelot, was refused
authorisation in 1804 because the plot concerned subjects who took
up arms against a usurper.[23] In 1810, the Ministry of the Interior
ordered that all calendars and almanacs should include the Fête of
Saint Napoleon on 15 August, as well as the anniversary of the
Emperor's coronation, set down for the first Sunday in December.
Other *fêtes* abolished by the Concordat were not to be mentioned.[24]
The press was wise not to mention Napoleon's second marriage, and
it was forbidden to advertise the existence of censorship itself.

Literary references to revolutionary violence were considered too
dangerous. The revolt in the the Vendée was taboo, and so was any
mention in the press of attempts to assassinate Bonaparte.[25] A work
on European history by Bordes came to the censor's attention in
1812. The author was asked to remove a list of the victims of the

---

*DOCUMENT 9.1   INSTRUCTIONS TO CENSORS FROM THE
MINISTER OF THE INTERIOR ON 22 DECEMBER 1812*

When a work is submitted to you, whether it be well or poorly
written, witty or not, containing ideas either wise or unreasonable,
these considerations have nothing to do with the motives which
should prompt you to recommend that publication be suspended
or halted. If the work is obscene, if its dissemination would violate
police regulations, only then are there grounds for proposing that
the text be modified, or that printing should not be permitted.

If the work has as its aim the revival of passions, the formation of
factions, or sowing the seed of domestic strife, then it presents a
risk which should alert you to demand that publication should be
prohibited.

The generous intention of His Majesty is that except in these
cases, the press should enjoy complete freedom.

Make clear, in a well-argued report, the tone (*esprit*), the merit or
the defects of the work presented for your censure, both from a literary point of view, and from the point of view of the various influences that it might exert.

You are, Monsieur, a member of the Republic of Letters, and no
less imbued than myself with the desire to see it flourish.

(Translated from Archives Nationales F[18].40, no.373)

Revolutionary Tribunal of 1794.[26] The régime's emphasis on unity
and reconciliation thus depended on anaesthetising readers against
the painful memories of France's recent upheavals.

The censors took great pains to protect France's current allies. Since
the incorporation of the Italian departments within the Empire, it was
not permissible to insult the Italians. One travel writer who indulged in
sarcastic comments about Italian religious practices was reprimanded
on this score.[27] Letters of Voltaire which compared the King of Prussia
to the notorious eighteenth-century bandit Mandrin had to be corrected.[28] As long as Russia remained an ally of the French, the literary
enthusiasms of anti-Tsarist Polish exiles also had to be restrained. It was
perfectly permissible, however, to insult Britain, as long as the attack
was not directed at the royal family. The censor felt it his duty to promote respect for *all* authority, even in an enemy country. He asked:
"Does there not exist a kind of secret agreement amongst all

governments which binds them mutually to respect each other, and not to allow themselves to be demeaned in the eyes of their subjects?"[29] By 1812, the Emperor Napoleon had left Bonaparte the Republican far behind. He now took his place (or so he thought) alongside the members of Europe's old established club of dynastic rulers.

Writers were not the only targets of Bonapartist literary coercion. Printers, publishers and booksellers (they were often the same people) were the object of new government regulations on the book trade in 1810 and 1811. The administration of book trade regulations was entrusted to a new official, the Directeur-général de l'Imprimerie. The first encumbent was Portalis, until he inadvertently allowed the publication of a Papal message attacking the Archbishop of Paris. He was succeeded by the Baron de Pommereul. The number of legally operating printshops was reduced; only sixty were at first permitted to practice their trade in the capital, although the number was extended to eighty.[30] To obtain a licence (or *brevet*) to work as a printer or a bookseller, the régime now required aspirants to take an oath of loyalty, provide trade references and a certificate of good conduct. Printers were compelled to declare the details of any work they intended to produce, including price, format, and print run, and they were obliged to send an advance copy to the Directeur-général for approval. The list of all approved works was published regularly in a new official publication, the *Bibliographie de l'Empire français*, which became an essential historical reference work, the *Bibliographie de la France*. This system of surveillance was enforced by a band of nine censors (rising to twenty by the end of the Empire) and the official inspectors of the book trade. There were six inspectors in Paris and another thirty in provincial France. To some extent, printers and booksellers welcomed the legislation. They needed security and some were grateful for the elimination of competitors. They welcomed state action to restrict imports and protect French publishing against pirate editions. They did not, however, bargain for the rigid administrative supervision of the imperial régime.

The philistinism of the Bonapartist dictatorship is notorious. Napoleon had little respect for the creative efforts of writers and artists. He wrote to Cambacérès: "People are complaining that we have no literature. It is the fault of the Minister of the Interior. He should see to it that some decent stuff gets written."[31] The censors' reports suggest that they took seriously the exhortation to encourage literary excellence. In a report of 1812, the censor had no hesitation in unconditionally recommending Ginguené's *Literary History of Italy* as one of the glories of French letters, in spite of the fact that the author was part of the liberal opposition "purged" in 1802. The censors also passed Madame de Staël's *De l'Allemagne* but Bonaparte overruled them. The censors could always be circumvented by Bonaparte, who had the power to organise unfavourable press reviews of items he did not favour. This was the tactic he adopted to deal with Madame de Staël's novels, *Delphine* and *Corinne*. The number of works mauled by Napoleonic censors should not be exaggerated (Document 9.2). In 1811, they refused publication to 11.6 per cent of the 697 manuscripts they considered. In 1812, they rejected 4 per cent, and in 1813 only 2.4 per cent, a tiny proportion of global literary output.[32]

DOCUMENT 9.2   A CENSOR'S REPORT

This extract is taken from the censors' weekly report on their work, dated 17 November 1810.

25 manuscripts have been examined by the censors.

19 have been returned to their authors or printers without amendment.

5 were corrected or cut.

The Director-General determined that the printing of the 25th should be prohibited.

The works returned after examination without amendment are ...

4. A novel entitled *Ellesmere*, translated from the English by Madame de Ste Hélène, in-12o. The different characters of this novel seem well drawn. Virtue is praised, honoured and rewarded and crime is punished. The purest sentiments of paternal affection, filial love and disinterested friendship breathe through every page. This is one of the few novels of which a woman need not blush to call herself the author or translator.

5. The end of the first and the second volume of the *Literary History of Italy* by Mr Ginguené, member of the Imperial Institute. This section of this important work contained the adventures of Dante, and a critical analysis of the *Divine Comedy* ... The style and taste of the author are in the very best traditions. They are enhanced, or rather they reach perfection as the interest of the work grows, and it approaches the great age of modern Italy ...

The works which are subject to amendment are
1. *Pessimism or the end of the 18th century*, by Mr Lepeintre. This
novel was critical, philosophical, freethinking, moral and historical in turn. Events pile up without any link, without order or
necessity ... Three kinds of changes are required of the author.
One relates to political circumstances and to the respect due to
the dead and to sovereign rulers. Another relates to the author's
philosophical principles. The third relates to matters of public
decency. First, the author makes Catherine II, Prince Potemkin
and other characters appear, and he draws them in the most
hateful and humiliating fashion. Then, he introduces ... the
memory of the war of the Vendée. It is considered that novels
should not be histories in disguise, and that no one should juxta-
pose famous names with imaginary narratives ... It is not appropriate in a novel to argue against the almighty power of God. It
has been a rule to set aside all works of this kind, which attack
the basis of natural religion. Novels form the libraries of the servants' quarters, and if they are contaminated by polemics against
the salutary belief in divine providence, then poor and violent
readers will have no fear of punishment. As Voltaire so well said,
they would then be fools if they did not murder their masters to
steal their silver ...
(Translated from Archives Nationales AFIV.1049)

It is fashionable to ridicule the régime's crass insensitivity to intellectual endeavour and works of creative imagination. To a large
extent, however, this insentivity was calculated. The régime had no
more intention of furthering the interests of an intellectual élite than
it had of listening to the demands of the political élite, whom
Bonaparte removed from the legislature in 1802. It was in the very
nature of the Bonapartist dictatorship by plebiscite to draw authority
from the people and not from elected politicians. In the same way, in
the literary sphere, it appealed over the heads of the intelligentsia to
public opinion as a whole. The Bonapartist dictatorship was determined that public opinion should be formed by the government
itself, and not by the antics of an irresponsible literary élite.
    One further question remains. Why did France tolerate the devel-
opment of the Bonapartist dictatorship? After all, the French Revolution had overthrown a monarch and destroyed the royal apparatus of

coercion in the name of freedom and popular sovereignty. Historians have stressed the importance of the creation of a public political sphere, an arena for the discussion of political ideas, the nature of liberty, equality, "les droits du peuple", sovereignty, republicanism and "le salut public". Parliamentary life and the burgeoning newspaper press established the framework for political debate, and drew an increasing number of readers and observers into the widening circle of participation. For the first time, a public opinion had been created. Politics was no longer the private concern of the monarch and his personal retinue; in a process which had begun under the Old Régime, it is argued, a new political space had been created and politics became part of public life. The Emperor, however, confiscated popular sovereignty and elevated himself as its sole interpreter. He had also, by 1813, closed down or at least severely restricted the political sphere opened up by the Revolution. The Bonapartist dictatorship cut short France's apprenticeship in parliamentary and democratic practice.[33]

If he achieved this with impunity, it was because the real significance of the French Revolution cannot be grasped through its political dimension alone. The Revolution, perhaps, did create modern politics and laid the ground rules for liberal and civil society, in the sense suggested by François Furet and others. But the French Revolutionary legacy was more complex than this. For a social revolution had also occurred. The monarchical state had indeed been transformed into a Bonapartist successor whose powers many consider potentially terrifying. At the same time, its social basis had irrevocably altered. Under Bonaparte, fortified by his revolutionary legacy, the privileged orders had permanently lost their grip on the state. Instead, social and political institutions were increasingly shaped by the revolutionary bourgeoisie, made up of administrators, lawyers and landowners, together with commercial interests.

In the Consulate, as we have seen, new law codes preserved the social aspirations of these groups towards equality of opportunity and promotion on merit. The Concordat with Rome had guaranteed the property transfers of the Revolution. A system of secondary education had been devised to train the sons of the bourgeoisie for state service. Legislation protected employers against strikers and labour agitation. If the Bonapartist dictatorship was permitted to develop beyond the Consulate, it was because the bourgeoisie now had a state which served its interests. The Consulate claimed to rest upon a pyramid of *notables* who now enjoyed new opportunities for advancement, profit and the quiet digestion of newly acquired real estate. The progressive satisfaction of bourgeois self-interest meant that the role of ideologies in politics was thereby weakened. This does not mean that the state was merely a passive instrument of a victorious social class. The Bonapartist state, for one thing, was equally an instrument of Bonaparte's personal will. For a time, Bonapartism succeeded because his personal destiny coincided exactly with the legacy of the bourgeois revolution and with the interests of France. The assumption of the imperial title in 1804 showed that this was not always to be the case; and the moments when his personal ambitions ceased to serve either France or the Revolution must be closely examined.

10 *Opposition: the Politics of Nostalgia*

The Bonapartist régime claimed to have united France and healed the wounds of a decade of revolutionary discord. The seizure of power in Brumaire, it was argued, was justified by the need to restore order and effective government, and to prevent any further degeneration into factionalism. Bonaparte claimed that he stood above political factions, and popular sovereignty was in theory exercised directly through the First Consul, undivided and undiminished. Were these claims legitimate? The lack of any genuine political opposition during most of the Empire certainly makes it appear that order and reconciliation had been achieved.

The opposition was most active when the régime seemed most insecure. Hence there were many threats to the Consulate in its early years and rumblings of discontent grew louder again after 1812, when defeat stared at Napoleon from the empty eyes of snowbound corpses on the retreat to the Beresina. The period between 1804 and about 1812, however, was one of comparative tranquillity. The history of the opposition therefore resembles a time-sandwich: it consists of two intense periods of conspiracy and intrigue, divided by a long interlude of imperial stability.

The anti-Bonapartists fall into three main groups: the royalists, the ex-Jacobins or republicans, and the liberals. Both the royalists and republicans were weakened by Bonaparte's ability to attract the support of moderates on the right and the left. The religious settlement, for example, isolated the extremists in both the anticlerical and ultramontane camps. The liberals were purged from the Legislature in 1802 and had little public support. The ex-Jacobins looked backwards to the revolutionary government of the Year 2, with its cheap bread, centralised government and patriotic fervour. A few, like the followers of Babeuf's conspiracy in 1796, hoped to establish a communist utopia, in which the produce of the soil could be owned and enjoyed in common. Bonaparte, as we have seen, prevented any repetition of the divisive violence of the Terror, but he harnessed *sans-culotte* patriotism for his own military objectives.

129

Royalists also looked backward to a mythical society held together by a common Catholic faith and family solidarity. Counter-revolutionary apologists like Bonald idealised the social harmony which supposedly existed in the Middle Ages. Then, it was claimed, "intermediary bodies" like provincial estates or the guilds protected France from despotism. But a conspiracy of philosophers and freemasons had allegedly undermined the power of Ancien Régime Catholicism, the introduction of divorce had destroyed the family, and economic individualism swept aside the guilds. Royalists looked back, too, to the era of monarchy, or at least to one of many versions of Old Régime monarchy. Some like the ex-minister Calonne preferred the enlightened, absolutist version. Others thought nostalgically of a more aristocratic monarchy – a model favoured by supporters of the defunct Parlements and the *émigrés*. Others were partisans of the kind of constitutional monarchy which had existed between 1789 and 1791, although many constitutionalists had rallied to Bonaparte. Royalist nostalgia, therefore, wore many crowns and tended to perpetuate the arguments of the 1780s between the King, his ministers and the Notables.

Bonaparte either neutralised this opposition, intimidated it, or stole its political platform in such a way as to persuade his opponents to join him. The Empire allowed no forum in which an opposition could legally express itself. The press was muzzled and during the Empire parliamentary institutions were a hollow façade. The Corps Législatif met for only seventeen days in 1811, and never in 1812.[1] The opposition thus found itself denied a voice and Bonapartist successes increasingly isolated it from popular support. It resorted to a series of futile conspiracies and abortive assassination attempts against Bonaparte. These tactics were symptomatic of impotence.

Royalism was always the most dangerous source of opposition for revolutionary and Bonapartist régimes, for two main reasons. First, it could rely upon enormous latent popular support, and second, it could draw on assistance and financial support from France's international enemies. The tragedy from the royalists' point of view was their complete inability to agree on common objectives, and to coordinate the divergent interests of Louis, the *émigrés*, the allies and the thousands of anti-revolutionary peasants within France. After all, peasants and aristocratic seigneurs had little in common. Peasants may have resisted conscription in the name of Church and King, but they had no wish to see tithes and seigneurial dues restored by their social superiors.

The coup of Brumaire Year 8 had raised monarchist hopes. Some royalists interpreted the Consulate as a stepping-stone to the restoration of the Bourbons. Bonaparte was compared to General Monk, the English general who had ensured the transition between the Cromwellian Commonwealth and the restoration of King Charles II in 1660. One reason why Napoleon's brother Lucien had fallen into disgrace in 1800 was his tactless publication of a pamphlet entitled *Parallels between Caesar, Cromwell, Monk and Bonaparte*.[2] For this error, Lucien was despatched to the embassy in Madrid.

The future Louis XVIII wrote to Bonaparte to sound out the possibilities for a monarchical restoration. Once Bonaparte had secured his position after the victory of Marengo, he rebuffed the royal overtures making it clear that he had no intention of acting as usher for a royal *entrée* into Paris. "I have received your letter, Monsieur," he wrote to Louis, "I thank you for the courteous things you say to me. You must not hope for your return to France; you would have to walk over one hundred thousand corpses. Sacrifice your interest to the peace and happiness of France; history will not overlook you."[3]

If Louis wanted to avoid returning over the dead bodies of 100 000 Frenchmen, he had to establish the monarchy as a credible alternative in the eyes of the revolutionary bourgeoisie which had accepted the Consulate. To achieve this, he needed to reassure all those who had voted for the death of Louis XVI that there would be no reprisals; and he needed to guarantee that the sale of ecclesiastical and *émigré* property (*biens nationaux*) was irrevocable. Only in 1804 did he begin to contemplate such concessions. Shunned by the European powers, who would not allow Louis to make political declarations on their territory, he retreated to a boat in the Baltic Sea. There he issued the Calmar Declaration, accepting the sale of the *biens nationaux*, but amnestying only those who had not taken part in the Revolution. Until Louis XVIII convincingly showed, however, that he was no longer living in the pre-revolutionary past, royalism was to remain effectively leaderless.

Popular royalism stood to profit from the high rate of desertion and brigandage in the last years of the Directory. Draft-dodgers were fugitives who risked imprisonment and could be recruited by royalist organisations, as they were in the forests of Normandy, and in the Indre-et-Loire, where a group of brigands calling themselves the "red army" offered them a refuge.[4] Deserters formed themselves into armed bands for protection, terrorising homesteads and travellers. They, too, were potential recruits for royalism, and the highway robberies they perpetrated sometimes had political motives. In the south, bands of deserters attacked tax officials and the purchasers of *biens nationaux*. Stagecoaches were held up between Toulouse and Bordeaux and elsewhere in the Midi: it is hard to distinguish common crimes from acts of rebellion, but sometimes the proceeds of tax collection would be stolen, while private passengers were left undisturbed. The small town of Joyeuse in the bandit country of the Ardèche was invaded by one band, the garrison disarmed and tax offices robbed.[5] In August 1799, the inhabitants of Barjac (Gard) openly celebrated the exploits of the royalist murder gangs, with a drunken parody of the Marseillaise, which began

Allons enfants de la Patrie,
Le jour des brigands est arrivé.[6]

After 1813, this atmosphere returned, encouraged by the approach of the armies of the European coalition. In the Gard Department in the south-west of France, counter-revolutionary bands resurfaced in 1815 to exact murderous vengeance against Protestants, public officials of the revolutionary period, and purchasers of *biens nationaux*. Confessional loyalties tended to overlap with political and economic ones, for the Protestants were prominent amongst the textile manufacturing élite of Nîmes, and they dominated local government there in 1815. Here, popular royalism expressed anti-Protestant hatreds that were centuries old. Continuity was assured by men like Froment, an enemy of the pro-revolutionary Protestants since 1790, and an instigator of the White Terror in the Gard in 1815.[7] Gwynne Lewis, historian of the Gard, invites a view of the Empire as just a brief episode of stability, inserted within a much longer story of eternal local antagonisms.

The threat to the Consulate was greatest in the west of France, infested by bands of *chouans*. It was almost impossible for the régime to prevent collusion here between the local population and the British navy, which was in direct contact with *chouan* leaders like Georges Cadoudal. British vessels had little trouble finding local pilots to guide them through western coastal waters. They could disembark from time to time with impunity, either to remove a gun emplacement or simply to buy fresh vegetables from the local inhabitants.[8]

A mixture of repression and concession brought the *chouan* counter-revolution to an end by 1802. The religious policies of the French Revolution had always been a principal cause of anti-revolutionary feeling in the fervently Catholic western departments. The clergy had agitated for the restoration of traditional Catholic worship, against the sale of church property and the introduction of civil marriage and divorce, as well as against the persecution of the clergy and the dechristianisation of the Year 2. Clandestine masses, baptisms and weddings were occasions for disseminating counter-revolutionary propaganda and maintaining the fury of anti-republicanism. Bonaparte's Concordat with the Pope was a master stroke which made much of that propaganda redundant. Catholic worship was restored and the *chouans* were offered an amnesty. To be sure, some Catholics continued to oppose the religious settlement, forming what was known as "La Petite Eglise" in defiance of the Concordat. The negotiations with the Pope, however, immediately removed one of the principal grievances on which the popular Counter-revolution was based.

It was now time to close down the *chouan* rebellion. General Brune introduced martial law in the west, and received orders to use the strictest severity in suppressing *chouannerie*. Villages which refused to cooperate with the army were to be burned down and captured rebels would be shot without trial. Meanwhile, in 1801, special military commissions were set up to try to execute criminal bands which were being rounded up elsewhere in the country. There would be no trial by jury for the brigands, and no appeal against the verdict of the special commissions.

The *chouans* were caught between concessions which undermined their support, and brutal counter-insurgency methods which threatened to eliminate them. They were gradually disarmed, even the most determined of them, the followers of Cadoudal in the Morbihan. The British concluded that there was no point for the time being in pouring further funds into the rebel cause.[9] It was the introduction of conscription which had originally sparked off the civil war in the spring of 1793; but when conscription was reintroduced in the west in the Year 12 (1804), there were virtually no disturbances. The great roar of popular Counter-revolution which had erupted in 1793 now fell silent for a decade.

The *chouan* leaders did not all give up. Deprived of their peasant guerrilla base in Brittany, they turned to conspiracies at the centre of government, aimed at the First Consul himself. The numerous plots and assassination attempts of the years 1800–2 might be seen as the last desperate throw of the *chouan* rebellion (they also verged on comic opera). There were plans by both royalists and Jacobins to assassinate Bonaparte on his way to Malmaison at the weekend (on the *décadi*). There were contingency plans for the seizure of power if Bonaparte should be killed in battle – the Treasury would be seized and Louis proclaimed King. There was a plan to assassinate Bonaparte at a military review on the Champ de Mars on 14 July 1800, but the grenadiers who had supposedly been hired obviously thought better of it, and no shot was fired. In August, one would-be assassin managed to infiltrate Malmaison disguised as a monumental mason (*marbrier*). There was a plot to stab Bonaparte at the theatre, and another to stab him as he *left* the theatre. In November 1800, Bishop Andrein, an ex-Conventionnel and the former constitutional bishop of Finistère, was murdered. A Senator, Clément de Ris, was kidnapped by Toulouse royalists, ransomed and abandoned unhurt.[10] The final act of the farce was a plot to shoot Bonaparte at the inauguration of memorials to Generals Kléber and Desaix, when scaffolding blocked the aim of the preposterous contraption built to fire the fatal bullet.[11]

Most of these schemes were wild fantasies, although the dead bishop of Finistère was real enough, and the First Consul only miraculously escaped dismemberment by bomb blast in the rue Niçaise at Christmas 1800. Some plots had nothing to do with the royalists; desperate ex-Jacobins were equally prone to such hallucinations about the death of Bonaparte. It is, however, in the nature of this mysterious nether-world of incompetent dreamers that ideological loyalties became intextricably confused. The borderline between Jacobins and royalists was frequently indistinguishable.

The police encouraged this kind of confusion, by using *agents provocateurs* and dubious spies of their own. One of the latter was Méhée de la Touche, who had served Louis XVI, before becoming a secret agent of Danton in 1792. He was employed by the Paris Commune at the time of the September Massacres, implicated in the Babeuf conspiracy, and would have been deported as a dangerous Jacobin, if the naval blockade had not prevented his departure. First Fouché, and then Bonaparte made use of Méhée. They placed him as a "mole" in the network of the British agent Drake, whom they knew was coordinating a royalist uprising in the eastern departments. In 1803, Méhée posed as a royalist, collected British secret service funds from Drake, and eventually exposed the fraud in order to have Drake recalled in disgrace to London.[12] We must be careful in assessing the conspiratorial opposition to Bonaparte: some of it involved royalists, some of it involved Jacobins, but some of it was probably manufactured by the police itself. The most serious royalist threat of the period, the Cadoudal plot of 1803–4, involved three key figures. One was the ex-*chouan* leader, Georges Cadoudal himself, who escaped detection in Paris for several months before he was betrayed. The second was General Pichegru, who had been sentenced to deportation after the Directorial coup of Fructidor Year 5 (1797). He was one of the very few deportees to have escaped from Guiana, and he made his way first to England and then to Paris. Their task was to make contact with General Moreau, whose loyalty to the Consulate was thought to be suspect, and to lure him into a plan to kidnap Bonaparte and put a royal prince on the throne.

Moreau was the victor of Hohenlinden, but his Rhine army had had little contact with Bonaparte and did not hold him in great affection. Moreau upset the royalist plans by refusing to be drawn into the conspiracy, although he did nothing to stop it, and Cadoudal later had the grace to exonerate him. No royal prince materialised on French soil either, and after the execution of the Duke of Enghien it was unlikely that any would in future. Forty-seven accused, mainly royalists, eventually appeared in the dock and twenty were sentenced to death. There had not been such bloodshed seen on the Place de Grève since the Terror of 1794.

Pichegru was not among them: he had been found garrotted in his prison cell, with Seneca's account of the suicide of Cato lying open rather too obviously on his cell table. No convincing explanation either for his murder or suicide has been provided, but this looks like the work of a zealous policeman with a classical education. Alternatively, Pichegru may have been murdered by royalists keen to stifle any further leaks of information.[13] Moreau was in the clear, and left for America. He later returned to Russia and died in action, fighting against France, in 1813. The main consequence of the débâcle was probably the return of Fouché to the Police Ministry in 1804.

The danger of Moreau's defection shows that like most dictators, Bonaparte had to be wary of discontent in his own armies. The conspiracies of General Malet underlined the vulnerability of the régime, although they failed like their predecessors. Malet had a reputation for republicanism. He was in Paris in 1808, under investigation for organising illegal gambling clubs in Rome. His first plot was to arrest Cambacérès, outlaw Napoleon (who was in Spain) and abolish conscription. As usually happened, Malet was betrayed by one of his own "associates" and spent four years in prison.

While Malet languished in jail, Fouché was again ousted from power, and as new Minister of Police Savary committed the indiscretion of allowing Malet to be transferred to a prison hospital, from which he promptly escaped in 1812. The resourceful Malet planned to announce the death of Napoleon in Moscow and establish a provisional government, which would immediately negotiate peace. Malet's supporters convinced the barracks in Popincourt in eastern Paris that the Emperor was indeed dead, and succeeded in putting both Savary and Pasquier the Prefect of Police behind bars, before an officer on the Place Vendôme called his bluff.[14] Fourteen suspects were executed, most of them military personnel. Malet had demonstrated that the régime was at risk while Napoleon was fighting in the far-flung corners of Europe. He had also revealed the irrelevance in 1812 of Bonaparte's dynastic policy. Throughout the eccentric progress of the Malet conspiracy, no one seems to have remembered that in case of the Emperor's death, his son was supposed to succeed him.[15]

The Jacobin leadership had been annihilated in the wake of the Opera Plot of December 1800, which had come very close to killing the First Consul. The régime's first reaction to the assassination attempt was to round up all known republican suspects. Within a week of the explosion, 600 republicans had been questioned in Paris alone. By the end of the month (Nivôse Year 8), 129 Jacobins had been deported. Only then, after Fouché had unmasked the real culprits, were the royalists responsible arrested as well. But the deportation of the Jacobins was not rescinded. A royalist assassination attempt had been manipulated in order to liquidate the Jacobin opposition.[16]

The deportation of the Year 9 removed the last band of *sans-culotte* militants, active since the Year 2. Almost half of those deported were ex-members of revolutionary committees during the Terror, and at least forty had been named as supporters of the Babeuf conspiracy of 1796.[17] Many were artisans from the luxury trades of the capital, which had been hard hit by the emigration and the Revolution. Repeated arrests and police harrassment had ruined whatever economic security they managed to recover in the intervals between interrogations.

The police reflex was always to investigate the same cluster of individual suspects, identified from lists of Jacobins drawn up in the

Thermidorean reaction, and used again after the Babeuf conspiracy. The effect was to focus regularly on the same group of militants, who by the Year 9 were demoralised. They were isolated as "terrorists" or "anarchists", and the domestic peace achieved by Bonapartism gave them no popular support.

There were a few examples of individual protest against the régime: Lafayette, for example, refused the Legion of Honour. Carnot, once a member of the Committee of Public Safety, accepted his but attacked the Life Consulate and the Empire.[18] Robert Lindet, the oldest member of the Committee of Public Safety in the Year 2, did not accept the coup of Brumaire, and he refused to join the government even in the Hundred Days, when many ex-Jacobins were prepared to support Napoleon.[19]

There are, however, just as many examples of Jacobins who rallied to the Consulate and the Empire. Prieur de la Côte d'Or, another ex-member of the Committee of Public Safety in the Year 2, briefly accepted a position in munitions, offered him by Carnot in 1800, but applied in vain for a post in the University in 1808.[20] His old colleague Bertrand Barère was more decisive and successful, at least until the Empire began to disillusion him. He had been in hiding during most of the Directory period but emerged to write pamphlets for Bonaparte, and was on the payroll of the Consulate until 1804. He was then elected to the legislature in his home town of Tarbes.[21] Barère is a clear example of Bonaparte's ability to win support from the ranks of moderate Jacobins.

The strength of the republican opposition cannot be assessed without raising the broader question of Bonaparte's relationship with his revolutionary legacy. It was an ambivalent relationship, as a study of republican symbolism will demonstrate. Bonaparte attempted to integrate some features of republicanism into the Consulate and Empire, such as its secularism and its nationalism, while rejecting others as divisive and seditious. He was thus able to divide republican supporters which nullified effective opposition. The inauguration of the Empire appears a significant moment, which encouraged disillusionment amongst republican democrats.

The Consulate inherited much of the political culture of republicanism. It absorbed a part of its symbolism and iconography. The tricolour flag, for example, was adopted and incorporated by the Consulate and Empire. Napoleon added the imperial eagle atop the flagpole.[22] Napoleon thus symbolically accepted his revolutionary legacy, and the standards which fluttered at Austerlitz and Jéna were

still those which revolutionary France had carried to victory at
Fleurus and Jemmapes. In this way, republican emblems started to
become the rallying points not of a political party but of the whole
French nation.

Changes, of course, were made. The imperial eagle replaced the
red phrygian bonnet, the revolutionary symbol of the emancipated
slave of antiquity, and of the *sans-culotte* of the Year 2. Even the republican calendar of 1793 which fell increasingly into disuse took many
years to disappear. The revolutionary calendar had divided the year
into equal months of thirty days each, with a few extra days left over
at the end of the year. Every week was decimalised: Sunday was abolished and the tenth day, or *décadi*, became the official rest day. The
calendar aimed to eliminate all traces of Christianity from the
calendar; it secularised time itself, proclaiming to the world that a
new historical epoch was beginning.

For six years, Bonaparte preserved the revolutionary calendar. In
the Year 8, many of the republican fêtes disappeared from it, but
14 July, the anniversary of the fall of the Bastille, was retained, as was
1er Vendémiaire, the first day of the year and the inaugural day of the
Republic itself. The obligation to work on former Sundays was abandoned; it had never been possible to enforce it. By 1804, the revolutionary calendar was rarely observed by ordinary citizens; it was only
recognised on memos and decrees emanating from the state bureaucracy. Nevertheless, even when the Republic came to an end in 1804,
Napoleon did not immediately discard the republican calendar. It no
longer served its original purpose, and the reconciliation with the
Catholic Church made its anticlericalism out of date. For Napoleon,
however, it had other advantages. He did not like to be reminded of
its revolutionary origins and insisted that it be refered to as the
"French calendar". He retained it until 1806 because it seemed an
appropriate instrument of a rational and secular bureaucracy. It was a
symbol not just of the Revolution but also of the well-ordered state.[23]

One republican symbol which retained its subversive and
democratic character was the Marseillaise. On the face of it, such an
aggressive military anthem seems well suited to the needs of
Bonapartism. The Marseillaise was indeed sung on the Italian
campaign, and used at the funeral of General Joubert, killed at Novi,
in the Year 7. It was played, too, on the march to Marengo. The
Marseillaise has always had a double-edged significance: it could
unite the nation, and yet it could inspire democratic movements
which threatened Bonaparte. He no doubt remembered that the

Marseillaise raised the spirits of the defiant deputies at St Cloud, as they faced the extinction of the Directory on 18 Brumaire.[24] The composer of the Marseillaise, Rouget de l'Isle, was kept under police surveillance. He was bold enough to vote *non* to the Life Consulate and was apparently distantly related to the intrepid conspirator General Malet. The Marseillaise was officially heard only rarely until 1814, when the Bourbons once again decamped from Paris, and its rousing tone was to accompany the last stand of the imperial guard at the Battle of Waterloo. Acceptable under the Consulate, discreetly avoided during the Empire, the Marseillaise was revived during the Hundred Days, only to be banned completely by the Bourbon Restoration. The fate of what was to become the French national anthem illustrated the contrasting ways in which every régime interpreted its own relationship to the French Revolution.

The liberal opposition had no connection either with the royalists or the Jacobins: it was made up essentially of middle-class intellectuals with no popular following. In spite of this, and despite the comprehensive defeat of the liberals in 1802, they have enjoyed a relatively high profile in the historiography of the Napoleonic period. This has been possible because they included writers, like Germaine de Staël and her insipid lover Benjamin Constant, who are regarded by critics as leading lights of nineteenth-century French literature.

De Staël was the daughter of the Old Régime finance minister, Necker, and the estranged wife of the Swedish ambassador to Paris. These connections enabled her to live in France, although she was Swiss, and to write at leisure, completely untroubled by anxieties of a financial nature. Her writings were a defence of enlightenment philosophy, eighteenth-century rationalism and sensibility. Together with Constant, she defended the political ideal of a representative parliamentary system, based on property ownership.[25] Through her writings and her Paris salon, she maintained a nagging criticism of Bonaparte's dictatorial pretensions, which enraged the First Consul and finally drove him to exile her.

There was, however, a certain amount of equivocation and opportunism about their liberalism. De Staël had been full of admiration for the victor of Italy and had written him enthusiastic letters, which Bonaparte later boasted to Las Cases were love letters (They have not survived.) Although she claimed retrospectively in *Ten Years of Exile* that she had diagnosed Bonaparte's frigid cynicism from the start, this cannot disguise the eagerness with which they greeted Brumaire and rushed to provide Constant with a seat in the Tribunat. Constant was getting used to praising *coups d'état* – a strange habit for a liberal – since in 1797 he had vigorously congratulated the Directory on the coup of Fructidor.[26] In a series of sulphurous clashes between De Staël and Bonaparte, the novelist's sensibilities regularly provoked dramatic outbursts of Corsican machismo. Bonaparte detested her criticisms of the Concordat, and her eulogies of Protestantism as a more liberal and tolerant creed than Catholicism. In addition, she repeatedly expressed a preference for the liberties enshrined in the constitution of his greatest enemy, Great Britain. She defended liberty and republicanism, called him an "idéophobe" and refused to be silent. He called her a devil (*coquine*), a crow and a trollop (*catin*).[27] But she refused to allow literature to become merely an instrument of his propaganda.

Bonaparte could not abide a republican coterie animated by a female intellectual. In an exchange between them reported by the poet Arnault in 1797, De Staël provoked him into his most notorious expression of mysogyny. "General," she taunted him, fishing blatantly for the compliment Bonaparte never knew how to give, "which woman do you love the most?"

BONAPARTE	My own.
DE STAËL	I grant you that, but which woman then do you respect the most?
BONAPARTE	The one who is the best housekeeper.
DE STAËL	I grant you that, too, but after all, who would you consider the first among women?
BONAPARTE	(turning his back on her) The one who produces most children.[28]

Bonaparte never made a secret of his dynastic priorities. Nor did he hide his opinion that women should not meddle in politics. Madame de Condorcet had answered this by explaining: "In a country where we cut their heads off, it is natural that women might like to know why." Bonaparte, however, reduced De Staël to speechlessness, as when he accosted her at a ball to which she was wearing a spectacularly low-cut dress. Staring at her cleavage, the First Consul remarked: "I suppose you breast-fed your children?"[29]

In 1802, Constant and the liberal opposition were removed from the Tribunat. In 1803, De Staël was expelled from Paris and forbidden to approach within a forty-mile radius of the capital. Her political power had rested on her Paris salon; to remove her from Paris was to finish her as a political threat, and she left for Germany. She had the resources and the talent to continue an illustrious international career. The French annexation of Geneva had deprived her family of its income from feudal dues, but Necker had made some shrewd investments in the United States. His daughter shared these, too – in fact she owned a part of the Bronx.[30]

In her writings of this period, De Staël had maintained her criticisms of the Concordat, the Life Consulate and what she saw as Bonapartist attacks on parliamentary freedom and independence. She dedicated her novel *Delphine*, published in 1802, to a reading public that was "silent but enlightened" (*à la France silencieuse mais éclairée*), a formula which seemed to defy Bonapartist attempts to control opinion. She kept alive the enlightenment idea of a critical community of intellectuals, outside the reach of the state, whose members were free to discuss and to judge political developments. Her fate shows that Bonapartism permitted independent intellectuals little space in which to operate.

The examples of opposition discussed in this chapter suggest that Bonapartist claims to have reconciled a divided nation were exaggerated. It may be true that while counter-revolutionary royalism tended to be an army without a leader, the liberals were all generals with no army. The plots against Bonaparte were nourished by fantasy and spurred on by lunatic desperation. Frenchmen and Frenchwomen, however, had not forgotten their revolutionary past. The scars of the Terror and civil war could not be erased by Napoleonic censors. They were to reappear in the dying phases of the Empire. In 1814, many ex-Jacobins saw in the approach of the allied armies a repetition of the threat of 1792–3, when the *patrie* was threatened by an invading coalition, representing the tyrannical monarchies bent on revenging Louis XVI. At the same moment, a resurgence of popular royalism took bloody vengeance on its past oppressors. The years of Empire were not able to prevent such a reenactment of the revolutionary drama. In 1815, as never before, the dead hand of the past weighed heavily on the spirits of the living.

11   The Empire in the Village

In 1814, Napoleon escaped from Elba and landed on the French coast at Fréjus. In early March, as he made his way north towards Paris, thousands of local inhabitants demonstrated their support. As he approached the city of Grenoble, 2000 peasants carrying torches lit up his route, and prepared a soft carpet of pine needles to line the road on which he entered the town.[1] In spite of Napoleonic taxation, and the burden of conscription throughout twenty years of almost continuous warfare, a section of the rural masses could still welcome back the Emperor in scenes of messianic adulation. The strength of peasant Bonapartism was a historical phenomenon which requires some comment and explanation.

There were, of course, many incidents of resistance in the countryside, too. Draft-dodging and desertion were two very common forms of disobedience, which necessitated the repressive measures put in place towards the end of the Empire. In general, historians have tended to neglect the growth of Bonapartist loyalties at the village level. Bonapartism in the village has sometimes been interpreted as the creation of a finely crafted propaganda effort to enlist the peasants in the years *after* 1815. This view implies that peasants were passive and gullible victims of the Napoleonic myth, and that their Bonapartism only became an important factor later on, as the 1848 Revolution approached.

Alternatively, some historical interpretations of the period have assumed that this was a period of rural depoliticisation. No doubt this assumption is partly justified. Napoleonic centralisation severely dented village autonomy. Local mayors, for example, were appointed by the prefects. The local justices (*juges de paix*) were elected until the Year 10, but otherwise, appointment from above was the rule when filling administrative positions, even at village level. State control thus stifled one possible outlet for the expression of political differences and local political quarrels. Even if the villages fell silent, however, this did not necessarily imply indifference to the Empire or to the person of the Emperor.

Peasant Bonapartism has also been overshadowed by the search for the sources of nineteenth-century Republicanism. Analyses of growing politicisation and Republicanism in the countryside sometimes tend to obscure the direction of peasant loyalties during the Consulate and Empire. They concentrate on two great moments in the history of rural politics: the acceptance of the Jacobin Constitution of 1793, and the legislative elections of April 1848 when 84 per cent of the electorate voted. The plebiscites of the Consulate disappear from view in between these two Republican landmarks, although about 50 per cent of the electorate voted in 1802 and 1804.[2]

Some liberal-democratic historians have been puzzled by the apparent illogicality of peasant support for Napoleon. Consider the case of Pont-de-Montvert, a tiny and remote village in the Cévennes, with a little over a hundred voters. The village faithfully provided the recruits demanded of it for the republican and imperial armies. A dozen conscripts were called up between 1803 and 1805, seven more in 1806, eight more in 1807, and about a dozen annually in the last four years of the Empire.[3] Seventeen sons of the village never returned, dying in battle, or more usually of disease, in the military hospitals of Spain. And yet the village voted unanimously in support of Bonaparte in 1800, in 1802, in 1804, and again in 1815.

Generalisations about the French countryside are fraught with difficulty. Pont-de-Montvert was a special case, perhaps, because it was a Protestant village. Regional variations all over France in such vital areas as religious observance, agrarian structure and patterns of landholding inevitably complicate the overall picture. The French countryside was a patchwork of regional economies, and in each square of the pattern a slightly different balance of agrarian power prevailed. In regional economies based on subsistence agriculture, rural communities were insulated from many outside forces and often resisted the pressures of national politics. In areas specialising in cash crops, on the other hand, the rural population, vulnerable to national or even international price fluctuations, might have broader horizons. This was sometimes the case in wine-growing areas.

The peasantry, as we noted in Chapter 5, was not a homogeneous class. It was composed of many different socio-economic strata, each of which had its own interests. Within this context of diversity, peasant Bonapartism was nevertheless unmistakable, and should be considered alongside the expressions of hostility towards the régime which have attracted plenty of attention. In order to address the problem, this chapter must consider the burden of conscription, the impact of the régime on the rural economy, and general levels of prosperity during the Empire. To outline the successes of *L'Empire au*

Village, we must also return to the question of Bonaparte's perceived relationship with his revolutionary legacy.

The Consulate represented a gradual return to normality. The wealthier peasants, whose authority had been shaken by the democratic politics of the revolutionary years, now recovered their pre-eminent position in the local community. In Jessenne's study of the cereal-growing area of Artois, the prosperous tenant-farmers, with 30 hectares or more at their disposal, re-assumed their traditional role as leading defenders of village autonomy.[4] These "coqs de village" were not necessarily important landowners; they were usually content to lease farms from one or more large proprietors. They dominated their villages, however, as employers of labour and since they also monopolised the ownership of horses, they controlled local plough-teams. Their political authority thus reflected their social and economic power. The Consulate brought them back to political life as mayors and municipal councillors.

The most telling aspect of Bonapartist "normalisation" in the countryside was the return to religious peace after the Concordat. Churches were reopened and religious festivals, pilgrimages and ceremonies resumed their traditional place in rural life. Although conflict with the Papacy was later renewed, Bonaparte effectively and officially restored Catholic worship as well as the religious calendar, which framed rural life and the agricultural year.

The Revolution had brought many benefits for the rural population, although they were far from evenly distributed. All rural inhabitants, however, stood to gain from the introduction of a rational administrative system, the end of clerical taxation and the abolition of seigneurialism. The French Revolution had abolished what remained of feudalism and Bonaparte protected this legacy. Bonaparte offered a guarantee that the end of seigneurialism would be permanent, and this was the key to his popularity in the French countryside.

The threat of a return to the Old Régime haunted the peasantry in the first half of the nineteenth century. They feared that the return of the Bourbons and the aristocrats would mean a reimposition of feudal obligations and the clerical tithe. This was not just a figment of their imagination. The *émigrés did* return to France in large numbers, after Bonaparte allowed them to do so with impunity. The imperial régime itself made attempts to rally the old nobility to its side. In the last years of the Empire, some ex-seigneurs were even appointed mayors in the villages they had once dominated as feudal landlords.[5]

All this was cause for alarm. So was the explicit way in which some landlords foreshadowed a return to the era of seigneurialism. During the Empire, leases sometimes included clauses describing what would happen to the tenant in the event of a return to pre-1789 conditions. Thus the Marquis de l'Isle stipulated in 1805 that leases on his estate at St Rémy-en-Plaine (Deux-Sèvres) would be null and void if feudal dues were restored.[6] The imminent collapse of the Empire in 1814 seemed to bring this eventuality closer. In the west of France, the clergy once again pressed their parishioners for the payment of the tithe. One catechism of 1814, in the diocese of Tarbes in the Pyrenees, told peasants that the non-payment of the tithe was a sin.[7] In this uncertain atmosphere, the revolutionary struggles of 1789–93 were reborn. In the Isère, châteaux were attacked. In the Auvergne and elsewhere, peasants feared that the return of the monarchy would lead to the restoration of tithes and seigneurial dues. Napoleon could be cast in the role of the saviour who would defend them against clericalism and the nobility. In Clermont-Ferrand, therefore, news of Napoleon's abdication was greeted with cries of "Vive l'Empéreur!"[8] As a bastion against a feudal revival, Napoleon could assume the mantle of revolutionary Jacobinism.

In spite of the food shortages of 1811–12, the Consulate and Empire were periods of relative prosperity in the countryside, accompanied by demographic expansion. The inflationary experience of Thermidor and the Directory had some advantages. It enabled indebted peasants to liquidate their debts relatively painlessly in devalued paper currency. Peasant proprietors who produced a surplus benefited from the rise in the price of agricultural produce. Between the Consulate (1798–1803) and the Bourbon Restoration (1817–20), cereal prices rose by about 18 per cent. The price of wine rose by 20 per cent, and that of beef by one third in the Napoleonic period. The consequences of conscription, moreover, were not entirely negative: the call-up contributed to labour shortages which forced up male wages. The real value of wages rose by at least 20 per cent during the Consulate and Empire.[9] In Vienne, agricultural wages were two-thirds higher in 1806 than they had been in 1789.[10] This improved the position of agricultural labourers who were looking for an opportunity to acquire a small plot. Higher wages enabled many to save enough to fulfil this ambition.

The régime naturally took a very positive view of its own contribution to better living standards. In *Statistiques élémentaires de la France*

(1805), Peuchet boasted that "more bread and meat are eaten in France today than formerly. The country-dweller who knew nothing better than rough food and unhealthy drink, today eats meat and bread and drinks good cider and beer."[11] These claims should be put in perspective; the average per capita meat consumption in France was only 18 kilograms in 1812.[12] In the long run, however, the abolition of feudal dues payable in kind may have released a surplus, which peasants could sell, to invest the proceeds in property. In this way, some peasant proprietors previously engaged in subsistence production could enter the market for the first time.

The prosperity of the Empire, however, was not universally shared. Rising cereal prices assisted commercial proprietors and rising wages benefited male day-labourers. These advantages were offset by rising rents. Rents rose, according to Chabert's calculation, by about 50 per cent during the Napoleonic period, which created difficulties for all tenants and sharecroppers.[13] The sharecropper usually did not have a marketable surplus to compensate him for higher rents. The small-scale tenant farmer also experienced higher labour costs if he employed a shepherd, a ploughman or other labourers on a casual basis. Differences in status within the peasantry itself must be taken into account when assessing levels of prosperity in the countryside. From the wage-labourer's perspective, the popularity of the Empire can be understood, but for the *petit propriétaire*, the situation is not so clear-cut.

Le Goff and Sutherland have taken a less optimistic view of French agriculture than the one implied by Peuchet's report, quoted above.[14] As a result of their suggestions, it is impossible to claim with confidence that agricultural productivity surged forward during the Napoleonic period. The value of leases is one possible indicator of rising productivity. If an estate produced increasing yields, lessors could raise their demands when leases came up for renewal. The evidence of leases on hospital land, paid sometimes in cash, sometimes in grain, suggests only an initial rise in value. At first, leases incorporated the clerical tithe and the payment of some seigneurial obligations. The value of hospital leases in Rouen and Langres (Haute-Marne) increased during the revolutionary decade, but then levelled off after 1803.[15]

The French population had risen from just under 28 million in 1789 to over 30 million in 1814. Agricultural productivity kept pace with this increase. In so doing, agriculture resumed the productive capacity it had lost in the revolutionary upheaval, but without surpassing its best performances at the end of the Old Régime. The Empire was thus a period of catching up, rather than a significant leap forward. There were many reasons why the régime's agricultural record had its limits. The urban population had contracted in the revolutionary years, thus reducing demand for foodstuffs. Another reason was the war, which temporarily distorted all economic activity. Normal trade routes were cut and the army itself made exceptional demands on provisions. Traditional textile production (except for cotton manufacture) continued to suffer deindustrialisation, which hit the countryside where much wool and silk manufacture, for example, were based.

Poor harvests intervened, although there was no repeat of the disastrous years of 1788, 1789 and 1795. The years between 1800 and 1805 were fair to good, except for the shortage of 1802–3. Then followed a poor harvest in 1806 and two good years before a depression and subsistence crisis in 1811–12. The harvest of 1812, however, was good, and that of 1813 exceptionally good.[16] The shortages of 1816–17, which have been labelled as Europe's last great subsistence crisis, were unusually severe, and underlined the fact that the Consulate and Empire had largely escaped traumatic famine.[17] This was a period relatively free of social conflict over food supplies.

Harvest yields did not markedly increase. In some areas of France, they would remain the case until the invention of chemical fertilisers. In the Lozère, seed yields were only about 3 to 1. Here, every hectare under cereal cultivation in the hills north of Mende required 2.5 metric tonnes of manure.[18] Methods of cultivation changed very slowly in the aftermath of the Revolution. Sickles had not everywhere been replaced by scythes. Oxen were commonly used for ploughing. The system of biennial crop rotation still used in many parts of France meant that large areas lay fallow. Population expansion continued to cause the fragmentation of landholdings. Meanwhile, short leases offered no incentive for investment. Nine-year leases were the maximum a tenant could expect; often farmers took leases shorter than this. On the more positive side, vineyards prospered from high wine prices, and exports could still continue in wartime under a licence system. New crops were promoted, like sugarbeet, to compensate for the inaccessibility of West Indian sugarcane. The livestock population expanded to its pre-revolutionary level.

The prosperity of French agriculture under the Consulate and Empire can therefore provide some clues to the régime's popularity.

But the prosperity of the period was relative. Productivity made up some ground lost in the revolutionary decade and provided for an expanding population. Traditional techniques, however, had not yet been transformed. Bonaparte had restored a sense of normality in many spheres of life, but he condemned France to a long war which blighted hopes of genuine economic progress for at least two decades.

The sale of the *biens nationaux* left a section of the peasantry well satisfied with the régime. The sale of nationalised ecclesiastical property, as well as the sale of property confiscated from *émigrés*, continued throughout the Republic, until a decree of the Year 11 (1803) gave the Church back its unsold property. One important consequence of Bonapartist rule was to guarantee the permanence of the revolutionary land settlement.

The chief beneficiaries of the sale of the *biens nationaux* were the bourgeois. They had the capital resources available to bid at auction for property which was rarely divided into small lots for the benefit of small investors. The bourgeois lived in the *chef-lieu*, where the auctions took place, and some of them had close connections with the administrators responsible for overseeing the sales. Some of them *were* local administrators, who had the chance to assign the choicest items to themselves. The inflation of the revolutionary paper currency, the *assignats*, had made sure that bargains were on offer for those with the liquidity and enterprise to seize the moment. Vastly depreciated paper money could be unloaded in the late 1790s, to acquire meadows, dairy farms or woods which had previously belonged to the Church.

Although the bourgeoisie was in a position to take greatest advantage of the sales, the peasantry, too, were purchasers. The peasants were already a large landowning class before the Revolution: they owned approximately one third of France's cultivable soil. The sale of the *biens nationaux*, however, further increased the number of small peasant proprietors. In the Périgord, for example, peasants succeeded in purchasing former properties of *émigré* nobles. Out of 570 purchasers of aristocratic property in the Périgord 62.3 per cent were peasants who bought up 29 per cent of the property on offer.[19] Many of these were wealthier farmers with the resources to buy a *métairie* (dairy farm) or even a château. Others, however, were relatively poor and sometimes illiterate peasants. Georges Lefebvre's study of the department of the Nord showed that 30 000 peasants acquired land during the Revolution, and 10 000 of them had not owned land previously.[20]

Historians continue to debate the economic consequences of these changes in the countryside. For some, like Peter Jones and Donald Sutherland, the revolutionary land settlement simply increased the number of micro-proprietors who owned small plots for subsistence purposes only.[21] According to this view, the revolutionary and Napoleonic periods accelerated the fragmentation of peasant landholdings. Thousands of peasants accumulated small properties without being incorporated into the network of commercialised exchange and capitalist agricultural production. Other historians, like McPhee, challenge the proposition that peasant land purchases strengthened subsistence agriculture without contributing to the transformation to capitalist production. They argue that the growth in the number of smallholdings did not inhibit capitalism, and cite the arguments of Soviet historians suggesting that the land sales helped to establish capitalist property ownership on a broader and more secure social base.[22] Whatever the long-term economic consequences, one political consequence was the creation of thousands of peasant landowners with a vested interest in maintaining the land transfers of the Revolution. The Napoleonic régime appointed itself the guardian of these interests.

In the village, as elsewhere, Napoleon pursued a compromise between revolutionary egalitarianism and Old Régime traditions. In Chapter 8, the implications of this compromise for rural inheritances was discussed. The Revolution had legislated for equal shares for all eligible heirs; Bonaparte, however, allowed peasant patriarchs some scope for favouring an eldest son who could preserve the family's holdings.

A similar compromise was reached over the problem of the enclosure of common land and the survival of collective rights. These were issues vital to the rural economy, and they mark the point where the bourgeois individualism of the French Revolution came into conflict with communal rights in the countryside.

Collective rights varied enormously from region to region. They were naturally different in areas of pasture, forest and arable land, but they were everywhere important to the smallholding peasantry. There was the customary right, for example, to graze livestock on pastures that were owned in common by the village community. This right usually belonged to all inhabitants of the village. There was also the right of *vaine pâture*, namely the right to graze livestock on abandoned or fallow land which belonged to other individuals. The *droit de parcours* allowed reciprocal grazing by two communities on each other's land. The collective distribution of manure (*nuits de fumature*) was also extremely valuable in an age when this was the only available form of fertiliser. In forested areas, some communities enjoyed the *droit de glandée* – the right to graze pigs, in seigneurial or other private forests rich in nuts and acorns, after St Michael's Day (29 September). They might also have the right to cut and gather dead wood to use as fuel (*affouages*). The right of *regain* allowed the collective cropping of any aftergrowth which appeared immediately after the cereal harvest.[23]

In August 1792, the National Convention introduced legislation intended to enforce the partition of common land. Local resistance, however, largely sabotaged this attempt to promote individual ownership. Furthermore, it raised serious problems: how was the land to be divided, amongst which inhabitants and on what basis? A partition of common land per capita seemed most egalitarian; but an alternative method was to divide it in proportion to existing landholdings, which would reflect and perpetuate existing inequalities.

A subsequent law of 10 June 1793 allowed local communities some decision in the fate of their common land. All non-wooded commons could be partitioned if one-third of the local inhabitants voted in favour. The law ordered that partition would then take place on a per capita basis, and women and children would be eligible for a share too. This legislation did not please everybody. Wealthier peasants often felt that access to common pasture was of greater benefit to them than a per capita partition of the land. Poorer peasants, too, would have preferred a division into household plots, rather than the extreme fragmentation that partition by head could produce.

The response to revolutionary legislation on the partition of common land was far from uniform, and historians have only recently begun to clarify its ramifications. In Picardy, a large number of landless labourers, proletarianised by the development of large commercial estates, welcomed the division of what common land was still available. Picardy was a cereal-growing area, but in Normandy, with its substantial dairy industry, livestock-owners hung on to their common pasture rights. In the Massif Central, partition was often resisted, because it was likely to give only very small and relatively infertile plots. Many partitions were later reversed because they became impractical, and grazing livestock gradually resumed occupation of miniscule, hard-to-maintain holdings. According to Georges Lefebvre, only seventy partitions were carried out in the department of the Nord, and of these over a half were later reversed. In the Oise,

Guy Ikni counted over a hundred communes which decided to partition their commons, a measure which arguably assisted thousands of
small-scale landowners. Nevertheless, even by 1826, more than half
(51 per cent) of the communes of the Oise department still owned
common land.[24]

Peasants were often indifferent to the chance to divide common
land because there was so little of it in the village to share. In many
villages of the southern Massif Central, common grazing land on
the mountainsides was simply not worth giving over to cultivation.
Transporting enough manure to higher altitudes to make hard soil
productive involved an effort out of all proportion to the meagre
results likely to be achieved. Furthermore, the disappearance of the
common flock would have a terrible consequence for all villagers:
they would not have enough manure to promote cereal-growing. In
Allègre (Haute-Loire), enclosures were repeatedly demolished by
local peasants in 1796, 1801 and 1802, and the common herd took
over the land again. The local authorities called in troops and levied
fines but they had a very limited effect.[25] The conflict between economic individualism and communalism thus became a struggle
between the competing needs of shepherds and cowherds on one
hand, and cereal cultivators on the other. Local economies might collapse and generate conflict if the scales were tipped too far in any
one direction. In Chauffort (Haute-Marne) in 1812, one rich farmer
invoked the right of *vaine pâture* to send his flock of 200 sheep to
graze on his neighbours' land. This inevitably caused a protest: fragile village economies were vulnerable to sudden disruptions to customary practices.[26]

Imperial legislation had to find a way through the maze of local
custom, village quarrels, land partitions which had succeeded, and
land partitions which had effectively lapsed. The result, as usual, was
a compromise with the past. Legislation of 1804 recognised partitions
which had been carried out legally under the provisions of 1793.
Many had reverted to heath and pasture since then, while others had
been forcibly reversed. Doubtful cases were to be examined one by
one.

The Empire thus retreated from the egalitarian individualism of
1793. It was compelled to recognise the strength of customary usages
and their importance to the rural economy. The Rural Law Code, it is
true, was based on the defence of private property. It assumed as its
basic premise that individual owners were entitled to enjoy complete freedom over their own property. In this sense, Napoleonic

legislation promoted bourgeois notions of freehold property in the countryside. *Propriétaires* who paid annual taxes of 100 francs or more were to enjoy hunting rights. Those who owned more than 25 hectares could own pigeons. Thus two of the most hated seigneurial privileges of the Old Régime were resurrected on a new basis.[27]

In practice, however, the Rural Code acknowledged a multiplicity of exceptions to its guiding principles. It could not legislate for all of France without taking into account a variety of local usages and the previous conflicts collective rights. Although the Code decreed the abolition of *vaine pâture* and the *droit de parcours*, it nevertheless allowed individual communes to suspend application of the legislation indefinitely, if this was to the benefit of local agriculture. Similarly, communal gleaning rights were also recognised for "the poor and needy, children, the aged and others who lack the strength to contribute to the work of the harvest".[28] These concessions mitigated the entrepreneurial thrust of revolutionary and Napoleonic legislation, although economic liberals took a negative view of this. François de Neufchâteau complained in 1806: "In vain has our Rural Code laid down the principle that the soil of France is as free as those who inhabit it; even today, traces of servitude and the remains of disorder are still visible in the countryside".[29]

Rural Bonapartism can therefore only be understood in the context of the religious settlement, the fear of a return to seigneurialism and a reversal of the sale of *biens nationaux*, and the deference shown by the Consulate and Empire to rural custom and collectivism in agriculture. The precise mechanisms, however, through which Bonapartist ideas were diffused would repay further study. Returning soldiers could reinforce Bonapartist loyalties. Conscription opened up new horizons, in Egypt, Italy, Spain and Russia, to peasants for whom their own village or valley had once contained the world. The Napoleonic veteran, who became a stock character in nineteenth-century fiction, returned during the Empire itself with new experiences of the outside world. Perhaps some of their stories were coloured by admiration for the glories of Napoleon's military achievements in which they had proudly shared. The role of Gondrin in Balzac's *Médecin de Village*, in which the crippled veteran of Bérésina asserts his claim for a disability pension, suggests that the Napoleonic legend could contribute to raising political consciousness in the countryside.

Lamartine's memoirs recall the visits of *colporteurs*, or peddlars, selling mementoes and cheap brochures, illustrated with crude woodcuts, which commemorated Napoleonic achievements. In his recollection, the *colporteur* had an important role in developing rural Bonapartism. Lamartine's memoirs betray a certain nostalgia and condescension towards the local peasantry. At the same time, they suggest that reports of Napoleonic glory were easily assimilated into traditional literary forms. In the description of Augereau leaping across the Rhine, for instance, the account of the battle resembles the fantastic tales of chivalry and romance which were part of the staple diet of popular reading matter in the countryside (Document 11.1).

DOCUMENT 11.1 LAMARTINE, POET AND FUTURE REPUBLICAN LEADER, RECALLS HIS CHILDHOOD

The hawkers of coloured engravings shouted their wares outside the houses: "Great battle against the French, led by General Bonaparte in Italy ...!" Then the peasant would come out of his cottage and, with eyes shining in wonder, would see a display of heroic portraits, listen to tales of combat, and for one *sou* he would buy the history of these feats of arms. He nailed them to the walls of his house, or had his wife sew them to the serge curtain around his bed; for him and for his family, this was the whole history of France in great deeds.

The first display of political enthusiasm I can remember struck me in a village courtyard beside the yard of our house. It was the enthusiasm of a young man, named Janin, slightly more educated than his neighbours, who taught the children of the parish to read. One day, to the sound of a clarinet and drum, he came out of the tumbledown building which served as a school. He gathered the boys and girls of Milly around him and showed them some pictures of great men which were being sold by a hawker. "There", he told them, "you can see the Battle of the Pyramids, in Egypt, won by General Bonaparte. He is the small, thin, dark man you can see, riding a golden horse which is prancing in front of these heaps of hewn stones known as the Pyramids".

But this didn't please the spectators as much as Augereau galloping on a white charger, crossing the Rhine in a single leap, as if he was being carried on the wings of victory, or Berthier, with his pensive air, tearing a swan's quill from his teetering plume, to write down the orders from high command. But Kléber, with his tall, drum-major's stance, made the best image of all, and drew murmurs of approval from the entire hamlet.

The hawker spent his morning selling these echoes of national glory while Janin explained them to the winegrowers. His enthusiasm communicated itself to the entire village. These were my first intimations of glory. A horse, a plume, and a long sabre would always be symbolic. For some time, these people thought they were soldiers, perhaps for ever. On winter nights in the stables, the hawker's goods were discussed and Janin was continually being invited to their houses to decipher the texts of these beautiful and truthful images.

(Translated from Alphone de Lamartine, *Memoires de Jeunesse, 1790–1815,* ed. Marie-Rénée Morin (Paris: Tallandier, 1990), pp.41–3)

In his book *La République au Village,* Maurice Agulhon emphasised the role of middle-class cultural intermediaries in aiding the penetration of republican ideals in the countryside during the early nineteenth-century.[30] Bourgeois and petit-bourgeois culture-brokers had the advantages of greater literacy and a knowledge of French (like Janin, in Lamartine's memoirs). The rural bourgeoisie may have fulfilled a similar role as disseminators of Bonapartism in rural society. There was a class of lawyers and notaries, for instance, in the countryside who were also landowners, capable of providing leadership.[31] It is not difficult to imagine such local hierarchies encouraging fears of a return to seigneurialism, in order to bolster support for the régime.

This model of cultural diffusion, however, is open to question. The idea of rural Bonapartism responding to the agency of local notables seems to deprive the peasantry themselves of any possibility of independent thought. It could be fatal to imply that villagers were simply passive receptacles for Bonapartist propaganda disseminated by their social superiors. There were many rural areas outside Agulhon's Provence where the population was widely dispersed, and where contact between peasant and bourgeois would have been a rare event. In other areas, local notables were in any case closet royalists. Peasants, as the French Revolution clearly demonstrated, were quite capable of making up their own minds, of resisting or interpreting propaganda according to a rational assessment of their own interests.

Peasant Bonapartism nevertheless seems surprising when the burden of conscription is taken into account. Continuous warfare took its toll. The Jourdan Law of the Year 6 had enabled the army to maintain its strength through a regular annual draft. All single men between 20 and 25 years old were eligible for conscription. Naturally enough, there was peasant resistance to conscription, and naturally enough the resistance encountered the full repressive weight of the Napoleonic state. Altogether between 3 and 3.5 million men were called up by the Revolution and Empire combined, and approximately 2 million of these were conscripted between 1800 and 1814. In other words, about 7 per cent of France's total population was called up.[32]

There were many ways of avoiding the draft. Marriage was one of them, as we saw in Chapter 5, since only bachelors were eligible for the call-up. In 1813, the fear of conscription completely revitalised the marriage market.

Conscripts could flee, but they risked recapture unless they could leave French territory altogether, as many did by escaping over the Pyrenees. Those who stayed but were desperate to avoid service could manufacture some physical deformity to secure exemption. Conscripts were turned away because they had severed a thumb or mutilated a foot in order to disqualify themselves. In five years of conscription before 1805, 35 per cent of all recruits were turned away because of ill-health or physical incapacity.[33]

Failing that, many pocketed the first instalment of their pay and then deserted. Desertion was simple. Recruits were given a starting allowance to buy clothes and to enable them to travel to their regiments. Many of them never arrived at the front. This kind of desertion en route to the army was especially popular in the south-west and the Massif Central. Before 1805, over half those called up in the Gironde, the Cantal, the Aveyron and the Lozère never reached their unit.[34] In the Year 8, 333 conscripts left the Ardèche department to join their regiment in Dijon, but only six arrived.[35] The army suffered a heavy price in lost manpower, as well as the rifles, uniforms, boots and even horses with which deserters absconded.

Deserters and draft-dodgers survived by sticking together, occasionally forming groups of bandits who resorted to theft or highway robbery to support themselves through years of outlawry. They survived best when supported by their local community. It was always an advantage to desert close to home; this ensured that the deserter could benefit from the protection of his native village. Rural society was generally much more hostile to conscription than were the cities. French villages needed all the manpower they could get at harvest time, and few communities could tolerate the loss of their strongest and most energetic labourers. In some villages, the official register of births mysteriously disappeared, so that it would be impossible to tell how many eligible conscripts the village could provide.[36] Rural society had a high level of tolerance for local deserters, even when they resorted to crime. The demands of the state confronted the needs of the rural community which valued its own economic survival as its highest priority. Villagers closed ranks against the *gendarmes* who came to flush deserters out of hiding. When the mayor of St Urcize in the Cantal helped to locate and arrest a conscript hiding in a local inn, public fury compelled him to resign, and no one could be found to take his place as an unpopular agent of repression.[37]

In spite of such challenges to authority, desertion declined in the later years of Empire. Harsher penalties, like years of hard labour, were imposed on fugitives who were recaptured. Methods of detection became more efficient. "Flying columns" of troops were used in 1811–12 to round up bands of draft-dodgers. By 1808, over 90 per cent of those called up were actually reaching their regiments, in complete contrast to the situation which prevailed at the end of the Directory period. The French Revolution had invented conscription; but Napoleon made it work.

In some rural areas, resistance to state demands was instinctive and unreserved. Nevertheless, the burden of conscription should not be exaggerated. The burden fell very unevenly in geographical terms. In the west and the south, where reluctance to obey the call-up could be expected, government demands were more lenient. In annexed territories, too, local susceptibilities were spared a heavy toll. In the eastern departments of France, however, where military service was a traditional source of employment, the régime could afford to make greater demands on the population. According to Sutherland, the government of the Year 9 (1801) demanded one conscript per every 860 inhabitants in the Haut-Rhin, one per 1204 in the south-western department of the Lozère, one per 2208 in the annexed departments of the Rhineland, and only one per 4930 in the Finistère, the most western department of Brittany.[38] The Bonapartist régime was sensitive to local hostility.

The rhythm of the state's demands was not consistent either. Annual conscription in the Consulate was light in comparison to the demands made by the Directory. Even by the Year 12 (1804), only about 200 000 had been called up, which was less than half the figure required by the *levée* of 1799.[39] Conscription intensified after 1812; the war was being lost in Spain and an army had vanished in Russia. Only then did resistance become significant and the régime was accordingly forced to adopt more intimidatory tactics.

There were legitimate as well as illegal methods of avoiding the draft. Those who were too short or not in good health were exempted: these exceptions favoured southerners who tended to be shorter than northerners, and they assisted lower-class males who were most likely to show the debilitating effects of malnutrition and poor living conditions. The demands of the Napoleonic state, however, gradually increased: Napoleon reduced the minimum height for conscripts to 4 ft 8 in.[40] Employment in munitions manufactures, military transport or other activities considered essential to the war also conferred immunity from the call-up. If none of these escape routes was available, officials could be bribed to release sons, brothers or cousins. In Aurillac (Cantal), over 7000 exemptions were granted between 1806 and 1810 alone. The members of the review panel responsible had all received bribes, and the local prefect was forced to resign when the scandal was exposed.[41]

Only the wealthy could afford to offer imperial officials inducements to circumvent the law. Similarly, only a few could afford to buy a replacement for a drafted family member, under the substitution system introduced during the Consulate. Perhaps between 5 and 10 per cent of conscripts were able to buy their way out of the army in this way. The fluctuating cost of substitution is a useful barometer of village responses to military service. Substitution was clearly becoming more expensive towards the later years of the Empire. In the Côte d'Or department, a substitute could be had for 1900 francs in 1805; by 1811, however, he would cost 3600 francs, which amounted to at least six times the annual income of a skilled labourer.[42] Agricol Perdiguier, son of a carpenter who was a veteran of the Italian campaign, recalled that his elder brother Simon drew a *mauvais numéro* in 1809. He paid 3000 francs for a replacement, a humble street-porter (*portefaix*). Simon was taking a gamble which failed. The porter never arrived at his unit and Simon was eventually forced to replace his own replacement.[43] In the south, the army was more unpopular and substitutes were harder to find. Thus the going rate in Avignon was already over 4000 francs by 1808.[44] For those who could not afford this sum, desertion was a better option.

A closer look at conscription thus reveals that it was not an unmitigated evil for rural France. Recruitment demands were not uniform in all areas or for all social classes. Exemptions could be obtained on a variety of grounds and the burden did not become very heavy until 1813. Even for those who could not escape the call-up, military life had its compensations. One was loot: the prospect of plundering Italian palaces and Russian churches appealed to recruits. The regularity with which Bonaparte issued menacing directives against looters in the army of Italy suggests that French soldiers were not slow to grasp and pocket the fruits of victory. Another compensation, perhaps, was sexual pleasure, if the high incidence of syphilis in the army is any indication.[45] Sexual conquest was regarded, it seems, as a natural sequel of victory on the battlefield. The French soldier passed, as the boast went, "du combat à l'amour et d'amour au combat".

Imperial taxation was just as likely as conscription to meet an angry response in the countryside. Napoleon's indirect taxation was especially provocative. In 1806, a tax on salt was re-established, reminiscent of the hated *gabelle*, the salt monopoly enjoyed by the Old Régime monarchy. In 1810, the government's tobacco monopoly was also revived. In 1812, Napoleon introduced the *droits réunis*, a package of duties on drinks and other consumables which again resembled a resurrection of Old Régime fiscal practice. Government duty on alcohol tripled during the Empire, which did not please southern winegrowers.[46] In 1814, there was considerable resistance to imperial taxation, and tax collectors risked being attacked by angry villagers, in scenes reminiscent of the antifiscal riots of the seventeenth century. "A bas la conscription! A bas les droits réunis!" shouted peasants as the régime fell. The Bourbon Restoration was expected to abolish the *droits réunis* but it did not oblige.

By 1812–13, therefore, the effects of continuous warfare started to take a heavier toll in the countryside, both in terms of men and money. Wartime industrial malaise, too, affected rural areas just as much as the cities. The war created an artificial economy: some sectors were temporarily advantaged by the acquisition of imperial markets, while in others the inaccessibility of overseas outlets accelerated long-term collapse. Industrialisation in some areas implied deindustrialisation in others. Some areas of textile production, for instance, declined, depriving rural areas of a valuable source of employment. The fall in silk prices, for instance, hit the Lyonnais, and the decline of the woollen industry also reduced rural incomes. Economic depression exacerbated the subsistence crisis of 1811–12, when vagrancy again became a serious problem on the roads of Normandy and northern France. Bands of beggars several thousand strong were reported on the roads near Dieppe and Le Havre in the winter of 1811. According to the Prefect of the Somme, 60 000 beggars had taken to the roads in his department, and in Brittany the weavers of Rennes were scouring the countryside for sustenance.[47]

Towards the end of the Empire, therefore, political uncertainty and military defeat aggravated the economic downturn. The increasing demands of the government made it unpopular in the countryside. Yet, just as official impositions increased, the fear of a return to monarchical rule came to Napoleon's assistance. His rule had stood for the definitive end of seigneurialism. The Bourbons, however, were associated with the re-establishment of tithes and seigneurial burdens on the peasantry. Allied armies, it was feared, would finally realise the programme of the *émigrés* and the Duke of Brunswick in 1792–3. A Jacobin, anti-Bourbon reflex worked in Napoleon's favour, and helps to explain why peasants could attack the *droits réunis* and at the same time vote for Napoleon's Acte Additionnel in 1815. Here, perhaps, is a clue to the success of the Empire at village level: in the last resort, it ensured the preservation of the essential gains of the Revolution. Peasant Jacobinism, suggests Peter Jones, was "sublimated" into peasant Bonapartism.[48] The republican militant Martin Nadaud later recalled the influence of his father, a journeyman stonemason, who bought the *Bulletins de la Grande Armée* in the local market in the 1820s.[49] Left-wing Republicans of the nineteenth century had a Bonapartist as well as a revolutionary heritage.

12 "Masses of Granite": The Sociology of an Elite

Gaps in our information about village life make it difficult to assess the impact of the Empire on the rural masses. The situation is quite different in the case of the social élites of the Empire. As is so often the case in historical research, the sources leave us well informed about the nature of the ruling classes, but piecing together a "history from below" demands considerable ingenuity. The membership of the élites whom the Napoleonic régime summoned to its defence is so well known that historians have been able to conduct a computer-based analysis of the career data of almost 70 000 *notables* of the Empire.[1]

Napoleon gathered to him an élite of wealth and talent, bound to the régime by personal allegiance to the Emperor and by a common aim of loyal service to the state. He gave them an institutional basis, in the imperial nobility, the legion of honour, and in the body of *notables* officially established by the Constitution of the Year 10. In so doing, he both recognised and rewarded their loyalty and service. These new institutions, and their prestigious members, were to be the "masses of granite" on which the régime relied.

The *notables* were the chief beneficiaries of the Consulate and Empire. The data processed by historians' computers helps to answer, in social terms, the question of who "won" the French Revolution. The status given to Napoleonic élites of landowners, functionaries and soldiers consecrated the triumph of the revolutionary bourgeoisie of administrators and professionals. This, however, is not just a study of social promotion since 1789; it is also a study of the survival of social groups who wielded power at the close of the Old Régime. The role of the old régime nobility under the Empire, for example, must not be obscured, and the continuity of élites must be acknowledged. The "masses of granite" represented a fusion of old and new, in which ancient geological strata combined with more recent deposits formed by the French Revolution.

Some historians have interpreted the formation of new social hierarchies in a more negative light. Jean Tulard viewed the creation of the

160

imperial nobility in 1808 as a decisive turning-point, which marked the beginning of the end for the Napoleonic Empire.[2] For some it represented not the fulfilment of the Revolution but a violation of its egalitarian principles. As we shall see, the new nobility was very different from the old. Even its "reactionary" features can be interpreted in the light of the ascending progress of the jurists and administrators who were the victors of 1789. Napoleon's tinsel aristocracy consummated the rise of the revolutionary bourgeoisie; but it also reflected the fact that once this bourgeoisie had achieved a dominant grip on the apparatus of the French state, it had ceased to be in any way revolutionary.

The Constitution of the Year 8 had envisaged three tiers of *notables*, elected at local, departmental and national level. This system was abandoned in the Constitution of the Year 10 which created electoral colleges in each department. These electoral colleges were to be elected from a list of the 600 largest taxpayers of the department. Since the land tax was by far the most substantial component of fiscal contributions, the list was inevitably a reflection of landed wealth. In the departmental colleges, the government thus provided itself with a pool of propertied supporters, from which it could select candidates for local administration and the national legislature. The lists of *notables* at departmental and *arrondissement* level, together with the lists of the 600 highest taxpayers in each department, confirmed the social importance of landownership. They are also a measure of the central role of land as a component of bourgeois wealth before the era of large-scale industrialisation.

The *notables* were not just chosen for the property they owned. They were chosen as candidates for state service, which meant that their political loyalties were another criterion for their eligibility. The prefect was usually the judge who advised the government on their political reliability. As *notables*, however, they enjoyed social influence but no real political power: the existence of the electoral colleges did not imply any dilution of central authority. They were expected to use their local influence to cement popular loyalty to the régime, as Roederer explained to the prefects in Prairial Year 10:

> One of the surest ways ... which can assist in revealing the state of public opinion, is to establish some idea of the civil life of the nation's greatest landed proprietors; because they are the ones who, exerting a threefold influence by means of their example, their speeches and the money they spend, determine opinion and the general feeling in periods of stability.[3]

The *notables* were fully expected to play their part in moulding docile and respectful imperial subjects. They were seen as a useful means of confirming Napoleonic hegemony. The typical *notable* of 1810 was a married man between 40 and 60 years old.[4] He belonged to the generation which had reached adulthood at the beginning of the French Revolution. He was too young to have any strong emotional attachment to the Old Régime, and his views of society and politics had been formed in the revolutionary years. Their professional status in 1810 is summarised in Table 12.1. Landownership was the group's chief defining characteristic. The *notables* were not all *propriétaires* on a large scale; they included quite modest landowners, too, which reflected the results of the sale of *biens nationaux* during the Revolution. The world of business and commerce provided only about one *notable* in ten, but a larger proportion of the *notables* than this had been involved in commerce at the end of the Old Régime.[6] In other words, a certain amount of business capital had been shifted into the acquisition of land, perhaps as a cautious response to the volatile economic conditions of the revolutionary years. Business élites, as Sutherland put it, had become "ruralised", and in the process they enjoyed the social promotion that landownership conferred on the leaders of eighteenth-century capitalism.[7] This emphasis on property effectively blocked any return to the society of orders of Old Régime France: state service and propertied wealth, not birth and inherited rank, would now determine the social and political hierarchy.

A second important category amongst the *notables* was that of public functionaries. Many of those who were old enough had served in the lower ranks of the civil or military administration under the Old

Table 12.1   Socio-professional Status of the *Notables* in 1810

33.9% were administrators or public servants
24.6% were landed proprietors (*propriétaires*)
14.4% were members of the liberal professions
10.8% were businessmen and tradesmen
 8.2% were owner-occupiers (*propriétaires exploitants*)
 2.4% were military personnel
 1.2% were members of the clergy
 4.5% belonged to other professional categories.[5]

Régime monarchy. These lesser bureaucrats of the old monarchy were joined by younger professionals and administrators at every level, from municipal government to the highest ranks of state service. As the British historian Alfred Cobban insisted, the French Revolution was led by lawyers and office-holders. This administrative and professional bourgeoisie emerged intact at the helm of the Napoleonic régime, and their importance was fully enshrined in the lists of *notables*.

Landowners, administrators, professional men and businessmen provided the four most solid elements of the "masses of granite". This Empire-wide generalisation, however, does not reveal the range of local variety which existed. Almost every department of the Empire offers some sociological variant in the composition of its élites. In the Haute-Garonne, for example, landed proprietors were completely dominant, making up over 60 per cent of the 600 largest taxpayers. About one-third had occupied some office under the Republic, Consulate or Empire, but about 45 per cent of the largest taxpayers were nobles, ex-parlementaires, or the sons of ex-parlementaires.[8] This suggests that most of the old régime ruling class in the *parlementaire* city of Toulouse weathered the Revolution without severe damage. Many in fact had prospered: one-third of the Toulousain *notables* had purchased *biens nationaux*.

In the relatively poor department of the Ain in eastern France, on the other hand, there were very few plutocratic landowners, and the Empire relied heavily on the local class of professional men, especially lawyers, most of whom had a record of participation in the Revolution. In the Ain, over one-third of the electoral college was made up of members of the liberal professions.[9]

A slightly different pattern emerged in the Rhineland, where imperial functionaries dominated the ranks of local *notables*. A new class of bourgeois administrators had emerged, formed from the personnel of both the defunct monarchy and the republican period. Thirty-one per cent of the electoral college of the Rhin-et-Moselle were imperial civil servants, and the proportion was even higher (40 per cent) in the *arrondissement* colleges of the annexed Ruhr department in the Year 12.[10] In the Bas-Rhin, prefects were careful to select a combination of *notables* which would not offend local religious susceptibilities. There was no rabbi and there were no Jews amongst the *notables* of the Bas-Rhin, and although one-third were Protestant, there was neither a Lutheran leader nor a Catholic bishop amongst their number.

These examples, from aristocratic Toulouse, the relatively poor and conservative departments of Savoy, and the culturally diverse Rhineland, do not represent the whole picture. They do not allow a full assessment of the position of business and commerce in the ranks of the *notables*. Their role has sometimes been undervalued by historians. Revisionist historians have thrown doubt on the theory that the French Revolution was a revolutionary transformation creating the conditions for future development towards a capitalist society. Thirty years ago, Alfred Cobban argued the opposite: that the French Revolution did more to retard than advance French capitalism.[11] In spite of the remarkably thin empirical basis on which Cobban relied, his ideas have been surprisingly influential. If businessmen and the commercial bourgeoisie do not figure prominently amongst Napoleonic *notables*, the link between the French Revolution and the future development of capitalism will look tenuous.

How significant, then, was the presence of commerce and industry on the lists of imperial *notables*? Their presence reflected the geography of French industry itself: there were high concentrations in a few areas. There remained an enormous contrast between a department like Mont-Blanc where businessmen, industrialists and artisans made up fewer than 10 per cent of local *notables*, and the highly urbanised Var department in mediterranean Provence where more than 30 per cent of the largest taxpayers were businessmen.[12]

In annexed Geneva, which became the department of Léman, the predominance of capitalist interests was even more spectacular. The bulk of the city's patrician oligarchy continued to dominate the list of largest taxpayers under French rule. In 1813, 42 per cent of Geneva's *notables* paid the *patente*, the tax on commercial licences, although wartime conditions and French protectionism had greatly reduced local industrial production. As a result, Swiss capital flowed into land. Nevertheless, three-quarters of Geneva's *notables* paid no land tax whatsoever.[13] In the departments of the Rhine and the Loire, between 15 and 20 per cent of *notables* were from commerce and industry.[14] Concentrations of manufacturing wealth appeared amongst the timber merchants of the Yonne in central France, the ironmasters (*maîtres des forges*) of the Haute-Saône, and in the textile-producing areas of Normandy.

The lists of *notables* therefore recognised the rise of the entrepreneur, even if the presence of merchants and manufacturers was not geographically consistent. Landownership and entrepreneurship were not necessarily mutually exclusive. The flight of capital into land was not always motivated by a cultural reflex which made the bourgeoisie a deferential admirer of the aristocratic lifestyle. It was often a rational investment decision. Moving money into land was a safe and profitable option at a time when Revolution and war increased business risk and could make profits elusive. Land could be mortgaged in the future as security for loans used to finance commercial enterprises. Transferring money into land, therefore, did not necessarily retard capitalist development; it could be a platform for progress, which would resume in calmer times.

A rigid distinction, therefore, between landed and commercial interests cannot easily be drawn. Merchants and industrialists were also *propriétaires*. Meanwhile, as studies of wills have shown, professional families and landowners by no means limited their capital investments to real estate. Most *notables* in Marseilles, for instance, held valuable letters of credit whether they were businessmen or not.[15] It is possible, then, that the information in Table 12.1 does not reveal the full extent of the social élite's involvement in entrepreneurial capitalism.

The lists of *notables* do not provide a completely trustworthy snapshot of France's wealthiest men; their composition was also a qualitative or political choice. This choice could also be dictated by bureaucratic expediency. The methods used by individual prefects to draw them up varied, and often tended to overlook businessmen whose wealth was not as conspicuous as that of the owners of large country estates. The commercial tax, or *patente*, was sometimes not taken into account at all in compiling the lists of the 600 largest taxpayers. This was the case in the Haute-Garonne, where the manufacturer Boyer-Fonfrède was surprisingly excluded.[16] Sometimes the prefects acknowledged insuperable difficulties in calculating taxable wealth which was not bound up in real estate. Barante, prefect of Geneva, confessed to such a problem in 1809:

> I have tried to select fairly evenly between the different sectors of the department, between civil and military functions and between the different circumstances of birth, wealth or service which carry influence and respect ... In a region where nearly all the wealth lies in moveable capital, it has been impossible for me to establish, with a degree of probability, any numerical measurement of the sum and value of such capital.[17]

A manufacturer who had no desire for administrative promotion might, of course, opt out of the lists of notability altogether. Others, who were both *négoçiants* and *propriétaires*, might find that their commercial wealth was not taken into consideration for reasons of bureaucratic convenience. Members of the old régime nobility figured strongly amongst the *notables* by virtue of their role as the greatest landowning class. The departmental list of leading taxpayers was often headed by an ex-noble, such as the Duke de Luynes in the Seine-et-Oise or the Duke de Choiseul-Praslin in the Seine-et-Marne. The old nobility now kept company with lawyers and entrepreneurs, but they included some of the largest individual property-owners in France. One such Croesus was the Duke de Choiseul-Praslin, previously mentioned, who did not merely head the list of leading taxpayers in the Seine-et-Marne but also headed the list in the department of the Sarthe, not to mention his considerable estates in the Côte d'Or department. In the Orne, the first twelve leading taxpayers were all nobles, and so were the first twelve in the Seine-et-Marne, eleven out of the first twelve in the Dordogne and ten out of the first twelve in the Seine-et-Oise.[18]

In spite of the survival of these upper aristocratic echelons, the imperial élite was open to talent. Its mixture of landowners, functionaries, lawyers and entrepreneurs registered the social transformation which the Revolution bequeathed to Napoleon. When the old monarchy had attempted a similar exercise, rallying its élites to the cause of limited reform in the ill-fated Assembly of Notables of 1787, the group then assembled had a rather different complexion. The notables of 1787 consisted of princes of the royal blood, dukes and peers of France, prelates, councillors of state, and leaders of the Parlements. The 144 hand-picked members represented only the privileged orders of old régime society. The Napoleonic notables were not representative of all ranks of French society either; but they did represent the triumphant professional, commercial and landowning bourgeoisie. Together with a section of the old nobility, they formed a cadre of *notables* who were to dominate French society until the 1848 Revolution. Their loyalty to Napoleon was far from guaranteed: in the Haute-Garonne in 1815, only fifty-four members of the electoral college answered Napoleon's call in the Hundred Days.[19] But their position and influence as *notables* continued long after the Emperor had departed from the scene.

The military did not figure largely in the ranks of the *notables*; they were not continuously present in their home departments, and thus were of limited value as a political instrument which would form local opinion. Their role as an emerging élite was more fully recognised in the creation of the imperial nobility, and especially of the *légion d'honneur*. The legion was established in 1802, and the first large batch of decorations was awarded at the military camp at Boulogne in 1804, when 2000 were so honoured. This occasion demonstrated the primary purpose of the *légion d'honneur*, which was to reward military service. Only a dozen of those decorated in Boulogne in 1804 were civilians.[20] Out of 38 000 promotions to the *légion d'honneur* between 1802 and 1814, only 4000 involved civilian personnel, most of them senators, politicians or councillors of state.[21] The legion had a military hierarchy of Grand Officers, Commanders, Officers and Legionnaires. It demonstrated the high regard in which the Napoleonic régime held military values, and it remains a respected badge of status in France today.

At the summit of the military hierarchy stood the Napoleonic marshals. They were an exclusive band: there were never more than sixteen of them active at any one time. As usual, political factors helped to dictate the Emperor's choice. Of the marshals appointed in 1804, seven were from the Rhine army, which had a reputation for Republicanism, and seven were from the army of Italy. Thus Napoleon's main military constituencies were equally satisfied.

According to Napoleonic mythology, the marshals were living proof of the new opportunities for social promotion opened up by the French Revolution, and seized by men of talent in the Consulate and Empire. Every French soldier, according to the cliché, carried a marshal's baton in his backpack. Talent, in other words, would inevitably rise and gather its true rewards, regardless of humble birth.

Not all Napoleon's marshals, however, came from humble backgrounds (see Table 12.2).[22] Augereau, it is true, was the son of a domestic servant, and Lefebvre was the son of a police *commissaire*. Only Lannes could genuinely claim a peasant background. But a handful of marshals, like Kellermann and Davout, had their social origins in the old régime aristocracy. A larger group still had backgrounds in the law and administration of the Bourbon monarchy, like Bernadotte or Brune, both descended from magistrates in provincial courts. The marshals formed a typically Napoleonic amalgamation of old régime lesser nobility, the sons of bourgeois and administrators, together with a few descended from lower social ranks. They enjoyed the titles, income and opportunity for imperial plunder which the Empire showered on its military élite.

Table 12.2 Napoleon's Marshals and their Social Origins

Name	Date promoted	Title	Father's profession
Augereau	1804	Duke of Castiglione	Domestic servant
Bernadotte	1804	Prince of Sweden	Attorney of the *sénéchaussée* of Pau
Berthier	1804	Sovereign-prince of Neuchâtel	Engineer, ennobled 1763
Bessières	1804	Duke of Istria	Doctor
Brune	1804	none	Magistrate of the *présidial* of Brive
Davout	1804	Prince of Eckmühl	Nobleman
Jourdan	1804	none	Surgeon
Kellermann	1804	Duke of Valmy	Ennobled 1788
Lannes	1804	Duke of Montebello	Peasant
Lefebvre	1804	Duke of Danzig	Police *commissaire*
Masséna	1804	Prince of Essling	Shopkeeper
Moncey	1804	Duke of Conegliano	*Avocat* of the Besançon Parlement
Mortier	1804	Duke of Treviso	Draper
Murat	1804	King of Naples	Innkeeper
Ney	1804	Prince of the Moskova	Cooper
Pérignon	1804	Count	Provost of the Constabulary of St Domingo
Sérurier	1804	Count	Petty nobleman
Soult	1804	Duke of Dalmatia	Notary
Victor	1807	Duke of Belluna	Usher in *bailliage* court
Macdonald	1809	Duke of Tarento	Scottish nobleman
Marmont	1809	Duke of Ragusa	Nobleman
Oudinot	1809	Duke of Reggio	Large farmer and brewer
Suchet	1811	Duke of Albufera	Silk merchant
Gouvion St Cyr	1812	Count	Tanner
Poniatowski	1813	Prince	Polish royal family
Grouchy	1815	Count	Nobleman

The largesse of Empire ended up in civilian hands, too. The Senators, for example, received plenty of material proof of the Emperor's gratitude. Appointments to the Senate had enabled Napoleon to pay his debts to his companions in Egypt and his supporters in Brumaire. Promotion to the Senate was offered to silence critics like Siéyès or reward ministers like Fouché and Roederer. The imperial Senate was expanded to receive new members from Italy, the Netherlands and Germany, as Napoleon used it to incorporate non-French élites. Some illustrious Senators were presented with *Senatoreries*, consisting of land and income which ensured a very comfortable retirement and the status of a local pasha.

The distribution of imperial princedoms and dukedoms (meaningless though these titles were), and the *Senatoreries*, suggest a division of the spoils among triumphant medieval warriors. They seem an anachronistic growth on a modern bureaucratic state. Even some of the prefectures were filled merely to satisfy the demands of loyal clients and patronage-seekers. In 1800, some prefectures were claimed by Bonaparte's companions from Egypt (the *égyptiens*), and seven were reserved for Joséphine's connections in the Beauharnais family. The other two consuls, too often thought of as mere shadows behind the throne, had their own clientèles to satisfy. According to Bergeron's calculations, Cambacérès controlled eight "pocket prefectures" in the Midi, while Consul Lebrun had a portfolio of ten to fill with his own supporters.[23]

The prefects were one of the most important sections of the Napoleonic élite considered here, because unlike senators, legionnaires or imperial nobles they wielded real administrative power. They embodied the presence and authority of the Napoleonic state in every French and imperial department. They, too, were a legacy of the French Revolution: of the first batch of prefects created in 1800, seventy had belonged to revolutionary assemblies, and their political loyalties ranged from the anglophile monarchism of Mounier to the republicanism of the ex-*montagnard* Jeanbon St André.[24] Sixty more of the early prefects had been involved in municipal or departmental administration under the Directory. If the entire consular and imperial body of 281 prefects are considered, and not just the early prefects, Whitcomb estimates that 30 per cent of all prefects had been members of a revolutionary assembly. Competent revolutionary politicians never went out of favour; they continued to enjoy promotion through the prefectoral corps, although old age took its toll. In 1814, only 19 per cent of the prefects had a revolutionary past.[25]

The prefects were a relatively young élite. Most of them were in their thirties or forties when they were first appointed. The early prefects, who belonged for the most part to the generation born between 1750 and 1770, gradually gave way to younger appointees who had no experience at all of the Old Régime or the early Revolution, but who had received most of their training in the Consulate and Empire. Many had served as auditors of the Conseil d'État, a nursery for future Napoleonic bureaucrats, and rose through the ranks and the sub-prefectures. The régime's medieval trappings should not deceive us: here was an increasingly professional body of administrators who now had their own specialised training and career structure.

The majority of prefects were recruited from Paris and northern France, although the expansion of the Empire meant that a small proportion were born outside France, in Italy, Belgium or the Netherlands. They were an increasingly stable and homogeneous group. Originally, they were recruited from politics, the law and the army, but a steadily rising proportion had an administrative background. They inevitably became more experienced as it became normal to serve in the same department for periods of four or five years. No fewer than thirty-three prefects actually served for more than twelve years. Whitcomb argues that this experience was part of a process of professionalisation which made the prefects better administrators. This may have been the case, but longevity in office and special training did not ensure that the prefects were sensitive to local needs, nor did they prevent the development of a stultifying bureaucratic mentality. In fact, they were more likely to encourage it.

The composition of the prefectoral corps confirmed the promotion of the administrative bourgeoisie. In spite of the presence in the prefectures of some noblemen, intellectuals and ex-soldiers, the bourgeoisie provided most of the cadres of imperial technocrats. The origins of the prefects are summarised in Table 12.3:

Table 12.3   Social Origins of Napoleon's Prefects

32% were recruited from the administration
20% were recruited from the legal profession
14% were recruited from politics
12% were recruited from the army
22% were recruited from other backgrounds (clerics, intellectuals, businessmen)[26]

61% were bourgeois in origin
39% were noble in origin

From the beginning of the Consulate onwards, a significant proportion of aristocrats joined the Napoleonic administration. La Tour du Pin, for example, a member of one of France's most illustrious families, was prefect of the Dyle department in 1808. Their number actually increased towards the end of the Empire. This was not, as is sometimes assumed, because they displaced the administrative bourgeoisie in a Napoleon-inspired aristocratic reaction. The influx of aristocrats into the prefectures was rather a function of imperial expansion: the aristocrats arrived in office in newly created non-French departments, where the régime tended to rely for support on the most conservative social elements.

In 1808, Napoleon created the imperial nobility, establishing a hierarchy of princes, dukes, counts, barons, and knights (*chevaliers*). By 1814, more than 3200 imperial titles had been created, most of them between 1808 and 1811. A clear majority of the new imperial nobles (58 per cent) were drawn from the bourgeoisie, while 20 per cent of the Napoleonic aristocracy came from the popular classes. A significant minority of 22 per cent of imperial nobles were members of the old régime nobility. For some aristocrats, Napoleonic titles would always be tawdry and cheapening. In Proust's novel, *In Search of Lost Time*, the Count of Jéna is ridiculed by high society aristocrats in St Germain because, it was snootily asserted, he was named after a bridge. Nevertheless, despite such ineradicable prejudices, Napoleon had some limited success in persuading the old nobility to support his régime.

A few industrial capitalists were ennobled, like the shipowner Begouën of Le Havre, who became a count in 1808, and the cloth manufacturer Poupart de Neuflize, mayor of Sedan and a baron in 1810. The banker Lecouteulx de Canteleu was a senator and a count, a promotion which may have been linked to the fact that he had supported the coup of Brumaire with loans to the tune of 12 million francs to the new government.[27] Fourteen Regents of the Bank of France were ennobled, most of them Protestant financiers grouped around Delessert, a Lyon textile tycoon. Eight baronetcies were offered to financiers in 1810 alone, probably in order to persuade the banks to lower interest rates at a time of economic crisis.

The promotion of the bourgeoisie, the *ralliement* of the old aristocracy: these are by now familiar characteristics of the "masses of granite". They apply, too, to the imperial nobility. The imperial nobility rewarded civil servants, and especially the military. Military officers made up 60 per cent of the imperial nobles, while another 22 per cent were from the highest ranks of the civil service, and the senators, prefects, bishops and mayors of important cities. The *notables* provided another 17 per cent of the imperial nobles.[28] Only a very small proportion of intellectuals or businessmen were elevated to the new upstart peerage.

The new hierarchy was very clearly defined at the outset in terms of state functions although, as a concession to the dynastic principle, the supreme title of Prince was to be accorded to members of the imperial family. Ministers, senators, life members of the Conseil d'État, archbishops and presidents of the Corps Législatif were eligible for promotion as Counts. Bishops, the mayors of three dozen important cities and presidents of electoral colleges could aspire to an imperial baronetcy. The Emperor, of course, could bestow titles personally on whoever he wished.

The creation of the imperial nobility has been seen as a retrograde betrayal of egalitarianism, a return to the hierarchical principle which the French Revolution had overthrown when it abolished all titles of nobility. Revolutionary principles were threatened further by the possibility of hereditary transmission of imperial noble status. Napoleon was attempting to create an élite with a vested interest in the preservation of the Empire and the bonapartist dynasty, but he appeared to many to be restoring some of the most detestable features of the Old Régime.

Resemblances between the imperial nobility and the Old Régime aristocracy, however, were superficial. State service, not family connections, was the criterion for promotion. This was a nobility of technocrats and functionaries rather than of ancient feudal lineage. The imperial nobles, unlike their eighteenth-century predecessors, enjoyed no tax exemptions and no legal privileges. They had a title, a donation of land in conquered territory and a coat-of-arms. Otherwise, the new nobility had none of the characteristic features of the old. Its members were not linked by ties of blood or intermarriage, and they came from a wide range of social backgrounds. Napoleon had sworn as part of his coronation oath to resist any reestablishment of the society of orders, which had been officially abolished on 4 August 1789. The imperial nobility was an open élite, not a feudal order. Napoleon told Cambacérès in 1807 that the new nobility was "the only way to uproot the old nobility entirely".[29] It welcomed defectors from the old ranks but was constituted on an entirely different basis.

State service earned an imperial title; but the holder qualified by virtue of his wealth, if he wanted to make his title hereditary. A duke needed an annual income of 200 000 francs to earn the right to a hereditary title. A count needed 30 000 francs per year, a baron 15 000 and a knight 3000 francs. Napoleon, as a young impoverished nobleman's son, had personal experience of the financial problems which constrained aristocratic pretensions. Decorations and distinctions were of little value without the liquid cash to maintain one's status.

There were many different ways of assembling the personal estate (*majorat*) which could justify the hereditary transmission of imperial nobility. Members of the old nobility often had enough property already to justify their new status. Riquet de Caraman, for example, formed a *majorat* from two soap manufactures in Marseilles, which made him eligible for a baronetcy.[30] The purchase of *biens nationaux* could also be used as the basis for the acquisition of hereditary titles. In a few cases, stocks and shares rather than landed property were used to constitute a *majorat*, which was the case for the banker Perregaux, and for the rare case of Louis Amiot in the Seine-et-Marne whose hereditary estate consisted entirely of shares in the Bank of France. In practice, only thirty-seven imperial counts and 131 barons registered a *majorat* to qualify for a hereditary title. Many knights (*chevaliers de l'Empire*) did so, however, and more than half of them were soldiers.[31]

If candidates were unable to muster enough personal property to justify a hereditary title, the Emperor could assist by providing them with generous state donations. The Grand Dignatories of the Empire received titles and imperial gifts carved out of annexed territory in Germany, Poland or Italy (see Table 12.4).

On paper, income from the Emperor's donations commonly constituted two-thirds of their personal estate. This was certainly the case for Marshal Masséna. In 1807, he received the income from seventeen Polish villages at Trombino, complete with woods and seigneurial dues. In 1808, he received a further donation of 70 000 francs annually from a former estate of the King of Prussia, at Hammersleben in Westphalia. When he became Duke of Rivoli, his estate needed to be enlarged further to match his new status, and the Emperor therefore endowed him with estates in Hanover. He finally became the imperial Prince of Essling, a title which would have looked incongruous on a pauper. In 1810, therefore, Masséna was accorded another half a million francs' annual income from estates and taxes in the province of Bayreuth.[32]

Table 12.4　The Grand Dignitaries of the Empire, est.1808

Great Elector	Joseph Bonaparte, King of Naples, then King of Spain (1808–13)
Vice-Elector	Talleyrand, Foreign Minister, then Prince of Benevento
Arch-Chancellor	Cambacérès, Consul, then Duke of Parma
Arch-Chancellor of State	Eugène de Beauharnais, Viceroy of Italy
Arch-Treasurer	Lebrun, ex-Consul, Duke of Piacenza
High Constable	Lucien Bonaparte, King of Holland (1806–10)
Vice-Constable	Berthier, Chief of Staff, Prince of Neuchâtel, then Prince of Wagram
Grand Judge	Regnier, Minister of Justice, Duke of Massa-Carrara
Grand Admiral	Joachim Murat, Grand-Duke of Berg, then King of Naples, married Caroline Bonaparte
Governor of the Departments beyond the Alps	Camillo Borghese, husband of Pauline Bonaparte
Governor of the Dutch Departments	Lebrun, ex-Consul, Duke of Piacenza

Marshals like Masséna discovered, however, that these immense riches were largely illusory. Not only did their grandiose titles mean nothing in terms of political authority, but the income that went with them was full of traps. It was very difficult to collect, especially in areas where there was considerable resistance to the French occupation. Local authorities in Westphalia or Hanover were not eager to help French officials extract rents from their own subjects, merely to fill the coffers of France's princely exploiters. After the bad harvest of 1812 only a fraction of the money due to the princes ever reached them. Even when the money was collected from Germany or Poland, the recipients lost a substantial percentage (up to 10 per cent) when it was converted into French currency. In 1813, the frontiers of the

Empire were contracting and the imperial dignatories received virtually no income at all.[33]

This group of dignitaries, however, had plenty of other opportunities to accumulate a fortune, some legal and some not. French imperial expansion offered victorious generals a chance to amass bribes, art treasures, and unofficial ransoms offered by occupied towns which wanted to buy protection from wholesale looting. Marshal Soult was particularly avaricious, and Napoleon regretted later in exile on St Helena that he had not had him shot as an example.[34] General Lamarque later recalled noticing a Raphael hanging in Soult's main reception room and related the following:

One admirer, standing before this painting, dared to ask the marshal how much he had paid for it. "It only cost me a couple of monks" ... and His Excellency explained that two cordelier monks had been compromised in a plot and were about to be hung, when their community offered to buy their freedom with this fine painting. The marshal allowed himself to be merciful [se laisser attendrir], he accepted the painting and the two monks were not hung.[35]

Soult's enormous collection of Spanish paintings was sold for a fabulous sum in 1852. In Florence, the town worthies planned to offer Brune a handful of paintings and engravings, together with a sumptuous necklace of jewellery for his wife, in order to avoid massive French appropriations from the Uffizi.[36] Brune had an eye for easy profit in Germany, too. During the continental blockade, he sold import licences which enabled Hamburg merchants to continue trade with Britain. In this instance, he lined his own pocket by subverting France's official economic policy.

Besides naked extortion, there were, of course, legal avenues to self-enrichment, like government salaries. A Marshal of France earned 40 000 francs per year, the prefect of the Seine received 100 000 francs, and councillors of state earned 30 000 francs. There was nothing to prevent individuals from accumulating several different lucrative positions, either in the military or civil branches of the imperial administration. Berthier was a good example of an imperial pluralist. Appointed Marshal in 1804, he was also Minister of War from 1800 until 1807. His chief position, however, was Chief of Staff of the Grande Armée. He was expected to be on call to respond loyally and promptly to the imperial will. On one occasion, he got up twenty-seven times in one night to take orders from the Emperor.[37] He was amply rewarded. He became Prince of Neuchâtel in 1806,

Vice-Constable in 1807, and Prince of Wagram in 1809. He received the Château of Chambord and the Château of Grosbois, in addition to his income of 1 million francs per year and his Paris town house on the rue des Capucines.

The dignatories of the Empire had the archaic medieval titles of Constable or Lord Chamberlain, but they remained an élite of state functionaries, not a caste of parasites. The Napoleonic Empire was a contradictory mixture of the ancient and the modern. On one hand, the apparatus of a professional bureaucracy was emerging. On the other hand, conquered territory was being handed out to avaricious military leaders as if they were tribal chieftains or followers of a Corsican clan. Titles plucked from the romanticised Middle Ages sat uneasily on officials of the most centralised and efficient government machine Europe had yet seen. The Napoleonic Empire was a modern technocracy dressed in the garb of Charlemagne.

The old nobility made the best of their new situation. They remained the largest landowning class, although now their eminence was challenged by officials, businessmen and the new élites among the imperial *notables*. One-third of Napoleon's ministers were ex-nobles, and at least a fifth of his generals were of noble birth.[38] Many aristocratic families began to reconstitute their fortunes and consolidate what remained of their estates after the Revolution.

The aristocracy had been sorely affected by the emigration; perhaps one noble family in four had a member who was an *émigré*.[39] A great deal of aristocratic land had been sold during the Revolution and much of it was irrecoverable, in spite of the efforts of a few loyal servants to keep the estates intact during the period of emigration. Living abroad as *émigrés* was expensive, and nobles who returned after 1801 had accumulated substantial debts over at least a decade. This burden of debt made it difficult for the aristocracy to borrow the money to buy back their land. Woodland was an exception. It had passed into the public domain, and was to be returned to the nobles by the Bourbon Restoration, but fertile and profitable estates had been snapped up and were irretrievable.

The Duke of Saulx-Tavanes is a good example of the nobility's predicament. When he returned from self-imposed exile in 1800, he found his Burgundian estates all sold, except for 5000 acres of forest which were in government hands.[40] All his arable and pasture land was gone for ever. He still had an income of 30 000 francs per year, which was about one-third of what he was able to command in 1789. Unfortunately for the duke, family squabbles had developed in his long absence. His two sisters claimed a share of the inheritance, according to the new egalitarian inheritance laws, and they had begun to sub-divide the property. The Duke of Saulx-Tavanes was less comfortably off than most of his class. According to Robert Forster, provincial nobles probably lost about a third of their income and one-fifth of their land in the French Revolution.[41] They had lost their seigneurial dues, which were admittedly of limited importance in many areas before 1789. On commercial estates like those of the Toulouse nobility in the rich cereal plains of the Lauraguais, seigneurial dues made up only about 8 per cent of the nobles' pre-revolutionary income. In the less fertile areas of central France, however, some provincial nobles lost more than a half of their income with the abolition of seigneurialism. In the Rouergue, dues in cash or in kind had made up over 70 per cent of seigneurial income in the Old Régime.[42] The profits of seigneurial justice disappeared, as did, of course, all the tax exemptions which had been enmeshed in the network of old régime privilege.

Most importantly, a social revolution had occurred which made the return of privilege and of aristocratic monopolies impossible. Nobles remained amongst the largest landowners in France, but their power, just like that of bourgeois landowners, now derived purely from their wealth. The nobles survived the Revolution and formed a new élite of *notables*, together with the successful bourgeoisie. They shared power, and above all, they did not share it on their own terms. The Duke of Saulx-Tavanes had not been systematically expropriated: he still had his château in the forest, but he was now a member of a bourgeois society which had completely redefined the basis of the social hierarchy.

13   Art, Propaganda and the Cult of Personality

Propaganda, as a means of shaping and controlling public opinion, is a familiar instrument of every modern government. Unlike twentieth-century régimes, imperial France had no Ministry of Propaganda, and no Ministry of Information, but Napoleon himself was responsible for supervising these essential functions of government. Every morning, we are told, Napoleon had the newspapers read to him as he shaved.[1] Much of what they printed would not have been "news" to the Emperor: he wrote some of the news items himself or commissioned others to write articles which he wanted to appear, specifying the desired content and argument. Napoleon, furthermore, was perhaps the first ruler to elevate propaganda into a weapon of war. It could harden the resolve of the embattled French, while the deliberate publication of false information in the European press could fatally mislead his enemies. Thus in 1805, when an invasion of England was still a possibility, the Dutch press was ordered to publish rumours that France was planning an expedition to the Near East.[2] At the height of Empire, the leading press organs of Europe were under French control, which placed a vast information machine at Napoleon's disposal.

Imperial propaganda was designed to praise the achievements of France and of the reign. Increasingly, however, it was expected to project a favourable image of the imperial dynasty and of the Emperor personally. The trend towards dynastically inspired propaganda was carefully supervised by the Emperor, who expected his remarriage and the birth of an heir to produce national rejoicing. His concern with the projection of a personal image amounted to what we might call, at the risk of anachronism, the development of a cult of personality. The construction of the myth of Napoleon had reference points in classical antiquity and in the Middle Ages; he slipped with ease from the role of a classical hero into the shining armour of a medieval knight. The audience for this propaganda was not taken in. By the last years of the Empire, when Napoleon most needed support at home, France was very slow to respond. Scepticism

1. Cradle of the King of Rome, 1811

2. *The Intervention of the Sabine Women*, 1796–9: J.-L. David

3. *Study for Bonaparte on the Bridge at Arcole*, 1796: A. J. Gros

4. (above) *Bonaparte Visiting the Victims of the Plague at Jaffa*, 1804: A. J. Gros

5. (below) *Napoleon at the Battle of Eylau*, 1807: A. J. Gros

6. *Napoleon Crossing the Great St Bernard*, 1801–2: J.-L. David

7. *Coronation of Napoleon I*, 1806–7: J.-L. David

8. *Coronation of Napoleon* (detail): J.-L. David

9. *The Emperor in his Study in the Tuileries*, 1812: J.-L. David

was so strong that he needed increased coercion to maintain the war effort. Nevertheless, Napoleon was original in his attempt to speak personally and directly to his subjects. Through the regular *Bulletins de la Grande Armée*, ordinary subects and soldiers could feel they were in contact with the destinies of France and of the Emperor.

The newspapers were expected to suppress ugly rumours which might foster opposition or unrest. Reporting rises in the price of grain, for example, could lead to panic and even food riots. Thus the *République démocrate d'Auch* was suppressed for mentioning that grain was dearer.[3] After 1811, no paper was permitted to print political news unless it had already appeared in the official *Moniteur.* Resistance to conscription was not widely reported and even reports of suicides were forbidden, presumably because they were considered potentially demoralising.[4]

Ugly rumours about France's enemies, on the other hand, were the staple diet of Napoleonic propaganda, and the press was expected to spread them on demand. The image of England presented in the imperial press was that of a backward and intolerant society. Britain was a refuge for royalists, it appeared to support black slavery in St Domingo, and it had restored Egypt to a state of ignorance after the departure of the enlightened French. England, French readers learned, had consistently oppressed the Irish Catholics. Britain's push for world dominion was responsible for the breakdown of the Peace of Amiens and later the war in Spain. British agents were suspected in the press of trying to assassinate Napoleon.[5] Here, official propaganda inherited some standard themes of the revolutionary period, when the hand of William Pitt was seen to be manipulating and financing the European counter-revolution.

Britain was not the only target of wartime propaganda. The Russian campaign produced a more desperate attempt to rally opinion in the wake of military setbacks. The press fed its by now blasé readers with a series of atrocity stories about the barbaric Russians. In 1812, according to the *Moniteur,* Count Rostopchin had freed 5000 criminals from prison, so that they could run riot, create mayhem and burn down Moscow. In 1814, when the Russians were on France's doorstep, the Cossacks were accused of feeding their horses with thatch from the roofs of peasants' houses. They were so cruel that they would also cut off peasants' noses if they resisted.[6]

It was an axiom of military propaganda that France was invincible. Losses were always attributed to a French inferiority in numbers, or to some accidental factor. If the French had retreated from Leipzig,

Napoleon claimed, this was merely a strategic withdrawal dictated by a temporary shortage of cannon balls.[7] Serious defeats like the Battle of the Nile would be blamed on subordinates, in order to protect Bonaparte's untarnished reputation as a military commander. Some defeats were never even reported to the French people. The French defeat at Vittoria in Spain in 1813, for example, was not publicised.[8] The *Bulletins de la Grande Armée* were used to propagate the official version of military encounters, and other papers all over France and Europe were expected to follow suit. The truth, of course, could not be obliterated, but it could be massaged, and the timing of reports became an important propaganda skill. The British victory at Trafalgar in 1805 could not be hushed up, but it was reported as late as possible, so that the news was eventually overshadowed by reports of the glorious French victory at Austerlitz.[9] In 1814, it was even thought advisable to report allied advances. French resistance would perhaps be stiffened by full and dramatic coverage of allied rapes, murders and other atrocities.

Historians conclude that by 1814 such horror stories carried no credibility for French newspaper readers.[10] The front of unrelenting triumphalism presented by the press, however, had already been fractured in 1812 by devastating revelations of French losses on the Russian front. This was not what the public was accustomed to reading. Suddenly, out of the blue, *Bulletin* no.29, issued in December 1812, announced serious losses to the French people for the first time. Even so, the *Bulletin* gave Napoleon a heroic role in the engagement, and concluded with an announcement that "The health of His Majesty has never been better" (Document 13.1).

DOCUMENT 13.1   THE DISASTER IN RUSSIA

(Reported in *Bulletin* 29, written 3 December 1812)

Up to November 6 the weather was perfect, and the movement of the army was executed with the greatest success. The cold began on the 7th; from this moment on, we lost each night several hundred horses who died in bivouac. We had already lost many cavalry and artillery horses by the time we reached Smolensk. More than 30,000 horses died in a few days. We had to destroy a good part of our guns, our munitions, and our food supplies.

The army, so fine on the 6th, was very different on the 14th, almost without cavalry, artillery or transportation. We had to march so as not to be forced to a battle which the lack of munitions prevented us from desiring. This difficulty, combined with an excessive cold which suddenly came upon us, made our situation grievous. Some men, of insufficiently strong temperament to rise above all the twists of fate and fortune, appeared shaken, lost their gaiety and good humour, and dreamed only of misfortunes and catastrophes.

The enemy enveloped all the columns with its Cossacks, who, like the Arabs in the desert, robbed the trains and the carriages which wandered to one side. This contemptible cavalry, which is good at making a noise but incapable of routing a company of riflemen, became redoubtable only through favourable cicumstances.

The enemy occupied all the crossings of the Berezina. Having deceived the enemy by various movements on the 25th, the Emperor had two bridges thrown over the river at daybreak on the 26th. The first brigade of the Partouneaux division got lost, went to the right instead of the left and was probably captured. This cruel misunderstanding cost us 2,000 infantrymen, 300 horses, and three pieces of artillery.

The conclusion of this exposé is that the army needs to reestablish its discipline, to reform, to remount its cavalry, artillery and supply wagons. Rest is its first need. The generals, officers and soldiers suffered much from fatigue and hunger. Many lost their baggage as a result of the loss of their horses, some by the ambushes of the Cossacks. The Cossacks have taken many isolated men.

In all these movements the Emperor always marched in the midst of his Guard, the cavalry commanded by the marshal Duke of Istria, and the infantry commanded by the Duke of Danzig. His Majesty was satisfied with the good spirit which his Guard showed ...

This devoted squadron, commanded by General Grouchy and under the orders of the King of Naples, did not lose sight of the Emperor in all the engagements.

The health of His Majesty has never been better.

Napoleonic propaganda presented a perfect picture of Napoleon himself. In the Year 8, the *Journal de Paris* reported that the First Consul worked eighteen hours per day, knew everything about the state of the country, and watched vigilantly over everyone's rights.[11] These themes found echoes later on in David's painting *Napoleon in his Study*, discussed below (Plate 9). When Châteaubriand rashly compared Napoleon to the Emperor Nero in 1807, Napoleon removed him from his position as editor of *Le Mercure*. An essential part of the Napoleonic myth, dating from this period, was that Bonaparte shared the sufferings of the common soldier, and would never subject him to any hardship which he himself was not prepared to endure. He was, according to official versions of his personality, invincible, clever, forceful yet compassionate. He was a man of action and at the same time a patron of the arts and sciences. His allies were perfidious and his subordinates were fallible, but Napoleon was an energetic, all-seeing hero.

Napoleon expected the press to express similar adulation of his family. He complained that it had not reported the immense joy of the troops when he produced a male heir. His second marriage was a particularly sensitive matter, especially given traditional Catholic views on divorce, and any statement with a hint of ridicule or criticism was dangerous. The dynasty was sacrosanct.

Napoleonic propaganda enjoyed a wide diffusion. The military *Bulletins* were posted up on town halls throughout France by the local prefects, as well as appearing in the official *Moniteur*. In the emergency of 1814, Napoleon ordered a nationwide distribution of *Bulletins* printed in small format, with a print run of 40 000 copies.[12]

The parish clergy were at first expected to play a role in disseminating news and propaganda for the régime, to a public which was illiterate and not necessarily French speaking. After 1805, however, the practice of reading military *Bulletins* from the pulpit was stopped. Napoleon had concluded by then that it gave the *curés* too great an influence. In other words, they could not be trusted to present the imperial viewpoint without making an adverse public comment at the same time. In the Loire-Inférieure, priests had refused to read them anyway, insisting that religious services should not be invaded by political matters.[13] In the Lozère, one unfortunate *curé* was driven from the pulpit when he attempted to deliver a sermon on the anniversary of the Battle of Austerlitz. Most of his outraged congregation in this part of the Massif Central consisted of the families of conscripts and draft-dodgers.[14]

"Every dictatorship," the Mexican poet and essayist Octavio Paz wrote with twentieth-century examples in mind, "by one man or by one party gives rise to two basic forms of schizophrenia: the monologue or the mausoleum." Was Napoleonic propaganda effective? Or did it indeed take the form of a monologue, conducted by Napoleon with himself, in the midst of a deaf or indifferent population? Official propaganda, it seems, would not succeed with the clergy, and judging by the violence of the Peninsular War it had little effect south of the Pyrenees either. Perhaps the *Bulletins* had the desired effect on the French army itself, and there are some suggestions that it did succeed in stirring up anti-British feeling in 1803.[15] It is also true that one reason why Louis XVIII was completely unknown to the French public on his restoration in 1814 was that the Empire's information services had effectively blotted the pretender out of French consciousness. Napoleon's *Bulletins* certainly did reach the masses, while the official press targeted bourgeois opinion. Roederer estimated the number of Parisian and departmental newspaper readers at about 300 000 – a tiny but influential audience.[16] Some of these, however, were administrators who were compelled to subscribe to the offical press; while others received copies free.

The audience's response is always difficult to measure, but there are a few indications of the limits of Napoleon's persuasive powers. On the occasion of his second marriage, the celebrations had to be carefully stage managed. The itinerary of the wedding party, for example, was routed to avoid Paris, in order to ensure the safety of the imperial couple and its entourage.[17] This does not suggest a high degree of confidence in popular support. In 1811, the birth of the King of Rome failed to distract a population suffering from a poor harvest and an economic slump. Finally, in 1812, the military *Bulletins* were issued at less and less frequent intervals – a sign perhaps that the public questioned their credibility and that the government knew it.

Napoleon wanted to bring all forms of literature under government tutelage. He once complained: "Popular literature is for me, but high literature is against me" (J'ai pour moi la petite littérature et contre moi la grande). Certainly, celebrated writers like Châteaubriand and Madame de Staël were thrown into opposition, but it was popular literature, after all, which had the widest circulation.

Bonapartism infiltrated some forms of popular culture more easily than others. Reading tastes changed slowly, but the popular song was a genre which proved receptive to the Bonapartist message. Under the Empire, Béranger was building a reputation as the leading composer and balladeer of the early nineteenth century. Béranger reached the height of his popularity in the July Revolution of 1830, but in the collection of songs he published in 1815, about one-seventh of his material was already overtly political.[18]

Béranger became the voice of the poor, idealising their simple life in songs like *Les Gueux* (The Beggars). Béranger himself was the son of a banker. He had got into debt and tried to revive his fortunes by buying a book-lending business (*cabinet de lecture*). His position does not seem to have improved much until 1809 when he achieved some security as a clerk in the Napoleonic University. His poems praised Bonaparte and the Concordat, which no doubt assisted his career, but from 1812 onwards he concentrated on the songs which made him famous. He was a member of the Caveau (The Cellar), one of the drinking clubs which produced popular songs of the bacchic or bohemian variety. In 1814, he produced a masterpiece, *Le Roi d'Yvetot* (Document 13.2), about a petty ruler who craved a simple life, without grandeur, ceremony, extravagance or glory. This was a moderate criticism of the declining Emperor. Later in 1814, he attacked the Bourbons and the Allies, in compositions like the very anti-English *Les Boxeurs ou l'Anglomane*. By 1815, his career as a nationalist and a Bonapartist was launched. His songs were an important vehicle for the transmission and consolidation of the Napoleonic legend.

Before the Revolution, a revival of interest in classical antiquity had exerted its influence on the fine arts everywhere in Europe. In

---

DOCUMENT 13.2:   LE ROI D'YVETOT

by Béranger, 1813

Il était un roi d'Yvetot
Peu connu dans l'histoire,
Se levant tard, se couchant tôt,
Dormant fort bien sans gloire,
Et couronné par Jeanneton
D'un simple bonnet de coton,
    Dit-on.
Oh! oh! oh! oh! ah! ah! ah! ah!
Quel bon petit roi c'était là!

Il faisait ses quatre repas
Dans son palais de chaume,

Et sur un âne, pas à pas,
Parcourait son royaume,
Joyeux, simple et croyant le bien,
Pour toute garde il n'avait rien
      Qu'un chien.
(*Chorus*)

Il n'avait de goût onéreux
Qu'une soif un peu vive;
Mais en rendant son peuple heureux,
Il faut bien qu'un roi vive.
Lui-même, á table et sans suppôt,
Sur chaque muid levait un pot
      D'impôt.
(*Chorus*)

Aux filles de bonnes maisons
Comme il avait su plaire,
Ses sujets avaient cent raisons
De le nommer leur père:
D'ailleurs il ne levait de ban
Que pour tirer quatre fois l'an
      Au blanc.
(*Chorus*)

Il n'agrandit point ses Etats,
Fut un voisin commode,
Et, modèle de potentats,
Prit le plaisir pour code.
Ce n'est que lorsqu'il expira
Que le peuple qui l'enterra
      Pleura.
(*Chorus*)

On conserve encore le portrait
De ce digne et bon prince;
C'est l'enseigne d'un cabaret
Fameux dans la province.
Les jours de fête, bien souvent,
La foule s'écrie en buvant
      Devant: (*Chorus*).

There once was a King of Yvetot,
Little known in history,
Who was early to bed and late to rise,
And slept in peace if not in glory,
Crowned by old Janet in a cotton night-cap,
So they say.
Oh! Ah! What a fine little king he was!

He took all four meals
In his thatched-roof palace,
And step by step, on a donkey's back,
He travelled through his kingdom,
Merry, simple, thinking well of all,
He had no retinue at all,
Except a dog.

He had no expensive taste
Except a rather eager thirst;
But kings who make their people happy
Have to live after all.
Alone at table, with no cronies,
He levied a full jug in tax
On each barrel.

He knew how to please
The daughters of fine families,
So his subjects had a hundred reasons
For calling him their father:
Besides he never called up his troops
Except four times a year
For shooting practice.

He never enlarged his dominions,
He was a genial neighbour,

He made pleasure his law-code
As an example to rulers.
Not until he breathed his last,
Did the people who buried him
Have cause to shed a tear.

The portrait of this good and worthy prince
Still survives
On a tavern-sign
Famous in the provinces.
Often on holidays,
The crowd drinks to it, singing: *Chorus.*

French schools, Roman history and the literature of the ancient world provided moral examples of wisdom, courage and self-sacrifice to be emulated. Students in Paris colleges studied Virgil's *Aenid*, Ovid's *Metamorphoses*, Cicero's *Orations*, as well as Livy, Tacitus and Plutarch. Classical references entered the vocabulary of every cultured eighteenth-century European. Speeches to the National Convention were full of allusions to classical history, and orators spoke next to a bust of Brutus. Place-names had been changed: several towns were renamed Brutus, and St Maximin, for example, became Marathon. Revolutionary street names and personal names also commemorated antique precedents. Revolutionaries suspected of favouring property redistribution were denounced, like the Gracchi, for supporting the "agrarian law". Some of those going to the guillotine thought of themselves as Socrates, or emulated other examples of the classical, patriotic suicide. Republicanism had been associated with an antique ideal of civic virtue, and a system of political ethics which stressed individual sacrifice for a patriotic ideal.

In the Consulate and Empire, however, the neo-classical style was evolving. Neo-classicism had lost any revolutionary or critical connotations it might have had under the Bourbon monarchy. It no longer provided a challenging visual vocabulary, and it had lost the didactic purpose and moral ardour identified with paintings by David, such as the *Oath of the Horatii*. The régime trivialised the noble austerity of neo-classicism, retaining its decorative trappings but abandoning its earlier substance. Bronze statuettes, for example, of David's *Oath of the Horatii* appeared on an Empire clock.

Official neo-classicism now referred to imperial as much as to republican Rome, a change which reflected the political transformation of Napoleonic France itself. Napoleon adopted the eagle, for example, as one of his emblems, together with lions and bees, and Egyptian motifs like the sphinx, which were in vogue after the French expedition of 1798. Meanwhile, marble busts of the Emperor himself were produced in Carrara, where Elisa Bonaparte organised the mass production of about 500 per year.[19]

The elaborate cradle designed in 1811 for the King of Rome (Napoleon's heir) was encrusted with contemporary Napoleonic symbolism (Plate 1). The legs consist of horns of plenty, supported by genii representing justice and strength. At the foot of the cradle, the infant would gaze on a small imperial eagle – an emblematic reflection of himself. Over the head of the cradle, a canopy is suspended by a goddess of fame. She has the world at her feet and holds up a laurel wreath. Fame and glory thus surround the child. The work, and the birth it commemorated, represented the union of the Bonapartist and Habsburg dynasties with the imperial city of Rome.

Napoleonic architecture was monumental in its scale, as typified by the hideous and expensive Arc de Triomphe. The arch celebrated the military victories of Napoleon, but it commemorated his generals and marshals, not the ordinary soldiers who died for the glory of France, and for whom Béranger had much more sympathy. We are today accustomed to ambitious presidents who wish to leave their mark on history in the form of some spectacular edifice, whether it is a cultural centre, a very large library or a complete *quartier* (as in Les Halles in central Paris). The Napoleonic ego, however, was satisfied with nothing less than an entire city. La Roche-sur-Yon, a town in the Vendée devastated in the civil war, was to be reborn as Napoléonville. A classically proportioned grid of streets would surround three main areas: the Place d'Armes for military parades, the prefecture and the market. This was an eloquent comment of the régime's priorities: the army, the administration and commerce, all devoted to the personal glory of the Emperor.

Napoleon imagined himself as a great patron of the visual arts. Painters and sculptors did receive official patronage and support under the Empire, but official taste in art tended to be narrow and unadventurous. The government sometimes bought paintings at the official Salon, the major exhibition and market-place for both aspiring and established artists. From 1798, the Salon jury was appointed by a government minister. Imperial patronage was supervised by Denon as Director-General of Museums. Rewards and decorations were granted to favoured artists. In addition, outstanding artists were exempted from military service.

Artists received official commissions, and some were given jobs in museum administration. A select few, like David, Vien (David's master) and the sculptor Houdon became members of the imperial nobility. In total, twenty-six artists received the legion of honour, including David, promoted to the rank of *officier*.[20] Their number included some of David's illustrious pupils, like Gros and Gérard, as well as the uncontroversial landscape artist Valenciennes. The régime therefore recognised the contribution of David's school, but otherwise rewarded traditional academic art. The elevation of Vien to the Senate was an indication of the régime's conservative taste and continuity with the artistic Old Régime. The distribution of decorations to artists under the Empire did not err on the side of generosity; under the Bourbon Restoration, honours distributed for artistic endeavour were to increase fourfold.

Eighteenth-century neo-classical painting, indelibly associated with the work of Jacques-Louis David, had advocated a new ideal of self-sacrifice and civic virtue. This was a rejection of sensuality in art, and of the frivolous decoration of the Rococo style. David's serious purpose and severe style contained an inherent moral critique of the decadent Bourbon court. Neo-classical painting promoted an ethic of duty to the state and public interest, which took priority over personal or family loyalties. Napoleon channelled this didactic purpose into the advancement of his personal legend.

His personal taste in art was simple and was determined by political needs. He favoured large-scale history paintings, the painters' equivalent of the monumental style of imperial architecture. "Nothing is beautiful," he told the Conseil d'État, "unless it is large. Vastness and immensity can make you forget a great many defeats."[21] Napoleon expected art to celebrate victory, generate optimism, and reflect his brilliant personal reputation. The response of the art world to these demands is best examined through the history of the great revolutionary propaganda artist David, and of his followers.

David had always been an accomplished portrait painter, as well as the greatest revolutionary artist of the period. In his treatment of *François de Nantes*, David produced a more representative image of imperial society than any of his large-scale propaganda commissions.

François de Nantes was a prefect, a councillor of state, and is painted as a count of the Empire, in the regalia of the legion of honour. The low angle of the painter's vision ensures that François looks down on the viewer, in the smug, patronising attitude of the imperial functionary.

At the end of the Directory, David had been working on his vast canvas, *The Intervention of the Sabine Women*, which can be seen as a plea for reconciliation after the factional strife of the revolutionary decade (Plate 2). The *Sabines* was put on exhibition in 1799; the 50 000 visitors who paid to see it over the next five years testified to David's personal reputation. The proceeds enabled him to buy a farm in the Seine-et-Marne.[22] The *Sabines* reproduced the contrast between stern male warriors and softer female observers, already apparent in his earlier *Brutus*. This time, however, the women are not passive spectators, privately weeping and mourning the dead. Instead, they actively invade male territory, to separate the gladiators and impose a truce. This message was entirely appropriate to the atmosphere of the Consulate which wanted to restore order and neutralise revolutionary divisions.

David sought to revive the simplicity of Greek art and he stated, "I want to create pure Greekness."[23] This aim created a tension, however, between his neo-classical austerity and the Empire's tendency to favour the more elaborate and florid style of imperial Rome. The régime was to prefer the Corinthian to the Doric, and Rome to Athens.

It was not very long before students of David began to establish reputations in their own right. Soon, artists like Gros and Girodet eclipsed the master himself, departing from the neo-classical path which David had pioneered. Both Gérard and Girodet, for example, completed paintings of Ossian (*Dream of Ossian* and *Ossian and his Warriors* respectively). Ossian was a rediscovered Celtic bard, whose poetry enjoyed a tremendous vogue in the Consulate, and was particularly enjoyed by Bonaparte himself. "Ossian" was in fact one of the most successful literary hoaxes of all time: the famous bard never existed and his work was fabricated by the Scottish poet Macpherson. Like his poetry, the works of David's pupils reflected late eighteenth-century romantic tendencies.

Gérard, who became portraitist to the imperial court, had assisted David during the Revolution, but broke with his master's heroic style. Girodet painted his *Apotheosis of the Fallen Heroes*, commissioned in 1801 for Bonaparte's residence at Malmaison, in which Napoleonic generals were welcomed to the Elysian fields by young maidens with lyres, and the ever fashionable Celtic bards complete with harps. This was followed by a romantic painting based on Châteaubriand's novel *Atala*, and the melodramatic *Scenes from the Deluge*, which won a prize in 1810 as one of the best pictures of the decade. It depicted a family trying to escape from a flood by clinging to a tree which was breaking.[24] A great age of romantic painting was dawning and an important artistic watershed can be discerned in this period, in the new departures taken by David's own disciples.

One of the most illustrious of these was Gros, perhaps the most important of the imperial propaganda painters and, one suspects, the one who best satisfied the Emperor's own tastes. Gros had met Bonaparte in Milan in 1796, and was given the mission of assessing Italian art treasures suitable for confiscation. This was the beginning of his association with Bonaparte as epic hero. In *Bonaparte at Arcole*, his young hero, grasping a standard, leads his troops onward (Plate 3). As in David's portrayal of the crossing of the St Bernard pass, Bonaparte's windswept hair lent him speed, energy and daring.

In 1804, Gros's *Bonaparte Visiting the Victims of the Plague at Jaffa* successfully developed another element in the construction of the mythical Napoleon (Plate 4). Napoleon comforts the plague-infected soldiers in an episode from the Egyptian campaigns. The scene is an exotic, Gothic cloister, and the subject-matter horrifying. Napoleon's gesture towards a plague victim parallels that of the medieval kings, whose charismatic touch was thought to cure their subjects of scrofula. Medieval chivalry and the spirit of the Crusades were thus appropriated by the propaganda myth. In *Napoleon at the Battle of Eylau*, Gros continued the epic, showing a sombre Emperor, still concerned to comfort his soldiers and care for the wounded (Plate 5). Eylau was a massacre: but Gros painted a victory.

David himself had a stormier relationship with Bonaparte. Like Gros, he was impressed by his first encounter with Bonaparte, at the time of the Italian campaigns, when the young general was cultivating the support of France's artistic and intellectual élite. In 1797, Bonaparte visited David's studio, when David announced to his students, "Voilà mon héros!"[25] "What a beautiful head he has," David enthused. "It is pure, it is grand, it is as beautiful as the antique. At last, here is a man to whom one would have raised altars in antiquity." Bonaparte invited David to join the Egypt expedition, but David was working on the *Sabines* and was too cautious to commit himself. He had perhaps learned a lesson from the Year 2, when he had sworn allegiance to Robespierre only days before Maximilien was condemned to the scaffold. This time he would wait until his hero's future was more secure.

By 1802, the relationship between the First Consul and David was closer. Bonaparte, however, refused to pose for the equestrian portrait of *Bonaparte Crossing the Great St Bernard* (Plate 6). He had only once condescended to sit for David, who thus produced the unfinished portrait of 1798. Achieving an accurate portrait was, after all, not the object of the exercise as far as Bonaparte was concerned. As he himself put it,

> It is not the exactness of traits, a wart on the nose, that makes a likeness. It is the character of the countenance, what animates a person that it is necessary to portray ... Certainly Alexander never posed for Apelles. No one knows if portraits of great men are likenesses. It is enough that their genius lives.[26]

It was not a question, therefore, of observing the real Bonaparte: what was at stake here was the manufacture of a public identity.

Bonaparte, astride a white horse, points the viewer onwards to glory over the Alps, in emulation of Hannibal and Charlemagne. The soldiers of his army are tiny, insignificant background details, compared to the calm, stylised rider who dominates the canvas. David's model was probably Falconet's equestrian portrait of Peter the Great of Russia. He borrowed Bonaparte's hat and coat and made his son pose in them. It was of absolutely no consequence that Bonaparte actually crossed the Alps on a mule, not on the fiery steed which helps to produce the tension and vigour of the composition. In 1803, David was made knight of the legion of honour.

The coronation of Napoleon was an even greater challenge to David. Begun in 1805, the *Sacre* was not completed until 1808 (Plate 7). With Napoleon's approval, David concentrated on the moment in the ceremony when Napoleon crowned Joséphine, with the Pope a mere spectator (Plate 8). At this stage, Bonaparte still respected his first wife enough to pay her this compliment. The coronation itself was meticulously stage managed. The columns of Notre Dame catheral were concealed by drapes, and Napoleonic emblems appeared everywhere; the painting shows an expanse of green velvet specked with bees. There was a fireworks display, a free distribution of food to the people of Paris, contributing to the "farces chinoises", which is how Madame de Staël dismissed it.

Protocol demanded that David include the imperial dignitaries. Talleyrand, Cambacérès and Eugène de Beauharnais are there front right; Berthier and the marshals stand with their plumes in the centre; the Bonaparte siblings stand behind Joséphine. In the galleries facing the painter sit their mother, Madame Mère, although she never attended the coronation, and she thoroughly detested the Beauharnais.[27] Behind her, as a final indulgence, David placed himself and his own family. This massive tableau had little ideological content. Its purpose was merely to display the pageantry of Empire. Napoleon was pleased. He told David, "You have understood my thoughts, you have made me a French knight."

Although, in 1804, David accepted the title of First Painter of the Empire, his financial demands now began to irritate the authorities. David had asked for 100 000 francs for the *Sacre*: he was only paid 65 000 francs, and he had to wait two years after the completion of the painting for them. Changes at the Louvre, which was renamed the Musée Napoléon, forced David to move his studio elsewhere in 1805. David was never invited to paint the great military victories of the Empire.

Nevertheless, two more propaganda paintings were to appear. The first was the very stilted *Distribution of the Eagles*, representing a ceremony at the Champ de Mars when the eagle standards were presented to regiments of the army and the National Guard. The painting was not finished until 1810, and so Joséphine, by then divorced, had to be painted out of the final version. The theatrical ritual of oath-taking had always appealled to David, but compared to his treatment of the Tennis Court oath or the oath of the Horatii, this time the adulation of the Emperor seemed empty and mechanical.

A different propaganda angle is taken by David's painting of a more corpulent *Napoleon in his Study* (1812). In this painting, the Emperor is working on his law codes, with a volume of Plutarch on the floor, as the candle burns low into the early hours of the morning. This assertion of Napoleon's industry and devotion to public administration is reminiscent of the story that Mussolini used to keep a light burning at all times in his office in the Quirinal, to show that the Duce worked indefatigably in the public cause while his subjects slept. The Emperor is wearing his legion of honour and Iron Cross (Plate 9).

David, perhaps, had himself become a victim of the personality cult he had helped to develop. In *Léonidas at Thermopylae*, he made a last attempt to rediscover his neo-classical roots. He searched once again for the archaic simplicity and celebration of patriotism which had once inspired him. The subject of the Spartans heroically holding the pass against the oncoming Persian hordes of Xerxes was a topical one in 1814, when the Allied armies threatened to overrun France. Napoleon hated it because he opposed any painting of a defeated army. The pass, however, could not be held for ever against the enemies of the Empire. In 1814, David cut and rolled the huge canvasses of the *Sacre* and the *Distribution of the Eagles* and smuggled them out of Paris. His relationship with Napoleon had never been easy. He struggled for the financial rewards to which he thought he was entitled, as he saw his younger students take over his place as France's leading artist. And yet he never compromised with the Bourbons, neither in the Hundred Days, nor in his later years in Brussels, where he took up residence after Louis XVIII sent him into exile in 1816.

14   The Unsheathed Sword, 1: War and International Relations, 1800–10

"The English want war," Napoleon said in 1803, "but if they are the first to draw the sword I will be the last to sheath it."[1] This sabre-rattling threat contained an accurate prediction of the bloodshed which was about to be inflicted on Europe for a further ten years. The Peace of Amiens, signed in 1802, lasted only fourteen months. It was no more than a truce separating two decades of international conflict, in which the European powers challenged first revolutionary and then Napoleonic France. Not until 1815, when Napoleon was definitively beaten at Waterloo in Belgium, was the cycle of continuous warfare closed.

This and the following chapter survey the history of international relations in this period, from the height of imperial success in 1805–7, to the slow agony suffered by the French in Spain, and the catastrophe in Russia in 1812. Our attention must now turn outward, to consider the objectives not just of France but of the other main belligerents who opposed her. The reasons for French military domination of Europe cannot be found in domestic politics alone. They also lie in the failure and reluctance of the major powers to unite against Napoleon.

The revolutionary wars had at first been envisaged as an international struggle on behalf of freedom and equality. In 1793, the Jacobins had offered to liberate the oppressed peoples of Europe from the yoke of Old Régime tyrannies. Napoleon, too, could be seen by some groups as a liberator: by the enlightened élite of Spain, for instance, or by the Poles whose state he resurrected. French rule and occupation had many complex consequences for those who were occupied (see Chapters 16 and 17). Under the Directory, attachment to France had sometimes entitled conquered territories to the dubious privilege of being exploited by greedy generals and army contractors. Napoleon's priority was imperial conquest and not ideological subversion. France's own military imperatives overrode the ambitions of revolutionaries in Holland, Switzerland or Italy. When the French armies came to the assistance of their revolutionary Dutch brethren by marching into Holland, the republican government in Paris had not been overcome by a fit of altruism. It had its eyes on two valuable prizes: the powerful Dutch fleet and the rich bank vaults of Amsterdam. As Schama put it, if the French offered Europe a fraternal embrace, it was fraternity on the terms laid down by the biggest brother.[2]

The underlying reasons for the success of French expansion have been suggested in Chapter 5. They derived from France's demographic strength and her rich material resources. Her productive capacities and huge reservoir of manpower made possible twenty years of almost continuous war and expansion. Except for the earliest and the final stages, the fighting took place on foreign soil and the French, like all conquerors, used the resources of annexed territories. When Masséna entered Zurich and St Gall in 1799, he requisitioned 800 000 bread rations, 20 000 bottles of wine, 10 000 bottles of brandy, 100 oxen and demanded 800 000 *livres* in payment as well. The unfortunate inhabitants had only just parted with 5 million florins for the previous occupier, the Austrian army.[3] In this way, the French population was spared the heaviest burdens of warfare for as long as possible.

This is not to say that personal factors, in particular the individual genius of Bonaparte, did not play a role in French victories. Bonaparte was a talented and inspiring general, but the French were not invincible. At Aboukir Bay (1798) and Trafalgar (1805), the war at sea was spectacularly lost to the British. At Bailen (1808) and Vittoria (1813) the French were defeated, admittedly in the absence of Napoleon himself. In Italy, in 1796–7, brilliant gambles and lightning strikes had guaranteed the famous victories which launched the Bonapartist legend. These striking successes were repeated in the campaigns of 1805–6. Military confrontations grew in scale, however, becoming more static and, at the same time, more murderous. At the massacres of Eylau (1807) and Borodino (1812), when Napoleon *was* in command, it is impossible to decide who was the victor. Twice, in Egypt and Russia, Napoleon was forced ignominiously to abandon the remnants of a demoralised army.

Napoleon was not merely an inspired military leader. He also knew how to exploit his victories, to extract the maximum advantage from those he defeated. French hegemony therefore relied on diplomatic successes as well as military achievements. Both were necessary to prevent the formation of a genuine European coalition against

France. Once the great powers all decided to combine their efforts, as they did only after 1813, then it was clear that not even the might of Napoleonic France could resist their united forces. The great achievement of French diplomacy, therefore, was to keep the coalition powers divided. If Napoleon could separate his opponents, he could pick them them off individually with ease. By means of bribery, offers of territory and temporary alliances, the French ensured that Prussia remained neutral until 1805, and that Russia was an ally from 1807 to 1812. Only Austria on the continent and Britain at sea were for different reasons persistent opponents of France. Napoleon conquered because he kept his enemies divided.

The Great Powers

The three great powers of central and eastern Europe – Prussia, Austria and Russia – had divergent long-term interests in central Europe and the Balkans. While Prussia and Austria competed for influence in Germany, Russia and Austria had conflicting designs on the Turkish Empire. At the same time, each power was determined not to allow any of its rivals to secure any unilateral advantage in the region. A gain of territory by Russia, for example, had to be compensated by territorial gains by Prussia and Austria, so that the overall balance of power was maintained. This was an axiom of eighteenth-century diplomacy, which doomed small and vulnerable states to become simply morsels thrown onto the scales to "balance" the appetites of more powerful and greedy predators. The mutual suspicions of the great powers had prevented any cooperative effort against France in the 1790s. Their expansionist aims had been satisfied at the expense of Poland, which was wiped off the map of Europe in the Polish Partitions of 1772, 1793 and 1795. As long as the powers were absorbed in the digestion of the annexed territory of their sacrificial Polish victim, they did not accord high priority to the threat posed by revolutionary France. None of the eastern powers wished to commit themselves in western Europe, since this would encourage a rival to snatch an advantage behind their back. These rivalries had complicated international relations throughout the eighteenth century; they were inevitably carried over into the Napoleonic era.

All the powers had quite different war aims. They had entered the war in 1792–3 ostensibly to restore Louis XVI and his successors to the French throne or, in the British case, to protect the Low Countries from French aggression. Behind these limited objectives, however, lay more fundamental interests. A glance at each of the major combatants will demonstrate the different policies and war aims which dictated their strategies. At times, their strategic interests dictated joining a European coalition against France; at other times, these permanent interests seemed better served by peace, neutrality or alliance with France.

Great Britain was primarily a maritime and overseas power. Her interests were global, and they centred on defending the profits of international commerce from India to the West Indies. Britain was therefore concerned with maintaining the naval supremacy which enabled it to dominate the sea routes to the Cape, the eastern Mediterranean and across the Atlantic. For Britain, the war against Napoleonic France was a war for oceanic hegemony. It provided an opportunity to seize French (as well as Dutch) colonies in the West Indies, and to reinforce the archipelago of strategic bases which linked London and the Near East, via Malta and Alexandria, or London and Bengal, via Ceylon and the Cape of Good Hope. The Battle of Trafalgar, in 1805, was for Britain a triumphant conclusion to the naval struggle.

Britain was correspondingly reluctant to engage an army on the continent of Europe. Instead, Britain offered subsidies to assist the mobilisation of its European allies, notably Austria and southern German states like Baden and Wurtemberg. For many years, therefore, Britain was able to concentrate on its vital interests at sea, by fighting the land war by proxy. France, however, could not ultimately be defeated except on land, and if Britain was serious about throwing France out of the Low Countries, it would have at some point to disembark an army in Europe. In addition, Britain always had one very important continental interest: the German state of Hanover, dynastically linked to the British crown, and coveted by Prussia. The fate of Hanover was a potential source of tension between Britain and the continental powers.

In 1809, London did at last decide to intervene in Europe. Britain's attempt, however, to land an army of 40 000 in Zeeland (the Walcheren expedition) was a fiasco. A total of 4000 died of disease in the Scheldt estuary and nothing was achieved.[4] The disaster provoked a duel between Canning and Castlereagh and helped to bring down the government. Britain entered the continental struggle much more effectively through the Portuguese door, Portugal being an old ally and an informal British colony, since it gave sustenance to

His Majesty's navy and welcomed substantial investments by some of his wealthier subjects. The Peninsular War opened up a "second front" which fatally stretched French resources from Moscow to Madrid. In spite of the importance of the Peninsular War in France's eventual defeat, however, the struggle from the British perspective was a contest for commercial supremacy. It expressed an economic rivalry which involved blockading the enemy coastline, and intimidating neutral shipping into steering clear of enemy ports. (The importance of the Continental Blockade will be discussed in Chapter 15.)

Russia's interests, like those of Britain, spanned more than one continent. The concerns of such a vast land mass can never be defined in European terms alone. Russia looked eastwards into Asia, and southwards as well, where the crumbling Ottoman Empire tempted many predators. Catherine the Great had nurtured her "Greek project", which aimed at establishing a Russian protectorate over Greece, giving Russia direct access to the Mediterranean. Other European powers would have viewed such a development with alarm, and Russia's ambitions in the eastern Mediterranean always risked antagonising powers like Britain, which had a strong commercial interest in Turkey through the Levant trade. In fact, the Ottoman Empire defied all predictions of its imminent collapse, enduring until the First World War, but the question of what to do when it fell and how to distribute the proceeds had already become "the Eastern Question", vexing European diplomats by the end of the eighteenth century.

Russia did not intend to be left out of the reckoning when the spoils were divided. Free passage through the Dardanelles was a vital Russian interest; it was the Black Sea fleet's outlet to the Mediterranean and was an important commercial route, especially for grain exports from the Ukraine. Russia could not afford to see the Straits fall into hostile hands. Russia had an official pretext for intervention in Turkish affairs, since she was the self-appointed custodian of the Christian communities and their holy places in the Near East. Any violation of Christian interests could be used to justify Russian interference.

In practice, it was the Egyptian campaign of 1798–9 which had brought Russia into the Second Coalition against France. Russia's interests had lain on Europe's periphery, but now Russian armies penetrated its very heart. The Sultan gave Tsar Paul I free passage for the Russian navy through the Straits. Paul immediately used this freedom to occupy the Ionian Islands, land troops in Naples and claim a protectorate over Malta, then governed by the Knights Hospitallers. Malta, too, was a potential point of Russo-British friction.

In 1801, Tsar Paul joined Sweden and Denmark in the Armed
Neutrality, an organised attempt to exclude Britain from the Baltic.
The Danes occupied Hamburg and Lübeck, which excluded Britain
from her German markets, and Prussia took the opportunity to
march into Hanover, which controlled the trade routes along the
Weser and the Elbe. This was a prototype of the Continental System,
later developed by Napoleon as an economic weapon against Britain,
and which had attractions for Russia.[5] Britain was extricated from
this serious situation in northern Europe partly by Nelson, who
bombarded Copenhagen into submission, and more fortuitously by
the assassin who conveniently removed Paul I from the scene. Under
his successor Alexander I, Russian policy was no longer systematically
hostile to Britain; but Russia was still tempted by the prospects of
expansion at the expense of the Ottoman Empire, and this remained
a constant feature of Russian diplomacy.

Austria was Napoleon's most consistent opponent, because she was
most threatened by French conquests in Germany and Italy. The
struggle against Prussia for domination of Germany had been the
main preoccupation of the Austrian Habsburgs since 1740, when
Frederick the Great had begun to tip the balance in favour of Prussia.
Even this objective, however, became less important than the fight to
avert the bleak future which French expansion offered the Habsburg
Empire. Austria's aim was to restrict France to her so-called "natural
frontiers", but French influence did not stop at the Rhine and France
annexed Austria's traditional dependencies in northern Italy. In
spite of repeated defeats at Marengo (1800), Ulm (1805), Austerlitz
(1805) and Wagram (1809), Austria, with the help of British
subsidies, tirelessly continued to put armies into the field.

In Italy, Napoleon had offered the Habsburgs Venice, but he had
based his satellite Cisalpine Republic in Milan. The very existence of
such a revolutionary Republic in Austria's ex-fief of Lombardy was
intolerable to Vienna. At the Treaty of Lunéville (1801), France's
strong position in Italy was confirmed, and the Italian Republic, soon
to become the Kingdom of Italy, swallowed up Parma, Modena and
the Papal Legations, as well as the Milanais (Map 14.1). Later the
Ligurian Republic was divided into departments of the French
Empire, while the states of Italy provided thrones for various members of the Bonaparte clan. The Treaty of Pressburg in 1805 excluded
Austria from Italy. (Map 14.2)

In Germany, too, French expansion completely destroyed the basis
of Austrian influence. The map of Germany was reorganised by
Napoleon, and the Habsburg Emperor lost his leading role in south-

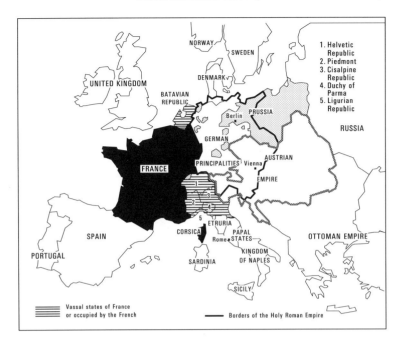

Map 14.1   Europe at the Peace of Lunéville, 1801

Source: François Furet, *La Révolution, 1770–1880* (Paris, Hachette, 1988).

ern Germany. In 1806, the new Confederation of the Rhine also made his influential position as Holy Roman Emperor redundant. Virtually expelled, then, from both Italy and Germany, Austria faced possible eclipse as a European power. Vienna could never accept a peace which reduced her to the status of a mere Balkan state. Lunéville and Pressburg were humiliating peace terms to which Austria could never resign herself in the long run. It is therefore not surprising that Austria was at the core of every anti-French coalition, and that the new-found unity of 1813–14 was negotiated by the masterful Austrian diplomat, Metternich. For Austria, the war was one of survival as a great power.

Prussia was as much focused on the struggle for domination of Germany as she was on the need to restrain French aggression. One explanation for French successes was that Prussia remained neutral in the conflict until 1805. This was essentially because French expansion offered Prussia tangible benefits which satisfied her wish to dominate Germany. Napoleon made sure that Prussia received a share from the secularisation of German ecclesiastical territories, he

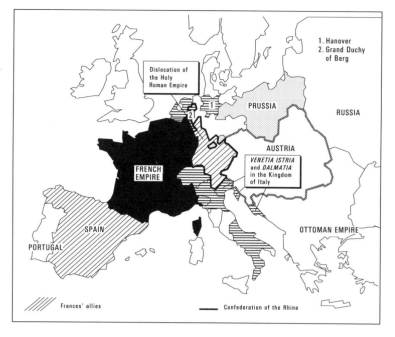

Map 14.2   Europe in 1806, after the Treaty of Pressburg

Source: François Furet, *La Révolution, 1770–1880* (Paris, Hachette, 1988).

held out the bait of Hanover to the Hohenzollerns, and promoted Prussian leadership in Germany at Austria's expense. Napoleon was very successful at offering other people's territory to his allies. There came a point, however, when the French cupboard was empty and the price of Prussian neutrality could no longer be paid. Prussia was eager for secure tenure of Hanover, and when it seemed that more German territory could be gained by opposing France than France was prepared to offer as a friend, then Prussia calculated that the moment had come to enter the coalition.

It can be seen, therefore, that the interests of the various coalition partners were divergent, if not incompatible. Hanover, Malta, domination in Germany, strategic and commercial control of the Baltic and the Mediterranean were all at stake; but they were arenas of conflict, not of consensus between the allied powers, in the wars against Napoleonic France. This enabled the French to exploit divisions and rivalries amongst her enemies. In addition, within every belligerent state opinion was divided. There were pro-war and pro-peace parties, hawks and doves. In Britain in 1802, there were Tories who were keen to pursue the struggle, and Whigs for whom a respite was necessary for financial recovery. In Russia, there were pro-French nobles and pro-English nobles who needed to sell their Baltic timber and grain to Britain. One group or the other might carry the day, depending on the circumstances and the mood of the volatile and unpredictable Tsar Alexander.

To pursue conquest and preserve French gains Napoleon needed to keep one of the German powers out of the conflict, and he needed the acquiescence if not the support of Russia. Until the death of Paul, he had both, in the shape of Prussian neutrality and Russian support for the Armed Neutrality. French success was to rely on Napoleon's continued ability to ensure the complicity of at least one of the leading powers in his expansionist project.

War and Diplomacy, 1802–10

The Treaty of Lunéville (1801) strengthened France's satellite republics – the Batavian Republic (Holland), the Helvetic Republic (Switzerland) and the Cisalpine (northern Italy). Austria accepted the French absorption of all territory on the left bank of the Rhine, and was powerless to prevent the division of Piedmont into departments of the French Empire. The enlarged Cisalpine Republic gave France effective control over northern and central Italy (see Map 14.1).

Prussia remained neutral and was ready to claim the reward for its compliance from the victorious French. In 1803, the French proceeded to redraw the map of Germany, simplifying and rationalising it, at the same time enhancing the authority of friends and weakening the influence of enemies. Talleyrand played an important role in the negotiations with German princes; which meant that their bribes helped to swell his considerable personal fortune. Germany had been a patchwork of more than 350 different states, principalities, bishoprics, self-governing cities and kingdoms. About half of them now disappeared, as Napoleon imposed a thoroughgoing secularisation. The ecclesiastical principalities were abolished. Amongst the Electors of the Holy Roman Empire, only one clerical Elector survived French reorganisation; he was the Archbishop of Mainz who was transferred to Ratisbon. Out of fifty-one free German cities in existence before the Napoleonic wars, only six remained. All the commercial tolls along the Rhine were abolished. Prussia received territory in Erfurt and Munster. The kingdoms of southern Germany also became beneficiaries, in an attempt to draw them away from traditional Austrian influence and into the French orbit. Baden received Mannheim and Heidelberg, and Bavaria was strengthened to counterbalance Prussian influence in Germany.

France had therefore achieved her aim of establishing French power on the Rhine at the expense of both Austria and Prussia. The acquiescence of Prussia and the German princes was bought by indemnifying them with confiscated ecclesiastical domains. Talleyrand grew rich, and French influence increased in southern Germany. Austria was compelled to accept this severe blow to her traditional leading position in Germany. There was now even a Protestant majority in the electoral college of the Holy Roman Empire. But with Prussia neutral and Russia cooperative towards France, Vienna had to submit.

In 1802, Britain had found herself isolated and forced to accept peace with France. Ireland had been invaded in 1798, Egypt had been attacked, while Austria had made a separate peace with Bonaparte. Without a continental ally, Britain faced war alone against France, Spain and Holland. In the long run, the British economy was sound enough to withstand the strains of prolonged warfare. The land tax had been increased and the first income tax had been imposed in response to the emergency. The government's credit remained solid. The Armed Neutrality, however, posed a new threat, cutting Britain off from markets and sources of materials in Scandinavia and Germany. Grain imports were in danger, at a time of poor harvests and food shortages. Britain was saved, as we have seen, by the bombardment of Copenhagen and the death of Tsar Paul. The Peace of Amiens was signed in 1802, but France could not expect peace to endure without an outright victory over the British.

Britain now faced the possibility of a French invasion across the Channel from the troops which Bonaparte assembled as the Army of Boulogne. France maintained the threat for two years but by 1805 it was clear that invasion plans had been shelved. The logistical problems were enormous. Special flat-bottomed boats had to be constructed if the invasion force was to disembark quickly on the Kent or Sussex coasts.[6] The invasion plan required clear weather and long dark nights, the first a feature of summer and the second of winter, but they rarely coincided. "Let us be masters of the straits for six hours," Bonaparte carelessly boasted, "and we will be masters of the world." In fact the crossing, it was estimated, would take ten hours, so the French force would have to ride two high tides.[7] The plan remained an enormous gamble as long as Britain continued to dominate the seas. Britain had fifty-five ships of the line in 1803, and

France could not hope to match this. In fact, the British succeeded in expanding their navy much faster than did the French, so that the naval armaments gap between the two powers widened rather than narrowed.[8] By 1804, it was becoming very likely that France would soon be facing another European coalition, and the projected invasion of England was no longer a priority. The inherent impossibility of the project was then recognised. Perhaps it had always been a bluff, a ruse which enabled Bonaparte to assemble a peace-time army without alarming the continental powers. Napoleon lent support to this view when he confessed to Metternich in 1810 that "the army assembled at Boulogne was always an army against Austria".[9] The defeats of both Britain *and* Austria, however, were essential if France was ever to achieve lasting peace.

The Peace of Amiens was no more than a truce; the struggle for possession of the French colonies simply suffered a brief postponement. In 1802, as soon as the treaty had been signed, Malmesbury had cynically prophesied to the Duke of York: "Peace, sir, in a week, and war in a month."[10] British commercial interests had hoped that the peace would once again open up European markets to them, but by 1803 this hope seemed delusory. Heavy duties were imposed on British imports in states allied to France or under French control – Holland, Spain, and northern Italy. As a result, British exports to Europe may have marginally declined in the peacetime years of 1802–03.[11]

Bonaparte seemed reluctant to meet the obligations of the treaty. The French did not carry out their promise to evacuate Holland because it was too costly to use French rather than Dutch resources to support the army. In addition, the French moved into Switzerland in 1803, in response to a revolution in the cantons. Bonaparte took the Helvetic Confederation under his military wing, which threatened Germany and Austria, and seemed to indicate a cavalier attitude towards the peace terms. Britain's response was a refusal to leave Malta which lay across the route from Toulon to Egypt. In 1803, The French occupied Hanover and Cuxhaven at the mouth of the Elbe, and after 1804 the British once again seized the French West Indies. As soon as Britain could be assured of the support of one continental ally, a resumption of hostilities was inevitable.

A new coalition was forming in which Russia was now drawn into the Austro-British alliance against France. Austria needed little more provocation: the proclamation of the French Empire in 1804 seemed a threat to the wounded pride of the Habsburg Emperor, while the assassination of the Duke of Enghien stirred the royal anger in every European court. The Cisalpine Republic had become the Kingdom of Italy, with Napoleon himself claiming the crown and appointing Eugène de Beauharnais as his Viceroy. This in itself was a violation of the terms of Lunéville. The French Empire annexed the Ligurian Republic, with its capital in Genoa, confirming that the French stranglehold on Italy allowed the Austrians no openings for the recovery of their authority in the peninsula. In 1803, Bonaparte had sent his fellow Corsican Sébastiani on a mission to the Near East. As a result, Tsar Alexander was apprehensive about French designs in the Ottoman Empire and was prepared to ally with Britain to deter the French. The Prussians, who still hung back, nevertheless had their sights set on Hanover. The new coalition was as usual cemented by the provision of British subsidies, and its agreed basis was British possession of Malta and the exclusion of France from the eastern Mediterranean. France was to be forced to retreat to her 1802 frontiers and Austria hoped to regain influence in Italy.

The Danube campaign of 1805 once more demonstrated France's extraordinary military capacity. Napoleon acted quickly to isolate the elements of the coalition, defeating Austria before she could receive substantial aid, and before the Prussian government had managed to resolve its own hesitation. The Austrians were crushed at Ulm (1805) and again (with the Russians) at Austerlitz (1805). At the Treaty of Pressburg (1805), Austria was forced to endure what was perhaps her most humiliating experience of the Napoleonic Wars. Austria lost all her remaining territory in Italy and Germany. Venice was lost, and the Austrian presence in the Tyrol and southern Germany was eliminated. Gradually, the French began to close the Italian ports to English trade: Livorno (in Tuscany), Civitavecchia (the port of Rome) and Ancona in the Papal States, as well as Naples. The Pope himself became a prisoner of France. Britain held on to Reggio in Calabria until 1808, but by then no independent states remained in existence in Italy. The new Confederation of the Rhine remained very much a paper constitution, but it signalled that France had replaced Austrian influence in Germany: the Bourbons would not have wished for more. The coalition's only consolation was that the Franco-Spanish fleet was destroyed at Trafalgar in 1805. Nelson, however, was fatally wounded, and the defeated Admiral Villeneuve committed suicide.

Prussia had hesitated while Austria suffered another spectacular defeat, and Prussian neutrality had been a major asset to Napoleon's success up to and including the campaign of 1805. Prussia's belated entry into the conflict, however, was as disastrous as that of Austria. Prussia had profited from the French reorganisation of the political map of Germany, but in addition sought a French guarantee that Hanover would become a permanent Prussian possession. France allowed Frederick William to occupy Hanover in 1804, but it was becoming clear to the Prussians that little more was to be extracted from cooperation with Napoleon. It was also alarmingly evident that Napoleon had little respect for anybody's neutrality. The abduction of the Duke of Enghien had occurred on supposedly neutral territory, and in 1805 French troops under Bernadotte violated Prussian territory by marching through Anspach. Prussia could not be pleased either by Napoleon's Confederation of the Rhine, which not only displaced Austria but also threatened Prussian ambitions. In 1806, therefore, Prussia, with the only continental army yet undefeated, entered the coalition against Napoleon.

The result was utter catastrophe at the Battle of Jena (1806). The implications of Prussia's defeat proved momentous, both for Prussia and for Germany as a whole. Jena demonstrated emphatically that the most powerful army of the Old Régime had been made completely obsolete by the changes wrought by the French Revolution and its heir Napoleon, in the nature of warfare and the composition of armies. But it was not just the Prussian army that was defeated; the entire social and political system, which the enlightened absolutism of Frederick the Great had striven to preserve, was now discredited. It had failed to meet the challenge posed by the egalitarianism and the democratic energies released by revolutionary and Napoleonic France. Prussian administrators like Stein and Hardenburg, Scharnhorst and Gneisenau, were not slow to draw the necessary conclusions. Prussian society was forced to adapt to the new world created by the French Revolution. Schemes were drawn up to transform the institution of serfdom, to break down social barriers and to rethink even the basis of military recruitment itself. Reforms were to be gradual and limited, but the movement was under way.[12] Jena put all of northern Germany under French control; but it also provoked a reassessment of the society of orders within old régime Prussia.

The peace settlement deprived Prussia of her territory between the Elbe and the Rhine, which became part either of the Grand Duchy of Berg or the Kingdom of Westphalia. The resurrection of Poland in the form of another French client state, the Grand Duchy of Warsaw, cost Prussia territory in the east as well. A war indemnity was imposed and the French army was to occupy Prussia until it was paid. Once again, the successful French army was able to live off conquered territory; the campaigns in Prussia and Poland cost the French taxpayer nothing.

The defeat of Austria and the collapse of Prussia left Russia alone to face the French. At Eylau (1807), France and Russia fought out an indecisive but bloody encounter in a snowstorm. When the snow cleared, 25 000 Russians lay dead and French losses amounted to 18 000.[13] Armed conflict was becoming increasingly expensive in terms of human sacrifice. The Grande Armée could no longer move with the devastating speed and efficiency of the illustrious Italian campaign of 1796–7. The army included a shrinking proportion of experienced veterans. It was now composed of many disparate elements – Dutch, Italians, Germans, Swiss, contingents recruited from all parts of the French Empire. It was no longer the streamlined national institution it had once been; it was a motley international conglomeration. The armies met again at Friedland (1807). This time, French victory was assured and the way was open for peace negotiations between Napoleon and Alexander.

The two Emperors met at Tilsit on a raft moored in the river Niemen, in an interview at which Napoleon believed he had made an indelible personal impression on Alexander. Their alliance, however, was always a fragile one (Map 14.3). Alexander gave up Russian interests in the Mediterranean, including the Ionian Islands, and Russia was to be incorporated within the continental system against British economic power (see Chapter 15). Napoleon thus gained an important recruit in the struggle against Britain, and won time to recover from the wars of 1806 and 1807. In return he gave Alexander vague promises of territory which was never his to offer. Alexander had a free hand in Turkey and the Baltic, and in 1808 he proceeded to invade Finland. In the long run, however, there were serious flaws in the alliance between the two giants of east and west. Little united them at Tilsit except, for the time being, mutual hostility towards Britain. The very existence of a new Polish state, established under French auspices, guaranteed conflict in the future.

The Empire, as an instrument of French hegemony in Europe, was at its height with the defeat of Austria, Prussia and Russia in 1805–7. Its revolutionary origins, however, were increasingly obscured by the trend towards a more dynastic form of imperial structure. The satellite republics were transformed into kingdoms, and new duchies and principalites were created. The Batavian Republic, for example, became the Kingdom of Holland in 1806, and the Cisalpine Republic, as we have seen, became the Kingdom of Italy. The new

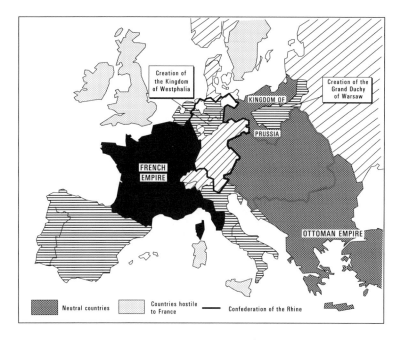

Map 14.3   Europe after the Treaty of Tilsit, 1807

Source: François Furet, *La Révolution, 1770–1880* (Paris, Hachette, 1988).

dynastic orientation of the Empire elevated the Bonaparte siblings to new titles and new thrones. Louis was enthroned as King of Holland (1806), and Jérôme as King of Westphalia (1807). It was even possible for members of the clan to rotate kingdoms. The elder brother Joseph, for instance, was King first of Naples and then of Spain. Eugène de Beauharnais, Napoleon's stepson, was adopted into the family and married Augusta of Bavaria before he ruled in Italy. A royal marriage was also arranged for Joséphine's cousin, Stéphanie de Beauharnais, with the ruling family of the kingdom of Baden.

    Male members of the clan who married outside this circle incurred the wrath of the Emperor. When Louis Bonaparte married Joséphine's daughter Hortense de Beauharnais, the match was approved. But Jérôme's marriage in 1803 to the American Elizabeth Patterson sent Napoleon into a furious defence of clan solidarity and honour. Jérôme was won back to the fold, however, by the lure of power. The dissolution of his first marriage in 1806 ensured there would be no Protestants within the dynastic élite, and he married the daughter of the King of Wurtemburg in 1807. If he had not so

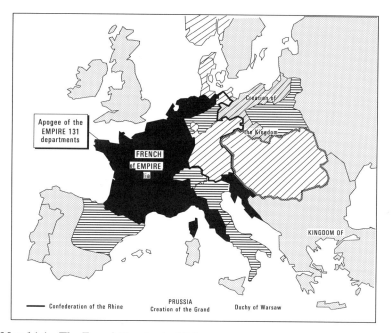

Map 14.4   The French Empire in 1812

Source: François Furet, *La Révolution, 1770–1880* (Paris, Hachette, 1988).

responded to his brother's rage, he might never have been considered for the Westphalian throne.

Lucien put himself beyond the pale by his second marriage to Alexandrine Jouberthon, ex-wife of a businessman, and the mother of his illegitimate son. The family had already objected in vain to his first marriage, to Christine Boyer, an innkeeper's daughter. Unlike Jérôme, Lucien refused to sacrifice his marriage to the dynasty, even for the kingdom of Italy, and was struck off the line of succession.[14] He never received a title from his resentful brother. The Bonaparte sisters also had their part to play in the new dynastic network. Elisa married an obscure Corsican officer, Felix Baciocchi, but became Princess of Lucca and Piombino and then Grand Duchess of Tuscany. Caroline married Murat and was eventually installed in Dusseldorf as Grand Duchess of Berg, before she became the Queen of Naples.

French imperial conquest looked less and less like the liberation of oppressed peoples, and more and more like an employment agency for members of a private patronage system. It provided prestigious assets to be divided amongst the Bonaparte kinship network. The members of that network meanwhile sought nothing more than assimilation by marriage into the traditional royal families of Europe.

If the Empire resembled a federation of fraternal kingdoms, this was merely a transitional stage because Napoleon increasingly subjected it to his central authority. Holland and the North Sea coast were annexed to reinforce the Continental Blockade, while Dalmatia and Catalonia were also absorbed as departments of France. At its height, the Empire had no fewer than 130 departments under its direct control. A new element was introduced when the King of Rome was born: the brothers Bonaparte grew uneasy about their position in an imperial future which would be reserved and nurtured for Napoleon's sole heir.

The Empire was at its height, but the new dynasticism showed one way in which Napoleonic success deformed his revolutionary heritage. The Emperor's obsession with his personal glory threatened to distort that legacy still further. The temptation to identify the fate of France with himself alone was to prove irresistible by 1812 (Map 14.4). Even at the point of its greatest achievement then, the Empire was already secreting a fatal poison – an unattainable dream of personal grandeur which would now propel it down the road to destruction (Tables 14.1 and 14.2).

Table 14.1   The Revolutionary and Napoleonic Wars

Wars and Coalitions
(with France's enemies or co-signatories)

1793–1795	War of the 1st Coalition	GB, Holland, Prussia, Austria, Spain, Savoy
1799–1801	War of the 2nd Coalition	GB, Russia, Austria, Naples, Baden, Mainz, Wurtemburg
1801	Treaty of Lunéville	Austria
1802–04	Peace of Amiens	GB
1805–07	Wars of the 3rd, 4th and 5th Coalitions	GB, Austria, Russia, Prussia, Naples, Sweden
1805	Treaty of Pressburg	Austria
1807	Treaty of Tilsit	Russia
1808–1814	Peninsular War	GB, Portugal, Spain,
1809	War against Austria	
1812	War against Russia	
1813	War of the last Coalition	GB, Russia, Prussia, Austria, Sweden

Table 14.2   Main French Victories and Defeats
(with France's principal antagonists)

1800	Marengo (Aus.)	Hohenlinden (Aus.)	
1805	Ulm (Aus.)	*Trafalgar (GB)*	Austerlitz (Aus.)
1806	Jena(Pruss.)	Auerstädt (Pruss.)	
1807	Eylau (Russ.)	Friedland (Russ.)	
1808	*Bailen (Sp.)*		
1809	Essling(Aus.)	Wagram (Aus.)	
1812	*Ciudad Rodrigo (GB)*		Borodino (Russ.)
1813	Lützen and Bautzen (Allies)		*Vittoria (GB)*
	Leipzig (Allies)		
1815	*Waterloo (Allies)*		

Note: Defeats are indicated in italic type.

15   The Unsheathed Sword, 2: Britain, Spain, Russia

The story of French dominance over the European continent has implications for the main theme of this study – the relationship between Napoleon and his revolutionary legacy. It is not easy to determine exactly when Napoleon abandoned his revolutionary legacy. For many years, his personal career coincided exactly with the needs of the Revolution for peace and consolidation, and it coincided, too, with the national interests of France. But at a certain point Napoleon's private ambition started to follow an independent trajectory, deviating both from the interests of the Revolution and those of France herself. The drive for personal glory eclipsed the revolutionary past and led France onwards to disaster.

When did Napoleon abandon the legacy of the recent past and sacrifice the spirit of the Revolution to his personal destiny? On the domestic scene, the inauguration of the Empire in 1804 was a significant turning-point. On the continental scene, several possibilities can be suggested. For Deutsch, there was a turning-point even before 1802, when Napoleonic policy had already become imperialist rather than nationalist.[1] Even before Bonaparte came to power, however, the Directory had already abandoned the goal of "natural frontiers", in favour of a more expansionist policy. The Empire arrived at another moment of decision in 1805, when the imposition of a humiliating peace on Austria condemned France to a further round of conflict, whose dynamism was not exhausted until 1815.

A crossroads was reached, it could be argued, in 1808, the beginning of French embroilment in Spain, which drained away French resources in the Peninsular War. In Bonapartist Spain, however, French rule still appeared to some as an instrument of rationalism and revolution. The Empire as a whole was enjoying success and stability in this period; not until its last years did it meet serious difficulties and opposition.

Another critical moment was Napoleon's marriage to Marie-Louise of Austria in 1810, signifying his desire for acceptance by the royal families of Europe. For the great usurper (as he remained in the eyes of the monarchies) and the scourge of the old régime dynasties clearly had dynastic ambitions of his own.

A more convincing choice is 1812, the date of the fateful Russian campaign. The decision to invade Russia was Napoleon's alone; he ignored advice to the contrary from Cambacérès and others. In terms of the defence of the Revolution, or of France's interests, the invasion of Russia was completely unnecessary; its logic lay in the relentless impetus of the war as Napoleon had pursued it, and in the obsessive fantasy of power which gripped him.

The Continental Blockade

Britain dominated the oceans and was reluctant to risk an army in continental Europe. An invasion across the Channel was a dangerous adventure. Nevertheless, Britain provided the financial support which animated the anti-French coalitions. Napoleonic France, therefore, could not expect peace unless Britain was defeated. One way to strike at Britain was to weaken her economic position in Europe. The Continental Blockade, or Continental System as it was more grandly called, represented a new kind of economic warfare, intended to bring Britain to her knees by stifling her overseas commerce.

Given that the balance of naval power remained heavily in Britain's favour, there was no possibility of blockading the British Isles themselves. France could not force the British merchant fleet to stay at home, but if France controlled the coastline of Europe British ships could be prevented from arriving and unloading in Hamburg, Livorno, Genoa or Rotterdam. The Continental Blockade was a *self*-blockade, an attempt to prevent British trade from gaining access to continental ports. The self-blockade, Napoleon hoped, would exclude Britain from her export markets and thus destroy her commercial wealth.

Several consequences would in theory ensue. If British exports could no longer reach their European destinations, Britain would suffer a severe crisis of overproduction, with resulting bankruptcies, unemployment and perhaps even a popular revolution. In addition, like any country with a large import bill and no export outlets, Britain would suffer a catastrophic balance of payments crisis, and her bullion reserves would soon be exhausted. A third aspect of the plan was France's imperialistic plan to take Britain's place on the continent, as leading provider of finished textiles, coal, colonial produce and other goods. The Continental System would thus eliminate France's main economic competitor from the European arena, allowing French industry to capture traditional British markets.

The plan contained some serious drawbacks and embodied at least one important contradiction. The contradiction was that both France and the rest of Europe were not completely self-sufficient. They needed the British goods which they tried to exclude, both raw materials and the colonial goods which Britain re-exported to continental Europe. France could not provide coffee, sugar and other colonial produce since the British had seized her colonies and, after Trafalgar, they could not be recovered. The self-blockade might therefore need to be broken if Europe was to maintain access to these goods.

The drawbacks were principally that British goods would always find some way of reaching European markets unless the French achieved total imperial domination of the continent. As a result, the Continental System had important consequences for the war: it dictated the need for further French conquests, in order to ensure that Europe was completely sealed off from British exports. The need to extend the Continental System implied the eventual invasions of Spain and Russia. Furthermore, France would have to coerce conquered states into accepting the complete rupture of their traditional economic connections with Britain.

There is little doubt that France could inflict serious damage on the sections of British industry which were most dependent on exports. These included cotton and wool manufactures, which usually exported approximately half of their product, as well as the cutlery and hardware industries of Sheffield and Birmingham.[2] A large proportion of British exports, however, was invulnerable because it went to destinations outside Europe itself. In 1805, Europe bought 33 per cent of British exports of home-produced goods, estimated according to their real value. Another 27 per cent were sold to the United States and 40 per cent to the rest of the world.[3] Napoleon could weaken Britain by denying her access to key trading partners in Germany and the Baltic, but without naval supremacy he could not prevent Britain from making up her losses in her own Empire, or in North and South America.

There was another problem: Britain and France could try to damage each other's merchant fleet as much as possible, but a great deal of produce could be carried in neutral ships. No blockade could be fully successful unless it included neutral shipping as well.

Both Britain and France accordingly took severe measures against neutral shipping, which was especially frustrating for the United States of America. By 1806, the French had extended the blockade to the Adriatic and the German coast, while the British blockaded all French ports and the northern coast of Europe as far east as the Elbe. In November 1806, Napoleon issued the Berlin Decree which ordered that every European port be closed not only to British ships but to *any* ships emanating from a port in Britain or her colonies. In addition, all British subjects found on French territory would be imprisoned and their property confiscated. Britain replied by Orders-in-Council (1807) which banned any maritime trade between one French-controlled port and another. All neutral ships destined for enemy ports were ordered to unload their cargo in a British port, to pay a tax and obtain a licence to continue to operate. By interrupting European trade with neutral powers, the British government hoped to compel continental customers to accept the British goods they needed. France responded to this broadside with a further volley: the Milan Decree (1807) ordered the confiscation of any ship which had succumbed to British regulations and put into a British port. Any neutral ship which had submitted to British demands could henceforth be seized anywhere at sea.

Tilsit brought Russia into the Continental System, the invasion of Spain threatened to seal off Spain and Portugal too, while after Wagram (1809) Austria could not resist either. In the Bayonne Decree (1808) Napoleon turned explicitly against neutral shipping and ordered the seizure of American ships entering French, Dutch or Italian ports. The Fontainebleau Decree (1810) marked a further escalation of the economic war against Britain, ordering up to ten years' penal servitude for smuggling, and the destruction of prohibited British goods. In Munich and elsewhere, British goods were publicly burned before uncomprehending local consumers.

One by-product of the economic war was the antagonism of neutrals, and eventually the Anglo-American war of 1812. In 1806, the United States began to exclude certain British imports, and in 1809 the Americans retaliated against the Berlin and Milan Decrees, and the Orders-in-Council, by closing their ports to both French and British shipping. But it is the impact of the blockade on the European conflict that is the primary concern here. How effective was the Continental System in weakening the British economy? The blockade was not consistently applied, but even so, there are signs that at certain moments in the struggle it seriously aggravated Britain's economic problems.

This was the case, for example, in 1808, after the Berlin and Milan Decrees, and the defection of Russia after Tilsit. The loss of the Baltic trade was especially damaging. The Baltic provided essential naval supplies, like hemp, tar and pitch. The timber, spars and yards of British naval vessels were manufactured from the fir and pine forests of northern Europe. Russia usually supplied two-thirds of British masts.[4] Portugal, Denmark and Prussia were incorporated into the Continental System, leaving Sweden as Britain's main European outlet. Exports to Europe declined to only 28 per cent of all British exports (measured in terms of value) in 1808.[5] These problems were aggravated by increasing Anglo-American hostility, but the British economy resisted well. The South American market looked promising, especially after the British briefly occupied Buenos Aires in 1806 and Montevideo in 1807. The extension of the Continental System in 1806–7 therefore caused only a temporary slump in the British economy in 1808 (Figure 15.1).

The Continental System hurt Britain much more in 1810–11. The British market was then flooded with unsold goods and there was a wave of bankruptcies. Industrial production fell by 20 per cent between 1809 and 1811, although the blockade was only one contributing cause. The severe depression caused unemployment and the outbreaks of machine-breaking in Nottinghamshire and the northern counties known as the Luddite Riots. Revolutionary conspirators succeeded in assassinating Prime Minister Perceval in 1812. Gold reserves fell as the war effort produced financial strain. Britain was committed to financing the Peninsular War, and by 1810 Wellington's army was absorbing over £5000 million per year. Walcheren had been costly, and the Austrian subsidy had amounted to £1188 million in 1809.[6] There was a worsening balance of payments deficit. The value of the pound fell over 25 per cent from 23 francs in 1808 to 17 francs in 1811.[7] Grain had to be purchased overseas to compensate for domestic food shortages. British exports tumbled to a new low in 1811 (see Figure 15.1), until the invasion of Russia once again signalled the relaxation of the Continental Blockade.

The blockade ultimately failed partly because of its own contradictions, and partly for reasons which were outside Napoleon's control. Although the blockade hurt Britain in 1808 and 1810–11, it was never consistently enforced. Napoleon was not capable of denying Britain access to every part of Europe. In attempting to achieve this, he committed France to further aggressive wars, initiated to make the blockade hermetic. The Spanish War opened up new avenues for English trade, and the collapse of the French alliance with Russia threw northern Europe open once again to Britain. Napoleon was responsible for both of these failures.

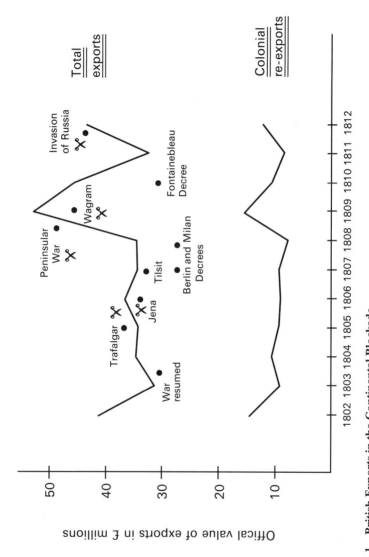

Figure 15.1   British Exports in the Continental Blockade

Source: Based on F. Crouzet, *L'Economie britannique et le blocur Continental*, 2 vols (Paris, PUF, 1958) pp. 883–7.

The blockade was regularly subverted, both by the British and from within the system itself. The British smuggled goods into Europe through Portugal, through Sicily or Malta or Heligoland or Gibraltar – through one tap or another which France could not shut off. Sugar, for example, found its way from Salonica through the Balkans, in small boxes carried by mules, via Vienna and onto French tables, where it understandably cost up to ten times as much as it did in Britain.

The French, too, violated their own blockade by allowing a limited amount of trade with Britain. A system of licences was introduced to permit merchants to sell goods in England. After all, France still needed to export her own wine, silk and luxuries. When Britain suffered food shortages, as in 1808–9, France sold wheat to England. (This could be justified as a way of draining Britain's liquidity, and also of enabling French agriculture to pay its taxes.) Europe, as we have seen, also needed to import British goods, and ways could be found to introduce such imports, either legally under licence or illegally as contraband. The Fontainebleau Decree (1810) had sentenced English goods to burn on continental bonfires, but German spectators resented the fact that in France itself legal loopholes in the blockade were officially tolerated. The Grande Armée had difficulty clothing its soldiers with uniforms and overcoats without British textiles. Holland and Germany were very reluctant to submit to French economic imperialism and protectionism, and so were the Russian noblemen who feared the profits of their timber trade with Britain would evaporate. When Napoleon had to withdraw troops from northern Europe, as he did in the 1809 campaign, French vigilance relaxed and British goods flooded in. Customs officials and French consuls were notoriously corrupt, and could be induced to let prohibited cargos escape their surveillance.

Europe was a vital market, but Britain had other export outlets which Napoleon could not touch. The United States was one of these. South America was rapidly becoming another. Involvement in the Peninsular War made Britain the guardian of the Portuguese and Spanish royal families. This helped to open up markets in Brazil, and South America in general, to British trade. When movements for independence from Spain and Portugal developed in South America, Britain gave moral support which was underpinned by a growing commercial connection. In the 1820s, Prime Minister Canning was the first to give the emerging independent states of South America official recognition – an indication of their new importance as an export market for Britain. Thus even if access to Europe was temporarily a problem, Britain could export elsewhere.

The British economy, therefore, with its sophisticated credit system and virtually impregnable sea power, managed to endure the pressure. Industrialisation continued and investment found new profitable outlets, in agriculture, public works, docks and canals. By the end of the war it was France who was in economic difficulty, short of raw materials, and with her overseas trade stifled. The French commercial bourgeoisie, just like the despised "nation of shopkeepers", was looking forward to peace, even if the return of the monarchy was necessary to achieve it.

The Spanish Ulcer and the Fate of the French Soldier

Spain was a vast, decaying Empire, ruled by a weak monarchy, a corrupt court, a wealthy and bigoted Church, and unpopular ministers. As France's closest economic partner, Spain appeared a vulnerable and at the same time an attractive prey. Furthermore, the forces of the Spanish Enlightenment, feeble though they were in comparison to their French equivalents, were sympathetic to France. Beyond Spain lay Portugal, a close ally of Britain, a major distribution point for colonial goods like sugar and spices, and one of the keys to the success of Napoleon's Continental System. But instead of shutting Britain out of Europe, the invasion of Spain showed the British the way back in.

The French intervention in Spain came at the Madrid government's own invitation. Chief Minister Godoy, anxious to bolster his own fading reputation, invited Napoleon to invade Portugal and share the spoils with Spain. The unpredicted results of French invasion were British intervention on the European continent, a fatal drain on French military resources, and disaster for the Spanish monarchy itself, which had opened the door to foreign control. In Kissinger's phrase, Austerlitz had shown how risky it was to be Napoleon's enemy; Jena demonstrated that it was fatal to remain neutral; but Spain proved it was disastrous to be France's friend.[8]

Charles IV was compelled to abdicate and Ferdinand VII claimed the throne. The French sent them both into exile. The French occupation, however, sparked a popular revolt. The memorable paintings of Francisco Goya present one version of the Madrid rising of May 1808 against French troops, and of the repression which followed. Thirty-one Frenchmen were killed and in retaliation Murat executed 100 Spaniards.[9] The occupying troops included Mamelukes, hated as descendants of Spain's Moslem conquerors. The revolt, in the name of Ferdinand VII, spread to the provinces, and the French soon faced a full-scale war. In 1808, a French army was astonishingly defeated at Bailen by Spanish regular troops. In 1809, Moore's British army was permitted to embark and escape to safety at Coruña.

Napoleon himself stayed in Spain less than three months. He crushed Madrid and installed his brother Joseph as King of Spain, but the guerrilla war went on. The support (or collaboration) of pro-French elements in the aristocracy and middle class (the *afrancesados*) seemed insignificant besides the violent forces of clerical obscurantism which were now unleashed. A revolt of peasants, shepherds and booty-seekers was encouraged by the clergy. The French were accused of being heretics, freemasons and agents of the devil. Torture and the massacre of civilians became commonplace in a barbaric struggle, in which Goya mourned his country and lamented the demise of enlightened hopes in Spain.[10] This was a civil war, as well as a struggle against the foreign invader, but the liberal intelligentsia was helpless before the atrocious slaughter (Document 15.1).

DOCUMENT 15.1   A SPANISH CATECHISM

This example of anti-French propaganda was published with the approval of the Junta of Seville.

Question : How is this child named?

Response : As a Spaniard.

Q : What is a Spaniard?

R : An honest man.

Q : How many duties does he have and what are they?

R : Three. To be a Christian of the Roman Catholic faith, to defend his religion, his King and his country, and to die rather than be conquered.

Q : Who is our King?

R : Ferdinand VII.

Q : With how much love should he be honoured?

R : With the greatest love, as his virtues and misfortunes have merited.

Q : Who is the enemy of our happiness?

R : The Emperor of the French.

Q : Who is he?

R : A new and infinitely evil ruler, a greedy chief of all evil men and the exterminator of the good, the essence and receptacle of every vice.

Q : How many natural forms does he assume?

R : Two. One a devil and the other human.

Q : How many Emperors are there?

R : There is one true Emperor, with three false faces.

Q : What are they?

R : Napoleon, Murat and Godoy.

Q : What are the characteristics of the first of these?

R : Arrogance and tyranny.

Q : And of the second?

R : Plunder and cruelty.

Q : And of the last?

R : Treason and disgrace.

Q : Who are the French?

R : Old Christians and modern heretics.

Q : What has brought them to this state?

R : False philosophy, and placing liberty above old customs.

Q : How do they serve their ruler?

R : Some feed his arrogance, and others are agents of his iniquity in the extermination of the human race.

(Translated from Sabino Delgado (ed.), *Guerra de la Independencia: proclamas, Bandos y Combatientes* (Madrid: Editora Nacional, 1976), pp.294–7.)

French units were isolated and ambushed by small bands of fighters who constantly harassed supply lines. The savagery of the French was exacerbated by their own constant fear of a menacing enemy who rarely came out into the open. When the French took Tarragona in 1811, 15 000 Spaniards were slaughtered.[11] When advancing or retreating, it was always unsafe to leave a military hospital, with sick and wounded soldiers, behind; in Spain either the inhabitants or the enemy would finish off the casualties. They were sometimes mutilated, hung from the trees, crucified or just sawn up. Wellington reputedly described his own army as "the scum of the earth"; adequate words could not be found to express what he thought of his appalling Spanish "allies". (Little love was lost between the Spaniards and the British, regarded as heretical Protestants who had made a cowardly run for it at Coruña; Spain hated *all* invaders.) What is more, food was short; everyone on both sides in Spain was always hungry. Soldiers looted what they wanted from local households and farms to fill themselves and keep warm. Their starving officers were often incapable of preventing this or unwilling to step in.

The Spanish resistance has often been portrayed as a patriotic and national struggle against the foreign invader. The less glamorous truth is that the struggle was not national but provincial and that unity was hard to realise. The Spanish monarchy had never achieved the complete integration of its domains and divisions were still apparent. The thirteen provincial *Juntas* rarely cooperated with each other. When the central *Junta* in Cadiz tried to impose conscription in 1811, it was very unpopular, and succeeded in raising only 100 000 men.[12] As a result, the only organised military force was the British army of 35 000, under Wellington, which lacked both cavalry and artillery. Since they faced up to 350 000 troops, a heavy burden fell on the guerrillas.[13] The Spanish word *guerrilla*, literally meaning a small war, originates in the Napoleonic period. It has come to refer to any similar struggle, in which groups of fighters emerge from the local population to frustrate and ambush a superior and better equipped enemy, and attack his sources of supply without risking a pitched battle. Some guerrilla bands grew into sizeable armies. Juan Martin Diaz, known as *El Empecinado* (the Stubborn One) led 5000 men, while Francisco Espoz y Mina had over 13 000 followers, who all escaped official control.[14]

Wellington's role was to defend Lisbon, which he did successfully in the campaign of 1810, using it as a base from which he could replenish his supplies by sea. He fought cautiously and defensively, unwilling to risk unnecessary casualties. Until 1812, he could make little impact on the general European conflict. The Peninsular War could not prevent the defeat of Austria in 1809, nor could it save Russia from invasion in 1812. After the French setbacks of 1812, however, he was not merely tying down French troops but advancing to push them out of Spain. In 1812, he moved to take Ciudad Rodrigo and Badajoz in Estremadura. He defeated Marmont at Salamanca (1812) and entered Madrid. In 1813, he decisively entered northern Spain. After Vittoria (1813), in the Basque country, Spain was free of the French forces.

Napoleon was slow to recognise the seriousness of the Spanish War. "The army," he wrote to Joseph, "seems to be commanded not by experienced generals but by postal inspectors."[15] But in 1812, there were between 33 000 and 50 000 Spanish partisans engaged in the struggle against France. They forced France to commit a substantial army to the occupation of the country. When the French wanted to send a convoy of supplies form Bayonne to Madrid in 1812, it took thirty-seven days to reach its destination, and it needed an escort of 4000 troops to protect it.[16] Manpower losses drained French strength. According to General Bigarré, an *aide* to Joseph Bonaparte, the French lost 100 men daily in Spain.[17] The onset of the Russian campaign meant that such losses could no longer be replaced. This was Napoleon's "Spanish Ulcer" – a suppurating wound which could not be cauterised, and which weakened the victim without being able to put him out of his misery.

The French faced almost insuperable supply problems in Spain. Although the guerrillas were poorly armed and badly organised, they could intimidate the local peasantry into withholding grain from the French, and as the French withdrew from rural areas in 1812 and 1813, they increasingly faced starvation. The dilemma faced by Marshal MacDonald in Barcelona was typical of the difficulties faced by the French. He needed 2 700 000 bread rations from Aragon. To make sure they arrived safely, however, he had to supply an escort of about 50 000 soldiers. In addition, he required a labour force to repair the Lerida–Barcelona road which had been damaged by guerrillas. The escort and the work-party also needed to be fed. They themselves would consume all the grain in the process of transporting it.[18]

No wonder many French soldiers deserted. By 1812, they were undernourished, demoralised and unpaid for at least a year. The Spanish government offered them money to desert, and *El Empecinado* claimed that thousands of French soldiers had defected to his own ranks.[19] The non-French contingents were most ready to desert. The Neapolitans deserted so fast that Napoleon put a stop to replacement from Naples. Recruitment in southern Italy for the Spanish campaign was simply helping to reinforce the enemy.

In reflecting on the sorry fate of French soldiers in Spain, it is worth remembering that death in battle was only one way of getting killed. Disease, rather than combat itself, was the real danger. Armies were vast insanitary camps where contagion spread fast. A typhus epidemic, for instance, followed the victory at Austerlitz. Napoleon did very little to improve medical services. In fact, the number of medical officers attached to the army was halved under the Consulate.[20] A medical service was provided for the elite of the Imperial Guard, and Napoleon encouraged the innovations introduced by the medical surgeon Larrey.

Larrey used "flying ambulances" to collect the wounded from the battlefield and give them treatment. Treatment very often consisted of the amputation of limbs shattered by cannon-shot. Larrey became a dedicated and energetic battlefield amputator. In the campaign against Prussia in 1806, he was quite capable of carrying out 200 amputations within an interval of twelve hours. At Friedland, his surgical operations were on a mass scale: a hundred surgeons amputated continuously for twenty-four hours. There were very good reasons for the popularity of this trend. Larrey hoped to keep the wounded out of the military hospitals, where he knew there was every chance of contracting a fatal infection. The amputations of mangled arms and legs, with or without the benefit of anaesthetic (usually alcohol), were a way of improving the chances of survival.

Napoleon's care and attention to the welfare of his soldiers was part of his legend. The Emperor looked after his veterans by providing them with pensions and, if necessary, accommodation in the soldiers' home, Les Invalides. Here Napoleon built on his revolutionary legacy. In 1790, the Revolution had made veterans' pensions a right for all. In 1815, 118 000 veterans were in receipt of a pension.[21] In 1812, however, there was a drop in the number of applicants for places in Les Invalides, because not many of the wounded survived the Russian campaign.

From Second Marriage to the Russian Campaign

Dynastic and personal considerations loomed ever larger in the administration of the Empire. After eight years with Joséphine, Napoleon was officially childless. His wife was now 46 and past child-bearing age. He needed a male heir, and his solution to this problem was to divorce Joséphine and remarry. Napoleon is believed to have informed Joséphine of his decision at a ball on New Year's Eve, 1809, exactly five years since the religious ceremony which had married them in the eyes of the Church. (The Napoleons had a mania for anniversaries.) The hunt was on for a new imperial bride.

The mother of the new upstart dynasty was to be sought amongst the most established and illustrious royal families of Europe. Napoleon, the heir of the Revolution, was joining the ranks of the old monarchies. Attention first focused on Alexander I's sister, who had the disadvantage of not being a Catholic, but opinion then favoured the 18 year-old Habsburg princess, Marie-Louise of Austria. The Bonapartes preferred the Russian, but the Beauharnais and apparently Joséphine herself leaned towards the Austrian candidate. In 1810, Napoleon and Marie-Louise were officially married, and within a year a son was born. In Vienna, Metternich may have hoped that the dynastic bond would lead to more cooperative Franco-Austrian relations. In France, supporters of the Revolution may have recalled the dire fate of a previous French monarch with an Austrian wife, and remarked apprehensively on the growing resemblance between the institutions of the Empire and those of the Old Régime.

One diplomatic consequence of Napoleon's second marriage was the end of the Russian alliance. Tsar Alexander's jealousy was aroused, and he feared Napoleon was drifting away from the per-sonal bond he imagined had been formed at Tilsit, towards a *rapprochement* with Vienna. The Tsar's suspicions led him once again to contemplate an alliance with Britain. Alexander raised tariffs on French goods, and it seemed that the marriage to Marie-Louise had made it very difficult to resolve the issues which divided Napoleon and the Tsar.

One of these was the Grand Duchy of Warsaw, a French client state and a revival of French old régime diplomatic policy, which had always aimed at countering the eastern powers with alliances with Poland and the Turks. Russia's interests had been well served by a Polish state dominated by the Tsar or, as a second-best scenario, the partition of Polish territory. The promotion of a Francophile Polish

Duchy, which was not willing to surrender any territory to the Tsar, created tension between Napoleon and Alexander.

Another point of difference lay in the Danubian Principalities (in modern-day Rumania), which Alexander believed himself entitled to occupy after the agreement at Tilsit. He discovered, however, that Napoleon was not prepared to support this move. There were further possible obstacles to Russian expansion in the Baltic. Bernadotte was elected to the throne of Sweden and his intentions were unclear (he was in fact to throw in his lot with the Tsar). In 1810, Napoleon brusquely annexed the Duchy of Oldenburg, whose integrity he had previously guaranteed. This was open provocation to Tsar Alexander.

There were several reasons, therefore, for the French invasion of Russia. France was unwilling to underwrite unlimited Russian expansion in the Baltic and the Ottoman Empire. Napoleon feared that Alexander would listen to the Russian aristocrats who were complaining about the damaging effects of the blockade on Russian agricultural exports. If Alexander veered once again towards cooperation with Britain, the Continental System would be in serious jeopardy. Above all, however, Napoleon's drive for power drew him onward into the empty spaces of Byelorussia. It was a huge risk to invade Russia without securing his Spanish front. He trusted too fervently in his own destiny and in his private vision of power in the east, which were soon to dissolve like passing reflections in the icy water of the river Beresina.

The army that invaded Russia was the largest Napoleon had assembled. The force of 700 000 included Germans, Swiss, Italians, Spanish, Portuguese, as well as 90 000 Poles and Lithuanians.[22] The Russian armies were outnumbered, and they retreated, drawing France further and further into Russia without daring to give battle. As the French advanced, their enormous army started to dwindle. Some of its foreign contingents disappeared, and many horses did not survive the long march either. The advance on Moscow in the heat was just as destructive as the retreat was to prove in winter.[23] Three hundred miles into Russia, one-third of the army had vanished. By the time they reached Smolensk, 400 miles into Russia, only 160 000 fit troops were still available. At Borodino, outside Moscow, an inconclusive battle was fought, in which the French and Russian artillery bombarded each other mercilessly. The French lost 30 000 men, and Kutuzov's army 50 000.[24] When Napoleon reached Moscow, parts of the city had been mysteriously burned, perhaps on the orders of Count Rostopchin, and the French entry was anything but a triumph. Napoleon waited a month in Moscow for Alexander to bend, but the Tsar doggedly refused to negotiate. There was shelter and food for the French in Moscow, not to mention fur, vodka and *objets d'art* in plenty, but Napoleon feared for his southern supply routes during the winter months. He decided to retreat.

On the retreat from Moscow, the French army crossed country which had already been exhausted by their passage eastward. They were shadowed by Kutuzov, a man of substance who needed several assistants to lift him into the saddle. Kutuzov, a cunning and lecherous general but hardly a military genius, studiously avoided a confrontation. In Soviet history, however, as well as in Tolstoy's *War and Peace*, Kutuzov traditionally appeared as a wise Russian patriot, leading the peasant resistance to the French in a "War for the Fatherland".[25] The French troops were harassed by Cossack cavalry, and also by partisans, who despatched deserters and stragglers. The winter temperatures reached minus 20°C and they were to drop further. The wounded and the exhausted froze where they fell, together with the useless jewels and icons they had plundered in Moscow. Clothing and footwear were inadequate. Starving soldiers sought some passing warmth by lying inside the carcasses of dead horses. The army disappeared in the snow and ice.

Only about 60 000 troops crossed the river Beresina, near Minsk, where the Russians almost caught the retreating French. It was a cruel irony that the winter climate moderated enough to thaw the Beresina, preventing the French from making an easy crossing over the ice. Tens of thousands of wounded and stragglers were left to die in the ice-floes, or be despatched by Cossacks, as the Imperial Guard and the other French units crossed on two improvised bridges. The Grande Armée had been destroyed. Over 400 000 men had been lost and another 100 000 taken prisoner.[26] In Paris, Malet had attempted to seize power by informing the capital of Napoleon's death, and the Emperor was now needed elsewhere. In any case, after the retreat from Moscow he no longer had an army to command.

In the night of 18 December 1812, a dishevelled, unshaven figure arrived at the Tuileries palace. When Marie-Louise had identified her husband, she received the devastating news of the military collapse (the 29th *Bulletin de la Grande Armée* had arrived but was not yet published). The Napoleonic Empire was now about to unravel.

16   The Napoleonic Revolution in Europe

The French Revolution only began in earnest outside France when the armies of the Directory or of Napoleon marched in. The ideals of social equality which had inspired the early revolutionaries of 1789–92 now swept across the Continent, with the French occupation of Italy, Germany, Spain and the Netherlands. The attack on privilege, seigneurialism and the power of the Church was carried to Europe in the wake of Bonaparte's all-conquering regiments. French expansion struck a series of damaging blows against the institutions of old régime Europe.

The impact of French revolutionary ideas was mitigated by many factors. The occupying power itself made contradictory demands on its newly acquired subjects. France had its own military and strategic interests to protect. The positive advantages of social change in the occupied territories were balanced by the military and economic exploitation to which they were subjected as parts of a Grand Empire ruled from Paris. Furthermore, revolutionary change was far from uniform: local traditions in many parts of the Empire were too powerful to ignore; and the revolutionary impetus could be very selective. The benefits of French administration were many and various, but they did not include the opportunity to put into practice new ideas of democratic self-government. Parliamentary rule had been brought to an end in France itself; Napoleon had no intention of fostering it elsewhere.

The revolutionary potential of the French presence in Europe will be examined in this chapter, alongside the many burdens it imposed. In the following chapter, the collaborators and resistors of the Empire will be identified as the social groups who stood to gain or lose from secularisation and the breaking down of feudal restrictions on social and economic development. Progress towards a more liberal and capitalist Europe demanded the creation of a wage-earning population free of seigneurial ties, and the defence of individual freehold property rights which were an inherent aim of the bourgeois revolution. In spite of its many contradictions, the Napoleonic Revolution in Europe is best considered in this context.

Models of Empire

Europe was to be remodelled by French arms and administration, but there were different and competing visions of the form that French-dominated Europe would take. For some, the French were liberators, for others, oppressors. The institutional forms of French domination evolved over time. The early republican model gave way to a more authoritarian model of Empire.

The republican model was adopted by France in conquered territories in the period before the Treaty of Lunéville in 1801. Republican France was then surrounded by a ring of republican "satellites", principally the Batavian Republic (the Netherlands), the Helvetic Republic (Switzerland) and the Cisalpine Republic (Lombardy and northern Italy). The satellites enjoyed some independence, but their political institutions were based on French models. The establishment of satellite republics gave encouragement to democratic forces in Holland, the Swiss cantons and Milan. As far as the Netherlands were concerned, for example, Simon Schama describes the period of 1798–1800 as one in which the Batavian Republic enjoyed an authentic representative democracy under French auspices.[1] The Dutch Constitution of 1798 provided for adult male suffrage and a single-chamber legislature. The Orange family was ousted, Jews were emancipated, and Roman Catholics were given full civil rights.

The republican model of French expansion was short-lived; it assisted the radical minority in the "liberated" territories, but it was also accompanied by exploitation and pillage which the government of the Directory could not or would not restrain. What the French government valued most about Holland, for example, was its fleet and the legendary wealth of the bankers of Amsterdam. The greed of French military personnel in Italy was one important cause of the wave of risings, the *insorgenza*, which helped to push the French out of Italy in 1799. Napoleon was to bring this republican period to an end. He would restrain the local radicals, curb aspirations towards local self-determination, and put an end to unchecked looting by his reckless subordinates.

Napoleon favoured a second model of Empire, which in his vanity he compared to Carolingian precedents. References to Charlemagne frequently appeared in official imperial rhetoric. The name of Carolus Magnus, for example, had been carved on the Alpine rock in David's famous portrait discussed in Chapter 13 (Plate 6). The comparison with Charlemagne emphasised Napoleon's desire to dispose of the thrones and dynasties of Europe as he pleased, especially in Italy. The Carolingian model had essentially a propaganda purpose; it intimidated the Pope and his supporters. In reality, Napoleon, unlike Charlemagne, never had a secure Spanish base, and the comparison was in any case extremely superficial. Charlemagne's loose Christian federation hardly resembled the modernising, technocratic adminis- tration of the centralised Napoleonic state.

Observers and historians have also offered their versions of the Napoleonic Empire. One conceptual model favoured by Napoleon's opponents was that of the Corsican clan. British propaganda, in par- ticular, frequently envisaged the Emperor as the head of a rapacious band of warriors, parcelling out territory in arbitrary fashion to reward his bandit chieftains, while reserving the choicest morsels for his closest family. The Empire, in this caricature, was nothing more than a vast system for the distribution of booty amongst a privileged kinship network. Napoleon's brother Louis received the throne of Holland, Joseph Bonaparte was King of Naples and of Spain, another brother Jérôme was King of Westphalia and Eugène de Beauharnais Viceroy of Italy. To focus exclusively on the Bonaparte family, how- ever, is to trivialise the important social and administrative reforms which they implemented. And to stress their Corsican origins is to miss the international aspects of French rule.

Finally, any overall view of the Napoleonic Empire must incorp- orate its modernising and rationalising tendencies, particularly emphasised by Stuart Woolf.[2] French administration, in this version, was progressive and enlightened, it embodied a scientific attitude to government and finance, and relied on predictable rules of law rather the personal whim of rulers or corrupt royal favourites. This model endows the Napoleonic Empire with predetermined object- ives and a great deal of forward planning. It does not interpret the Empire as an improvised machine for conquest and exploitation, but it credits Napoleon with a vision and a plan. Woolf's discussion of this modernising model may serve as a warning against any aspirations towards European uniformity.

This model, however, is useful if we bear in mind two major reser- vations (of which Woolf is incidentally very much aware). First, the French administrative model, regarded by the French themselves as the most superior form then available, was forced to accommodate local differences wherever it attempted to impose a uniform struc- ture on the Empire. Second, the French themselves undermined "the Napoleonic Project" for Europe. Territory was reserved for the grand imperial dignatories, while the demands of the Continental System distorted economic development and subordinated it to France's war needs. European diversity and French military hegemony therefore tended to sabotage the Empire's civilising powers.

This was always a very ethnocentric model of imperial expansion. The French believed that the French Revolution had given them the secrets of enlightened government, and that they alone had access to the code for social equality and progressive values. Other nations who failed to appreciate the benefits of the French Revolution were pitied or condemned as idle, superstitious peoples who were not yet ready to emerge from feudal darkness. Attacks on the retreating French in 1799, for example, seemed part of a struggle between enlightened French progress and a rising tide of Italian backwardness. According to Masséna, "Only the efforts of France can stop Europe from falling back into the barbarism into which her enemies are plunging her."[3] French administrators thought the Tuscans were lazy and the Neapolitans corrupt. In the Dalmatian provinces, it was even more difficult for the chauvinistic French to assist the poor inhabitants to throw off their oppression. The intendant of Ragusa (Dubrovnik) condescendingly complained:

> We have to deal with peoples who are too ignorant, too distant from civilisation and above all too poor to hope to be able to reach perfection suddenly and without shocks ... their intelligence is not sufficiently developed ... the methods of healing must be in proportion to the strength of the patient.[4]

For "perfection" read rationalism as defined by the Enlightenment, and the revolutionary social reforms of 1789–91; for "too distant from civilisation" read "too far from Paris".

At its fullest extent, the Napoleonic Empire included 130 departments and ruled about 44 million subjects. The French impact on this vast area, however, varied according to the length of time the French stayed before being driven out. The Rhineland, for example, had a long exposure to French reforms and institutions, and was permanently transformed as a result. In Spain, in contrast, the French had only a weak and transient grip on affairs. In 1810, King Joseph optimistically divided Spain into departments, but he was never able to appoint prefects. Catalonia, Aragon, Navarre and Biscay were removed from his royal jurisdiction and placed under military control, while Marshal Soult enjoyed unlimited authority in Andalusia. So the short-lived Bonaparte Kingdom of Spain then consisted only of Castile. Spain was never subdued and King Joseph, who repeatedly offered Napoleon his resignation, achieved little.[5]

The intensity of French domination further depended on the type of government, direct or indirect, adopted for a given territory. Political changes in the Empire closely followed developments in metropolitan France itself. The transition from Republic to Empire in 1804 was therefore of crucial importance outside as well as inside France. It paralleled a transition away from satellite Republics towards monarchy in the dependent territories. The Italian Republic was transformed into the Kingdom of Italy in 1806, and in the same year, the episode of the Batavian Republic was formally terminated by the elevation of Louis Bonaparte to the throne of Holland. Some parts of Napoleonic Europe were forced to undergo a third stage, when sections of the Empire were directly annexed to France. As Napoleon attempted to tighten the web of the Continental Blockade against Britain, he annexed the Ligurian coast, where Genoa was an important Mediterranean port to be secured in the struggle to keep out British goods.[6] For similar reasons, the French absorbed Tuscany (then the Kingdom of Etruria) in 1807 and the Papal States in 1809. Much to King Louis's disappointment, Holland was also transformed into French departments ruled directly from Paris.

The French occupation thus took various forms, ranging from satellite republic to satellite kingdom, including the special intendancies of the Illyrian provinces and the resurrected Polish state, the Duchy of Warsaw. Some territories were administered directly as French departments, while Prussia was subjected to a military occupation which was exceptionally rigorous. In some areas the Bonapartes ruled; but in the Kingdom of Italy, Napoleon was an absentee monarch. The Italians demanded that the thrones of France and Italy be separated; as Napoleon remained King of Italy, they were only partially satisfied. Uniformity of treatment was hard to achieve. French influence was always likely to be weaker in satellite states like the Duchy of Berg than it was in those areas subjected to direct annexation, like the Rhineland, where existing social structures were effectively destroyed and new élites promoted.[7]

The novelty of French legislation depended additionally on the strength of indigenous reform in the period *before* French conquest. The French attack on the old régime social structure was most profound in areas which had already experienced enlightened reform. The Netherlands had already had their own Patriot Revolution in the 1780s, when the lower bourgeoisie of artisans and small merchants had challenged the monarchy and the ruling Dutch oligarchies, inspired by a mixture of enlightenment ideals and Calvinist evangelism.[8] In Tuscany, Leopold of Habsburg had already abolished clerical tithes, and established free trade in grain, one of the main objectives of late eighteenth-century liberal economists. In Belgium and Piedmont, only the vestiges of seigneurialism still remained at the time of the French Revolution. In the Italian kingdom, French reforms took root because they continued initiatives already begun by eighteenth-century reformers.[9] Elsewhere, however, in Naples or in the Grand Duchy of Berg, the powers of aristocratic landowner-ship were very solidly entrenched. Here, the French presence accordingly had much greater revolutionary potential, but in the long run its impact was less far-reaching.[10]

All these factors conditioned the impact of the Napoleonic Revolution: the many faceted institutional character of the French régime, the time available to French administrators in occupied territory, as well as the force of local traditions and antecedents. These considerations compel historians to be careful before making generalisations about the whole of French-occupied Europe. Such nuances must be borne in mind when evaluating the major social revolution introduced by the French.

As was the case in revolutionary France, this revolution was generally supported by the bourgeoisie and enlightened sections of the nobility, but was frequently resisted by the Church and sometimes by the peasantry. But in Italy and Germany, there was to be no equivalent of the Vendean War of 1793, even in 1814, when resistance was at its height.[11]

The Napoleonic Empire and Social Reform

Seigneurial dues and seigneurial justice were abolished in French-dominated Europe. In Belgium and in the Batavian Republic, they had already been abolished as early as 1795. They were under attack in occupied Italy during the *triennio* of 1795–9. Elsewhere in Europe, the attack on feudal rights resumed in earnest after 1804. In Berg, serfdom was abolished, and Bavaria officially followed suit. Landed élites, however, expected to be compensated for the loss of these rights. In Berg and Westphalia, only personal obligations like labour services were abolished outright, whereas feudal burdens on land had to be "redeemed" by compensation payments.[12]

The destruction of seigneurial burdens promoted individual property rights and was a potential boost for agricultural development. The specific terms of French legislation in Germany, however, forced the peasants to pay for at least a part of their freedom. The French reforms thus respected the interests of the landowners, making it difficult for a class of free landowning peasants to emerge. Inevitably, the influence of local landowners often prevailed. Count Beugnot in Westphalia urged his impatient Emperor to consider the peculiar local conditions in which he was obliged to operate:

> The feudalism that exists in your state of Westphalia is not the weak and almost extinct feudalism that existed in France in 1789, where one could only observe privileges and honorific rights. Here feudalism is part of the social order, it is at its roots ... All reforms must be slow and measured; this is one of those matters where time is required for success.[13]

In Poland, similarly, serfdom was abolished in the Grand Duchy of Warsaw in 1807, which potentially liberated the agricultural labour market. *Corvée* (compulsory labour) contracts, however, remained.[14] A law of 1806 abolished the personal rights of seigneurs in the Kingdom of Naples, and swept away seigneurial justice, too, although the landlords were to be compensated for this. Traditional élites were extremely well entrenched in Naples, and income from seigneurial rights was highly concentrated. At the end of the eighteenth century, 80 per cent of all feudal revenue in the kingdom was collected by only 600 families.[15] The landowning aristocracy was rich, powerful and very compact. This made fundamental reform difficult, even under French occupation.

Aristocratic privileges were abolished, except in Poland. They were decreed out of existence in Berg and Westphalia in 1809, which meant that the nobility's fiscal immunities were destroyed, paving the way for a rational and more equitable system of taxation. In the ex-Prussian parts of Germany, the abolition of privilege also removed the social barriers which had prevented the bourgeoisie from buying land, and deterred the nobles from engaging in industry and commerce. The society of orders was thus under attack, and the French reforms undermined the corporations and privileged intermediary bodies which exerted so much influence in the Old Régime. The guilds disappeared, and the collective rights of the peasants would also give way to the partition of common land. The Napoleonic Revolution thus promoted both social equality and individualism, although it did not

necessarily aim at increasing the number of peasant proprietors.
The personal dependence of the peasantry on their landlord was
weakened, but without redistributing property in favour of small
landowners. The material condition of the peasants was sometimes
even worsened by the loss of common pasture land. The partition of
common land could provoke rural disturbances, where peasants
defended their collective rights against the French promotion of
agrarian individualism.[16]

The new Napoleonic law codes were transplanted into conquered
territory, together with all the social upheavals they registered. The
equality of all citizens before the law was recognised and the jury system was introduced. Civil marriage and divorce were made legal.
Individual property rights were protected and the division of inheritances was also introduced. Some of these ideas were bound to provoke misgivings and opposition in old régime Europe. In Dusseldorf
(Duchy of Berg), Count Beugnot pleaded for more time before the
code became law. Divorce, he reminded Napoleon, was still scarcely
known, even in non-Catholic areas. Napoleon would not wait: he
ordered full implementation by 1810.[17]

In Naples, too, King Joseph knew that divorce and civil marriage
would appear shocking innovations. The idea of equally divided
inheritances would also strike at the power of aristocratic landowners
to guarantee the continued domination of their extensive family
estates. As a result, Joseph avoided the full implementation of the
Code Napoléon for as long as he could.[18] In 1810, however, Napoleon
insisted that Joseph's successor Murat should implement the code in
southern Italy, even including the controversial legalisation of
divorce. The Civil Code was not fully applied in Rome, either,
although the judicial rights and privileges of the clergy were abolished by the French.

The introduction of the entire corpus of Napoleonic law codes,
with the abolition of privilege, Jewish emancipation, the end of primogeniture and the entailing of aristocratic estates suddenly over-
turned some of the basic certainties of old régime society. Stuart
Woolf concludes: "Reading the collections of decrees and laws
issued in these years creates the impression of a total abolition of
the past and the writing of a new page in the history of the Italian
peninsula."[19]

In Catholic Europe, French rule redefined relationships with the
Papacy as versions of the Concordat between Napoleon and the Pope
were implemented. A measure of French-style secularisation was

introduced everywhere except in Poland where there was no strong bourgeois class and, once again, the Church and nobility survived well. The Church lost its control of the registration of births, marriages and deaths, as well as its income from clerical tithes and its monopoly over education. In occupied Rome itself, the political authority of the cardinals was broken. The property of convents and religious orders was nationalised, and the clergy forced to take an oath of allegiance to the state, just as in France itself. The disappearance of the Papal court during the period of French annexation caused an economic as well as a political crisis. The Holy See had provided employment for merchants, artisans and professional men. The Roman bourgeoisie, as well as the popular classes, had some material reasons to lament the French attack on the Pope's spiritual and temporal authority.[20]

French legislation threatened a similar shock in Catholic Spain. Convents and monasteries were suppressed but, in addition, the French abolished the Spanish Inquisition. In so doing, they satisfied a long-standing liberal aspiration, and removed one of the hated targets of the eighteenth-century Enlightenment. At the same time, however, they deprived the clergy and traditional Catholics of (as they saw it) their protection against Jews and heretics.

In Spain, Italy and Germany, the property of religious orders was put on sale, just as the *biens nationaux* of the clergy had been sold in France after 1790. In one respect, however, the sale of clerical property in French-administered Europe did not imitate the auctions of *biens nationaux* in France. It was much rarer outside France for the sales to enlarge the number of small peasant proprietors. In general, the chief beneficiaries were either speculators or wealthy landowners who already had the liquidity to invest. The sale of national properties helped to rally the support of the élites to the French cause, tempting the landowning *notables* on whom the French hoped to base their rule.

Sometimes a considerable amount of property changed hands. In the four Rhineland departments, for example, the property sold has been estimated at 6.6 per cent of the surface area, and about 12 ½ per cent of all available agricultural land.[21] In the Department of Jemappes (Belgium), 11 per cent of cultivated land came up for sale.[22] In Jemappes, about one quarter of the land sold was bought by French bankers and army contractors, and three-quarters went to local bourgeois and administrators. In Hainault in Belgium, the clergy themselves bought 16 per cent of properties, and the bourgeoisie

57 per cent. The peasants' share was only 9.5 per cent.[23] Resales of property, however, by those who had bought early only to make a quick profit, may have indirectly increased the chances of peasants to acquire more property. This was apparently the case in the Saar–Mosel region.[24]

In Piedmont and the Kingdom of Italy, too, noble and bourgeois landowners took advantage of property sales. The poorer peasants were once again usually spectators, and sometimes victims, because land sales allowed agricultural entrepreneurs to concentrate their estates and economise on labour. The sale of church lands in the Cisalpine Republic and the Kingdom of Italy was a stage in the formation of a new landed élite, composed of the older aristocratic landowners, and a newly emerging class of non-noble *possidenti*, benefiting from the favourable conditions (land sales and the extension of public offices) of French rule.[25]

The impact of secularisation was quite different in Protestant Europe. In the Catholic heart of Europe, in Belgium or Italy, the land sales represented an unprecedented opportunity for enrichment and social mobility. In Holland, however, there was very little property to nationalise. In Britain, too, we might speculate that the French would not have succeeded in rallying the same support as they did in the Po valley. If Napoleon had successfully invaded the Kent coast, and installed Talleyrand as prefect of a hypothetical Department of the Thames, there would have been virtually no *biens nationaux* to sell. Britain, like Holland, had long since had its Protestant reformation.

Religious toleration for Protestants and Jews was another French innovation which meant much more in Italy or Germany than it did in the Batavian Republic or the Kingdom of Holland. The French completely redrew the political map of Germany, forcing Catholic and Protestant communities to live together under the same secular authority. In the Belgian departments, Jews and Protestants were given complete freedom of worship for the first time. As a result of French imperial influence, the revolutionary and Napoleonic period remains a landmark in the emancipation of European Jewry. The spirit of their emancipation, however, was that of the rational, utilitarian, eighteenth-century reformers, and it in no way resembled late twentieth-century liberal attitudes, which value cultural pluralism and respect for difference. The Jews were emancipated in order to make them available for assimilation as citizens of a modern, secular society. They were now available for conscription, and they were taxed on the same basis as other citizens. This was seen by their liberators as the beginning of a process of complete absorption into the host society.

The new French educational system was introduced wherever the French had the time and the money to devote to schooling. As in France, the attention of governments hardly stretched beyond the provision of secondary schooling following the model of the *lycées*. *Lycées* were established in the Kingdom of Italy and in Belgium, where the French language took up most of the first year's curriculum, and its use was essential for administrative employment.[26]

As far as university education was concerned, however, French rule did not always deliver what it promised. French *lycées* were established in the Duchy of Berg, but a new university in its capital, Dusseldorf, never materialised. Furthermore, political economy, taught in most German universities, was banned by Napoleon as a subversive discipline.[27] In Italy, the French established learned societies, engineering schools and veterinary training colleges.

The French improved roads and canals, and invested in public works for military purposes, and also for civilian and progressive ends. They organised the crossing of the Simplon pass and improved the Dutch dykes. In the Kingdom of Naples, the excavation of the Roman site at Pompeii continued, and the export of artefacts, which the Bourbon monarchy had been unable to prevent, was banned. The French literally brought enlightenment to the city of Naples: 1700 oil lamps were installed in the streets of the capital, and the Corso Napoleone was built.[28]

The French Empire therefore brought to its subjects a rational system of public administration, based on the unit of the department, governed at the superior level by a class of bureaucrats with international experience. Napoleonic rule relied on a class of professional administrators, competent to serve wherever needed as prefects, consuls, or ministers. One was Saliceti, a fellow Corsican-in-arms with the Bonapartes since the French Revolution, who was appointed as Minister in Lucca, Genoa and Naples. Another was Count Beugnot in Westphalia and Berg. Roederer, too, had an impressive career as a professional international bureaucrat, acting as minister in Switzerland and Holland, then reforming the finances in Naples before serving in Berg. Lebrun, the former consul, was another peripatetic imperial trouble-shooter, charged with overseeing the digestion by the Empire first of Liguria (1805–7) and then of Holland (1810–13).

The Conseil d'État in Paris welcomed trainee personnel from annexed territory, and helped to produce a pan-European governing class. Its members were expected to use modern techniques of government, by collecting detailed information and statistics on harvest yields, economic resources, and the wealth and political affiliations of local notables. Much of this was the work of the local prefect who was a vital link in the imperial administrative hierarchy. In the annexed departments, the prefect was expected to make an annual tour of his department and was directly responsible to the Minister of the Interior. He supervised conscription, police, religious affairs, economic life and the workings of the judiciary.

French administration aimed to provide prompt action, based on full access to information and a clear definition of the functions of each official concerned. The civil service was to operate according to expectations generated by regular practice and observance of the rule of law. If local finances needed overhauling, the French decreed it. In Naples, for example, Roederer simplified the fiscal system in two decisive blows: he abolished the wasteful system of tax-farming and levied a single uniform land tax. In many parts of Europe outside Prussia, the arrival of the French provided a first experience of efficient administration along rational lines.

The French campaign to familiarise local populations with the benefits of smallpox vaccination stands as a symbolic illustration of the clash between French rational administration and the anachronistic values of old régime Europe. In the Trasimeno Department, Roederer *fils* attempted to have everybody vaccinated, in an area whose previous ruler, the Pope, had refused to allow the practice, since it was decreed contrary to religious principles. In 1812–13, the French administration nevertheless succeeded in vaccinating one-third of new-born babies in the department.[29] But when the Pope was restored to power in 1815, vaccination was again officially condemned.

The Burdens of Occupation: Conscription and Taxation

Conscription and taxation provided the resources the Empire needed to keep the old régime powers at bay. Conscription was uneven, as it was in France, and the demands of the occupying power were moderated in practice by the local population's capacity to resist. Conscription had, after all, contributed to the bloody rising in the Vendée in March 1793, and similar civil strife was likely to erupt elsewhere in Europe. In Belgium, for instance, the introduction of the Jourdan conscription law in 1798 had sparked off a revolt. A similar rising occurred in the Tyrol in 1809, and military recruitment was at least one contributing factor. Joseph and Murat, wishing to raise the esteem in which they were regarded by the Neapolitans, introduced a rather muted form of conscription into the Kingdom of Naples. Only one conscript was drafted per every 1000 inhabitants.[30] But conscription *was* introduced eventually, in the Italian Republic in 1802, in the Duchy of Berg in 1807 and in Holland in 1810.

Every territory had its own way of dealing with French demands, although obedience was successfully enforced. The Neapolitans recruited convicts (who frequently deserted in Spain), and Louis Bonaparte conscripted orphans and foreign prisoners of war, and hired German mercenaries, in order to spare the indigenous Dutch population. In the Rhineland and Germany, which traditionally provided the shock-troops of several old régime armies, conscription was relatively heavy. Almost 5 per cent of the population of the left-bank Rhineland departments were called up between 1802 and 1814; at the same time, desertion rates were very low here: only 10 per cent deserted from the department of the Rhin-et-Moselle in 1808–9, an indication of the degree of acceptance of French rule in the peak years of imperial success.[31] Westphalia, with a population of just 2 million, made a sizeable contribution to the Empire in terms of manpower. Seventy thousand were drafted between 1808 and 1813 and 30 000 volunteered for military service. They were attracted by higher pay and more considerate treatment than they were used to, and perhaps by the fact that even in the imperial army they would be commanded by German officers. Westphalian contingents suffered heavy losses in Spain, Russia and the campaign of 1809: a high price to pay for rational taxation and internal free trade in the Empire's model German state.[32]

The mixed national composition of the Grande Armée of 1812 has already been remarked (Chapter 15). The army was a kind of international melting-pot, a social institution which brought together peasants from isolated villages all over the continent. It was an integrating institution, which could foster national or even international solidarities. Those who marched to Spain or Russia had a privileged view of the world, which was much broader than the very narrow horizons of the fellow villagers they left behind. Many different old régime German states were represented in the German contingents, and the Italian units did not respect the old political frontiers. Italy was resigned to conscription which swelled the army of the Italian Kingdom, although desertion rates were high. The French established military academies at Modena, Pavia, Bologna and Lodi, so that sons of bourgeois families could aspire to become career officers. In this way, French military demands may have unwittingly fostered the notion of a common Italian identity, within the ranks of the Grande Armée itself. At the highest level of command, the imperial armies were led by an international élite. Their generals included 70 Italians, 32 Poles, 15 Swiss, 18 Dutch, 10 Belgians, 20 Germans, and 19 English or Irish who had traditionally furnished French and continental armies with military careerists.[33]

French administration signified a French taxation system, or at least a system more rational than that of the Old Régime, put in place in an attempt to meet at least some of the Empire's military demands. Instead of the fiscal immunity of the nobility, which had made old régime taxation so inequitable and its revenue so inelastic, the Empire could now try to levy a single uniform tax on land. The territories dominated by France borrowed the French model, in which the main land tax was supplemented by taxes on commercial licences (*patentes*), moveable property and some luxury items. When this failed to meet the heavy demands of war, the proceeds of the sale of *biens nationaux* helped to cover the deficit, and new indirect taxes could be invented, although they invariably made the occupiers unpopular with consumers.

The huge sums spent on war in the period tend to disguise how much more efficient tax systems became under rational French inspiration. The revenues of the Kingdom of Italy, for example, rose by 50 per cent between 1805 and 1811, although the deficit still increased much faster, from 1 million to 5 million lire.[34] In Naples, Roederer replaced a tangled web of over 100 different Bourbon taxes with a single tax on land and industry. In Holland, the fiscal reformer Gogel introduced a uniform land tax, fixed at 25 per cent of all rental value. Death duties were levied, as well as taxes on *patentes*, movable property and an eighteenth-century equivalent of a wealth tax, a tax on servants. His project included a personal tax of 10 per cent on all other sources of income.[35] Holland was a society with a rich mercantile oligarchy whose interests were protected by Gogel's scheme; commercial profits were taxed at a lower rate than agricultural revenue.

In the Kingdom of Italy, the Piedmontese finance minister, Prina, also levied a single land tax, and even managed to balance the budget for a short time. It is of course true that he did not have the problems encountered in Poland or Westphalia, where substantial tracts of land were handed to imperial dignatories, so that their revenues could not be touched by the government. There was plenty of peasant resistance to Prina's indirect taxes: the tax on milling flour provoked the disturbances of 1809. Prina was to pay a high price for the exactions which made him the most successful finance minister of the Napoleonic Empire. There were attacks on the collectors of consumption taxes (*droits réunis*) in 1813–14, and an angry Milan crowd dragged Prina into the street and murdered him like a dog.

Modernising fiscal reformers like Prina and Gogel did not, therefore, make friends everywhere. In a sense, their hands were tied by the contradictory policies of the Empire itself. Financial success was very difficult when warfare devoured revenue faster than anyone could collect it. In addition, the estates delivered as rewards to imperial marshals and functionaries created large enclaves which severely limited the resources of some satellite states. By 1809, about a quarter of all such land donations were endowments of Westphalian properties.[36] As they were administered directly from France, and not by the Westphalian government, these entailed estates made it impossible to balance the budget in what had been hailed as a "model" Napoleonic state. Similar gifts were made from confiscated royal domains in the Duchy of Warsaw and handed to Davout, Lannes and Lefebvre, the new Duke of Danzig. It has been estimated that the Duchy of Warsaw was thus deprived of one-fifth of its potential revenue.[37] The reforming impulses of imperial expansion were thus paradoxically thwarted by Napoleon's need to exploit his conquests and distribute largesse to his victorious henchmen. The "Corsican clan" model of the Empire, as an apparatus for the acquisition and distribution of booty to the privileged few, was here in conflict with the reforming, modernising possibilities of French expansion.

17   The Napoleonic Empire: Collaboration and Resistance

Centralisation and Conservatism

French rule brought old régime Europe face to face with revolutionary notions of equality and individualism, the end of privilege and seigneurialism, and the secular state. One effect of this was to impose a uniform system of values on a very wide variety of European cultures and traditions. European societies under French rule were given the same law codes, the same system of secondary education, similar fiscal structures, and a version of the Concordat with the Catholic Church. The Napoleonic bureaucracy was inspired by a passion for rational regulation which could, at its worst, smother independent initiatives and inhibit the development of a pluralistic Europe. The French even recommended this standardising tendency as a virtue. The rulers of Bavaria and Baden were advised that "the adoption of the Napoleonic Code will be a blessing for the peoples of these states as it will eliminate the variety of customs that rule them."[1] Local customs were here identified with feudal obscurantism.

Some of the new subjects of the Empire, however, doubted the hegemonic assumption that French precepts could be universally transplanted into any kind of soil from Portugal to Cairo. In Berg, the German jurist von Allmedingen objected that "Perfect laws are the beautiful and free forms of the interior life of a nation: they come out of life itself. The Civil Code has not come out of the life of the German nation."[2] This firmly organic conception of law and administrative practice offers a valuable corrective to the Napoleonic Empire's impressive reforming record. It is a suitable preface to a discussion of some of the more profound implications and drawbacks of French domination: its centralisation, the lack of opportunity it provided for genuine self-determination, and Napoleon's social conservatism.

Paris remained the brain of the Napoleonic Empire. The existence of satellite republics or kingdoms implied at least some devolution of authority, but Napoleon insisted that their rulers should account to him regularly and frequently for all their decisions.

244

Eugène de Beauharnais, appointed Viceroy of Italy in 1805, was told to write daily to Napoleon, and to do nothing without prior permission. "If Milan were on fire," he was instructed, "you should let Milan burn and wait for instructions ... [do nothing without authority] even if the moon is about to fall on Milan."[3] Perhaps Eugène was too young and inexperienced to be allowed his freedom. At least Count Beugnot, who took over the Duchy of Berg in 1808, only reported to the Emperor every *week*. Napoleon, however, personally supervised the movements and organisation of his regiments in Berg, and demanded to be kept informed of budgetary details, down to the Duchy's monthly income. All the minutes of the council of state meetings in Dusseldorf were depatched to Paris.

This degree of centralised control inevitably produced delays. Requests for approval had to travel from the outer reaches of the Empire to the appropriate ministry in Paris, if not to Napoleon personally, and back again, before action could be safely taken. The hospital of Santa Maria Nuova in Florence was a particularly patient victim of bureaucratic procrastination. The hospital waited for fourteen months to get Napoleon's permission to sell off a few houses to pay its debts.[4] The Emperor's absences on military campaigns could impose further delays. Napoleon spent only 900 days out of a possible 3500 in Paris between 1805 and 1814. The year 1810 was the only one in this period when he remained in France without interruption.[5]

On the other hand, the Emperor's travels did not prevent him from personally galvanising local administrators into action. His passage through an important centre could be a shattering experience for his subordinates. In 1811, for example, the Emperor descended on Dusseldorf, and in the course of a two-day visit ordered the installation of the French judicial system, the establishment of a university, a *lycée*, four or five other secondary schools, and the implementation of a Concordat.

Occasionally, however, satellite rulers could undermine uniformity and the imperial will by developing their own independent policies. Louis in Holland and Murat in Naples both attempted to do this. Murat was an ostentatious soldier with a huge ego and a sartorial sense that made courtiers cringe. His garishly coloured uniforms, gigantic plumes, his capes and sabres earned him the nickname of "the Chief Bedouin" from Madame de Staël. Murat had been promoted because he was married to Caroline Bonaparte, who proved just as independent as her braggart of a husband, entertaining a series of lovers who included General Junot and probably prince Metternich. Murat, like King Louis, was reluctant to enforce the Continental System as rigorously as Napoleon required. Both attempted to cultivate a local following. Murat even went so far as to replace the French tricolour with the Neapolitan flag in 1811, and ordered all foreigners holding office in his kingdom to take Neapolitan citizenship. This incensed Napoleon, and his anger with Murat helped to provoke the latter's flamboyant attempts to forge a separate Italian destiny for himself as the Empire collapsed. Neither Louis nor Murat was ultimately successful. If Napoleon insisted, he could do as he did in 1810, forcing Louis to abdicate the throne of Holland so that France could annex his short-lived kingdom.

The French did not share all the benefits of the great Revolution with their imperial subjects. They paradoxically offered Europe no apprenticeship in the principles and practice of popular sovereignty. In France, Napoleon claimed that he alone personified the popular will. His imperial policy was similarly authoritarian, except that his rule was justified by conquest and not by plebiscite. He had come to power by liquidating the Directory's experiment in parliamentary representation, and he increasingly preferred to govern with the advice of technical experts. The same was generally true in the Empire, where representative institutions enjoyed only a token existence, if indeed they were tolerated at all.

The Polish example for once illustrates a general imperial pattern. The Polish Diet remained in existence in the Napoleonic Duchy of Warsaw, because the Emperor was unwilling to challenge the social and political eminence of the landowning nobility. According to the 1807 Constitution, the nobles were to elect sixty out of 100 members in the second chamber. This was merely window-dressing because real power lay with the professional bureaucracy. The Polish Diet met for only two weeks every two years and it enjoyed no legislative initiative.[6]

The French did not therefore look for support from democrats and republicans, to whom they allowed little or no political voice. Instead, they cultivated men of substance, the conservative and patrician landowners of Italy and central Europe. There was an apparent contradiction here, since the French Empire, as we have seen, swept away the feudal bases of élite power. The French, however, offered plenty of compensation to conservatives: they strengthened their social pre-eminence, offered the property of the Church for sale, maintained order and held radical forces in check.

Two individual examples of French success in securing the assistance of conservatives are those of Schimmelpennick in Holland, and Melzi in northern Italy. Both these leaders accepted that French rule was progressive, but they hoped at the same time to preserve the special identity of their territory. Schimmelpenninck, who was appointed Grand Pensionary of Holland in 1805, was a wealthy Amsterdam patrician and a substantial landowner in Overijssel. He worked to secure the departure of occupying French troops, a plebiscite which would test the legitimacy of the idea of monarchy in Holland, and access to office for the Dutch.[7] Schimmelpennick was gambling on squeezing some concessions out of the French in return for his compliance. He had agreed to become a political puppet, hoping to salvage some independence for the Dutch in the process. But he had little to show for his collaboration. French forces did not withdraw and the French rejected his republicanism.

The career of Melzi d'Eril was very similar. Melzi was a Milanese aristocrat and a strong anticlerical who became vice-president of the Italian Republic. He saw that cooperation with the French had several possible advantages. The French presence would help him to crush the radical threat and build a large independent state in northern Italy. He would open careers to talent and gradually break down the urban separatism that had for so long paralysed the Italian peninsula. Like Schimmelpenninck, Melzi was valuable to France as a representative of local conservative leadership who welcomed Napoleonic rule. Melzi believed that Italian interests would be better served by working with the French instead of against them.[8] Like Schimmelpenninck, Melzi was poorly rewarded by Napoleon. Napoleon would not allow the Republic of Italy to establish its own diplomatic corps, nor would he withdraw French troops. Melzi managed to create an Italian army, but was forced to send contingents to prepare for the invasion of Britain. French power thus would not tolerate the kind of independence envisaged by local conservative leaders like Schimmelpenninck and Melzi. The threat of direct annexation was enough to ensure their obedience to Paris. As officials of Holland or Italy, they could at least preserve the illusion of separate status. That status would be altogether lost if their territory was administered directly from Paris like any other French department.

The victims of this unequal alliance between Napoleon and local conservatism were the democratic movements which had emerged in the 1790s (or earlier in the Dutch case). Napoleon gave the supporters of Italian unification no freedom to move, and no forum in which to express themselves. The patriots of Milan were restrained as far as possible and hopes for Italian unity received a humiliating snub in the Treaty of Campoformio in 1797, when Napoleon handed Venice to the Habsburgs. In so doing, he showed as little regard for the wishes of the inhabitants of the *Serenissima* as any dynastic ruler of the Old Régime. Proposals for democratic reform, including the introduction of a system of poor relief, fell upon deaf ears.[9]

Collaboration and Resistance

The Napoleonic Empire had many collaborators, as well as some resistors. Broadly speaking, serious resistance to the French was confined to the 1790s and the dying years of the Empire. Between 1804 and at least 1810 there was a trend towards closer collaboration with the French (except in Spain). The French victories of 1806 and 1809 gave the Empire an aura of invincibility which encouraged cooperation with the occupying power. There was nothing in this "middle" period to compare with the anti-French upsurge of the late 1790s.

The social profile of Napoleon's supporters and his enemies, however, needs to be clearly defined. Many social groups welcomed French rule as a liberating force. The Jews, for instance, achieved legal emancipation, even if they were still the object of suspicion and hatred. In Livorno, a cosmopolitan port whose international trade collapsed as a result of the blockade, anti-French feeling intensified as economic stagnation worsened. The Jewish community, though, remained pro-French. Those who hated the French also hated French sympathisers. As a result, anti-French hostility overlapped with antisemitism.[10]

In general class terms, those who collaborated with the French belonged to the same social groups on whom the Napoleonic régime relied for support in France itself. French rule employed and cultivated the support of an élite of notables, consisting of administrators, landowners and businessmen. They were mainly of bourgeois origin, but they included members of the nobility who also saw advantages in supporting the French. In particular, the property transfers of the period assisted both the consolidation of existing élites and the promotion of the bourgeoisie.

The Rhineland provides a good example of the Empire's appeal to merchants and manufacturers. On the annexed left bank of the Rhine, the textile manufacturers of Aachen and Krefeld enjoyed an unprecedented boom under French rule. They profited from an extraordinary situation: as part of France, they had access to a new and unified market, while their chief competitors were disadvantaged: British goods were officially excluded from continental markets, and German competitors were obstructed by the tariff barriers erected by the French along the Rhine. By 1811, the Department of the Ruhr was one of the most industrialised in the entire Empire.[11]

The businessmen of the Rhineland departments did not share the anti-French feelings being nurtured by German intellectuals in university centres like Heidelberg. They experienced an administration which offered a complete break with the past and incorporated their interests in departmental administration, even at the local level. They took advantage of the nationalisation of ecclesiastical property to expand their concerns, setting up new workshops in church buildings. As the statistician Demian remarked in Cologne in 1815: "The convents, once devoted to the cultivation of holy indolence, now resounded with the deafening noise of industrial activity."[12] Between 1789 and 1881, the value of Aachen's wool production doubled. The number of silk-manufacturing enterprises in Krefeld doubled, too, and seven new cotton-spinning firms were established in Cologne between 1799 and 1805. Rhenish businessmen were in close contact with political officials. As Jeffry Diefendorf demonstrates, they had found a state apparatus which responded to their interests.[13]

When the French withdrew, the Rhineland business community had to accommodate to their new masters the Prussians. Belderbusch, who had become Mayor of Bonn, and the Krefeld silk manufacturer von der Leyen, who had been elevated to the imperial nobility, had no difficulty in swearing loyalty to Prussia in 1815.[14] Even under Prussian rule, there was no question of turning back the clock on the French reforms of the previous decade. The social gains of the French period became permanent.

The bourgeoisie and the nobility stood to benefit from the secularisation of church property, in their role as landowners. Members of the urban bourgeoisie could extend their businesses or make lucrative investments in rural real estate. The commercial classes bought 31 per cent of the land sold in Piedmont, and the liberal professions accounted for another 19 per cent.[15] Speculators with ready capital could cream off a large portion for resale. In the Ruhr, the entrepreneur Daniel Brammarz made no fewer than 197 of such speculative purchases. Brammarz and those like him emerged as members of a new class of landowning capitalists in the region.[16]

The nobility was not slow to consolidate its landholdings either. In the Arno department, 39 per cent of land purchasers were aristocrats.[17] The peasantry benefited very little in northern Italy, but traditional landowners joined with merchants and administrators to seize the opportunity for enrichment offered by French rule. For this reason, some Marxist historians have seen the episode of the land sales as a colossal missed opportunity, in which the chance for a substantial property redistribution in favour of smallholders was discarded.[18] The attack on seigneurialism left the nobles and the wealthy bourgeois as dominant powers in northern Italian society.

Many aristocrats, then, rallied to the Napoleonic régimes. The most reactionary nobles forced the French to compromise, to delay the implementation of the law codes, and to guarantee adequate compensation for the abolition of seigneurial dues. The most enterprising amongst them supported French reforms, entered state service and made substantial material gains. One example is that of the Piedmontese family of the Cavours, which in the next generation was to produce Count Camillo, a leading figure in the Italian *Risorgimento*, and later to become Prime Minister of Piedmont and Italy. The Cavours were firm supporters of the French. They bought *beni nazionali* and became successful aristocratic capitalists. They were innovative agronomists who bred horses, introduced merino sheep, and developed the manufacture of linen. French was Cavour's first language and he later put into practice further measures of secularisation in Piedmont, as well as engineering Piedmontese expansion under the auspices of the third Napoleon.

Germany, too, provides similar examples of the consolidation of the business and landowning classes under Napoleonic rule. The Treaty of Lunéville of 1801 expropriated fifty-six princes and seigneurs on the left bank of the Rhine. Many nobles promptly emigrated from French territory. In the Ruhr, however, large numbers of aristocratic businessmen or landowners stayed and rallied to the French. The abolition of seigneurial dues clearly did not have a drastic effect on their sources of income in this region. There were still four old régime aristocrats among the five highest tax-payers of the Ruhr department, and seven nobles among the eight leading tax-payers of the Rhin-et-Moselle department.[19]

In Westphalia, most of the prefects appointed were aristocrats, but there were limits to their commitment to the new régime. They were often reluctant to leave their locality and their family estates. They would often therefore refuse postings or promotions which took them out of their native territory. Civil servants drawn from the noble classes were not geographically mobile, and so they rarely joined that band of peripatetic international bureaucrats encountered in Chapter 16. They were quite prepared to serve as sub-prefects or local mayors, as they did for instance in Liège or Brussels. Wherever they were located, in Italy, Germany or elsewhere, the landowners were terrified of popular disturbances. This, too, drove them into the arms of the French, who guaranteed law, order and their protection against the unruly subordinate classes.

The professional and administrative bourgeoisie must also be classed amongst the strongest supporters of the French. French administration offered new posts in a well-oiled bureaucratic machine. In 1805, the financial administration of the Kingdom of Italy alone employed over 5000 public servants. The expanding imperial bureaucracy welcomed the Italian élite and thus helped to establish the regime on a solid local base.[20] The sons of the bourgeoisie were keen to serve the administrative apprenticeship offered by the French. In the case of the Tuscan bourgeoisie, for example, or the French sympathisers (the *afrancesados*) in Spain, Napoleonic administration promised to continue the enlightened principles of late eighteenth-century government.

Opportunities for educated, middle-class functionaries were limited only by the French insistence on reserving sensitive posts for candidates of French origin. In other words, the highest posts in finance, justice and other branches of the administration tended to be given to Frenchmen by preference. In Piedmont, the French struggled to establish an impartial magistracy which could arbitrate in the tangled web of local vendettas.[21] Trials of brigands in Umbria were entrusted to French military courts and not to local magistrates who, it was assumed, might be susceptible to intimidation, or be lenient towards criminals who were local personalities.[22]

The prefectoral corps, however, was gradually internationalised. Altogether, there were thirty-two prefects from territories outside the frontiers of pre-Napoleonic France. They were rarely appointed in their own region; three Belgians were posted to the Hanseatic departments, and Italian prefects were nominated in Belgium. Thirteen prefects came from Italy, 9 from Belgium, 7 from the Netherlands, 2 from Switzerland but only 1 from Germany.[23] As well as being internationalised, the prefectoral corps also became more professional. The prefects appointed by Melzi, when he was vice-president of the Italian Republic, were drawn from his own network of aristocratic families. Eugène de Beauharnais, as his successor, looked instead for candidates with administrative experience, although he still drew his prefects from the conservative élite.[24]

The collaborators of the Napoleonic Empire therefore emerged from several social groups. They included the commercial and industrial bourgeoisie in economically developed areas like the Rhineland. They also included the administrative bourgeoisie, who might be expected to favour a régime which embodied the end of feudal restrictions and the opening up of careers to talent. Aristocrats also figured amongst the collaborators, and the French sought the support of the landowning élites. These élites, including the gentry or *galantuomini* of the Mezzogiorno, did not always enjoy a broad basis of support. They were threatened in the last years of French rule by resistors, representing the forces of the Old Régime, and above all by the local peasantry.

There were essentially two main kinds of resistors to the Napoleonic régime in Europe: the traditionalists and the radicals. The radicals and nationalists failed to present a real threat to imperial stability and can be briefly dealt with. Just as Napoleon had purged the Tribunat of the liberal opposition in Paris in 1802, so the transformation of the sister republics into satellite kingdoms tended to silence the opposition on the left. There was a Jacobin rising in Bologna in 1802, provoked by the French order to disband the local National Guard, and led by a secret society of *stilettanti* (stiletto-holders).[25] The rising was crushed by French troops. Radical ideas were discussed throughout the period in secret societies like the *carbonari* (charcoal-burners) in southern Italy, or the guelphs in central Italy. They drew their membership from amongst army officers and freemasons, but they never enjoyed a wide enough basis of support to seriously worry the French. The secret societies survived the Empire, and in the period of the Restoration nourished the liberal conspiracies which produced some of the early heroes and martyrs of the movement for Italian unification.

Serious resistance to the French did not develop until the last years of Empire, when anti-conscription disturbances occurred in many areas. Such riots occurred in Holland in 1811–12, and after the Dutch losses of the Russian campaign revolt became more generalised. The retreat of the French after 1813 encouraged rebellion to come out into the open. In Amsterdam, customs-houses were burned down and the property of collaborators was destroyed. In Overijssel, the Russian troops were welcomed as liberators from the French.[26] A similar pattern can be found in the Duchy of Berg, where in 1813 the workers of Solingen shouted their support as the Cossacks arrived.[27] The timetable of radical resistance in the Empire thus closely paralleled the rhythm of liberal opposition in France. Crushed by 1802, the ex-Jacobins only re-emerged as the Empire foundered after 1812.

The traditionalist and especially clerical resistance to the Napoleonic régime was more widespread. Unlike the Jacobin opposition, which was inspired by frustrated hopes of reform, the clerical backlash was a response to the French attack on the solidly entrenched position of the Church in old régime society. Ecclesiastical taxation (tithes) had been abolished, which left many priests destitute. The sale of church property undermined the church's role as a landowner and a temporal power, and reduced its capacity to act as a source of health care and charitable relief for the poor. The Church lost its monopoly of education, while the registration of births, marriages and deaths was secularised. Divorce was introduced, while Protestants and Jews were emancipated – measures which were anathema in fiercely Catholic countries like Spain and Belgium. It is not surprising, therefore, that much of the anti-French resistance was clerical in its inspiration. In Rome and in Belgium, it was difficult to find collaborators amongst the Catholic élites; in Spain, it was almost impossible.

In Belgium, the oath of hatred of monarchy imposed by the Directory met widespread hostility from the Catholic clergy. Deportation orders were issued for thousands of priests, although only 445 were actually deported.[28] After the French invasion of the Papal States, and the captivity of the Pope, it was even more difficult to persuade Catholic leaders to accept French legislation. In Italy, too, priests joined the opposition to the French in 1813, if not before. "Al diavolo gli scommunicati," demanded clerical propaganda, "May the devil take this excommunicated race", and the French were denounced as notorious freemasons and despoilers of God's Temple.[29] In Spain, as we have seen, the property of convents was confiscated and the Inquisition abolished. Both priests and the upper clergy joined the resistance to the French, and monks were to be found amongst the guerrillas. One-third of the membership of the rebel Cortes of Cadiz was made up of Spanish bishops.[30] In Spain, the French forces therefore confronted long-standing traditions of medieval bigotry. The guerrilla war against the French was a struggle between the Counter-Reformation and the French Revolution.

Enlightened French ideas appealed most to the urban bourgeoisie; making them acceptable to the rural masses of Europe was a daunting task. In Spain, Belgium and southern Italy, the clergy seemed to have

privileged access to the peasantry, and to be more successful in mobilising the rural population than were the French administrators and
their agents. Thus the gap between the collaborators and resistors was
a social one, between educated bourgeois and progressive aristocrats
on one side, and the clergy and peasantry on the other. There was
sometimes also a cultural chasm between pro-French collaborators
and their enemies. The world of popular belief proved very resilient
towards the rational, reforming ideologies of learned culture.

The sale of clerical land, as we have seen, profited the landowning
and commercial élite, but did not usually produce substantial material benefit to peasant proprietors. The liberalisation of the economy
promoted values of individual property ownership which were often
alien to rural communities dependent on the enjoyment of collective
rights and common pasture. In these ways, peasants were likely to feel
excluded and challenged by new revolutionary bourgeois ideologies.
Peasant interests in the preservation of communal rights, the acquisition of land, and price controls lay squarely in the path of the capitalist and individualist values which underpinned French social
reforms. In the south of Italy, the reformers and the Jacobins were, in
the eyes of the peasantry, wealthy urban property-owners who had no
point of contact with humble villagers. An oft-quoted local jingle
expressed popular hostility to well-heeled, educated reformers:

> He who has bread and wine
> Has to be a Jacobin.[31]

In 1799, the Neapolitan Jacobins had attempted to bridge the gap
between the urban revolution and a suspicious peasantry. They faced
similar problems to those with which middle-class revolutionaries had
grappled in France: how to educate people in the new ideas of freedom, equality, popular sovereignty, the rights of citizens, and the new
role of religion in a secular society. A great popularising effort had to
be launched, but in Naples, as elsewhere, it was undertaken by a
small, educated minority who were attempting to revitalise a *basso
popolo* thought to be still heavily sedated by clerical influence. In fact,
propagandists for the reforming cause at first relied on enlightened
clergymen to spread the word. The best way to disseminate new ideas
was to use age-old methods of oral transmission, speak to the masses
in local dialect, in their traditional meeting-places, the churches and
the village squares. The message of the new secular state had to be
mediated through a variety of channels, including priests, municipal
officers, doctors and other *galantuomini* (gentry). In Venetia, for

example, the parish clergy were ordered by their bishops to collaborate with the French. Whatever the channels of diffusion, the message
of individualist egalitarianism remained an alien one, and it had a
fatal weakness in that it rested on the importation of foreign models
from France. As Vincenzo Cuoco wrote:

> The opinion of the patriots and those of the people were not the
> same; they had different ideas, different customs and even differ-
> ent languages. This same admiration for foreigners which had
> slowed down our culture in the time of the king was the same that
> formed, at the beginning of the Republic, the greatest obstacle to
> the establishment of Liberty.[32]

The attacks on the French in 1799, and during the imperial period,
showed the failure of bourgeois collaborators to bridge the enormous cultural abyss which separated them from the peasantry.

The "two nations" of the propertied and the popular remained far
apart in occupied Europe. The Italian kingdom has so far provided
us with illustrations of collaboration, but the extreme south of the
Italian peninsula will serve as an example of the complexities of
peasant resistance to French rule. The peasants often resisted
French taxation in isolated and sporadic risings, just as they had
always resisted Bourbon, Papal or Austrian taxation. Antifiscal protest, in other words, was nothing new. Insurrection, Napoleon
warned his brother Joseph, was inevitably to be expected sooner or
later. It could be dealt with, he advised, by burning a few villages and
carrying out a few exemplary executions (which worked everywhere
except in Spain).[33] What the French added to this situation was the
burden of conscription, which sparked off the Tyrolean resistance of
1809. The situation in the south was complicated by the presence of
the British fleet, which continued to use Sicily as a base of operations. The British did not scruple to give Calabrian rebels financial
assistance.

Peasant revolt, however, was multifaceted, and it is unwise to reduce
its cause to any single factor whether it be taxation, conscription or
hatred of the French foreigners. In the Tyrol, for example, the resistance to conscription was clericalised and exploited by Austria, and the
peasants fought for the unlikely slogan "God, Emperor and Fatherland", as well as against Jews and Protestants.[34] In Calabria, they fought
out of poverty, despair and in reaction to the land shortage. Their
resistance to the French was superimposed on more fundamental
local struggles. Sometimes these took the form of long-term social

conflicts between lords and peasants in the countryside. At other times, wealthy graziers themselves might condone brigandage, supporting the preservation of communal pastures from enclosures and the spread of cereal cultivation.[35]

Peasant resistance (except in Spain) could usually be localised, contained and crushed by the French. In Calabria, banditry was endemic, and the exceptional circumstances of the French period temporarily turned it into a widespread political revolt. Bandit gangs, formed from the remnants of the Papal and Bourbon armies and using their uniforms and weapons, attacked tax-collectors, local officials and customs officers. One of the most notorious bandit leaders of the period was Pezza, nicknamed Fra Diavolo (Brother Devil), although he had no connection with holy orders. In the rebellion of Fra Diavolo, pagan superstition merged with antifiscal protest. His father had been killed in the French repression of the rising of 1799, so that his rebellion also took the form of a traditional family vendetta against the French.[36]

In 1799, Fra Diavolo had gathered a band 1700 strong which dominated the countryside north of Naples. He waylaid anyone venturing on the road from Rome to Naples, and blocked the French garrison in the coastal town of Gaeta. He was eventually arrested, but then escaped, which added to the growing legend of his invulnerability. Fra Diavolo, it was believed, carried the dried head of a viper wrapped in silk as a charm which magically protected him from danger.[37]

In 1806, the French occupation of Naples provoked a resurgence of banditry. With the approval of the Bourbon monarchy, and with English aid, Fra Diavolo continued to plunder and carry out brutal assassinations against the French. The bourgeoisie, fearful of a more widespread popular insurrection, and struggling with the dead weight of the feudal past, did nothing to enlist popular support. Fra Diavolo's resistance appealed to the lower clergy, as well as the rural population, and mobilised their resentments against both the French and local landowners. At the height of his activity in Calabria, he tied down 10 000 French troops and was responsible for a series of hideous atrocities. He massacred the French garrison at Itri, some of whom were found with their hands tied behind their backs and disembowelled.[38] He was eventually captured and hung in 1806, much to the relief of Neapolitan property-owners.

He had been given a licence to kill by the British and King Ferdinand and was able to operate on a large scale, because a class war in the countryside briefly coincided with opposition to foreign invasion.

Brigandage was by no means created by the French but their presence helped to give it mass support in the Kingdom of Naples. The French briefly found themselves in the position of defending landowners against a peasant jacquerie. Meanwhile, the impotent pro-French bourgeoisie was caught helplessly between popular violence on one hand, and the powerful forces of agrarian conservatism on the other.

The Napoleonic Empire and Nationalism

In exile on the island of St Helena, Napoleon posed as the far-sighted and benevolent sponsor of national aspirations in Italy. He asserted:

> As for the 15 million Italians, their unification was already very advanced; it was necessary only to watch, as the convergence of ideas and legislation grew daily towards maturity amongst them, together with that sure, infallible cement of all human societies, unity of thought and feeling. The reunion of Piedmont, Parma, Tuscany and Rome to France was only intended as a temporary stage, and had no other object but to oversee, guarantee and promote the national education of the Italians.[39]

The patronising tone of this reflection hardly needs emphasis, and it also illustrates the French assumption that they were the sole repositories of political wisdom, which was noted in Chapter 16. Napoleon's comments do not represent an analysis of past events so much as an attempt to construct a myth of Napoleon as the friend of emerging nationalities. His nephew, Napoleon III, was to be the chief beneficiary of this myth, when the Piedmontese sought his support in the 1850s.

Napoleon's comments on St Helena represent a mystification of events because, as we have seen, the Empire leaned on conservatives, and discouraged or repressed the radicals or Jacobins who aspired to national unity. In Prussia, furthermore, ideas of nationalism developed in intellectual circles *in opposition* to the very exacting French military occupation. Ideas of nationalism, however, in Prussia or elsewhere, had as yet no popular appeal. They existed only in the writings and imagination of a small group of writers and intellectuals who, as we have seen, were sometimes separated from the ordinary masses by a huge cultural divide. Popular revolt in Spain showed the European intelligentsia what barbarity could be unleashed if national insurrections against the French were encouraged, and they recoiled in horror from the consequences.

French rule did, however unwittingly, assist the development of the nation-state in nineteenth-century Europe, although it did not help nationalists in the way Napoleon later implied. The incorporation of small political communities in a large international Empire helped to break down the local and provincial loyalties which were obstacles to the growth of a wider consciousness. The maps of Germany and Italy were redrawn, not of course in order to unite them, but the result, in spite of the French, was to open up the possibility of further steps towards national unity. In the Rhineland, ninety-seven petty states and jurisdictions were replaced by just four French departments of roughly equal size. The Kingdom of Italy brought together a popula- tion of 7 million Italians under a common government. In this pro- cess, some proud cities lost their special status as they were merged into a larger territorial unit. This kind of dislocation happened in Cologne, Bonn, or Bologna which very much resented the fact that Milan was the seat of government. Nevertheless, in spite of them- selves, the French were contributing to the erosion of municipal par- ticularism. The armies and the administrative services of the Empire also helped to break down old barriers. In the Kingdom of Italy, for instance, Tuscans, Genoese, Piedmontese, and Romans could all compete for jobs and find employment in a common administrative enterprise.

Social and economic transformations under the French also showed the way forward to greater unity. The weakening of the soci- ety of orders and the elimination of special privileges undermined aristocratic resistance to the emergence of a modern nation-state in the future. In establishing internal free trade, the French helped to open up regional economies. It must be admitted that the Napo- leonic Empire imposed new tariff barriers which disrupted trade pat- terns, but the French did rationalise and reduce the many customs tolls levied on navigation up the Rhine. Internal customs dues were abolished in Naples in 1807, and in Berg in 1808. The simplification of the political and commercial geography of Germany was a per- manent achievement of the Napoleonic period.

The Napoleonic states of Europe did not then collapse because of a widespread upsurge of nationalist sentiment against them. Nationalist ideologies meant very little to workers and peasants in the first half of the nineteenth century. It was not until the very end of the century that nationalism acquired a mass following. The Belgians did not expel the French in the way that they later rose against the Dutch monarchy which ruled them between 1815 and 1830. There was no decisive revolt in Italy either. In 1806, when the Neapolitan army was defeated, there was no movement in support of the Bourbons. When, in 1813, the English landed at Viareggio, in an attempt to hasten the disintegration of the Empire, no popular movement occurred in Tuscany.[40] There was no revolution against Eugène de Beauharnais in the Italian Kingdom in 1814. Murat's last-ditch attempt to rally pan-Italian support met with little response. The French withdrew from Italy not in response to internal resistance, but as a result of French military defeats elsewhere in Europe.

They left after laying the foundations for the later development of the nation-state. New social structures had been put in place all over French-dominated Europe. The peasantry had been emancipated from seigneurial burdens, and new opportunities for advancement beckoned the educated bourgeoisie. Many obstacles to commercial and industrial development had been removed. The interests of landowning élites had everywhere been protected, and so the means of production (both landed and industrial capital) remained very largely in the same hands as before. There was one important exception to this, however, which was the sale of ecclesiastical lands during the French régimes. Schools, taxes, law courts and judicial procedures, as well as the role of the Church, had been reformed, and a large number of Europeans had had some practical experience of the modern secular state, with its professional bureaucracy and conscripted armies. In areas like the Rhineland, which had experienced twenty years of French rule, the legacy of the French Revolution was permanent and there would be no return to the structures and institutions of the old régime.

18   The Economy at War

France never had an industrial revolution. At least, she did not experience an industrial revolution in the British sense of a sudden sharp
rise in economic growth and manufacturing output, associated with
industrial concentration, widespread factory-building and rapidly
accelerating urbanisation. Instead, the rhythm of France's industrial
growth was more gradual and more consistent. It had begun in the
mid-eighteenth century, when most industrial activity still took place in
the countryside, and it continued at a steady pace throughout the nineteenth century. Not until the 1930s was the number of people engaged
in agriculture surpassed by the size of France's industrial workforce.[1]
The period of the Consulate and Empire, although turbulent, was too
short to have a profound impact on these long-term trends.

The Revolution had redefined the nature of individual property and
destroyed seigneurialism. It had established a legal and social environ-
ment in which capitalist agriculture and commercial development could
potentially prosper. At the same time, however, it produced a decade of
war and upheaval in which normal economic activity was severely disrupted. The economic benefits of revolutionary change, postponed by
war and political trauma, were not apparent until the more peaceful
years of the nineteenth century. In the space of fifteen years between
1800 and 1815, then, there were only patchy signs that a radical break
had occurred in the growth pattern of the French economy.

War dominated the economic life of the period. Although agricultural development appeared static, trade and industry were shaken
by the consequences of war and conquest: the exploitation of
conquered markets, enforced protectionism, and greater state control. The colonial trade, which had been the leading sector of the
French economy in the Old Régime, collapsed and did not recover.
The steps taken towards free trade at the end of the Old Régime, cul-
minating in the Pitt–Vergennes Treaty of 1786 with Britain, became
obsolete in the era of the Continental Blockade. We must resist the
tendency to make Napoleon's Continental System responsible for all
the evidence of economic decline in the period. The blockade confirmed trends which were already present: it did not cause, for

example, the decline of Venice or Holland's industrial malaise. Regardless of the war, their decline was irreversible anyway.

War had positive as well as negative effects, as this chapter will show. Some sectors of the economy were ruined but others flourished, and a few were significantly modernised. Some specific areas, such as cotton manufacture, experienced a decisive phase of mechanisation and industrialisation in this period. Dynamic sectors must be distinguished from the sluggish, and those stimulated by the war from those depressed by the abnormal conditions it imposed. This can be attempted by considering trade and industry under the Napoleonic Empire as a tale of three cities: Bordeaux, Strasbourg and Ghent, representing in turn the victims of war (the port of Bordeaux), the temporary beneficiaries (the transit trade of Strasbourg) and those who collected permanent dividends from it (the textile masters of Ghent).

Agriculture

Agriculture made a slow recovery after the upheaval of the revolutionary decade, but overall productivity levels did not exceed those of the 1780s.[2] As seen in Chapter 11, a rise in agricultural wages was partially cancelled out by the accompanying rise in rents and prices of essential foodstuffs. Higher rents and prices produced healthy profits for large commercial landowners. They were a sign that the expanding population was increasing consumer demand. By 1814, France's total population was over 30 million.[3]

Table 17.1   A Provincial Labourer's Wages, 1790–1819 (measured in 5-year averages, indexed to 1790–4)

Years	Wheat	Wages
1790–94	100	100
1800–04	121	140
1805–09	98	158
1810–14	132	171
1815–19	139	167

Source: T.J.A. LeGoff and D.M.G. Sutherland, "The Revolution and the Rural Economy", in A. Forrest and P. Jones (eds.), *Reshaping France: Town, County and Region during the French Revolution* (Manchester: Manchester University Press, 1991), p.73

As Table 17.1 nevertheless suggests, good harvest yields made the Consulate and Empire a period of relative prosperity. In spite of the crisis of 1810–11, nothing approached in severity either the famine and high mortality of 1795 or the disaster of 1817 (Document 17.1).

DOCUMENT 17.1   THE PROBLEM OF FOOD SUPPLIES

The Minister of Commerce and Manufactures reports on the problems of feeding the population of Rouen in the 1812 crisis.

Paris, 20 March 1812

Sire,

I feel obliged to acquaint Your Majesty with the present situation in the Department of the Seine-Inférieure, with respect to food supplies.

The Prefect informs me that the price of grain has risen so high at recent markets that bread is being sold in his department at 6 ½ to 7 *sous* per lb.; that in Rouen, the local authorities have managed so far to keep it at 5 ½ *sous*; but that they have been forced to allow an increase, to assist the bakers, and prevent the population of surrounding areas from arriving *en masse* at the doors of Rouen bakeries, where bread can be obtained more cheaply than in outlying areas.

Measures have been taken to forestall disturbances and prevent excesses. The police are on constant alert. The Guard of Honour is ready to mount up if needed. Platoons of National Guards, consisting of well-known citizens can be quickly assembled. The instigators of trouble, should there be any, will be immediately arrested.

The Prefect believes that these measures would prevent any disorder, if it were not for a more serious problem which must be addressed.

The farmers of Louviers, Andely, Des Andelys and Pontaudemer (Eure) who traditionally supply Rouen and who desire to continue to do so, dare not send their grain, because supply wagons have already been looted on the highways. The Prefect urgently requests that a detachment of 2 or 300 cavalry be despatched to Rouen, to enlighten the attitudes of the people and to protect the circulation of grain.

On the 6th of this month, the French corsair *L'Epervier* captured and brought into Cherbourg an American vessel carrying 2,717 barrels of flour destined for London.

Could not the government use this flour, reimbursing its value at a later date to whoever has a claim on it? ...

Your Majesty granted some licences at my request to merchants of Le Havre to export goods to England, on the condition that they returned with rice.

One of their ships entered Le Havre on the 12th of this month, with a cargo of 695 sacks and 249 barrels of Carolina rice. Other vessels with similar cargoes are expected.

I will not hesitate to execute the orders which Your Majesty sees fit to give me on the proposals which I have the honour of submitting to him,

I am, Sire, with the profoundest respect, the very loyal and very obedient servant and subject of Your Royal and Imperial Highness,

Count Collin de Sussy.

(Translated from Archives Nationales AF IV.1059)

The war and the maritime blockade deprived France of supplies of colonial goods, including sugar and dyes, which were heavily in demand from the expanding cotton-manufacturing industry. Substitute crops were introduced, to provide domestic sources of these goods. These were the only serious attempts at crop innovation in the period, and they met with mediocre success. Sugar-beet was planted in the north, but the return of peacetime conditions after 1815 put an end to this experiment. Dyes like indigo were developed in the Vaucluse with more success. These crops, like the potato, were still of minor importance. Although potatoes took up 8 per cent of cultivated land in the Moselle department, they were still seen primarily as animal-feed.[4]

No striking breakthrough occurred in the rural economy. Even the most pessimistic analysts of the revolutionary period, however, cannot deny the enormous success of the wine industry. The prosperity of viticulture under Napoleon is all the more impressive, since government revenue from consumption taxes on alcohol more than doubled in the Empire.[5] Rising domestic demand was paralleled by increasing demand for exported wine. Champagne sales to eastern and central Europe soared; after the Peace of Amiens in 1802,

Europe rushed to replenish its champagne cellars. Exports accounted for three-quarters of all champagne sales in this period.[6] Bordeaux vineyards similarly exported about one-third of their vintage, and trade was boosted by peace, and by very good harvests in 1802 and 1803.[7] In Alsace, too, wine growers prospered, selling regularly to thirsty French armies, and to markets in Bavaria and the rest of Germany. The Haut-Rhin department exported one-eighth of its vintage in 1807.[8]

The overall impact of the French Revolution on agriculture is a hotly debated issue. Marxist-oriented historians, like Soboul or McPhee, argue that the Revolution created the conditions which made possible, in the long run, the development of commercialised agriculture along capitalist lines. The end of seigneurialism and its burdens enabled farmers to produce a marketable surplus, and to invest in specialised production for urban consumption.

On the other hand, critics of this thesis claim that the Revolution did very little to transform the structure of agricultural production. Some, like Alfred Cobban, insisted that the legislation of the period even retarded agricultural capitalism in France, by creating a proliferation of small inefficient peasant proprietors.[9] McPhee has described this school of thought as the "minimalist school", because it argues that the Revolution changed next to nothing. Le Goff and Sutherland, for example, point out that there was no increase in France's sheep and cattle population after the Revolution.[10] Since the surplus previously extracted in seigneurial dues or clerical taxation was often incorporated into lease contracts, tenants and share-croppers had no more disposable income than before the Revolution.

The evidence from the Consulate and Empire cannot resolve this continuing debate. The period is too short to provide data which will weigh heavily in the balance on either side. This was an exceptional interlude, made up of fifteen years of almost uninterrupted warfare, which temporarily distorted many features of France's growth. These were not the circumstances in which historians should go looking for an economic miracle.

Two comments on the "minimalist" interpretation may be offered. First, the benefits of the Revolution were unevenly spread. Agricultural labourers and share-croppers saw little immediate material benefit, but for more substantial landowners, the picture was different. The whole nature of their tenure was changed by the abolition of feudal burdens and the enforcement of new individualistic bourgeois notions of freehold property. Second, there is perhaps no automatic equation between smallholdings and inefficient agriculture. Large concentrated estates, held by aristocratic absentee landlords were just as likely to resist capitalist methods as small proprietors were. Perhaps, as Bergeron suggests, the medium-sized properties prospered most in this period. Calignon, a former tenant of the Duc de Saulx-Tavanes at Arc-sur-Tille in the Dijonnais, cultivated his own 60-hectare property personally and dramatically raised its yield to three times the average by 1801.[11]

Outside France's frontiers, the demands of the armies stimulated agricultural production. In northern Italy, the creation of a much larger unified market also encouraged the production of cereals, olives and rice. As was the case in France itself, greater productivity was achieved by extending the area under cultivation, rather than by applying more sophisticated or intensive methods.

The sales of *biens nationaux* (the nationalised property of the Church and the *émigrés*) made the acquisition of new land an attractive investment opportunity. It was easy to buy new farms, or enlarge existing ones, so that there was little incentive to pursue technical improvements. As a result, there were no spectacular advances in the agricultural sector, as there were to be in industry. French society, as was seen from the lists of notables, was dominated by landowners rather than merchants and manufacturers. Land was a good investment, and there was plenty of it for sale. Diverting capital investment into real estate, however, did not necessarily inhibit commercial or industrial development. Landed property could provide the security for high-risk capitalist ventures, and it could be a solid basis for raising credit to develop a business. There was nothing to stop an entrepreneur like Boyer-Fonfrède being a shipowner, textile manufacturer and a purchaser of *biens nationaux* all at once.[12] Many cotton-mills were set up in the nationalised property of the religious orders, like his in the Dominican convent of Toulouse.

International Trade

Naval war and the Continental Blockade severely disrupted patterns of international trade. The blockade of French ports, together with British measures against neutral shipping, ruined the colonial trade on which the prosperity of the ports of the Atlantic seaboard had rested. On the other hand, the French grip on continental markets stimulated trade through inland entrepots like Strasbourg.

Trade with the French West Indian islands of Martinique, Guadeloupe, Tobago and St Domingo (better known today as Haiti) had provided the wealthy mercantile bourgeoisie of Bordeaux, Nantes and Le Havre with an international role. They imported sugar, coffee, cotton and indigo, and re-exported three-quarters of it all over Europe. Between 550 and 600 French ships arrived at their principal destination, St Domingo, each year in 1787 and 1788.[13] They took cargos of milled flour or manufactured articles for the settler population, together with salted beef (much of it of Irish origin) for the black slaves. They also supplied the plantations with a human cargo of slaves from Angola, Mozambique or the west African coast, in exchange for colonial goods. At the end of the Old Régime, traders disembarked 28 000 negro slaves per year in St Domingo.[14]

British sea-power stifled this prosperous and expanding commerce, but it had been severely damaged long before Bonaparte came to power. In 1791, the slave revolt in St Domingo threatened merchants in colonial goods with ruin. Capital invested in the West Indies was immobilised or lost altogether, while the Atlantic ports stood idle. The life-blood of Bordeaux drained away as its merchants confined their activities to a limited, regional sphere. The war with Britain made the situation worse, but trade briefly improved after the Peace of Amiens. The resumption of hostilities and the introduction of Napoleon's Continental System confirmed the decline of Bordeaux as an international trading centre. As soon as war broke out in 1803, sixty-three Bordeaux ships were captured at sea by the British. A visitor from Hamburg lamented in 1801: "The ancient splendour of Bordeaux is no more."[15]

Bordeaux survived, at least until the Continental Blockade became truly effective after 1806, by using neutral shipping. Colonial produce arrived in French ports from neutral European ports, or on American ships. Lisbon, for example was a staging-post for Pernambuco cotton; Hamburg received West Indian produce. United States ships and middlemen were extremely active in the colonial trade, inserting themselves more and more into the exchange network between Europe and the Americas. Bordeaux dealers set up offices in Baltimore and Philadelphia, while American companies established connections with Nantes and Bordeaux. The importance of the Caribbean, and the enticing prospects offered by the American market itself, helped to make New York an increasingly important international commercial centre from this period onwards. In 1805, 201 American ships anchored in Bordeaux, as well as 247 Danish vessels. Between them, Danish and American carriers accounted for a half of Bordeaux's foreign trade. The maritime war hurt neutral shipping and its true implications were felt by 1808. Wine exports virtually halted in that year and only six United States vessels entered Bordeaux.[16]

Stagnation affected not merely Bordeaux itself, but also the industries which supported its international shipping. Shipyards now lay idle. In the hinterland of Languedoc and Aquitaine, ropemakers and sailmakers had supplied Bordelais merchantmen, while wine exports depended on a host of rural industries like cork-making, glass manufacture and barrel-making. Many industries like these, geared to oceanic trade, disappeared in the revolutionary and Napoleonic wars. Tonneins had 700 ropemakers in 1789 but only supported 200 by 1801.[17] Flour mills devoted to production for the Caribbean plantations went out of business, as did the sugar refineries which processed imported sugar from St Domingo. The collapse of Bordeaux as an international commercial hub ruined these ancillary industries, and thus affected economic life over a very large geographical area. This contributed to the economic underdevelopment of the region, and it threatened the south-west with deindustrialisation, or "pastoralisation", as François Crouzet termed it.[18]

The only resources were smuggling or privateering – in other words, arming cargo ships to run the gauntlet of the British naval blockade. This was, of course, a high-risk business, and the profits, if any, were correspondingly inflated. Between 1793 and the end of the Empire, 163 privateers left the port of Bordeaux; the number which safely returned is unknown, but their shareholders could expect to realise profits of up to 240 per cent.

Bordeaux was exemplary: its fate was shared by other international seaports in France and the Empire. Nantes, for example, lost its slave trade. The port of Amsterdam was severely affected. In 1806, 1349 ships had docked in Amsterdam, but in 1809, there were only 310 arrivals. Trade in contraband (illegally imported British goods) kept the port alive, and King Louis Bonaparte complained that maintaining a self-blockade was as futile as trying to "stop skin from sweating".[19] Smuggling, however, could not restore Amsterdam's international trading position.

The purpose of the Continental System, as discussed in Chapter 15, was to prevent Britain from exporting her manufactured goods to Europe, and thereby to choke the British economy in a glut of unsaleable products. This, however, was not the only objective of

Napoleon's grand design. The Continental System was also a method of destroying Britain's leading market share in Europe, and capturing that market for France. Europe under French domination was a source of raw materials for French industry and a market for French manufactures. With the deliberate exclusion of British competition, France would be free to colonise European markets.

French commercial priorities had been revised: in 1805–6, a turning-point was reached. France was victorious on land but her sea power was destroyed. Trafalgar and Austerlitz were the disaster and the triumph which forced a re-evaluation of European markets. As the Chamber of Commerce of Marseilles argued in 1806, "The loss of our principal colony St Domingo must further enhance the value of the outlets which our industry and manufacture can preserve in Europe."[20]

Eastern France now lay at the crossroads of imperial trade. New commercial centres in this region were to play an important role in the conquest of markets in Germany and Italy. Strasbourg was one such centre, with a prosperous future within Napoleon's scheme to make the entire continental economy subservient to French interests. Strasbourg was the main reception point for Balkan and Turkish cotton – which was at a premium when Indian and American supplies were scarce. It also lay near the north–south trade axis of the Rhine, and was a launching-pad for French penetration of markets in Switzerland, Germany and eastern Europe. Strasbourg, unlike Bordeaux, was an example of urban and regional prosperity under the Empire.

Strasbourg accordingly enjoyed a sustained economic expansion in the years between 1807 and 1810, in conditions which favoured exports across the Rhine or into Italy. The down-river Rhineland trade to Mainz and Frankfurt also entered a boom period. Wines and local tobacco were exported and industrialisation accelerated in the textile industry in the upper Rhine. Strasbourg handled one-third of all France's imports, and exports from one-third of France's territory passed through the city.[21] After 1810, there was a widespread trade recession, aggravated in Alsace by the introduction of the government tobacco monopoly which ended private tobacco processing. The importation of Levantine cottons was now also prohibited, but exports nevertheless recovered to reach a new peak in 1812.

This boom was an artificial one, induced by the particularly favourable conditions of the Continental System. Strasbourg's prosperity depended on the exclusion of British goods (France's main competitor), and the imperial control of Germany and Italy. After 1815, the boom was over. Strasbourg no longer found itself at the hub of a huge Empire, but shrunk once again to assume its former persona as a frontier city. While Bordeaux stagnated, therefore, Strasbourg was revitalised. The experience of the Empire in these two urban examples had political consequences. After the way the south-west had suffered during the war, it was no wonder that Bordeaux welcomed first Wellington and then the Bourbons as liberators. In Alsace, the reaction was the contrary. Here, the Bourbon Restoration and peace in Europe heralded a return to mediocrity. Eastern France was to remain a permanent Bonapartist stronghold.

In the rest of the Empire, Napoleon's attempt to colonise European markets was particularly successful in Italy. The wars and unrestrained plunder of the late 1790s had devastated economic life in the peninsula. Under the Consulate and Empire, the situation was more tranquil, but French economic imperialism exploited Italy's resources to the full. Italy was used to supply France with food and raw materials, such as wheat, rice, leather and oil, as determined by the imperial administration. Thus even when the price of bread soared in Milan in 1810, the French refused to stop wheat exports to France, which drained supplies in Italy and put up the price of food there even further. French consumers had priority.

Italian raw silk was monopolised by Lyon manufacturers. Silk represented over 40 per cent of the value of exports from the Kingdom of Italy in 1812.[22] At the same time, Italian markets were the preserve of French goods. Italy was herself hardly industrialised and could not compete with the French industrial products she had to buy, except possibly in the case of silk manufacture. In 1808, a customs treaty between France and the Kingdom of Italy imposed terms which ensured the French monopoly of Italy as an export market. The Italian market was especially valuable in the later years of the Empire, when the war in Spain deprived France of one important export market.

As for Italy itself, the demands of the French Empire encouraged commercial agriculture, but production of silk, wheat and leather were northern specialities. In the south, poverty and low agricultural productivity remained the norm. The gap between the more prosperous and urbanised north, where capitalist agriculture was developing, and the poorer more traditional south was not narrowed under the Empire: if anything, it widened. The Napoleonic Empire, however, cannot be blamed for all of Italy's problems, least of all the eternal problem of the *mezzogiorno*. The Italian economy had suffered for centuries from localised markets and political fragmentation. The French Empire at least created a single market in the Kingdom of Italy, with its population of over 6 million.

Industrial Change

The period of the Consulate and Empire marked a decisive phase in the history of French capitalism, according to Louis Bergeron.[23] The loss of Canada and India in the the eighteenth century, and naval defeat at the hands of Britain in the Napoleonic wars ended the era in which France competed with Great Britain for global commercial supremacy. Relegated to a secondary role as a trading nation, France now began to emerge as a modern industrial power. She found that here, too, Britain had already established a significant lead which she did not relinquish for a century and a half.

Industrial production rose to 50 per cent above the levels attained in the 1780s.[24] Industrial advance, however, was localised and confined to certain sectors. One of these was cotton, but modernisation of cotton manufactures failed to drag the rest of the economy in its wake.

The most important industry of all was the textile industry, which probably accounted for one half of France's industrial domestic product at the end of the eighteenth century.[25] The protectionist tariffs imposed in the Continental Blockade created an exceptional situation in which France's main rival in textile manufactures was removed from the competition. While British goods were excluded from Europe, French textiles, and cotton in particular, enjoyed spectacular expansion. In Rouen, for example, production of printed cottons (*indiennes*) had by 1810 reached triple the level of 1789.[26]

It was British technology, paradoxically, which made this expansion possible. In the 1790s, Boyer-Fonfrède had not only adopted British machines like Crompton's mule and the flying shuttle, but he also imported British workers to install and operate them. He had recruited eight workers in Manchester and appointed Isaac Gouldbroof of Leeds to direct his Toulouse workshop.[27] In wartime, these international borrowings were difficult to repeat without conducting industrial espionage. The machines had to be smuggled to France or imitations had to be built, sometimes with the assistance of

British émigrés. The mule-jennies (*mulgénies*) constructed in France in this period were mutations based on older British cotton-spinning machines.

The expansion of cotton production responded to a new demand for cheaper printed materials. The greatest success stories were those of manufacturers who seized new fashion opportunities by meeting consumers' desires for more accessible cotton products. Oberkampf, on the other hand, was reluctant to follow changing tastes. His company declined because of his insistence on maintaining traditionally high standards of quality and design, which made his prices uncompetitive.[28] By concentrating on *articles de qualité*, Oberkampf failed to compete at the lower end of the market and he ran into difficulties.

Expansion was very evident in the east of France, particularly in Mulhouse and surrounding parts of Alsace. Before the Revolution, Mulhouse had belonged to the Swiss cantons, but in 1798 it voted to become part of France, which gave its products easy access to the huge French market. A new élite of manufacturers emerged here, principally from the Protestant bourgeoisie. The favourable conditions of the blockade, and access to the all-important French consumer market were crucial to the success of cotton masters like Dollfuss-Mieg and Koechlin. They also took advantage of the captive market in Italy. In Mulhouse, the number of cotton enterprises tripled between 1786 and 1810, and between 1798 and 1810 the population of the city rose by 35 per cent. Mulhouse was dubbed "the French Manchester" and in 1811 22 000 were employed in the city's textile industry.[29]

Mechanisation in the cotton industry began with the printing process and worked backwards. Printing had previously been a laborious process carried out at printing "tables", where the cotton cloth was laid out and worked. Oberkampf was responsible for introducing the cylindrical printing process for the first time in France, at his mill at Jouy-en-Josas. Spinning was revolutionised to keep up with the new pace of printing. The first water-powered cotton mills were established in Alsace in 1802, and steam-power followed. In 1812, Dollfuss-Mieg used the first steam-engine built in France, for cotton-spinning. In 1789, there had been only six mechanised cotton-mills in France; by the end of the Empire there were no fewer than 272 – a striking rate of progress.[30]

The most imaginative entrepreneurs took control of all parts of the production process at once. Liévin Bauwens of Ghent was one who combined spinning, weaving, bleaching and printing under the same roof. His spinning-mills gave work both to domestic weavers in the countryside, and to others in his weaving-mills; some of them were inmates of the local prison where he happened to be the warden.[31] They in turn provided work for Bauwens's calico printers. Manufacturers found that there was one aspect of production they could not control: the supply of raw cotton. The Continental Blockade eliminated British India as a source, and supplies had then to be secured from Brazil, Louisiana or the Levant (Turkey or Georgia).

Mechanisation was much slower in the weaving process, which still tended to be dominated by domestic production. Urban dealers "put out" work to handloom weavers in the villages, who worked for piece rates, returning the finished cloth to middlemen. The flying shuttle increased productivity and the increasing pace of production led to the gradual decline of the "putting-out" system. This was to have drastic consequences for employment possibilities in the countryside, where peasants had been accustomed to supplement their earnings as part-time domestic textile workers. Female employment was particularly hit, although the new cotton-mills employed female as well as child labour. Women's expertise was especially valued in the printing and colouring process.

The involvement of women in cottage industry had been vital to the peasants' family economy in textile-producing areas, although rates of pay never reflected their true importance. In the Pays de Caux, in northern Normandy, a clear division of tasks along gender lines had operated: the men were weavers, and the women worked as spinners, without interrupting their agricultural work.[32] The rapid mechanisation of spinning caused a serious crisis of female employment. Since the men tended to be higher earners and more mobile, their gravitated to the spinning mills which opened in urban centres, leaving the women at home. There many women took up weaving, reversing traditional roles. Mechanisation had thus inverted the previous sexual division of labour, but the low level of female wages meant that males continued to enjoy greater mobility and financial independence.

There were forty-four cotton-mills in Paris alone in 1814, and cotton transformed the capital for the first time into a leading industrial centre. There were more than 12 000 cotton workers in Paris by 1807, and almost two-thirds of them were at the gigantic Richard–Lenoir enterprise. The partnership of Richard and Lenoir was far from typical, in an industry in which a handful of modernising entrepreneurs stood out from a mass of small workshops. Most firms of the capital still employed less than 100 workers each.[33] Unlike most family companies, Richard–Lenoir started on borrowed capital, setting up production in religious establishments they had acquired as speculative investments in *biens nationaux*. By 1815, Richard had 15 000 wage-earners at his command. In an example of industrial concentration which was remarkable for the period, Richard–Lenoir drew their labour force from a wide area. Nevertheless, many of these thousands of wage-earners were domestic producers, working for the company in Picardy, the Manche, Cambrai or St Quentin. Domestic and factory production continued side by side within the same enterprise.

Male wage-earners enjoyed a strong bargaining position under the Empire, when conscription reduced the number of those seeking jobs. They improved their wages and ignored employers' demands in a host of invisible ways, like stealing materials or going absent. Mutual aid funds were set up in Mulhouse, and when they were officially banned in 1811 workers organised a 24-hour shutdown.[34] This kind of insubordination provoked complaints from employers that "anarchy" was taking over their businesses. The introduction of the worker's passbook (*livret*) in 1803 was designed to police the workforce and restrict workers' mobility. It became more difficult for individual workers to leave one employer without notice in order to take up a better paid job with another.

The factories posed new problems for workers and employers. Employers sought to prescribe long and clearly defined working hours and to tie each man or woman to the close surveillance and maintenance of the machine. Systems of fines for lateness and non-observance of factory rules were imposed. All this constituted a new discipline of labour, to which peasant workers, used to more informal and irregular work rhythms, were not accustomed. In Alsace, for example, a 13 ½-hour working day was common at the beginning of the century. A worker absent for one day from the mill might be docked two days' pay. A worker absent for two days would be automatically dismissed.[35] Needless to say, there were wide discrepancies in the wages earned by men and women. A male weaver, for instance, earned three times as much as a female weaver, who in turn earned double the pay of a child.

The complete transformation of peasant into proletarian still lay in the future. The early factories were at a transitional stage in the evolution of the workforce into the atomised agents of assembly-line production. In Ghent, for example, a leading spinner would be responsible for the work and the machinery of a team of workers. He would pay them himself, and the group as a whole would be paid piecework rates.[36] In a sense, therefore, the new cotton-mills simply incorporated (and multiplied) traditional production methods inherited from the craft workshop.

The manufacture of other textiles, such as woollen cloth, was far less successful than cotton production. Only cotton experienced genuine structural transformation in this period. In fact, parts of France's textile industries went into terminal decline. Cloth production in Languedoc, for example, collapsed after the Turkish and then the Spanish markets were cut off.[37] Small scale industries, employing outdated technology, did not survive the conditions of the naval blockade. The linen industry of St Quentin and the Nord suffered, and Rheims wool only survived because the region produced a very wide variety of cloths.[38] The Revolution had destroyed the market for legal and clerical robes, but the looms of Rheims continued to produce cloth for National Guardsmen's uniforms, as well as making naval bunting. The Belgian town of Verviers was perhaps the exception to this pattern of stagnation in the woollen industry: its textile industry experienced rapid growth in the years of the Consulate.[39] Elsewhere, the difficulties experienced by traditional textile production in the Old Régime were accentuated in the Napoleonic era.

The industrialisation of one sector, then, could mean the deindustrialisation of another. A new geographical concentration of industry was developing. The industries of Languedoc and the south-west were disappearing from the industrial map of France. Instead, new centres were establishing their importance in the nineteenth-century industrial economy. One was the growing textile conurbation of Lille–Roubaix–Tourcoing. Another was Paris itself, which was becoming an important banking and industrial centre, attracting capital investment which the seaports were now failing to absorb.

Paris recruited southern banking families like Perregaux and Laffitte, Swiss capitalists like Delessert, and for the first time Jewish banking interests from the east – James Rothschild installed himself in Paris in 1812. Bankers no longer made their money solely by lending to the State, as they had done in the Old Regime. They invested increasingly in commerce and industry. Paris was a cotton-producing centre, as well as housing the traditional luxury industries which made it famous: porcelain, tapestries, clocks and jewellery.

In heavy industries like coal, iron and steel, there was some mechanisation and industrial concentration, but technological advances were limited. The coke-smelting process had not yet been perfected.

War stimulated increases in iron and steel production, but they evaporated after peace pulled down the wall of protective tariffs which had sustained them. Coal production increased, too, and by the end of the Empire France produced about 900 000 tonnes annually. This achievement is put into perspective when it is realised that at the same period, Britain produced almost 17 million tonnes. French production did not reach that level until 1874.

In Belgium, the Continental System had a dramatic impact on heavy industry. Access to imperial markets accelerated production of both coal and textiles in the Belgian departments. In fact, by 1815, Belgium was the engine-room of the Napoleonic Empire; the Belgian departments of Jemappes, Ourthe, Forêts and Sambre-et-Meuse produced one half of all the Empire's coal, and one quarter of all its iron.[40]

The expansion of Belgian textiles transformed Ghent from a market town into an energetic industrial centre. The cotton-master Bauwens was the eldest of twelve children of a Ghent tanner, although he established his first mill in Passy, outside Paris. In 1801, he opened a second mill in Ghent, and in 1803 a third at Tronchiennes.[41] He created a small empire, in which he built spinning machinery for other producers, many of whom were his relatives. Ghent's new fortunes were the result of the Empire and the Continental Blockade; the city's manufactures were now tied to the French market. This, together with the obstacles placed in the way of English competition, ensured its emergence as a new industrial zone.

Areas which lay outside the tariff wall surrounding the Grand Empire suffered. This was the fate of the Grand Duchy of Berg and the Ligurian Republic. Berg textiles found it hard to compete with production in the Rhineland departments. Genoa felt disadvantaged by Nice, which began to take the Piedmontese trade. Here, merchants and industrialists argued for their inclusion within the protective ring of the French departments, to share the benefits seized by towns like Strasbourg and Ghent.

Assessments of the impact of the Continental System must therefore vary according to particular industries and regions. Maritime trade was ruined by the war; but the inland trade across imperial Europe prospered. For those producing goods for sale within the rich French market, like the manufacturers of Ghent, profits beckoned; but for those competing against it, like those of Berg, life was difficult. Cotton production went through a rapid phase of concentration and mechanisation, and producers had favourable export markets at their mercy in Germany and Italy.

The Empire and the Continental System cannot be blamed for all economic problems of the time. Many of them long pre-dated Bonaparte. Nothing could redeem the decline of the Netherlands. Its impoverished textile industry and ailing dairy production were developments of the eighteenth century rather than of the Napoleonic period. Nor could the efforts of the Continental Blockade close the lead taken by industrial Britain. Neither increased coal production nor a huge rise in cotton production could alter the long-term reality of British industrial supremacy. The impact of the Empire therefore has to be placed in the context of the long duration (*longue durée*), in which agricultural methods did not undergo structural change, and France's position relative to Britain remained constant.

One consequence of the Empire was to reinforce the dependence of business and banking circles on the state. The role of the state under Napoleon was a new one: since the age of Louis XIV, the monarchy's policy had been to regulate and prod the domestic economy, but to follow a foreign policy in pursuit of *la gloire* which took scant account of France's economic interests. Under Napoleon, this situation was reversed. The Empire, like the Revolution, favoured economic liberalism at home, together with a European policy fully geared to France's economic needs. The state provided an "artificial" climate in which French entrepreneurs could hold their competitors at bay, and proceed to conquer new markets. What the state could not yet provide was a sophisticated credit system, in spite of the creation of the Bank of France. But in 1811, the government did in an emergency lend money to Richard–Lenoir to rescue the company from bankruptcy.[42] Industrialists were used to soliciting the state for aid.

The fragility of industrial growth was exposed in the later years of the Empire, especially when markets and the Empire itself contracted. In 1810–11, the crisis which struck all Europe was largely the result of overproduction. The economy took a downward turn, in which silks, cottons and wines could not find an outlet. By 1811, the slump was severely aggravated by a bad harvest. Bankruptcies and widespread unemployment ensued. In 1811, Bauwens found himself financially overextended, the market saturated, and sales falling. He was bankrupt. Lousberg, another bankrupt Ghent cotton-master, committed suicide by drowning in the river Lys.[43] There were 270 bankruptcies in the Seine department alone in 1810. Workers were dismissed everywhere. The mills of Mulhouse gradually fell silent, as two-thirds of the city's textile workers were unemployed.[44] Neverthe-less, 1812 witnessed a recovery, sometimes forgotten by historians, who tend to see the last years of Empire as unrelieved decline. The Italian market was still secure, and the textile mills of Ghent, Mulhouse and elsewhere picked up production. River trade on the Rhine reached a new peak in 1812, only to be interrupted by the mil-itary setbacks of 1813.

The Consulate and Empire were overall periods of economic growth, highlighted by the economic contraction of the Revolution and Restoration which framed the period. France lost her strong commercial position overseas and agricultural productivity changed only slowly. Nevertheless, mechanisation and modernisation in a few areas signalled a new phase of industrialisation.

In Europe as a whole, the economic balance had shifted perma-nently from west to east, as Crouzet has argued.[45] In the eighteenth century, the Atlantic ports had been the most dynamic sector of Europe's economic life. Now, French maritime trade and its support-ing industries had collapsed. The port of Bordeaux was stifled and the industries of south-western France decayed. The vital productive areas were now on France's eastern borders. They lay, as we have seen, in Belgium with its industrialised coal and textile industries, and in the Rhineland and eastern France which were advantaged by the policies of Empire. The core of economic production in contin-ental Europe now lay where it is to be found today: enclosed roughly within an inverted triangle, which has its apex near Milan and its base running from northern France through Belgium to the north of Germany. The Rhine rather than the Atlantic ocean kept Europe's wealth afloat.

19 Débâcle and Resurrection, 1813–15: Napoleon the Liberal

"If the Bourbons return," Bertrand Lhodiesnière warned his fellow Normans in 1814, "you will have to pay tithes and feudal dues again, and after dark, they will make you keep the frogs quiet so that milord and milady can get a good night's sleep."[1] Lhodiesnière enjoyed considerable local status. He had been a Girondin deputy in the Convention, survived the Terror, and through the purchase of *biens nationaux* had become a substantial landowner in the Orne department. And yet, in spite of his obvious hostility to the Church and aristocracy, he was apparently no friend of Napoleon Bonaparte. As a defiant deputy in the Council of 500, on 19 Brumaire Year 8, he had been one of the last representatives of the people to be thrust out of the window of the chamber when Bonaparte's troops seized power. Now, in 1814, he had suddenly become a supporter of the Napoleonic régime.

There were others like him – ex-revolutionaries who had seemed "allergic to Bonapartism", as Chaumié calls them, but who rallied to support the Emperor in 1814. Military defeat, foreign invasion and the return of the Old Régime revived revolutionary loyalties and made Napoleon their focus. The integrity of France and the gains of the French Revolution were once more at stake. Napoleon had distanced himself from his revolutionary past when he became hereditary Emperor in 1804, married a Habsburg in 1810, and invaded Russia in 1812. In 1814, however, he returned to the true origins of his power, which lay in the Revolution of 1789. The events of 1814–15 presented France with the stark truth that Napoleon was the only alternative to monarchy and aristocratic reaction. In these circumstances, Napoleon was reborn as the embodiment of revolutionary sentiment and of the defence of the nation. In its last months of power, Bonapartism found within itself the strength to become a revolutionary force again.

The régime was pushed to this extremity by the military defeats which followed the Russian campaign. Napoleon had been able to resist all previous coalitions of the European powers because he had kept them apart, through alliances with Prussia, Austria or Russia. In 1813, he still hoped that his marriage would keep Austria neutral, but in this he was to be cruelly disillusioned. It was no longer possible to divide and conquer. For the first time, the European powers were united against France, and for the first time they were able to inflict a decisive defeat on the Emperor.

This unity was largely the work of two men and three treaties. The men were Metternich, Austrian foreign minister since 1809, and Castlereagh, a rare example of a British minister who was thoroughly immersed in the affairs of the European continent. Austria had lost her traditional eminence in Germany and Italy, as well as her outlet to the sea. A general coalition was essential to Austria's recovery as a great power, as long as she could prevent Russia from confiscating for herself the profits of France's defeat. Metternich aimed to restore legitimate rulers to their thrones and make Europe safe from revolution; Castlereagh's objectives were less ideological. They consisted of restoring a European balance and containing French aggression.

The three treaties were signed at Teplitz in 1813, at Kalisch in February 1814, and at Chaumont where the Allies (Britain, Austria, Russia and Prussia) looked forward to twenty years of mutual cooperation. The basis of the new coalition was, as ever, a British subsidy of £5 million to keep the armies of the continental powers on a war footing. Britain looked forward to retaining her colonial conquests and restoring Prussia and Hanover. Metternich wanted to restore Habsburg influence in Germany and Italy, to restrain Prussian designs on Saxony, and to counter Russian domination of Poland. Germany would be liberated up to the Rhine and the Holy Roman Empire would be resurrected. Most importantly, the members of the coalition vowed they would not make a separate peace with Napoleon.

At the end of 1812, this new unity still had to be negotiated and exploited. After the retreat from Moscow in December 1812, Tsar Alexander was determined to press home Russia's advantage. In February 1813, the Prussians and Austrians allowed the Russians to occupy Warsaw. Prussia's hand was now forced by risings against the French occupation in Brandenburg and East Prussia. The Prussian Estates formed popular militia (*Landwehr*) to resist the French. About 120 000 men were mobilised in a citizens' army.[2] Intellectuals and students enthusiastically joined a patriotic movement, which German nationalist historians described as a *Befreiungskrieg*, a war of liberation against the French. The idea of German unity had as yet little popular support, and its democratic tendencies antagonised rulers like

Frederick William of Prussia. Prussia joined Russia in alliance against France: at Kalisch, the Tsar promised to secure the resurrection of Prussia. Sweden also joined the coalition on Russia's side.

In May 1813, in the battles of Lutzen (near Leipzig) and Bautzen (near Dresden), Napoleon repulsed the allies with heavy losses on both sides. The victory was only partial: he had not eliminated the enemy. Metternich now posed as mediator between Napoleon on one side, and the Prussians and Russians on the other. He proposed to Napoleon the surrender of Poland to Russia, the abandonment of the Illyrian provinces to Austria, and a recognition of the independence of the Hanseatic towns. If Napoleon had ceded at this point, he may have staved off defeat by keeping Austria neutral. But he refused; after all, in spite of the Russian campaign, Lutzen and Bautzen, he was not yet defeated, and still had the wit and power to defy Europe. His refusal brought Austria into the coalition. When Metternich next offered peace terms, they would not be so generous.

Napoleon had collected a new army to replace the losses of the Russian campaign. As imperial territory shrank, however, he could no longer spare metropolitan France the worst rigours of conscription. France itself was called on to provide more and more men and supplies. Napoleon withdrew troops from Spain, mobilised the National Guard, and increased taxation. There was rising opposition to conscription in 1813, and rioting against consumption taxes (*droits réunis*). He raised money from the sale of import and export licences, reducing the Continental System to a mere device for collecting revenue. In spite of these efforts, he remained critically short of cavalry.

The decisive conflict would be played out in central Europe, where the armies of the eastern powers converged. When Napoleon faced the coalition army of 320 000 troops outside Leipzig in October 1813, he was outnumbered by two to one. The "Battle of the Nations" raged for three days. The French were routed by allied troops who showed new-found purpose and determination. Napoleon's German and Italian contingents defected to the coalition. The French army was cut to pieces in a headlong and murderous retreat over the river Elster, where Marshal Poniatowski was drowned. Perhaps only a quarter of Napoleon's army lived to fight another day. Yet another army would have to be created.[3]

Retreating troops brought a typhus epidemic to France and the Rhineland. Jeanbon St André, prefect of Mainz, was one of 20 000 victims. The Empire collapsed, creating a complete power vacuum. Spain was lost. Fouché abandoned Illyria and fled to Venice. Prussia occupied Saxony. Bavaria and Wurtemberg joined the allies. The French were thrown out of their satellite states, the Duchy of Berg and the Kingdom of Westphalia. In November, an uprising began in Holland as the French withdrew. It had taken only one significant defeat to achieve this; but there was now nothing left of the Grand Empire except Belgium and Italy, which was conspicuous for the lack of agitation against the French. The army of the Kingdom of Italy mutinied rather than submit to the Austrians. The year 1814 was not 1799: there were no sweeping purges and the administrative machinery left by the French remained intact.[4]

British and colonial goods began to flood into Europe as the Continental Blockade dissolved like a sandcastle at high tide. Harvests were good in 1813, and business prospects appeared rosy on the British side of the Channel. Castlereagh put the promised subsidies at his allies' disposal through the German banks. In 1817, a grateful Habsburg Emperor ennobled the Frankfurt Rothschilds for their services to the coalition.

In Italy, Metternich had entered negotiations with Murat, who disowned Napoleon in an attempt to save his Neapolitan throne from the débris of the Empire. The British found it expedient to give Murat his head, and in 1813 he tried to gather support for a movement for Italian unification. Having marched north from Naples, he declared Italian independence at Rimini in April 1815. His call awoke no popular response and his position remained very ambiguous. If Murat was to convince the allies that he had renounced Napoleon, as Bernadotte had done in Sweden, he was obliged to make war on Eugène's Kingdom of Italy. This was a step which he was ultimately not prepared to take. The Austrians defeated his army near Tolentino and the British entered Naples. Eugène was allowed to evacuate his kingdom and Murat fled. When he foolishly tried to return, he was captured and shot. The road to Italian independence was to be strewn with victims of such wild and gratuitous gestures.

As we have seen, in 1813 France was crushed at Leipzig in the Battle of the Nations. Napoleon had thus lost the campaign for the Rhine. In 1814, against very unfavourable odds, he lost the campaign for France itself. On 31 March 1814, Paris itself capitulated. The Senate deposed Napoleon, who abdicated in favour of his son. On 6 April, at Fontainebleau, abandoned by the bourgeoisie and its representatives, he was obliged to accept an unconditional abdication. Paris declared for the Bourbons, who were now restored by the victorious coalition powers.

Metternich had entertained the idea of a settlement based on France's "natural frontiers", that is to say, the Alps, the Pyrenees and the Rhine. When the French were forced to abandon Holland, this idea became redundant. The defeat at Leipzig had in effect cost France the Rhine frontier. Castlereagh arrived in Basle to promote a new peace plan. France would be reduced to the frontiers of 1792, and would be encircled by a ring of independent states which would act as buffers against French aggression. Belgium would be incorporated in a new Kingdom of Holland, Prussia would acquire territory in the Rhineland, and a neutral Switzerland and the Kingdom of Savoy would complete the ring. This was the essence of the peace later imposed on France by the Treaty of Vienna (Map 19.1).

Lombardy and Venetia were restored to Austrian rule and the Habsburgs were returned to the Duchy of Tuscany. The ancient Republics of Genoa and Venice were sacrificed to cement Habsburg authority in the Italian peninsula. Poland was to be divided between the three eastern European powers, although Russia secured the largest share. Prussia eventually annexed about half of Saxony, Westphalia and the left bank of the Rhine. Metternich was reluctant

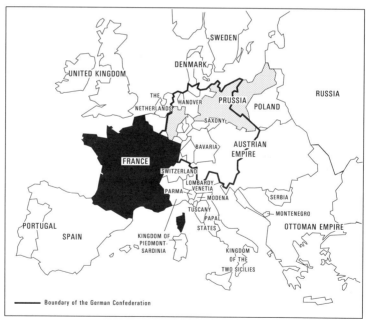

Map 19.1   Europe after the Congress of Vienna, 1815

Source: As Map 14.1.

to accept Russia's renewed grip on Poland, and the Prussian annexation of part of Saxony, but his pill was considerably sweetened by Austria's new role as the guardian of Italy.

Napoleon himself was sent to the Mediterranean island of Elba, not as a prisoner but as an independent sovereign. Marie-Louise, whom he never saw again, was consoled with the tiny Italian Duchy of Parma-Guastalla. This was rather better treatment than that reserved

---

DOCUMENT 19.1   THE BETRAYAL OF THE GENERALS

In 1814, Napoleon's greatest supporters came to terms with the new regime, attempting to guarantee continuity and protect their own careers.

Proclamation of Marshal Augereau to His Army, 16 April 1814

Soldiers!

On 2 April, the Senate, interpreter of the will of a nation weary of the tyrannical yoke of Napoleon Bonaparte, pronounced his abdication and that of his family.

Bonaparte and his despotism will be replaced by a new monarchical Constitution, strong and liberal, and by a descendant of our ancient Kings.

Your ranks, honours and distinctions are guaranteed. The legislative body, the Grand Dignatories, the marshals, generals and all the corps of the Grande Armée, have given their support to the decrees of the Senate, and Bonaparte himself has abdicated the thrones of France and Italy on behalf of himself and his heirs.

Soldiers, you are freed from your oaths, both by the nation in whom sovereignty resides, and by the abdication of a man who, having sacrificed thousands of victims to his cruel ambition, refused to die like a soldier.

The nation calls Louis XVIII to the throne. Born French, he will honour your glory and will proudly surround himself with your leaders. As a son of Henry IV, he will have his courage: he will love his soldiers and his people.

Swear loyalty to Louis XVIII and to the Constitution which he offers us. Raise a flag which is truly French, and put away all symbols of a sterile revolution. Soon you will find, in the gratitude and admiration of your King and your Country, a just reward for your noble endeavours.

(Translated from *Le Moniteur,* 23 April 1814)

for deposed dictators in the twentieth century, who have been strung up on meathooks or shot with their family after summary trial. It was also better treatment than many of his English enemies believed he deserved. *The Times* of London felt that "such a wretch would be a disgrace to Botany Bay".[5]

The Napoleonic adventure seemed over. Napoleon had seen close associates, relatives and trusted marshals manoeuvre for position as his fall became imminent (Document 19.1). They were obliged to make peace with his royal successor, but the Emperor was humiliated by their betrayal. On 12 April 1814, he attempted suicide by poisoning himself, according to Caulaincourt his last foreign minister.[6] As his carriage passed through Provence, there were popular demonstrations against him. On Elba, Napoleon busied himself managing the island's small budget and refurbishing the accommodation. Such tasks could only emphasise the new disgrace into which the master of Europe's fortunes had now fallen. He was visited by the curious as a tourist attraction. He kept in touch with events in France; if an opportunity arose, he would return.

The Bourbons were restored to the throne of France twice: first in 1814 and then again after Waterloo. On both occasions they were enthroned not by popular demand, but by order of the victorious allied powers. Louis XVIII had spent a quarter of a century in exile and was a stranger to his own people. The Bourbons' main virtue was that they represented peace at last, while Napoleon had condemned France to a cycle of perpetual warfare which could only be closed by French humiliation on the battlefield. As a ruler, however, who owed his legitimacy to a double French defeat, Louis XVIII could not expect to find his task easy.

The main task of the restored Bourbons was to reconcile the Old Régime with the French Revolution. This was to prove beyond their meagre personal talents. Some steps towards reconciliation were taken. For example, Louis XVIII was compelled to accept that the sale of the *biens nationaux* was permanent. If he had not accepted this important pre-condition, the French bourgeoisie would not have tolerated his restoration. Louis XVIII had no intention either of abandoning the Napoleonic administrative system which had transformed and strengthened the apparatus of the state.

The monarchy also gave France the Charter of 1814 which established a two-chamber parliamentary system, incorporating a house of hereditary peers and a Chamber of Deputies elected by limited suffrage. The King, however, accepted no limitations on his appointment of ministers, and he would not necessarily be bound by the will of the elected majority. Furthermore, the Charter failed to recognise the revolutionary principle of the sovereignty of the people. Louis XVIII conceived his new representative system not as something to which the French had a right, but as a gift, graciously bestowed on his people by a benevolent sovereign.

By taking the title of Louis XVIII (Louis XVII had never ruled), the King was asserting that the Bourbons' legitimate claims were unbroken by the Revolution and the execution of Louis XVI. This did not augur well for the future. The Bourbon's task was made immeasurably more difficult by the fact that the monarchy's greatest supporters demanded much more than Louis offered. The returning *émigrés*, and other reactionary supporters of the Old Régime, known as the Ultra-royalists, despised the Charter's concessions to constitutional liberalism. They aimed at a reconstruction of the Old Régime, urging reprisals against those who had purchased the property of the Church and the *émigrés*, and against all those revolutionaries who had voted the death of Louis XVI in 1793. Tactlessly, the régime planned a memorial to the victims of Quiberon Bay, the site of the failed invasion by a counter-revolutionary *émigré* army in 1795. Rumours spread that tithes and seigneurialism would be restored, and the *biens nationaux* returned to their former owners. The Bourbons made a further important mistake. They generously promised the abolition of the hated consumption taxes (*droits réunis*), but then in view of their financial situation withdrew the promise. This played into the hands of those who increasingly recognised Napoleon as their protection against a monarchist and clerical reaction.

The real question of the First Restoration, as Carnot rightly saw, was not how representative or how valuable was the Charter of 1814, but how permanent was it likely to prove? Louis XVIII seemed incapable of resisting the demands of *émigrés* and Ultras.[7] In the south-west, the Duke of Angoulême exploited popular royalism and the disillusionment of extreme royalists with their compromising monarch. Protestants and other revolutionary sympathisers were not safe in Languedoc, where Angoulême commanded like an independent ruler.[8] Moderates like Carnot were prepared in 1814 to support a constitutional monarchy, but the Ultras seemed bent on vengeance, their bitter knives sharpened by twenty years in the wilderness.

At the end of February 1815, Napoleon left Portoferraio on the island of Elba, and on 1 March he landed with over 1000 men near Fréjus on

the south coast of France. Louis XVIII waited for the country to rise
against the usurper, but instead it welcomed him. The King fled to
Belgium and the Duke of Angoulême decamped to Spain. Napoleon
was ready to capitalise on disaffection with the Bourbons, and the
fears of a return to feudalism illustrated by Bertrand Lhodiesnière at
the opening of this chapter. The whirlwind journey to Paris which followed met no resistance, and has entered Napoleonic mythology as
"The Flight of the Eagle". To avoid the anti-Bonapartists in Marseilles
who had insulted him on his way south in 1814, Napoleon took the
Alpine route, via Digne and Grenoble. He promised his supporters a
new beginning in which he would restore liberty to France.

His return, however, condemned France to another war against the
coalition. The threat of foreign invasion and conscription loomed
again. Peace in Europe had always been Louis XVIII's strongest card,
and for this reason France hesitated. Most of the bourgeoisie, whose
support Napoleon was desperately seeking, would wait for the outcome of his sudden resurrection. They feared this new adventure as
much as they were apprehensive about the intentions of the
Bourbons. For others, the military threat revived the patriotic spirit
of 1792 and 1793, when the motherland was in danger and the entire
French Revolution at risk.

A new revolutionary movement thus developed during the Hundred
Days of Napoleon's return to power, which rallied support behind the
new liberal face of Bonapartism. New elections were ordered and the
émigrés were once again driven out. The representatives of the people
were summoned to the Champ de Mars in a ceremony intended to
recall the gigantic federation of National Guardsmen which had
gathered there in 1790. "I have come," Napoleon claimed, adopting
the rhetoric of Jacobinism which he had so rarely used since his days at
the siege of Toulon, "to save Frenchmen from the slavery in which
priests and nobles wished to plunge them. Let them beware. I will
string them up from the lamp-posts."[9]

Elections to a new Chamber of Deputies brought a host of old
revolutionaries out of the woodwork. Lafayette was elected, along
with Lanjuinais, and Bertrand Barère, ex-member of the Committee
of Public Safety during the Terror. Different revolutionary groups,
Feuillants, Girondins and Jacobins, who had been at each other's
throats in 1791–4, united behind Napoleon and against the monarchy and foreign invasion. In Toulouse the ex-terrorist Vadier, aged
80, came out of retirement to join the movement against royalism.[10]
As a symbol of Napoleon's new political orientation, the new govern-

ment included two ex-terrorists, Fouché and Carnot, the organiser of victory in 1793 who now found himself in an unaccustomed role as Minister of the Interior. Within a month, the administration was purged. About three-quarters of the prefects appointed or retained by Louis XVIII had been dismissed.[11]

The case of Lanjuinais, the ex-Girondin Conventionnel, is particularly instructive in assessing Napoleon's new sources of support in the Hundred Days. The Girondins had traditionally been strong defenders of decentralisation, which made them the natural enemies of the Napoleonic state. Several ex-Girondins, however, rallied to the Emperor. Lanjuinais did so as a confirmed liberal. He had opposed the coup of Brumaire, voted against the Life Consulate and against the hereditary Empire. In 1814, he had even called for the deposition of Napoleon.[12] Louis XVIII made him a peer of France, and then, in the Hundred Days, Lanjuinais was elected president of the Chamber of Deputies. Perhaps Napoleon found an alliance with such liberals uncomfortable; in the Consulate, after all, he had unceremoniously eliminated them from political power. Circumstances and a common enemy now brought them together again.

How much support did Napoleon enjoy during the Hundred Days? This question can be answered with a three-part hypothesis : first, the bourgeoisie, the *notables* of the Empire, were on the whole extremely reluctant to commit themselves. Second, there was a strong groundswell of popular support for Napoleon, particularly in the army, where his charismatic appeal was strongest and where there was some acceptance of Napoleon's claim that France had been betrayed, not defeated, in 1814.[13] Popular Bonapartism, however, was challenged by the strength of popular royalism in the Midi. Third, a revolutionary movement emerged in support of the Empire, which united elements both of the pro-revolutionary bourgeoisie and the lower classes, especially in the cities. Carnot described the situation as "a struggle between the drawing-rooms and the mass of the people", in which the people supported the Emperor.[14] Napoleon was extremely reluctant to arm the popular classes; he preferred an alliance with social élites, which proved difficult to secure.

His supporters can best be analysed through the *fédéré* movement, which sprang up spontaneously in various parts of France in the Hundred Days, and in the response to the Acte Additionnel, which was Napoleon's new Constitution of 1815.

The *fédérés* came together to maintain order, resist royalism and to protect the integrity of France against possible invasion. Everywhere, they embodied a revival of the revolutionary and patriotic impulses of the 1790s. Regicide Conventionnels were found among the leaders of thirteen provincial federations.[15] In the west of France, where the reintroduction of conscription provoked a revival of the Vendean rising of 1793, the *fédérés* supported the government to resist royalism and prevent civil war. In Brittany, *fédérés* made an active contribution to suppressing *chouan* rebels. The conflicts of the 1790s were being replayed, although the alliance of the western bourgeoisie with regular troops now looked to Napoleon rather than to a republican government.

Elsewhere in France, the motivation of local Bonapartists varied. In Burgundy, they supported the government's attempts to resist invasion. In Languedoc, they rallied to combat royalist reprisals against Protestants and purchasers of *biens nationaux*. In Nîmes, Protestant textile workers, known as the yellownecks (*collets jaunes*), conducted operations from a café named the Isle of Elba.[16] The *fédérés* swore oaths of loyalty to the Emperor, planted liberty trees, sang revolutionary songs and fought royalists in the streets. In Paris, there were several different federations, but the 13 000 federated riflemen (*fédérés-tirailleurs*) armed by the government deterred anti-Bonapartists, and were a potential weapon in the hands of Napoleon against the Chamber of Deputies.

There were hundreds of thousands of *fédérés* all over France, although the largest contingents were formed in Brittany, Burgundy and Paris.[17] In Rennes, they were composed very largely of middle-class recruits, students, administrators, professional men and merchants. In Dijon, however, their social composition was not exclusively bourgeois. Artisans and shopkeepers formed 30 per cent of the Dijon *fédérés*, in a renaissance of the bourgeois and *sans-culotte* alliance which had been typical of provincial Jacobinism in 1793.

They came together spontaneously until the government took over the role of sponsorship, partly in order to circumscribe their activities. The manufacturer Boyer-Fonfrède, a leading Bonapartist in Toulouse during the Hundred Days, pointed out the dangers of this neo-Jacobin support for Napoleon. In a letter to Fouché he wrote:

> The people will join the federations *en masse*, that is certain, but it is for you to judge how far that should go, for there is a tendency to repeat the events of '93. The people sees that it is resisted by the privileged classes, and this spurs it to action, and you know better than anyone the danger that can result if one is not in control of it.[18]

The strength of popular Bonapartism in the Hundred Days cannot be doubted, but the attitude of the authorities towards it was sometimes ambiguous. The prefect of Toulouse informed Carnot on 18 May 1815 that "only the rabble (*la canaille*) supports the Emperor", in language which suggested the huge social chasm between the *notables* and the people.[19] Georges Lefebvre long ago accused Napoleon of not wishing to exploit the popular movement in his favour.[20] The problem was starkly posed in Paris itself, where the federated riflemen of the suburbs of St Antoine and St Marceau were overwhelmingly of lower-class origin. About 44 per cent of them were manual labourers and 38 per cent of them artisans.[21] Napoleon gave them weapons, but was keen to limit the scope of their intervention in domestic politics.

Napoleon had promised to defend French liberties, but the constitution he offered, the Acte Additionnel, only partially fulfilled his promise. Napoleon recognised that liberal gestures were now required. It was essential that he should offer France more than the Bourbons. The Acte Additionnel thus needed to outbid Louis XVIII's Charter of 1814.

Napoleon renewed contact with constitutional liberals like Benjamin Constant. Constant was always the opportunist. In 1813, he had been linked with Bernadotte, King of Sweden, who saw himself as a possible pretender to the French throne. As late as March 1814, he published an article in the *Journal des Débats* comparing Napoleon to Attila and Ghengis Khan.[22] But within a month, he was bowing before the Emperor, appointed councillor of state, and drafting the Acte Additionnel which was nicknamed "la Benjamine".

The Acte Additionnel, as its name implied, was envisaged as a supplement to previous Napoleonic constitutions. It did not, therefore, replace the centralised and authoritarian structures on which the Empire was based. Some liberal reforms were incorporated, like the freedom of the press, the publicity of parliamentary debates and the irremovability of judges. A two-chamber parliament was retained, with an upper house of peers appointed by the Emperor. The lower house, chosen by electoral colleges in a process of indirect election, would be renewable every five years. The Chamber of Deputies, however, was to have no formal control over the appointment of ministers.[23] The Bourbon monarchy, the return of seigneurialism and the annulment of the sale of *biens nationaux* were all declared unconstitutional.

It is doubtful whether this succeeded in strengthening Napoleon's position. He reintroduced universal suffrage, but the wealthy bourgeoisie preferred a parliamentary system in which voting was restricted to substantial property-owners. Liberals noted with regret the lack of provision for genuine ministerial accountability. The Jacobins revolted against the idea of maintaining the hereditary peerage. Napoleon's quest for the loyalty of the *notables* looked unconvincing.

This became quite clear when the Acte Additionnel was submitted for popular approval in a plebiscite. Conditions were not favourable for a peaceful consultation with the electorate, which the government could manipulate as it had done in 1802 and 1804. War seemed imminent. Clergy and royalists opposed the plebiscite and urged deliberate abstention. The west was close to civil war, and the Vendean rebels tied down 30 000 government troops who were sorely missed at Waterloo. In the Midi, many royalist mayors flatly refused to conduct the vote, or else sent in completely blank electoral registers. Those who supported the régime often felt isolated and impotent. The mayor of Montours, near Fougères in Brittany, wrote in his blank voting register: "There wasn't any point in recording my vote because it would have been the only one."[24]

Votes in favour of the Acte Additionnel totalled 1.55 million, and those against 5740. This level of support, representing about 21 per cent of the electorate, was well below the level of the plebiscites of 1802 and 1804.[25] Bonapartism still appeared strong in the east of France and in Burgundy, as well as parts of the rural centre and southwest, like the Haute-Vienne and the Creuse. Elsewhere, Napoleon suffered a major setback. In the north there was little support, while Brittany and the west had been completely lost, and the south remained predominantly royalist. Merchant cities whose economies had suffered under the Empire gave Napoleon little support. There was massive abstention in Marseilles and Bordeaux.[26] On the whole, France had abstained, either in response to royalist pressure or else out of a desire to wait and see the result of Napoleon's final gamble.

The importance of the Acte Additionnel cannot be measured simply in terms of its impact during the Hundred Days. Its significance went beyond this brief episode. Napoleon had added a new persona to his mythical repertoire – that of Napoleon the liberal. In 1815, he again tapped the original source of his power – the legacy of the French Revolution – by gathering the support of ex-revolutionaries of various political hues. The main historical significance of the Hundred Days lies in this convergence of Bonapartism with the liberal aspirations of the revolutionary movement.

The Hundred Days were therefore a brief but fertile period. They revealed the depth of popular fears of the *émigrés* and the return of feudal impositions. Napoleon's return exposed the country's indifference and hostility to the Bourbon dynasty and the pre-1789 past which it represented. It presented the bourgeoisie with an insoluble dilemma: how to preserve careers open to talent, equality of opportunity, the end of privilege, and the revolutionary land sales, all of which Napoleon represented, and still remain at peace with Europe? The Hundred Days polarised politics and made a tranquil transfer of power to Louis XVIII unlikely. In 1814, the King had found it expedient to forgive many imperial supporters; in 1815, those who had rejoined the Bonapartist ranks in the Hundred Days could not be tolerated. Here, for royalist historians, lay the political irresponsibility of Napoleon's return from Elba: it made a peaceful transition to Bourbon rule impossible.[27] The difficulties of the restored Bourbons, however, owed more to the excesses of their own supporters than to Napoleon.

As a result of the Hundred Days, nineteenth-century Bonapartism could nourish and inspire liberal–revolutionary aspirations. "Vive le petit tondu, merde pour le roi!" (long live little baldy, shit to the king) shouted the *fédérés* of Blagnac near Toulouse, and a stamp duty collector of Salies echoed the sentiment, shouting, "Let's polish Napoleon's boots with Bourbon grease." The Restoration described this individual as an "unbridled jacobin, anti-priests, immoral, singing the Marseillaise with such fury that he makes women cry."[28] Through a multitude of such rebellious characters, Bonapartism retained a democratic and populist potential.

In June 1815, Napoleon attacked the allied armies massed in Belgium, hoping once again to divide the Prussians from Wellington's army of English, Dutch, Belgians, Hanoverians and Brunswickers. The coalition managed to maintain coordination on the battlefield. Napoleon did indeed force the Prussians to retreat but he could not exterminate them. Blucher, the Prussian commander, had his horse shot from under him. While he recovered from the fall, his deputy Gneisenau wisely ordered a retreat northwards which would still keep the Prussians in touch with Wellington's army. This order, Wellington later told the King of the Netherlands, was "the decisive moment of the century".[29]

Wellington waited in the vicinity of the small village of Waterloo, about 15 kilometres south of Brussels. His squares of well-drilled Anglo-German infantry repulsed repeated French cavalry charges, and the timely intervention of the Prussians secured the defeat of Napoleon. The allies lost over 20 000 and the French about 35 000 killed, wounded or taken prisoner.[30]

In Paris, Lafayette persuaded parliament to declare a state of emergency and demand the abdication of the Emperor. Marshal Davout now urged Napoleon to defy the chamber, and disperse it with the aid of the federated riflemen, but Napoleon refused.[31] He abdicated, and gave himself up to the English, hoping to end his days in Britain or the United States. This time, however, the allies were not so lenient. Napoleon was imprisoned on the Atlantic island of St Helena, an altogether bleaker prospect than Elba. There, he started to dictate his memoirs, which proved a powerful instrument in the development of the Napoleonic myth.

The Bourbons, returning once again, were in a considerably less generous mood than the allies. The Hundred Days had reinforced ultra-royalist demands for reprisals. Bonapartists were (with some difficulty) disarmed and the regicides were exiled. Marshal Ney, who had first promised to bring Napoleon back to Paris in an iron cage and then defected to the Emperor, was shot. This was no more than a political assassination, argued Lanjuinais, showing considerable moral courage.[32] So it was, just as the execution of the Duke of Enghien had been in 1804. In Toulouse, in August 1815, General Ramel was shot and wounded outside his house by royalist paramilitaries, who finished him off later indoors. A White Terror against revolutionaries and their sympathisers began in the Rhône valley. In Avignon, the *fédérés* of the Hundred Days were massacred, and so was Marshal Brune.

The victorious powers reduced France to her revolutionary frontiers, depriving her of Savoy. France was to pay a war indemnity and suffer an army of occupation for three years. The Bonaparte dynasty was to be excluded for ever from the French throne. The reaction was installed all over Europe. In Piedmont-Sardinia, Victor Emmanuel I abolished all the French legislation affecting his kingdom (but French administrative structures remained in place in spite of this gesture).[33] Bourbon reaction returned to Spain and Naples. The Duke of Modena resumed his antisemitic policies. The Pope abolished the Napoleonic code, along with other evils of the day, like smallpox vaccination and streetlighting. Ferdinand VII tried to re-establish the Spanish Inquisition.

In France itself, there were still genuine fears of a seigneurial reaction, and a severe subsistence crisis developed in 1816–17. No wonder, perhaps, that many thought of Napoleon with nostalgia, or refused to believe in his disappearance. Napoleon was "sighted" several times in the early years of the Second Restoration, in Spain, Italy, Toulon, Lyon, and Brussels. He was rumoured to be leading a huge army of Turks and Americans, well supplied with grain, against the monarchy. There had already been a second coming, so why not a third?[34] Some still entertained a messianic hope that the Emperor would materialise again, like the woman of Villemur near Toulouse, who declared like many others: "We'll have him soon (*Nous l'aurons*), and we'll be celebrating *(nous ferons la fête)*, but we won't plant poplars like the royalists, we'll plant oaks which will last much longer."[35] This feeling became a powerful political myth, which Louis-Napoleon III later harnessed for his own ends.

In 1821, Napoleon died on St Helena. This was not so much a conclusion as an introduction to the history of Bonapartism in nineteenth-century France. But that is another story.

20   Conclusion

"What a novel my life is!" Napoleon once exclaimed. The irresistible rise and fall of Napoleon Bonaparte was a drama which captivated, inspired and occasionally revolted the artistic minds of all Europe. Byron wrote poetry about him, Beethoven dedicated and then undedicated a symphony to him. His personal charisma had at times mesmerised both the humble French infantryman and the Tsar of all the Russias himself. Long after his death, he came to represent a Promethean force – Napoleon *was* the power of individual will and energy over circumstance and the inertia of the world. The universe of the great novelist Balzac, in the 1830s and 1840s, was full of Napoleonic models. Vautrin was the Napoleon of crime, Nucingen the Napoleon of finance, while Balzac himself, in the scope of his creative energy, resembled a Napoleon of the pen.[1]

This study has argued, however, that Napoleon's individual trajectory cannot be understood outside the historical forces which helped to direct it. Napoleon Bonaparte, whatever his personal destiny, was a part of the history of the French Revolution. His relationship with that legacy was the determining feature of his career. The revolutionary ideals of freedom and equality, the notion of popular sovereignty, the goal of rational administration and the rule of law, the liberation of Europe from feudal oppression, and above all the poisoned legacy of war – all these inheritances formed the basis of his power, and at the same time limited his options. At times he tried to depart from the revolutionary past or else to subject it to his personal ambition. Whenever he did so, the result was a disaster and nothing permanent was achieved. The lasting contributions of Napoleon Bonaparte were those made when his personal destiny conformed with the needs of France and of its revolutionary history.

Napoleon, then, did not step outside the river of history. He was immersed in its stream, buoyed up by its currents, unable to reverse their direction. His career should not be interpreted as a single immutable "block", for it evolved through several distinct phases. The young Corsican nobleman, first, was part of a family whose fortunes depended on sending its sons into service in France, Tuscany or Rome. The Revolution found him a young officer, already in his early twenties, and gave him his opportunity, as it did to so many talented and frustrated men like him. In 1793, Bonaparte was a Jacobin, a Montagnard and a follower of the Robespierre brothers at the siege of Toulon. In 1796–7, he had mellowed into Bonaparte the republican, supporter of the Directory, but discovering in Italy the political possibilities of military glory. As First Consul, Bonaparte's persona was that of the creative statesman, the lawgiver who brought France peace, reconciliation, and the consolidation of the French Revolution's social reforms. After 1804, he was transformed into the Emperor Napoleon, more authoritarian, concerned to protect his dynasty and eager to dominate Europe itself. A final transformation occurred in 1815, when the circumstances of the Hundred Days forced a new metamorphosis into Napoleon the liberal.

Throughout this evolution, two main themes stand out. Napoleon was, as he is often described, the founder of the modern state. His régime was also the fulfilment of the bourgeois Revolution of 1789–99.

The new state, which emerged from the Revolution and was shaped by Napoleon, was a secular state, without a trace of the divine sanction which had been one of the ideological props of the old régime monarchy. It was a state based on a conscripted army and staffed by a professional bureaucracy. Administration was "rationalised", in the sense that corruption and favouritism were officially outlawed. The affairs of all citizens were dealt with in principle on a basis of equality and according to fixed regulations, instead of being at the mercy of a monarch's whim. Above all, the modern state was a well-informed state, which used its own machinery to collect data on the lives and activities of its subjects. As it knew them better, it policed them more closely and it taxed them more efficiently.

The value of this achievement was clearly demonstrated by the restored Bourbon monarchy, which saw no profit in dismantling the Napoleonic state structure. Through the prefects and the rest of the Napoleonic bureaucracy, the state now dealt directly with individuals, instead of through a confusing layer of corporations and intermediary bodies. Whatever sentimental attachment the Bourbons may have had to the corporate society of the Old Régime, they recognised that the Revolution and Napoleon had vastly increased the power of the French state. Instead of putting the clock back to 1789, the Bourbons intended to reap full benefit from this new state power.

In Napoleon's hands, however, the state had become the instrument of dictatorship. Although lip service was still paid to the principle of popular sovereignty, Napoleon negated its democratic essence by claiming that he alone embodied the indivisible rights of the people. He manipulated a series of plebiscites to consolidate his personal authority. Bonapartism was not, then, a military dictatorship, for its power was characteristically derived from repeated consultations with the popular will, in 1800, 1802, 1804 and 1815.[2] It was, however, a régime which brought parliamentary life to an end, and expressed utter contempt for the liberal intellectuals who defended the representative style of democracy. The imperial years of Bonapartism were anti-parliamentary and anti-liberal. In addition, the information media were strictly controlled by Napoleon's popular dictatorship.

The revisionist historians of the French Revolution argue for the continuities between the centralising tendencies of the Napoleonic state and the absolutism of the old régime monarchy. For François Furet, the Revolution and Napoleon completed the work of the Bourbons, by destroying the power of the privileged orders, the Church and the nobility, and building an egalitarian despotism on their ruins. Napoleon in fact enjoyed personal power that was more absolute than that of the so-called absolute monarchs themselves. Furet sees Napoleon as the successor of the Sun King, "the Louis XIV of the democratic state".[3]

In this interpretation, the liberals who opposed the Napoleonic dictatorship are praised as the torch-bearers of the democratic and pluralistic political culture promised by the Revolution. Furet therefore erects his hero Benjamin Constant into a man of prophetic vision and integrity, the only one to foresee the dictatorial implications of the coup of Brumaire.[4] This book, in contrast, has tried to expose Constant's hesitancy and sheer opportunism.

To compare Napoleon with the Bourbons is to sin by anachronism. Turning Napoleon into the last of the Enlightened Absolutists of the late eighteenth century means ignoring the momentous events that separate them. The French Revolution was a decisive historical rupture which places Louis XVI and Napoleon Bonaparte in totally different spheres. The historical role of the Enlightened Absolutists had been to rationalise the confused and creaking old régime state structure. Their aim was to squeeze more resources from it, without disturbing its fundamental framework which was based on inequality and privilege. They had no intention of undermining the society of orders itself. On the contrary, they stood at its pinnacle, and its existence justified their authority.

When Bonaparte came to power, the society of orders had been completely transformed by the French Revolution. Legal privilege and tax exemptions had been destroyed – a fact which Napoleon emphatically confirmed. Bonaparte's task was not to extract more resources from a traditional social structure; that traditional social structure, along with noble privilege, the guilds, the Parlements and provincial autonomies, had been swept away by the Revolution. The role of the Enlightened Absolutists was to rationalise the Old Régime, but Napoleon's was to rationalise the new one. His task was not to safeguard the social prestige of the aristocracy (to which the monarchies were dedicated, and to whom in 1789 Louis XVI had linked his own fate). Napoleon's role was rather to build the institutions which would realise new forms of equality of opportunity.

This is not to evade a central historical problem: how did the ideals of the French Revolution lead to personal dictatorship?

This problem can only be addressed by considering the Revolution's social dimension, as well as its political aspects. The Revolution had assumed several different institutional manifestations: the constitutional monarchy of 1791, the Jacobin Republic of 1793–4, the parliamentary Republic of 1795–9, and then the Consulate and the Empire. But these régimes did not exist in a vacuum; they were linked to a whole social arena in which the aspirations of revolutionary supporters competed for supremacy. They were the institutional forms of the Revolution: conflicting social forces and social aspirations gave them substance and infused them with purpose. The same applies to the Napoleonic state: the social forces which underpinned it must be considered. Its social basis is what distinguishes the Napoleonic régime from the Bourbon monarchy, and makes it the heir of the Revolution. The social foundations of the Napoleonic régime, as this book has argued, lay in the bourgeois and peasant revolution of 1789.

The Consulate and Empire rested on the support of the *notables*, whom the régime itself helped to define and cultivate. The *notables* were gathered from the successful revolutionary bourgeoisie of landowners, professional men and administrators, together with elements of the commercial and manufacturing élites. They supported Napoleon because he preserved the social gains of the Revolution. He himself was an enduring symbol of careers open to talent. He perpetuated the abolition of seigneurialism and of aristocratic privilege. He confirmed the material gains of the bourgeoisie, especially

the sale of the *biens nationaux*. He established a legal code which
embodied equality before the law, and he introduced a system of secondary education which served the interests of the professional and
administrative élite. The creation of the new imperial nobility
seemed to many to be a retrograde step, but it could also be interpreted as an assertion of new social priorities. The new imperial
nobility was intended to bury the old. The society of orders was
obsolete and archaic. Instead of birth and connections, society now
declared its new criteria for distinguished status: propertied wealth,
personal talent and service to the state.[5]

The victorious revolutionary bourgeoisie accepted Napoleon's
dictatorship because it guaranteed their social promotion. They
found in it a state apparatus which assisted their advancement and
acted in their broad interests. "We have finished the romance of the
Revolution," Napoleon told the Council of State in language perfectly comprehensible to the practical, empirical bourgeois. "Now we
must begin its history, looking only for what is real and possible in
the application of principles and not what is speculative and hypothetical. To pursue a different course today would be to philosoph-
ize, not to govern."[6] Napoleon restored law and order, ending the
civil war in the west, pacifying France, and reconciling the factions
which had divided the country. His realistic agreement with the
Pope ended religious schism and removed another serious threat to
the stability of the revolutionary achievement. Napoleon's pragmatic
view of religious questions was in tune with the Voltairean attitude of
the French bourgeoisie. Religion was not a matter of doctrine or
faith, but it was essential for social cohesion and the subordination
of the lower classes. "Deprive the people of their faith," Napoleon
said, "and you will be left with nothing but highway robbers."[7]

Napoleon was the consolidator of the bourgeois Revolution, but he
was not the passive instrument of any class or social group. His personal agenda coincided with national and revolutionary interests, but
at various moments in his career his own ambitions diverged from the
cause of the Revolution. The exact timing of this divergence is under
dispute. For Jean Tulard, Napoleon abandoned his legacy in 1808
when he established the imperial nobility and plunged into Spain.
For others, the Habsburg marriage of 1810, signifying a wedding with
dynasticism, was a crucial departure from his revolutionary legacy.
This study prefers to emphasise two other moments when Napoleon's
"star" left its revolutionary orbit. One was 1812, when a mirage of
supreme power dictated the catastrophic invasion of Russia. The

other was 1804, the transition from Republic to hereditary Empire. This was a symbolic change which seemed to close a period of innovation and creativity. It had serious repercussions, too, on other parts of Europe under French influence, where the satellite Republics gave way to Bonapartist kingdoms.

All that Napoleon did solely to satisfy his own thirst for glory and power was swept away in his fall. The conquests disappeared and the Bonapartist dynasty was outlawed. What endured was the social and administrative structure he put in place to preserve the Revolution. The law codes long outlived him, as did the Concordat, the *lycées*, and the prefects. This made the period rather more than a mere "episode" in French history, as Louis Bergeron called it.[8] "Everything," Furet concluded, "or nearly everything lasting in French history that Bonaparte did was accomplished between 1800 and 1804."[9] The inauguration of the Empire was a turning-point in his own career, and in the history of his relationship to his revolutionary legacy.

One part of that legacy was continuing warfare. The Peace of Amiens, which greatly enhanced Napoleon's popularity, proved illusory. The fate of the whole régime depended on continual warfare and repeated victories. France had the wealth and demographic resources to support an exceptional military effort, although conquered territories were forced to contribute their share of the sacrifices. Napoleon's talent and the conflicts which divided the European powers ensured a string of spectacular victories. As soon as the great powers united, after 1813, victory was no longer assured. One defeat brought the Empire to an end.

The special conditions of war profited some sections of the economy, but perpetual warfare was not in the general interests of France or its bourgeoisie. There was a clear contradiction between Napoleon's role as executor of the bourgeois Revolution and the very non-bourgeois character of his military genius. By the Hundred Days it was evident that the French bourgeoisie was not prepared for another round of general hostilities, and it witheld support for Napoleon.

The posthumous myth of Napoleon further exposed the gap between the mundane and materialistic realities of bourgeois society and the romantic hero, who epitomised adventure, daring and action. The Napoleonic myth seemed to focus on all that was unlike contemporary prosaic reality.[10] For Julien Sorel in Stendhal's novel *The Red and the Black*, Napoleon represented colour, action and nobility of spirit which contrasted with the narrow mediocrity of Restoration

society. His memory also symbolised the possibilities for social promotion, now eliminated by the return to power of the *émigrés*, and the
reinstallation of old hierarchies.

In 1840, Napoleon's ashes were brought back to France from
St Helena. The monarchy of Louis-Philippe believed that the Napoleonic myth could be enlisted for its own purposes, to strengthen the
government at a time when opinion was focused on diplomatic conflicts with Britain. Where were the imperial remains to be buried?
The Pantheon had too many Republican connotations. St Denis, the
resting-place of French monarchs, was considered, but the suggestion
offended legitimists who felt the presence of a usurper would pollute
the royal crypt. Instead, Napoleon came to rest in a specially designed
tomb in the Invalides, which was politically neutral, and appropriate
enough as the home of the veterans of the imperial armies.[11] Louis-
Philippe felt no danger in attempting to incorporate the Napoleonic
memory into the dominant ethos of the July Monarchy. Napoleon was
ceasing to become the reference point for a particular political
group; he was already being appropriated as an asset who belonged to
the entire nation.

Notes

Chapter 1. Introduction

1. Jean Tulard, *Le Mythe de Napoléon* (Paris: Armand Colin, 1971), pp.47, 51 etc.
2. Addicts may consult Jean Savant, *Napoléon* (Paris: Veyrier, 1974); Frank Richardson, *Napoleon, Bisexual Emperor* (London: Kimber, 1972); Arno Karlen, *Napoleon's Glands and Other Ventures in Biohistory* (Boston: Little Brown, 1984).
3. J.M. Thompson, *Napoleon Bonaparte* (Oxford: Blackwell, 1988), p.389.
4. J. Tulard, *Napoleon: The Myth of the Saviour*, trans. T. Waugh (London: Methuen, 1985), p.449. For the poisoning allegations, see Sten Forshufvud and Ben Weider, *Assassination at St Helena: The Poisoning of Napoleon Bonaparte* (Vancouver: Mitchell Press, 1978), and Frank Richardson, *Napoleon's Death: An Inquest* (London: Kimber, 1974).
5. G. Ellis, *Napoleon's Continental Blockade: The Case of Alsace* (Oxford: Clarendon Press, 1981); Alan Forrest, *Conscripts and Deserters: The Army and French Society during the Revolution and Empire* (New York: Oxford University Press, 1989); Michael Broers, *The Restoration of Order in Napoleonic Piedmont, 1797–1814*, unpublished Oxford D.Phil.thesis, 1986.

Chapter 2. Bonaparte the Jacobin

1. J. Boswell, *An Account of Corsica, the Journal of a Tour in that Island and Memoirs of Pascal Paoli* (London, 1768).
2. Peter A. Thrasher, *Pasquale Paoli: an Enlightened Hero, 1725–1807* (London: Constable, 1970), e.g. pp.98–9.
3. D. Carrington, "Paoli et sa 'Constitution' (1755–69)", *AhRf*, 218, October–December, 1974, 531.
4. J. Tulard, *Napoleon: The Myth of the Saviour* (London: Methuen, 1985), p.24.

5. S.F. Scott, *The Response of the Royal Army to the French Revolution: The Role and Development of the Line Army during 1789–93*, (Oxford, 1978).

6. J.M. Thompson, *Napoleon Bonaparte* (Oxford: Blackwell, 1988), p.8.

7. Ibid., p.10.

8. Thrasher, *Pasquale Paoli*, chapter 18.

9. Eugène Déprez, "Les Origines républicaines de Bonaparte", *RH*, 97, 1908, 319.

10. Jean Defranceschi, *La Corse française (30 nov. 1789–15 juin 1794)* (Paris: Société des études robespierristes, 1980), p.90.

11. Ibid., p.142.

12. Tulard, *Napoleon: The Myth of the Saviour*, p.39.

13. William Scott, *Terror and Repression in Revolutionary Marseilles* (London: Macmillan, 1973).

14. M.H. Crook, "Federalism and the French Revolution: The Revolt of Toulon in 1793", *History*, 65, 1980, 383–97.

15. A. Aulard, "Bonaparte républicain", in his *Etudes et Leçons*, vol.9 (Paris, 1924), pp.71–92. This article was written in 1921.

16. A. to M. Robespierre, Nice, 16 Germinal Year 2, in Georges Michon (ed.), *Correspondance de Maximilien et Augustin Robespierre* (Paris: Nizet & Bastard, 1926), no.371, p.274.

17. Martyn Lyons, *France under the Directory* (Cambridge: Cambridge University Press, 1975).

18. Harvey Mitchell, "Vendémiaire – a Re-evaluation", *JMH*, 30, 1958.

Chapter 3.   Bonaparte the Republican

1. Georges Six, *Les Généraux de la Révolution et de l'Empire* (Paris, 1947).

2. Martyn Lyons, *France under the Directory* (Cambridge: Cambridge University Press), pp.50–1.

3. *Note sur l'Armée de l'Italie*, cited by J.M. Thompson, *Napoleon Bonaparte* (Oxford: Blackwell, 1988), p.60.

4. Ibid., p.62.

5. Napoleon, *Correspondance*, 32 vols (Paris, 1858–70), vol.1, no.91, p.118, proclamation from headquarters in Nice, 7 Germinal Year 4.

6. A. Aulard, "Bonaparte républicain", in his *Etudes et Lezons*, vol.9 (Paris, 1924), pp.82–3; V. Daline, "Marc-Antoine Jullien après le 9 Thermidor", *AhRf*, 185, 1966.

7. For brief summaries of the Italian campaign, see Lyons, *France under the Directory*, pp.196–200; Denis Richet, "The Italian Campaign", in F. Furet and M. Ozouf (eds), *A Critical Dictionary of the French Revolution*, trans. A. Goldhammer (Cambridge, Mass.: Harvard University Press, 1989), pp.81–93; Jacques Godechot, *La Grande Nation: l'expansion révolutionnaire de la France dans le monde de 1789 à 1799* (Paris, 1956) 2 vols.

8. Ferdinand Boyer, "Les responsibilités de Napoléon dans le transfert à Paris des oeuvres d'art de l'étranger", *Rhmc*, 11, 1964, 241–62.

9. Richet, "The Italian Campaign", p.86.

10. J.R. Suratteau, "Le Directoire a-t-il eu une politique italienne?", *Critica Storica*, 27:2, 1990, 351–64.

11. G. Vaccarino, *I Patrioti "anarchistes" e l'idea dell'unità italiana (1796–99)* (Turin, 1955).

12. U. Marcelli, "La crisa economica e sociale a Bologna e le prime vendite dei beni ecclesiastici, *Atti e memorie della deputazione di storia patria per le province di Romagna*, new series, 5, 1953–4.

13. Renzo de Felice, "La Vendita dei beni nazionali nella Repubblica Romana del 1798–9", *Storia ed Economia*, 8 (Rome, 1960).

14. Napoleon, *Correspondance*, 2, no.1321, p.264, letter to Directory, Milan, 28 December 1796.

15. Richet, "The Italian Campaign", p.87.

16. Marcel Reinhard (ed.), *Avec Bonaparte en Italie, d'après les lettres inédites de son a.d.c. Joseph Sulkowski* (Paris: Hachette, 1946), p.95.

17. Jacques Godechot, *The Counter-Revolution: Doctrine and Action, 1789–1804* (Princeton, NJ: Princeton University Press, 1981), pp.303–8.

18. V.E. Giuntella, "La Giacobina Repubblica Romana, 1798–9: aspetti e momenti", *Archivio della società romana di storia patria*, 73 (Rome, 1950).

19. A.B. Rodger, *The War of the Second Coalition, 1798–1801: A Strategic Commentary* (Oxford, 1964); Jean Thiry, *Bonaparte en Egypte* (Paris: Berger-Levrault, 1973), pp.109–11.

20. Thompson, *Napoleon Bonaparte*, p.98.

21. Y. Laissus, "Gaspard Monge et l'expédition d'Egypte", *Revue de Synthèse*, 81, 1960.

22. Edward W. Said, *Orientalism* (Harmondsworth: Peregrine, 1985), pp.80–7.

23. Napoleon, *Correspondance*, 4, no.2723, p.270, Alexandria, proclamation of 2 July 1798.

24. Thiry, *Bonaparte en Egypte*, p.201.
25. F. Charles-Roux, *Bonaparte: Governor of Egypt* (London, 1937).
26. Napoleon, *Correspondance*, 4, nos.2723, 2733, pp.271, 281, Alexandria, orders of 14 and 15 Messidor Year 6; Thiry, *Bonaparte en Egypte*, pp.251–2.
27. Thiry, *Bonaparte en Egypte*, pp.272–3.
28. Ibid., pp.379–80.

Chapter 4. The Coup of Brumaire

1. Martyn Lyons, *France under the Directory* (Cambridge: Cambridge University Press), chapter 11; Georges Lefebvre, *Le Directoire* (Paris, 1946); A. Goodwin, "The French Executive Directory – a re-evaluation", *History*, 22, 87, 1937.
2. C.H. Church, "The Social Basis of the French Central Bureaucracy under the Directory, 1795–99", *P&P*, 36, 1967.
3. C.H. Church, "Bureaucracy, Politics and Revolution: The Evidence of the Commission des Dix-Sept", *FHS*, 6:4, 1970.
4. P. Boucher, *Charles Cochon de Lapparent* (Paris, 1969).
5. I. Woloch, *Jacobin Legacy: The Democratic Movement under the Directory* (Princeton, 1970); Lynn Hunt, D. Lansky and P. Hanson, "The Failure of the Liberal Republic in France, 1795–1799: The Road to Brumaire", *JMH*, 51:4, 1979, 734–59.
6. Félix Rocquain, *L'Etat de la France au 18 Brumaire* (Paris, 1874).
7. R.C. Cobb, *Reactions to the French Revolution* (London: Oxford University Press, 1972), chapter 5.
8. Lyons, *France under the Directory*, chapter 11.
9. Colin Lucas, "The First Directory and the Rule of Law", *FHS*, 10:2, Fall 1977, 231–60.
10. Raymond Guyot, "Du Directoire au Consulat: les transitions", *RH*, 111, 1912.
11. S.T. Ross, "The Military Strategy of the Directory: The Campaigns of 1799", *FHS*, 5, 1967.
12. Lyons, *France under the Directory*, pp.228–9.
13. Pierre-Louis Roederer, *Mémoires sur la Révolution, le Consulat et l'Empire*, vol.3, ed. O. Aubry (Paris: Plon, 1942), p.105.
14. Jean-Denis Bredin, *Sieyès, la clé de la Révolution française* (Paris: Le Fallois, 1988), pp.437, 441.
15. Ibid., p.444.

16. Sergio Moravia, *Il Tramonto dell'Illuminismo* (Bari, 1968); S. Moravia, *Il Pensiero degli idéologues: scienzia e filosofia in Francia (1780–1815)* (Florence, 1976).

17. Gohier, *Mémoires des contemporains* (Paris, 1824), 2 vols.

18. Albert Ollivier, *Le Dix-huit Brumaire* (Paris: Gallimard, 1959), pp.149–52.

19. Jacques Godechot, *Les commissaires aux armées sous le Directoire* (Paris, 1937), 2 vols.

20. Bredin, *Sieyès, la clé de la Révolution,* p.447; Edgar Quinet, *La Révolution* (Paris: Belin, 1987), pp.690ff.

21. Bredin, *Sieyès, la clé de la Révolution,* p.79.

22. Ibid., p.454.

23. See L. Sciout, *Le Directoire* (Paris, 1895–7), 4 vols.

24. Ollivier, *Le Dix-huit-Brumaire,* p.209.

25. Aulard, "Bonaparte et les poignards des Cinq-Cents", *Etudes et Leçons,* vol.3, 1906, pp.271–89.

26. Ollivier, *Le Dix-huit-Brumaire,* p.222.

27. Aulard, "Le Lendemain du 18 brumaire", *Etudes et Leçons,* vol.2, 1906, p.223.

28. Ibid., pp.213–52.

Chapter 5. France in 1800

1. Jacques Godechot, *La Grande Nation: l'expansion revolutionnaire de la France dans le monde de 1789 à 1799* (Paris, 1956), 2 vols.

2. J. Dupâquier, "Problèmes démographiques de la France napoléonienne", *Rhmc,* 17, 1970, 340–1.

3. Ibid., p.354.

4. Ibid., p.356.

5. Catherine Rollet, "L'Effet des crises économiques sur la population", *Rhmc,* 17, 1970, 391–410.

6. M. Lachiver, *La Population de Meulan du 17e au 19e siècle: étude de démographie historique* (Paris, 1969), pp.193–208.

7. George D. Sussman, *Selling Mother's Milk: The Wet-nursing Business in France, 1715–1914* (Urbana: University of Illinois Press, 1982), p.116.

8. R. Monnier, "Ouvriers", *DN,* 1287.

9. J. Houdaille, "Le Problème des pertes de guerre", *Rhmc,* 17, 1970, 411–23.

10. Dupâquier, "Problèmes démographiques de la France napoléonienne", p.346.
11. Jacques Dupâquier (ed.) *Histoire de la Population française, vol.3, De 1789 à 1914* (Paris: Presses Universitaires de France, 1988), pp.71–2.
12. Dupâquier, "Problèmes démographiques de la France napoléonienne", p.351.
13. Louis Bergeron, *L'Episode napoléonien (aspects intérieurs), 1799–1815* (Paris: Seuil, 1972), p.120.
14. André Armengaud, "Les Mariages de 1813 à Toulouse", in *Sur la Population française au XVIIIe et au XIXe siècles: hommage à Marcel Reinhard* (Paris: Société de Démographie historique, 1973), p.13.
15. P. McPhee, *A Social History of France, 1780–1880,* (London: Routledge, 1992), p.15.
16. Dupâquier, *Histoire de la Population française,* vol.3, p.6.
17. A. Armengaud, "Mariages et naissances sous le Consulat et l'Empire", *Rhmc,* 17, 1970, 373–90.
18. Jacques Dupâquier, *Histoire de la Population française,* vol.3, p.67.
19. E. LeRoy Ladurie, "Démographie et 'funestes secrets': le Languedoc (fin XVIIIe – début XIXe siècle)", *AhRf,* 182, 1965, 385–400.
20. J. Dupâquier and M. Lachiver, "Sur les débuts de la contraception en France ou les deux malthusianismes", *AESC,* 5, 1969.
21. Bergeron, *L'Episode napoléonien,* p.124; Dupâquier, *Histoire,* vol. 3, pp.301–73.
22. J. Godechot in report of discussion, *Rhmc,* 17, 1970, 466.
23. Marie-Noëlle Bourguet, "Race et Folklore: l'image officielle de la France en 1800", *AESC,* 31:4, 1976, 802–23.
24. Stuart Woolf, "Statistics and the Modern State", *Comparative Studies in Society and History,* 31:3, July 1989, 588–604; Marie-Noëlle Bourguet, *Déchiffrer la France: la statistique départementale à l'époque napoléonienne* (Paris: Archives Contemporaines, 1990); Jean-Claude Perrot and S. Woolf, *State and Statistics in France, 1789–1815* (London: Harwood Academic, 1984), e.g. pp.22, 87–90.
25. J.-N. Biraben, "La Statistique de la Population", *Rhmc,* 17, 1970, 359–72; Marcel Reinhard, "La Statistique de la Population sous le Consulat et l'Empire", *Population,* 5:1, 1950, 103–20.
26. Dupâquier, "Problèmes démographiques", p.348.
27. Jean Vidalenc, *Le peuple des campagnes, 1815–48* (Paris: Rivière, 1970), p.40.

28. Michel Vovelle, "Villes, bourgs, villages: le reseau urbain–villageois en provence (1750–1850)", *AM*, 90:3–4, 1978, 431–4.

29. Alain Corbin, *The Foul and the Fragrant: Odor and the French Social Imagination* (Cambridge, Mass.: Harvard University Press, 1986).

30. David Garrioch, *Neighbourhood and Community in Paris, 1740–1790* (Cambridge: Cambridge University Press, 1986).

31. Bergeron, *Episode napoléonien*, p.126.

32. J. Coppolani, "Bilan démographique de Toulouse de 1789 à 1815", *Contributions à l'histoire démographique de la Révolution française*, 2e série (Paris, 1965).

33. L. Goron, "Les Migrations saisonnières dans les départements pyrénéens au début du 19e siècle", *Revue géographique des Pyrénées et du Sud-Ouest*, 4, 1933.

34. Roger Béteille, "Les Migrations saisonnières", *Rhmc*, 17, 1970, 433.

35. Ibid., p.439.

36. P.M. Jones, *The Peasantry in the French Revolution* (Cambridge: Cambridge University Press, 1988), pp.259–63.

37. Vidalenc, *Le peuple des campagnes, 1815–48*, p.219

38. Ibid., p.309.

39. Ibid., p.50.

40. R. Monnier, "Ouvriers", *DN*, p.1281.

41. Fernand Braudel, *L'Identité de la France, vol.1, Espace et Histoire* (Paris: Arthaud, 1986), chapter 1.

42. J.P. Aron, P. Dumont and E. LeRoy Ladurie, *Anthropologie du conscrit français* (Paris, 1972).

43. Hervé Le Bras and Emmanuel Todd, *L'Invention de la France: atlas anthropologique et politique* (Paris: Livre de poche, collection Pluriel, 1981).

44. Abbé Grégoire, *Rapport sur la nécessité et les moyens d'anéantir les patois et d'universaliser l'usage de la langue française*, presented to National Convention, 16 Prairial Year 2.

45. P. Chaunu, *La civilisation de l'Europe des lumières* (Paris, 1971), p.144.

46. Martyn Lyons, "Regionalism and linguistic conformity in the French Revolution", in A. Forrest and P. Jones (eds), *Reshaping France: Town, Country and Region during the French Revolution* (Manchester, 1991), chapter 11.

47. P. McPhee, "A Case-study of Internal Colonisation: The Francisation of Northern Catalonia", *Review*, 3, 1980.

48. Adeline Daumard, *Les Bourgeois de Paris au XIXe siècle* (Paris: Flammarion, 1970), pp.20–2.

49. A. Cobban, *The Social Interpretation of the French Revolution* (Cambridge: 1964).
50. W. Scott, "The Urban Bourgeoisie in the French Revolution: Marseille, 1789–92", in Forrest and Jones, *Reshaping France*, chapter 5.
51. Françoise Ours, "Aux origines de l'industrie textile vizilloise: la manufacture des Périer de 1776 à 1825", and Bernard Bonnin, "Un bourgeois en quête de titres et de domaines seigneuriaux: Claude Périer dans les dernières annés de l'Ancien Régime", in M. Vovelle (ed.), *Bourgeoisies de Province et Révolution* (Grenoble: Presses Universitaires de Grenoble, 1987), pp.55–77.

Chapter 6.   Republic of Notables

1. Jean-Denis Bredin, *Sieyès, la clé de la Revolution francaise* (Paris: Le Fallois, 1988). pp.466–7.
2. Irene Collins, *Napoleon and his Parliaments, 1800–1815* (London: Edward Arnold, 1979), p.12.
3. Louis Bergeron, *Épisode napoléonien (aspects intérieurs), 1799–1815* (Paris: Seuil, 1972), p.78.
4. Bredin, *Sieyès*, pp.488–9.
5. Ibid., pp.476–7.
6. Georges Lefebvre, *Napoleon*, vol.1 (London: Routledge and Kegan Paul, 1966), p.77.
7. Collins, *Napoleon and his Parliaments, 1800–1815*, pp.19–22.
8. Cambacérès, *Lettres inédites à Napoléon, 1802–1814*, ed. Jean Tulard (Paris: Klincksieck, 1973), in 2 vols.
9. Bredin, *Sieyès*, p.480.
10. Lefebvre, *Napoleon*, vol.1, p.73.
11. Bredin, *Sieyès*, p.463.
12. Louis Fougère (ed.), *Le Conseil d'Etat: son histoire à travers les documents de l'époque, 1799–1974* (Paris: Centre national de la Recherche scientifique, 1974), pp.56, 74.
13. Cited in. André Latreille, *L'Eglise Catholique et la Révolution française*, 2 vols, (Paris, 1946–50), vol.2, chapter 1.
14. Edward A. Whitcomb, *Napoleon's Diplomatic Service* (Durham, North Carolina: Duke University Press, 1979), p.32.
15. Fougère, *Le Conseil d'État*, pp.55–6, 175–7.
16. Clive H. Church, *Revolution and Red Tape: The French Ministerial Bureaucracy, 1770–1850* (Oxford: Clarendon Press, 1981), p.273.

17. A. Aulard, "La Centralisation napoléonienne: les prefets", in his
     Etudes et Leçons, vol.7 (Paris, 1913), pp.132–3.
18. Maurice Agulhon *et al.*, *Les Maires en France du Consulat à nos jours*
     (Paris: Sorbonne, 1986), pp.38–41.
19. Jacques Godechot, *Les Institutions de la France sous la Révolution et
     l'Empire* (Paris, 1968), p.556.
20. Claude Langlois, "Le Plebiscite de l'an VIII, ou le coup d'état du
     18 Pluviôse an VIII", *AhRf*, 207, 1972, 43–65.
21. Langlois, op.cit., *AhRf*, 208, 1972, pp.233–5.
22. J.M. Sydenham, "The Crime of 3 Nivôse (24 December 1800)", in
     J.F. Bosher (ed.), *French Government and Society, 1500–1850: Essays
     in Memory of Alfred Cobban* (London: Athlone Press, 1973),
     pp.295–320.
23. Aulard, "Centralisation", op.cit., p.121.
24. P.-L. Roederer, *Mémoires sur la Révolution, le Consulat et l'Empire*,
     vol.3 (Paris, 1942), p.145.
25. Quoted in Bredin, *Sieyès*, p.486.

Chapter 7.   The Concordat

1. S. Bianchi, *La Révolution culturelle de l'an 2* (Paris: Aubier, 1982).
2. Michel Vovelle, *Religion et révolution: la déchristianisation de l'an II*
    (Paris: Hachette, 1976).
3. M.Vovelle, "Le tournant des mentalités en France 1750–1789 – la
    sensibilité pré-révolutionnaire", *Social History*, 5, 1977.
4. M.Vovelle, *Piété baroque et la déchristianisation en Provence au XVIIIe
    siècle* (Paris: Plon, 1973).
5. Jacques Houdaille, "Un indicateur de pratique religieuse: la
    célébration saisonnière des mariages avant, pendant et après la
    Révolution française (1740–1829)", *Population*, 33:2, 1978, 367–
    80.
6. Ralph Gibson, *A Social History of French Catholicism, 1789–1914*
    (London: Routledge, 1989), p.229.
7. O. Hufton, "The Reconstruction of a Church, 1796–1801", in G.
    Lewis and C. Lucas (eds), *Beyond the Terror: Essays in French
    Regional and Social History, 1794–1815*, (Cambridge: Cambridge
    University Press, 1983), pp.21–52.
8. Jean Godel, *La Reconstruction concordataire dans le diocèse de
    Grenoble après la Révolution (1802–1809)*, (Grenoble: CNRS, 1968),
    pp.246–80.

9. G. Cholvy and Y.-M. Hilaire, *Histoire religieuse de la France contemporaine*, 3 vols (Toulouse: Privat, 1985), vol.1, p.14.
10. Ibid., pp.17–18.
11. Ibid., p.23.
12. Claude Langlois, *Le Diocèse de Vannes au XIXe siècle, 1800–1830* (Paris: Klincksieck, 1974).
13. E.E.Y. Hales, *Napoleon and the Pope* (London: Eyre & Spottiswoode, 1962), pp.156–7.
14. E.E.Y. Hales, *Revolution and Papacy, 1769–1846* (London: Eyre & Spottiswoode, 1960), p.143.
15. R. Secher, *Le génocide franco-français: la Vendée – vengé* (Paris: PUF, 1986); J.-C. Martin, *La Vendée et la France* (Paris: Seuil, 1986); Hugh Gough, "Genocide and the Bicentenary: The French Revolution and the Revenge of the Vendée", *Historical Journal*, 30:4, 1987, 987.
16. Langlois, *Dioèse de Vannes*, p.102.
17. A. Latreille, *L'Eglise catholique et la Révolution française*, 2 vols (Paris, 1946–50), vol.2, chapter 1, part 3.
18. Hales, *Napoleon and the Pope*, p.70.
19. Latreille, *L'Eglise catholique et la Révolution française*, p.252–5.
20. Godel, *La Reconstruction concordataire*, p.139.
21. C. Langlois, "Portalis", *DN*, p.1365.
22. Gibson, *A Social History of French Catholism, 1789–1914*, pp.105–7.

Chapter 8.   Law Codes and Lycées

1. R.B. Holtman, *The Napoleonic Revolution* (Philadelphia: Lippincott, 1967), p.89.
2. Jean Imbert, "Code Civil", *DN*, 429.
3. Joseph Goy, "Civil Code", in F. Furet and M. Ozouf, *Critical Dictionary of the French Revolution* (Cambridge, Mass.: Harvard University Press, 1989).
4. R. Phillips, *Family Breakdown in late 18th Century France: divorces in Rouen, 1792–1803* (Oxford: Clarendon Press, 1980), p.4.
5. Ibid., pp.44–58; L. Hunt, "The Unstable Boundaries of the French Revolution", in M. Perrot (ed.), *History of Private Life*, Vol.4 (Cambridge, Mass.: Belknap, 1990), p.33.
6. R. Phillips, "Women's Emancipation: The Family and Social Change in Eighteenth Century France", *Journal of Social History*, 12, summer 1979, 553–67.

7. Yvonne Knibiehler, "Les Médecins et la 'nature féminine' au temps du Code civil", *AESC*, 31:4, 1976, 824–45.

8. J. Limpens, "Territorial Expansion of the Code", in B.Schwarz (ed.), *The Code Napoléon and the Common-Law World* (New York: New York University Press, 1956), pp.92–109.

9. Jean Carbonnier, "Le Code Civil", in Pierre Nora (ed.), *Les Lieux de Mémoire*, Vol.2-2 (Paris: Gallimard, 1986), p.297.

10. Ibid., p.309.

11. Martyn Lyons, *France under the Directory* (Cambridge: Cambridge University Press, 1975), chapter 6.

12. Quoted in J. Godechot, *Les Institutions de la France sous la Révolution et l'Empire* (Paris, 1968), p.637.

13. Daniel Milo, "Les Classiques scolaires", in Nora, *Les Lieux de Mémoire*, Vol.2-3, p.530.

14. Holtman, *Napoleonic Revolution*, p.148.

15. G. Clause, "Lycées", *DN*, p.1102.

16. Holtman, *Napoleonic Revolution*, p.160.

17. Clause, "Lycées", p.1103.

18. D. Julia, ed. *Atlas de la Révolution française, vol.2, L'Enseignement, 1760–1815* (Paris: Ecole des hautes Etudes en Sciences Sociales, 1987), p.35.

19. Nicole and Jean Dhombres, *Naissance d'un Pouvoir: sciences et savants en France (1793–1824)* (Paris: Payot, 1989). See also Maurice Crosland, *Gay-Lussac: Scientist and Bourgeois* (Cambridge: Cambridge University Press, 1978); the same author's *The Society of Arcueil: a view of French science at the time of Napoleon I* (London: Heinemann, 1967) and Dorinda Outram, *Georges Cuvier: Vocation, Science and Authority in Post-Revolutionary France* (Manchester: Manchester University Press, 1984).

Chapter 9. Dictatorship by Plebiscite

1. Frédéric Bluche, "Plébiscite", *DN*, pp.1338–9. Bluche excludes the vote of the armed forces from his calculations, to arrive at a swing of 118 per cent in Bonaparte's favour in 1802, a swing of 14 per cent against him in 1804, and a swing of 35 per cent against him in 1815.

2. Ibid.

3. Archives Nationales (AN), BII.11.

4. AN BII.46.

5. AN F^1.cIII. Haute-Garonne.

6. AN BII.515/516.
7. AN BII.722 and F¹c.III. Haute-Garonne.
8. AN BII.887a.
9. Collins, *Napoleon and his Parliaments, 1800–1815* (London: Edward Arnold, 1979), p.46.
10. J.-L. Halperin, "Tribunat", *DN*, p.1656.
11. Cited in J. Tulard, *Napoleon: The Myth of the Saviour,* (London: Metheun, 1985).
12. Marcel Le Clère, "Fouché", *DN*, pp.746–51.
13. E.A. Arnold, jr, *Fouché, Napoleon and the General Police* (Washington: University Press of America, 1979), pp.154–6.
14. Le Clère, "Fouché".
15. S. Kaplan, "Refléxions sur la police du monde de travail, 1700–1815", *Rh*, 261, 1979, 17–77.
16. R. Monnier, "Ouvriers", *DN*, pp.1284–5.
17. André Cabanis, *La Presse sous le Consulat et l'Empire* (Paris, 1975), p.9, n.1.
18. Alfred Fierro-Domenech, "Edition", *DN*, pp.641–3.
19. J. Tulard, "Censure", *DN*, p.395.
20. Cabanis, *La Presse*, p.66.
21. James Smith Allen, *In the Public Eye: A History of Reading in Modern France, 1800–1940* (Princeton, NJ: Princeton University Press, 1992), p.94.
22. AN F18.39, censor's reports of 6 Pluviôse An 13, 19 July and 11 December 1807.
23. AN F18.39, censor's report of 28 Vendémiaire An 13.
24. AN F18.10A, circular of 20 September 1810.
25. Cabanis, *La Presse*, pp.205–30.
26. Bibliothèque Nationale, Nouvelles acquisitions françaises (BN.naf) 10739, 8 April 1812.
27. BN.naf.5001, no.39.
28. BN.naf.5001, no.9.
29. BN.naf.5001, no.82.
30. Bernard Vouillot, "La Révolution et l'Empire: Une Nouvelle Réglementation", in H.-J. Martin and R. Chartier (eds), *Histoire de l'Edition française, vol.2* (Paris: Promodis, 1984), pp.526–35.
31. Napoléon, *Correspondance*, vol.13 (Paris, 1858–70), p.689, no.11287, 21 Nov. 1806.
32. Fierro-Domenech, "Edition".
33. Louis Bergeron, "Napoléon ou l'état post-révolutionnaire", in Colin Lucas (ed.), *The French Revolution and the Creation of Modern*

Political Culture: vol.2, The Political Culture of the French Revolution (Oxford: Pergamon Press, 1988), chapter 23.

Chapter 10.   Opposition: the Politics of Nostalgia

1. D.M.G. Sutherland, *France, 1789–1815: Revolution and Counter-revolution* (London: Fontana, 1985), p.390.
2. J. Tulard, *Napoleon: Myth of the Saviour* (London: Methuen, 1985), p.114.
3. Cited in Jacques Godechot, *The Counter-revolution: Doctrine and Action, 1789–1804*, trans. S. Attanasio (London: Routledge & Kegan Paul, 1972), p.364.
4. Sutherland, *France, 1789–1815*, pp.340–1.
5. Ibid., p.341.
6. Gwynne Lewis, *The Second Vendée: The Continuity of Counter-revolution in the Department of the Gard, 1789–1815* (Oxford: Clarendon Press, 1978), p.104.
7. Ibid., pp.167, 178.
8. Jean Vidalenc, "L'Opposition sous le Consulat et l'Empire", *AhRf*, 60, 1968, 472–88 (see p.480).
9. Sutherland, *France, 1789–1815*, pp.349–50.
10. Godechot, *Counter-revolution*, pp.367–8.
11. Henri Gaubert, *Conspirateurs au temps de Napoléon Premier* (Paris, 1962).
12. Godechot, *Counter-revolution*, pp.370–2.
13. Gaubert, *Conspirateurs*, pp.223–5.
14. Ibid., pp.289–343.
15. Sutherland, *France, 1789–1815*, p.398.
16. R.C. Cobb, "Note sur la répression contre le personnel sans-culotte de 1795 à 1801", *AhRf*, 134, 1954, p.28.
17. Raymonde Monnier, "De l'An III à l'An IX, les derniers sans-culottes", *AhRf*, 257, 1984, 386–406.
18. Marcel Reinhard, *Le Grand Carnot: vol.2, De Thermidor à l'Exil* (Paris: Hachette, 1952), chapter 10.
19. Huntley Dupré, *Two Brothers in the French Revolution: Robert and Thomas Lindet*, (Hamden: Archon, 1967).
20. Georges Bouchard, *Un Organisateur de la Victoire: Prieur de la Côte d'Or, membre du Comité du Salut Public* (Paris, 1946).
21. Leo Gershoy, *Bertrand Barère: A Reluctant Terrorist* (Princeton: Princeton University Press, 1962).

22. Raoul Girardet, "Les Trois Couleurs", in P. Nora (ed.), *Les Lieux de Mémoire*, vol.1, (Paris: Gallimard, 1986) p.14.
23. Bronislaw Baczko, "Le calendrier républicain, in Nora, *Les Lieux de Mémoire*, vol.1. pp.74–9.
24. Michel Vovelle, "La Marseillaise", in ibid., pp.102–5.
25. Simone Balayé, *Madame de Staël: lumières et liberté* (Paris: Klincksieck, 1979), chapter 3.
26. Ghislain de Diesbach, *Madame de Staël* (Paris: Perrin, 1983), p.200.
27. Balayé, *Madame de Staël*, p.118.
28. Diesbach, *Madame de Staël*, p.202.
29. Ibid., p.239.
30. Ibid., pp.207–8.

Chapter 11. The Empire in the Village

1. D.M.G. Sutherland, *France, 1789–1815: Revolution and Counter-revolution* (London: Fontana, 1985), pp.433–4.
2. P. McPhee, "Electoral and Direct Democracy in France, 1789–1851", *European History Quarterly*, 16, 1986, 77–96.
3. Patrice L.-R. Higonnet, *Pont-de-Montvert: Social Structure and Politics in a French Village, 1700–1914* (Cambridge, Mass.: Harvard University Press, 1971), pp.90–2.
4. Jean-Pierre Jessenne, *Pouvoir au Village et Révolution: Artois, 1760–1848* (Lille: Presse Universitaire de Lille, 1987).
5. Maurice Agulhon, *Histoire de la France rurale: vol.3, Apogée et crise de la civilisation paysanne, 1789–1914* (Paris: Seuil, 1976), pp.51–8.
6. Albert Soboul, "Survivances féodales dans la société rurale du 19e siècle", in his *Problèmes paysans de la Révolution (1789–1848)* (Paris: Maspéro, 1976), p.155.
7. Ibid., pp.156–7.
8. Bernard Ménager, *Les Napoléons du Peuple* (Paris: Aubier, 1988), chapters 1–2.
9. A. Chabert, *Essai sur les mouvements des revenus et de l'activité économique en France de 1798 à 1820* (Paris: Génin, 1949), 2 vols.
10. J. Tulard, *La Vie quotidienne des Français sous Napoléon* (Paris: Hachette, 1978), pp.30–1.
11. Quoted in J. Tulard, *Napoleon: Myth of the Saviour* (London: Methuen, 1985), p.188.
12. Agulhon, *France rurale*, vol.3, p.112.

13. Chabert, *Essai sur les mouvements des revenus.*
14. T.J.A. Le Goff and D.M.G. Sutherland, "The Revolution and the Rural Economy", in A. Forrest and P. Jones, *Reshaping France* (Manchester, 1991), chapter 4.
15. Ibid., pp.64–6.
16. Ibid., p.59 and Chabert, *Essai sur les mouvements des revenus.*
17. J.D. Post, *The Last Great Subsistence Crisis in the Western World* (Baltimore: Johns Hopkins University Press, 1977).
18. Peter Jones, *Politics and Rural Society: The Southern Massif Central, c.1750–1880* (Cambridge: Cambridge University Press, 1985), p.52.
19. Réné Pijassou, "La crise révolutionnaire", in A. Higounet-Nadal (ed.), *Histoire du Périgord* (Toulouse: Privat, 1983), pp.266–7.
20. G. Lefebvre, *Les paysans du Nord pendant la Révolution française* (Bari, 1959), pp.519–21.
21. Le Goff and Sutherland, "The Revolution and the Rural Economy" and P. Jones, *The Peasantry in the French Revolution* (Cambridge: Cambridge University Press, 1988), p.254.
22. P. McPhee, "The French Revolution, Peasants and Capitalism", *American Historical Review*, 94, 1989, 1265–80.
23. Peter Jones, "Common rights and Agrarian Individualism in the Southern Massif Central, 1750–1880", in G. Lewis and G. Lucas (eds), *Beyond the Terror: Essays in French Regional and Social History, 1794–1815* (Cambridge, 1983), chapter 5; and J.-J. Clère, "La vaine pâture au 19e siècle: un anachronisme?", *AhRf*, 247, 1982, 113–28.
24. G. Ikni, "Sur les biens communaux pendant la Révolution française", *AhRf*, 247, 1982, 92.
25. P. Jones, "Common rights", p.136.
26. Clère, "Vaine pâture", pp.123–4.
27. Françoise Fortunet, "Le Code Rural ou l'impossible codification", *AhRf*, 247, 1982, 110–1.
28. Ibid., pp.108–9.
29. Cited in Clère, "Vaine pâture", p.120.
30. M. Agulhon, *The Republic in the Village: The People of the Var from the French Revolution to the Second Republic* (Cambridge: Cambridge University Press, 1982).
31. P. Jones, *Politics and Rural Society*, pp.77–86.
32. As Sutherland reminds us, this was only a quarter of the proportion drafted in the First World War. See Sutherland, *France, 1789–1815*, p.378, and Alan Forrest, *Conscripts and*

Deserters: the army and French society during the Revolution and Empire (New York: Oxford University Press, 1989), pp.20–1.

33. Forrest, *Conscripts and Deserters*, p.45.
34. Ibid., p.71.
35. Ibid., p.170.
36. Ibid., p.134–5.
37. Ibid., p.227.
38. Sutherland, *France, 1789–1815*, p.377. This last figure may not take into account naval recruitment, which was substantial in Brittany.
39. Ibid., p.377.
40. Forrest, *Conscripts and Deserters*, p.44.
41. Ibid., p.48.
42. Sutherland, *France, 1789–1815*, p.379.
43. A. Perdiguier, *Mémoires d'un compagnon* (Paris: Maspéro, 1977), p.40.
44. Forrest, *Conscripts and Deserters*, p.59.
45. Colin Jones, "The Welfare of the French Foot-soldier", *History*, 65, 214, 1980, 212.
46. Sutherland, *France, 1789-1815*, p.381.
47. R.C. Cobb, *The Police and the People: French Popular Protest, 1789–1820* (Oxford: Oxford University Press, 1970), pp.105–6.
48. Jones, *Peasantry*, p.268.
49. Martin Nadaud, *Les Mémoires de Léonard, ancien garçon maçon* (Paris, no date), pp.44–6.

Chapter 12.   "Masses of Granite"

1. Louis Bergeron and Guy Chaussinand-Nogaret, *"Les Masses de Granit": cent mille notables du 1er Empire* (Paris: EHESS, 1979).
2. J. Tulard, *Napoleon: Myth of the Saviour* (London: Methuen, 1985), pp.248–53.
3. Cited in G. Chaussinand-Nogaret, L. Bergeron and R. Forster, "Les notables du 'Grand Empire' en 1810", *AESC*, 26:5, 1971, 1068.
4. Bergeron and Chaussinand-Nogaret, *"Masses de granit"*, p.14.
5. Ibid., p.43. These figures are based on information about 63 683 individuals.
6. Ibid., p.29. Of the *notables* who were old enough to be professionally active in 1789, 16.4 per cent were from the commercial classes.

7. D.M.G. Sutherland, *France, 1789–1815* (London: Fontana, 1985), pp.385–6.

8. Pierre Bouyoux, "Les 'six cents plus imposés' du département de la Haute-Garonne en l'an X", *AM*, 70, 1958, 318, 322 and 324.

9. Jean-Michel Lévy, "Les Notables de l'Ain sous le Consulat et l'Empire", *Rhmc*, 17, 1970, 726–40.

10. Roger Dufraisse, "Les Notables de la rive gauche du Rhin à l'époque napoléonienne", *Rhmc*, 17, 1970, 766–7.

11. A.Cobban, *The Social Interpretation of the French Revolution* (Cambridge: Cambridge University Press, 1964).

12. André Palluel-Guillard, "Les Notables des Alpes du Nord sous le premier Empire", *Rhmc*, 17, 1970, 756; Maurice Agulhon, "Les Notables du Var sous le Consulat", *Rhmc*, 17, 1970, 720–5.

13. Palluel-Guillard, "Les Notables des Alpes" pp.750–2.

14. Geoffrey Ellis, "Rhine and Loire: Napoleonic élites and social order", in G. Lewis and G. Lucas (eds), *Beyond the Terror: Essays in French Regional and Social History, 1794–1815* (Cambridge, 1983) pp.265–7.

15. F. Spannel, "Les Eléments de la fortune des grands notables marseillais au début du XIXe siècle", *Provence historique*, 7, 1957, 96–8.

16. Bouyoux, "Les 'six cents plus imposés'", p.319. Boyer-Fonfrède would have been eligible on his payment of the *patente* alone.

17. Cited in Palluel-Guillard, "Les Notables des Alpes du Nord" p.742.

18. Anne-Marie Boursier and Albert Soboul, "La Grande propriété foncière à l'époque napoléonienne", *AhRf*, 245, 1981, 406–11.

19. Bouyoux, "Les 'six cents plus imposés'", p.326.

20. Bergeron, *France under Napoleon* (Princeton: Princeton University Press, 1981), p.64.

21. Sutherland, *France, 1789–1815*, p.367.

22. Tulard, *DN*, "Maréchaux". Lannes died in action in 1809, as did Poniatowski in 1813. Bessières died in 1813, and Brune was assassinated in 1815.

23. Bergeron, *France under Napoleon*, p.57.

24. Ibid., p.58 and Bergeron, *L'Episode napoléonienne: aspects intérieurs* (Paris: Seuil, 1972), p.71. There is a discrepancy between French and English versions. Unfortunately, the English translator seems to have read "soixante-dix" as "soixante-deux".

25. Edward A. Whitcomb, "Napoleon's Prefects", *AmHistRev*, 79, 1974, 1091–103 for this section.

26. Ibid., p.1097.
27. Michel Bruguière, "Finance et noblesse: l'entrée des financiers dans la noblesse d'Empire", *Rhmc*, 17, 1970, 664–70.
28. Tulard, *Napoleon: Myth of the Saviour*, pp.248–53.
29. Cited in Bergeron, *L'Episode napoléonienne*, p.84.
30. J. Tulard, "Les composants d'une fortune: le cas de la noblesse d'Empire", *RH*, 513, 1975, 121–2.
31. Pierre Durye, "Les chevaliers dans la noblesse impériale", *Rhmc*, 17, 1970, 678.
32. Archives Nationales 311 AP.80–82, *Papiers Masséna*.
33. Tulard, "Les composants d'une fortune", pp.126–7; Monika Senkowska-Gluck, "Les Donataires de Napoléon", *Rhmc*, 17, 1970.
34. Napoleon, *Correspondance*, vol.32 (Paris, 1858–70), p.369.
35. Cited in *DN*, p.1584.
36. Tulard, "Les composants d'une fortune", p.132.
37. *DN*, p.204. In 1815, the Allies kept Berthier prisoner in Bamberg Castle in Bavaria, to prevent him from going back to Napoleon during the Hundred Days. He died there after falling or jumping in despair from a third-floor window.
38. Sutherland, *France, 1789–1815*, p.389.
39. Robert Forster, "The Survival of the Nobility during the French Revolution", *P&P*, 37, 1967, 75.
40. R. Forster, *The House of Saulx-Tavanes: Versailles and Burgundy, 1700–1830* (Baltimore: Johns Hopkins University Press, 1971), pp.193–6.
41. Forster, "Survival of the Nobility", p.82.
42. P. Jones, *The Peasantry in the French Revolution* (Cambridge: Cambridge University Press, 1988), p.49.

Chapter 13.   Art, Propaganda and the Cult of Personality

1. André Cabanis, *La Presse sous le Consulat et l'Empire* (Paris, 1975), pp.196–7.
2. Ibid., p.261.
3. Robert B. Holtman, *Napoleonic Propaganda* (Baton Rouge: Louisiana State University Press, 1950), p.46.
4. Cabanis, *La Presse*, p.224.
5. Holtman, *Napoleonic Propaganda*, "The Message".
6. Ibid., pp.8–9.
7. Ibid., p.22.

8. Ibid., p.197.
9. Cabanis, *La Presse*, pp.299–300.
10. Ibid., pp.314–16.
11. Holtman, *Napoleonic Propaganda*, p.33.
12. Ibid., p.95.
13. Ibid., p.143.
14. Ibid., p.211.
15. Ibid., p.205.
16. A. Cabanis, *La Presse*, pp.313–14
17. Holtman, *Napoleonic Propaganda*, p.236.
18. Jean Touchard, *La Gloire de Béranger*, 2 vols (Paris, 1968), pp.199–200.
19. Hugh Honour, *Neo-Classicism* (Harmondsworth: Penguin, 1968), pp.170–9.
20. Bruno Foucart, "L'Artiste dans la société de l'Empire: sa participation aux honneurs et dignités", *Rhmc*, 17, 1970, 709–19.
21. Warren Roberts, *Jacques-Louis David, Revolutionary Artist* (Chapel Hill: University of North Carolina Press, 1989), p.137; A.Brookner, *Jacques-Louis David*, (London: Chatto & Windus, 1980).
22. Luc de Nanteuil, *Jacques-Louis David* (London: Thames & Hudson, 1990), p.31.
23. Roberts, *Jacques-Louis David, Revolutionary Artist*, pp.112–16.
24. Walter Friedlaender, *David to Delacroix* (Cambridge, Mass.: Harvard University Press, 1952), pp.42–3.
25. Roberts, *Jacques-Louis David, Revolutionary Artist*, pp.126–7.
26. Ibid., p.144.
27. Ibid., pp.159–60.

Chapter 14. The Unsheathed Sword, 1

1. Harold C. Deutsch, *The Genesis of Napoleonic Imperialism* (Philadelphia, 1975), p.129.
2. Simon Schama, *Patriots and Liberators: Revolution in the Netherlands, 1780–1813* (New York: Knopf, 1977), p.8.
3. Geoffrey Best, *War and Society in Revolutionary Europe, 1770–1870* (London: Fontana, 1982).
4. G. Lefebvre, *Napoléon* (Paris: Presses Universitaires de France, 1965), p.311.
5. Hugh Ragsdale, "A Continental System in 1801: Paul I and Bonaparte", *JMH*, 42:1, 1970, 70–89.

6. J.M. Thompson, *Napoleon Bonaparte* (Oxford: Blackwell, 1988), pp.229–30.
7. J. Tulard, *Napoleon: Myth of the Saviour* (London: Methuen 1985), p.136.
8. Jacques Lovie and André Palluel-Guillard, *L'Episode napoléonien: aspects extérieurs 1799–1815* (Paris: Seuil, 1972), 48–56; Lefebvre, *Napoleon*, vol.1, pp.176, 186.
9. Deutsch, *Genesis of Napoleonic Imperialism*, p.174.
10. Ibid., pp.36–7.
11. Ibid., p.99.
12. W.M. Simon, *The Failure of the Prussian Reform Movement, 1807–19* (New York, 1971); G.S. Ford, *Stein and the era of Reform, 1807–15*; Gordon A. Craig, *The Politics of the Prussian Army, 1640–1945* (Oxford, 1955).
13. Lefebvre, *Napoleon* (French ed.), p.241.
14. In 1809, Lucien, fearing a worse fate at Napoleon's hands, tried to get away to the United States but was captured on the way by the British. He lived in England until 1814, when he returned to support Napoleon in the Hundred Days. He died in Italy in 1840. Owen Connelly (ed.), *Historical Dictionary of Napoleonic France, 1799–1815*, (London: Aldwych, 1985).

Chapter 15.   The Unsheathed Sword, 2

1. Harold C. Deutsch, *The Genesis of Napoleonic Imperialism* (Philadelphia, 1975).
2. François Crouzet, *L'Economie britannique et le blocus continental (1806–1813)*, 2 vols (Paris: PUF, 1958), pp.63–5.
3. Ibid., p.68.
4. Hugh Ragsdale, "A Continental System in 1801: Paul I and Bonaparte", *JMH*, 42:1, 1970, 70–89. p.83.
5. Crouzet, *Economie britannique*, p.386.
6. Ibid., p.534.
7. J. Lovie and A. Palluel-Guillard, *L'Episode napoléonien: aspects exterieurs, 1799–1815* (Paris: Seuil, 1972), pp.122–3.
8. H. Kissinger, *A World Restored* (London: Gollancz, 1973), chapter 3.
9. Michael Glover, *Legacy of Glory: The Bonaparte Kingdom of Spain, 1808–1813* (London: Leo Cooper, 1972), p.23.

10. Gwyn Williams, *Goya and the Impossible Revolution*, (London: Allen Lane), 1976.
11. G. Best, *War and Society in Revolutionary Europe, 1770–1870* (London: Fontana, 1982), p.102.
12. G. Lefebvre, *Napoléon* (Paris: Presses Universitaires de France, 1965) pp.339–40.
13. Lovie and Palluel-Guillard, *L'Episode napoléonien*, pp.124–5.
14. Best, *War and Society*, p.174.
15. Letter of 16 August 1808, in Glover, *Legacy of Glory*, p.52.
16. Gabriel H. Lovett, "The Spanish Guerrillas and Napoleon", *PCRE*, 1975, pp.80–90.
17. Don Alexander, "The Impact of Guerrilla Warfare in Spain on French combat strength", *PCRE*, 1975, pp.91–103.
18. Ibid., p.96.
19. Ibid., p.97.
20. Isser Woloch, *The French Veteran from the Revolution to the Restoration* (Chapel Hill: University of North Carolina Press, 1979), part 3, pp.196–203.
21. Ibid., pp.205–6.
22. Lefebvre, *Napoleon*, vol.2, pp.311–13; Owen Connelly, *Blundering to Glory: Napoleon's Military Campaigns* (Wilmington, Delaware, 1987), p.159.
23. Irene Collins, "Variations on the theme of Napoleon's Moscow campaign", *History*, 71, 1986, 39–53.
24. Lefebvre, *Napoleon*, vol.2, p.315.
25. Barry Hollingsworth, "The Napoleonic Invasion of Russia and Recent Soviet Historical Writing", *JMH*, 38:1, 1966, 38–52. Soviet history drew a deliberate parallel with Stalin's resistance to Hitler's invasion in 1941.
26. Lefebvre, *Napoleon*, vol.2, p.317.

Chapter 16.   The Napoleonic Revolution in Europe

1. Simon Schama, *Patriots and Liberators: Revolution in The Netherlands, 1780–1813* (New York: Knopf, 1977), p.361.
2. S. Woolf, *Napoleon's Integration of Europe* (London and New York: Routledge, 1991).
3. S. Woolf, "French Civilisation and Ethnicity in the Napoleonic Empire", *P&P*, 124, 1989, 106; S. Woolf, "The Construction of a

European World-View in the Revolutionary-Napoleonic Years", *P&P*, 137, 1992, 72–101.

4. Woolf, "French Civilisation and Ethnicity", p.113.

5. Michael Glover, *Legacy of Glory: The Bonaparte Kingdom of Spain, 1808–1813* (London: Leo Cooper, 1972), p.101.

6. S. Woolf, *A History of Italy, 1700–1860: The Social Constraints of Political Change* (London: Methuen, 1979), pp.192–4.

7. Wolfgang Schieder, "Sécularisations et Médiatisations dans les quatre départements de la rive gauche du Rhin, 1794–1814", *AhRf*, 286, 1991, 484, a condensation of the same author's *Säkularisation und Mediatisierung in den vier rheinischen Départements. Edition des standardisierten Datenmaterials der zu veräussernden Nationalgüter,* 4 vols (Boppard, 1991).

8. Schama, *Patriots and Liberators,* chapter 3.

9. John A. Davis, *Conflict and Control: Law and Order in Nineteenth-century Italy* (Atlantic Highlands, NJ: Humanities Press International, 1988).

10. Albert Soboul, "Problèmes sociaux des pays sous occupation française, 1799–1814", *PSDF,* pp.4–5; Pasquale Villani, "L'Abolition de la féodalité dans le Royaume de Naples", *AhRf,* 41, 1969, 229–38.

11. Y.-M. Bercé (ed.), *La Fin de l'Europe napoléonienne, 1814: la vacance du pouvoir* (Paris: Veyrier, 1990).

12. Soboul, "Problèmes sociaux", pp.4–5; H.A.L. Fisher, *Napoleonic Statesmanship: Germany* (Oxford: Clarendon Press, 1903), pp.203–5.

13. Woolf, *Napoleon's Integration,* p.119.

14. Boguslaw Lesnodorski, "Le Processus de l'abolition du régime féodal dans les territoires polonais aux 18e et 19e siècles", *AhRf,* 41, 1969, 300–1.

15. Angelo Massafra, "La Crise du baronnage napolitain à la fin du 18e siècle", *AhRf,* 41, 1969, 222.

16. Davis, *Conflict and Control,* p.46.

17. Fisher, *Napoleon Statesmanship,* pp.197–8.

18. Owen Connelly, *Napoleon's Satellite Kingdoms* (New York: Free Press, 1965), p.78.

19. Woolf, *History of Italy,* p.209.

20. A. Fugier, *Napoléon et l'Italie* (Paris: Janin, 1947).

21. Schieder, "Secularisations et Médiatisations", p.490.

22. Woolf, *Napoleon's Integration,* p.202.

23. R. Devleeshouwer, "Le cas de la Belgique", *Occupants–Occupés, 1792–1815, Colloque de Bruxelles, 1968* (Université Libre de Bruxelles, Institut de Sociologie, 1969) pp.58–9.
24. M. Müller, *Säkularisation und Grundbesitz. Zur Sozialgeschichte des Saar–Mosel–Raumes, 1794–1813* (Boppard, 1980), cited by Woolf, *Napoleon's Integration*, p.205.
25. C. Capra, "Les Collèges électoraux de la république italienne et du royaume d'Italie, *AhRf*, 230, 1977, 566–86.
26. Devleeshouwer, "Le cas de la Belgique", pp.23–4.
27. Fisher, *Napoleonic Statesmanship*, pp.210–11.
28. Connelly, *Napoleon's Satellite Kingdoms*, pp.92–95.
29. Y.-M. Bercé, "Société et police dans l'ombrie napoléonienne", *AhRf*, 220, 1975, 239–40.
30. Connelly, *Napoleon's Satellite Kingdoms*, p.88.
31. R. Dufraisse, "Les Départements réunis de la rive gauche du Rhin, 1797–1814", *PSDF*, pp.48–52.
32. Helmut Berding, "Le Royaume de Westphalie, Etat-modèle", *Francia*, 10, 1982, 345–58.
33. Georges Six, *Dictionnaire biographique des généraux et admiraux français de la Révolution et de l'Empire, 1792–1814* (Paris, 1934).
34. Woolf, *Napoleon's Integration*, p.105.
35. Connelly, *Napoleon's Satellite Kingdoms*, p.149; Schama, *Patriots and Liberators*, p.505.
36. H. Berding, *Napoleonische Herrschafts- und Gesellschaftspolitik in Königreich Westfalen 1807–1813* (1973), cited in Geoffrey Ellis, *The Napoleonic Empire* (Atlantic Highlands, NJ: Humanities Press International, 1991), pp.90–1.
37. Monika Senkowska-Gluck, "Les donataires de Napoléon", *Rhmc*, 17, 1970, 680–93.

Chapter 17. The Napoleonic Empire

1. Napoleon, *Correspondance* (Paris, 1858–70), vol.16, 31 octobre 1807.
2. S. Woolf, *Napoleon's Integration of Europe* (London and New York: Routledge, 1991), p.107.
3. O. Connelly, *Napoleon's Satellite Kingdoms* (New York: Free Press, 1965), p.29.
4. Woolf, *Napoleon's Integration*, p.38.

5. M. Dunan, "Napoléon et le système continental en 1810", *Revue d'histoire diplomatique*, 1946, 1.
6. A. Soboul, "Le Duché de Varsovie, 1807–1813: structures juridiques et réalités sociales", *PSDF*, p.174.
7. S. Schama, *Patriots and Liberators: Revolution in The Netherlands, 1780–1813* (New York: Knopf, 1977), pp.459–70.
8. Connelly, *Napoleon's Satellite Kingdoms*, pp.25–6; S. Woolf, *A History of Italy, 1700–1860* (London: Methuen, 1979), pp.191, 204.
9. M. Leonardi, "Democrates et masses populaires à Bologna (1796–1802)", *AhRf*, 230, 1977, 528–39.
10. J.-P. Filippini, "Les Livournais et l'occupation française sous le premier Empire", *AhRf*, 220, 1975, 203–30.
11. R. Dufraisse, "Départements réunis de la rive gauche du Rhin, 1797–1814", *PSDF*, pp.52–7.
12. R. Dufraisse, "Elites anciennes et élites nouvelles dans les pays de la rive gauche du Rhin à l'époque napoléonienne", *AhRf*, 248, 1982, 247.
13. Jeffry M. Diefendorf, *Businessmen and Politics in the Rhineland, 1789–1834* (Princeton, NJ: Princeton University Press, 1980), pp.156, 182–4.
14. Dufraisse, "Elites anciennes", pp.263–5.
15. P. Notario, *La Vendita dei beni nazionali in Piemonte nel periodo napoleonico, 1800–1814* (Milan: Banca Commerciale Italiana, 1980).
16. W. Schieder, "Sécularisations et Médiatisations dans les quatre départements de la rive gauche du Rhin, 1794–1814", *AhRf*, 286, 1991, p.492.
17. F. Mineccia, "La vendita dei beni nazionali in Toscana (1808–1814)", in I. Tognarini (ed.), *La Toscana nell'età rivoluzionaria* (Naples, 1985).
18. A. Soboul "Napoléon et l'Italie ou la Révolution manquée", *PSDF*, pp.81–2.
19. Dufraisse, "Elites anciennes", pp.254–7.
20. Woolf, *Napoleon's Integration*, p.110; J.A. Davis, *Conflict and Control: Law and Order in Nineteenth-Century Italy* (Atlantic Highlands: Humanities Press International, 1988), pp.25–6.
21. Michael Broers, "Revolution as Vendetta: Napoleonic Piedmont, 1801–1814", *Historical Journal*, 33, 1990, 787–809.
22. Y.-M. Bercé, "Société et police dans l'ombrie napoléonienne", *AhRf*, 220, 1975, p.245.
23. Woolf, *Napoleon's Integration*, pp.76–7.

24. L. Antonielli, "Le choix de prefets dans la république italienne et le royaume d'Italie", *AhRf*, 230, 1977, 548–65.
25. Woolf, *History of Italy*, p.201.
26. Schama, *Patriots and Liberators*, p.635.
27. H.A.L. Fisher, *Napoleonic Statesmanship: Germany* (Oxford: Claredon Press, 1903), p.221.
28. Devleeshouwer, *PSDF*, pp.25–8.
29. Bercé, "Société et police", p.239.
30. Pierre Vilar, "L'Espagne devant Napoléon, 1808–14", *PSDF*, p.239.
31. Quoted e.g. by Woolf, *History of Italy*, p.184.
32. V. Cuoco, *Saggio storico sulla Rivoluzione Napoletana del 1799* (2nd ed. 1806), ed.F. Nicolini (Bari, 1926), p.90.
33. Woolf, *History of Italy*, p.230.
34. Ibid., p.233.
35. J.A. Davis, *Conflict and Control: Law and Order in Nineteenth-Century Italy* (Atlantic Highlands: Humanities Press International, 1988), chapter 3.
36. Gaetano Cingari, *Brigantaggio, proprietari e contadini nel Sud (1799–1900)* (Reggio Calabria: Editori meridionali riuniti, 1976).
37. Ibid., p.46.
38. Ibid., pp.73–4.
39. Las Cases, *Mémorial de Ste Hélène* (Paris: Garnier, 1961), vol.2, p.546.
40. Filippini, "Les Livournais et l'occupation française sous le premier Empire".

Chapter 18. The Economy at War

1. Georges Dupeux, *French Society, 1789–1970* (London: Methuen, 1976), pp.20–22.
2. T.J.A. Le Goff and D.M.G. Sutherland, "Revolution and the Rural Economy", in A. Forrest and P. Jones (eds), *Reshaping France* (Manchester, 1991), pp.58–60.
3. D.M.G. Sutherland, *France, 1789–1815* (London: Fontana, 1985), p.383.
4. L. Bergeron, *L'Episode napoléonienne (aspects intérieurs), 1799–1815* (Paris: Seuil, 1972), p.182.
5. Sutherland, *France, 1789–1815*, pp.380–1.
6. Bergeron, *L'Episode napoléonienne*, p.185.

7. Paul Butel, "Crise et mutation de l'activité économique à Bordeaux sous le Consulat et l'Empire", *Rhmc,* 17, 1970, 540–4.
8. Paul Leuilliot, *L'Alsace au début du XIXe siècle: Essais d'histoire politique, économique et religieuse, 1815–30,* vol.2 (Paris: SEVPEN, 1959), p.120.
9. A. Cobban, *A Social Interpretation of the French Revolution* (Cambridge: Cambridge University Press, 1964).
10. Le Goff and Sutherland, "Revolution and the rural economy", pp.61–2; Peter McPhee, *A Social History of France, 1780–1880* (London: Routledge, 1992).
11. R. Forster, *The House of Saulx-Tavanes: Versailles and Burgundy, 1700–1830* (Baltimore: Johns Hopkins University Press, 1971), pp.188–9.
12. H. Causse, "Un industriel toulousain au temps de la Révolution et de l'Empire: François-Bernard Boyer-Fonfrède", *AM,* 69, 1957, 121–2.
13. P. Butel, "Revolution and the Urban Economy: Maritime Cities and Continental Cities", in A. Forrest and P. Jones (eds), *Reshaping France* (Manchester, 1991), p.39.
14. P. Butel, "Succès et déclin du commerce colonial français de la Révolution à la Restauration", *RE,* 40:6, 1989, 1080–4.
15. Butel, "Crise et Mutation", p.541–6.
16. Ibid., p.549.
17. F. Crouzet, "Les Origines du sous-développement économique du Sud-Ouest", *AM,* 71, 1959.
18. F. Crouzet, "Wars, Blockade and Economic Change in Europe, 1792–1815", *Journal of Economic History,* 24, 1964, 573; and "Les origines".
19. O. Connelly, *Napoleon's Satellite Kingdoms* (New York: Free Press, 1965), pp.145–6.
20. G. Ellis, *Napoleon's Continental Blockade: The Case of Alsace* (Oxford: Clarendon Press, 1981), p.116.
21. Ibid., pp.153–4.
22. S. Woolf, "L'Impact de l'occupation française sur l'économie italienne (1796–1815)", *RE,* 40:6, 1989, 1115; Max Tacel, "La Place de l'Italie dans l'économie impériale de 1806 à 1814", in M.Dunan (ed.), *Napoléon et l'Europe* (Paris: Brépols, 1960), pp.21–39.
23. L. Bergeron, "Problèmes économiques de la France napoléonienne", *Rhmc,* 17, 1970, 469.
24. Ibid., p.496.

25. Denis Woronoff, "L'Industrialisation de la France de 1789 à 1815: un essai de bilan", *RE*, 40:6, 1989, 1048.

26. Ibid., p.1049.

27. Causse, "Un industriel toulousain au temps de la Révolution et de l'Empire", p.123.

28. L. Bergeron, *Banquiers, négociants et manufacturiers parisiennes du Directoire à l'Empire* (Paris: Mouton, 1978), chapter 9.

29. Leuilliot, *L'Alsace au début du XIXe siècle*, vol.2, p.366.

30. Woronoff, "L'Industrialisation", p.1052.

31. J. Dhondt, "The Cotton Industry at Ghent during the French régime", in F. Crouzet, W.H. Chaloner and W.M. Stern (eds), *Essays in European Economic History, 1789–1914* (London: Edward Arnold, 1969), p.21.

32. Gay L. Gullickson, *Spinners and Weavers of Auffay: rural industry and the sexual division of labour in a French village, 1750–1850* (Cambridge: Cambridge University Press, 1986).

33. Bergeron, *Banquiers*, pp.212–14.

34. Leuilliot, *L'Alsace au début du XIXe siècle*, vol.2, p.491.

35. Ibid., pp.488–91.

36. Dhondt, "The Cotton Industry at Ghent", p.43.

37. Jean-Pierre Poussou, "Les activités urbaines en France pendant la Révolution", *RE*, 40:6, 1989, 1069.

38. Georges Clause, "L'Industrie lainière rémoise à l'époque napoléonienne", *Rhmc*, 17, 1970, 547–95.

39. R. Devleeshouwer, "Le Consulat et l'Empire: période de "take-off" pour l'économie belge?", *Rhmc*, 17, 1970, 613.

40. Ibid., p.615.

41. Dhondt, "The Cotton Industry at Ghent", pp.15–52.

42. Bergeron, *Banquiers*, pp.209–13.

43. Ibid., p.294.

44. Sutherland, *France 1789–1815*, p.415.

45. Crouzet, "Wars, Blockade, etc.", pp.586–7.

Chapter 19.   Débâcle and Resurrection, 1813–15

1. Jacqueline Chaumié, "Les Girondins et les Cent Jours", *AhRf*, 205, 1971, 355.

2. G. Lefebvre, *Napoléon* (London: Routledge & Kegan Paul, 1966), p.539.

3. Ibid., p.553 gives French losses as 60 000, in addition to 23 000 taken prisoner. The Allies lost 60 000 killed or wounded.

4. Yves-Marie Bercé (ed.), *La Fin de l'Europe napoléonienne, 1814: la vacance du pouvoir* (Paris: Veyrier, 1990).

5. J.M. Thompson, *Napoleon Bonaparte* (Oxford: Blackwell, 1988), p.359–60.

6. There may also have been another suicide attempt on 8 April – J. Tulard, *Napoléon: The Myth of the Saviour* (London: Methuen, 1985), p.325.

7. M. Reinhard, *Le Grand Carnot* vol.2 (Paris: Hachette, 1952), p.298.

8. M. Albert, *La Première Restauration dans la Haute-Garonne* (Paris, 1932).

9. Cited by Henry Houssaye, *1815 – Les Cent Jours* (Paris, 1901), chapter 19.

10. Martyn Lyons, *Révolution et Terreur à Toulouse* (Toulouse: Privat, 1980), p.258.

11. Reinhard, *Carnot*, p.314.

12. Chaumié, "Les Girondins et les Cents Jours", p.346.

13. H. Houssaye, *1815 – Waterloo* (London: Black, 1900), pp.42–8.

14. Reinhard, *Carnot*, p.321.

15. R.S. Alexander, *Bonapartism and the Revolutionary Tradition in France: The Fédérés of 1815* (Cambridge: Cambridge University Press, 1991), pp.13, 93.

16. G. Lewis, *The Second Vendée* (Oxford: Clarendon Press, 1978), p.178.

17. Alexander, *Bonapartism and the Revolutionary Tradition in France* pp.95–8.

18. Ibid., p.37.

19. Archives départementales de la Haute-Garonne, (ADHG) 4 M 34.

20. Lefebvre, *Napoléon*, pp.575–6.

21. Alexander, *Bonapartism and the Revolutionary Tradition in France*, p.205; K.D. Tonnesson, "Les fédérés de Paris pendant les Cent Jours", *AhRf*, no.249, 1982, p.395.

22. Paul Bastid, *Benjamin Constant et sa doctrine*, vol.1 (Paris: Armand Colin, 1966), p.280.

23. Frédéric Bluche, *Le Plébiscite des Cent Jours, avril-mai 1815* (Geneva: Droz, 1974), pp.4–8; S. Rials, "Acte Additionnel", *DN*, pp.32–4.

24. Bluche, *Plébiscite*, p.29.

25. Ibid., pp.37–8.

26. Ibid., pp.56, 61.

27. G. Bertier de Sauvigny, *The Bourbon Restoration*, trans. L. Case (Philadelphia: University of Pennsylvania Press, 1967).
28. ADHG 4 M 35.
29. Houssaye, *Waterloo*, pp.132–3.
30. Ibid., pp.435, 443–4.
31. Alexander, *Bonapartism and the Revolutionary Tradition in France*, pp.201, 207.
32. Chaumié, "Les Girondins et les Cents Jours", p.363.
33. S. Woolf, "L'Italie en 1814", in Y.-M. Bercé, *La Fin de l'europe napoléonienne, 1814: La vacance de pouvoir* (Paris: Veyrier, 1990), p.240.
34. Bernard Ménager, *Les Napoléon du Peuple* (Paris: Aubier, 1988), pp.20–3.
35. ADHG 4 M 35.

Chapter 20. Conclusion

1. Jean Tulard, *Le Mythe de Napoléon* (Paris: Armand Colin, 1971), pp.82–3.
2. Frédéric Bluche, *Le Bonapartisme* (Paris: PUF – Que sais-je?, 1981).
3. F. Furet, *La Révolution: de Turgot à Jules Ferry, 1770–1880* (Paris: Hachette, 1988), pp.227–36.
4. Ibid., pp.217–19.
5. F.L. Ford, "The Revolutionary and Napoleonic Era: How Much of a Watershed?", *AmHistRev*, 49:1, 1963.
6. Cited in F. Furet and M. Ozouf, "Napoleon Bonaparte", *Critical Dictionary of the French Revolution* (Cambridge, Mass.: Harvard University Press, 1989), p.279.
7. Ibid., p.282.
8. Bergeron, *L'Episode napoléonien (aspects intérieurs), 1799–1815* (Paris: Seuil, 1972).
9. Furet, *La Révolution*, pp.254–5.
10. Pierre Barbéris, "Napoléon: structures et signification d'un mythe littéraire", *Revue d'histoire littéraire de la France*, 70e année, 1970, 1034–5.
11. J. Tulard, "Le Retour des Cendres", in P. Nora (ed.), *Lieux de Mémoire – La Nation* (Paris: Gallimard, 1986), vol.2:iii, pp.97–8; Stanley Mellon, "The July Monarchy and the Napoleonic Myth", *Yale French Studies*, 26, 1960, 70–8.

Recommended Further Reading

This select bibliography offers suggestions for further reading designed for the English-reading student. Works in languages other than English, and more specialised works, are detailed in the notes. Titles with an asterisk* have a useful bibliography.

Most general histories of the period deal either with Napoleonic France itself or with the Empire but rarely span both. The best introduction to Napoleonic France is Louis Bergeron, *France under Napoleon*, trans. R.R. Palmer (Princeton, NJ: Princeton University Press, 1981), which conveniently summarises recent research on the *notables*. The best on Napoleonic Europe is the up-to-date synthesis by Stuart Woolf, *Napoleon's Integration of Europe** (London and New York: Routledge, 1991). These can be supplemented by the lively Jean Tulard, *Napoleon: The Myth of the Saviour**, trans. Teresa Waugh (London: Methuen, 1985), which conveys only a fraction of the author's immense erudition in the area.

Other serviceable general works are Irene Collins, *Napoleon, First Consul and Emperor* (London: Historical Association pamphlet, 1986), Robert B. Holtman, *The Napoleonic Revolution* (Philadelphia: Lippincott, 1967), and David H. Pinckney, *Napoleon, Historical Enigma* (St Louis, Missouri: Forum, 1978). A useful attempt at a broad overview was made by Franklin L. Ford, "The Revolutionary and Napoleonic Era: How Much of a Watershed?", *AmHistRev*, 49:1, 1963. More exciting, however, is François Crouzet, "Wars, Blockade and Economic Change in Europe, 1792–1815", *Journal of Economic History*, 24, 1964, by an author whose work on the Continental Blockade remains fundamental. Students should also enjoy the short but magisterial treatment by J. McManners, "Napoleon", in his *Lectures on European History, 1789–1914: Men, Machines and Freedom* (Oxford: Blackwell, 1966). Georges Lefebvre's *Napoleon* (London: Routledge & Kegan Paul, 1969), in 2 volumes, stands out for its broad French and European coverage, but it is a substantial opus.

General histories of France or of the Revolution which have something to contribute include Peter McPhee, *A Social History of France, 1780–1880** (London: Routledge, 1992), and at the other end of the political spectrum, François Furet and Mona Ozouf, *A Critical Diction-ary of the French Revolution*, trans. A. Goldhammer (Cambridge, Mass.: Harvard University Press, 1989). D.M.G. Sutherland, *France, 1789–1815: Revolution and Counter-revolution* (London: Fontana Modern History of France, 1985) is preferred to M.J. Sydenham, *The First French Republic, 1792–1804* (London: Batsford, 1974), which has a limited focus on political history. For the English student, two refer-ence works are suggested: Owen Connelly (ed.), *Historical Dictionary of Napoleonic France, 1799–1815* (London: Aldwych, 1985) and Barry Rothaus and S.F. Scott (eds), *Historical Dictionary of the French Revolu-tion*, 2 vols, (Westport, Conn: Greenwood, 1985).

For the history of the Directory, consult Martyn Lyons, *France under the Directory** (Cambridge: Cambridge University Press, 1975). Similar in its coverage is Denis Woronoff, *The Thermidorean Regime and the Directory* (Cambridge: Cambridge University Press, 1984), although this has more on economic history, which is the author's speciality. Two important articles, which have appeared since *France under the Directory*, are Lynn Hunt *et al.*, "The Failure of the Liberal Republic in France, 1795–1799: The Road to Brumaire", *JMH*, 51, 1979, 734–59 and Colin Lucas, "The First Directory and the Rule of Law", *FHS*, 10:2, 1977, 231–60.

The religious history of the period is still capable of provoking pas-sionate reactions. Among the most balanced are Adrien Dansette, *Reli-gious History of Modern France*, 2 vols, trans. J. Dingle (London: Nelson, 1961), and the excellent J. McManners, *The French Revolution and the Church* (London: SPCK, 1969). Ralph Gibson, *A Social History of French Catholicism, 1789–1914* (London: Routledge, 1987) makes no secret of the author's hostility to the Catholic Church. In addition, see two books by E.E.Y. Hales, *Revolution and Papacy, 1769–1846* (London: Eyre & Spottiswoode, 1960), and *Napoleon and the Pope* (London: Eyre & Spottiswoode, 1962).

On the history of divorce, the leading authority is Roderick Phillips, *Family Breakdown in late 18th Century France: Divorces in Rouen, 1792–1803* (Oxford: Clarendon Press, 1980). This monograph can be read in conjunction with the same author's article "Women's Emancipa-tion, the Family and Social Change in Eighteenth-Century France", *Journal of Social History*, 12, 1979, 553–67.

There are a number of monographs in English by administrative historians on Napoleonic élites and institutions, including Clive Church, *Revolution and Red Tape: The French Ministerial Bureaucracy, 1770–1850* (Oxford: Clarendon Press, 1981), and Irene Collins,

Napoleon and his Parliaments, 1800–1815 (London: Edward Arnold, 1979). More specialised are Edward A. Whitcomb, *Napoleon's Diplomatic Service* (Durham, N. Car.: Duke University Press, 1979) and Eric A. Arnold, Jr, *Fouché, Napoleon and the General Police* (Washington: University Press of America, 1979). On the collection of statistical information, see Jean-Claude Perrot and Stuart Woolf, *State and Statistics in France, 1789–1815* (London: Harwood Academic, 1984). Robert B. Holtman, *Napoleonic Propaganda* (Baton Rouge: Louisiana State University Press, 1950) considers the control and suppression of information. Two important groups are analysed in Jean-Paul Bertaud, "Napoleon's Officers", *P&P*, 112, 1986 and Edward A. Whitcomb, "Napoleon's Prefects", *AmHistRev*, 79, 1974, 1089–118.

Aspects of the economic history of this period are treated by Sutherland (see above), and some of the articles in Alan Forrest and Peter Jones (eds), *Reshaping France: Town, Country and Region during the French Revolution* (Manchester: Manchester University Press, 1991). For the countryside, consult the indispensable Peter Jones, *The Peasantry in the French Revolution* (Cambridge: Cambridge University Press, 1988); and the same author's monograph *Politics and Rural Society: The Southern Massif Central, c.1750–1880* (Cambridge: Cambridge University Press, 1985). Robert Forster, "The Survival of the Nobility during the French Revolution", *P&P*, 37, 1967, 71–86 should not be ignored.

The standard history of the Counter-revolution is Jacques Godechot, *The Counter-revolution: Doctrine and Action, 1789–1804*, trans. S. Attanasio (London: Routledge & Kegan Paul, 1972). Problems of disorder and resistance, however, have been discussed with considerably more verve by British historians influenced by Richard Cobb. Apart from R.C. Cobb himself, *The Police and the People: French Popular Protest, 1789–1820* (Oxford: Clarendon Press, 1970), see Gwynne Lewis, *The Second Vendée: The Continuity of Counter-revolution in the Department of the Gard, 1789–1815* (Oxford: Clarendon Press, 1978), and Alan Forrest, *Conscripts and Deserters: The Army and French Society during the Revolution and Empire* (New York: Oxford University Press, 1989). There is a similar emphasis on local conflicts in Michael Broers, "Revolution as Vendetta", *Historical Journal*, 33, 1990 – two articles on revolutionary and Napoleonic Piedmont.

On painting see Walter Friedlaender, *David to Delacroix* (Cambridge, Mass.: Harvard University Press, 1952). On David there is Anita Brookner, *Jacques-Louis David* (London: Chatto & Windus, 1980), but Warren Roberts, *Jacques-Louis David, Revolutionary Artist*

(Chapel Hill: University of North Carolina Press, 1989) is particularly recommended.

Addicts of the military history of the period will find plenty to think about in Geoffrey Best, *War and Society in Revolutionary Europe, 1770–1870* (London: Fontana, 1982), Owen Connelly, *Blundering to Glory: Napoleon's Military Campaigns* (Wilmington, Delaware: Scholarly Resources, 1987) and Isser Woloch, *The French Veteran from the Revolution to the Restoration* (Chapel Hill: University of North Carolina Press, 1979), part 3.

On the Empire, Stuart Woolf's *Napoleonic Integration of Europe* (recommended above) has eclipsed Owen Connelly, *Napoleon's Satellite Kingdoms* (New York: The Free Press, 1965), and the shorter Geoffrey Ellis, *The Napoleonic Empire** (Atlantic Highlands, NJ: Humanities Press International, 1991). Add Stuart Woolf, "French Civilisation and Ethnicity in the Napoleonic Empire", *P&P*, 124, 1989, 96–120. English students of the Rhineland are very well served by two fine monographs by Jeffry M. Diefendorf, *Businessmen and Politics in the Rhineland, 1789–1834* (Princeton NJ: Princeton University Press, 1980), and Geoffrey Ellis, *Napoleon's Continental Blockade: The Case of Alsace* (Oxford: Clarendon Press, 1981). On Spain, the quality varies, but try Michael Glover, *Legacy of Glory: The Bonaparte Kingdom of Spain, 1808–1813* (London: Leo Cooper, 1972), and Don W. Alexander, *Rod of Iron: French Counter-insurgency Policy in Aragon during the Peninsular War* (Wilmington, Delaware: Scholarly Resources, 1985). An interesting insight into Spanish problems is provided by Gwyn A. Williams, *Goya: The Impossible Revolution* (London: Allen Lane, 1976). On the Netherlands, the best (but most verbose) work is Simon Schama, *Patriots and Liberators: Revolution in the Netherlands, 1780–1813* (New York: Knopf, 1977). English students of Italy should consult Broers (above), but must rely on Stuart Woolf, *A History of Italy, 1700–1860: The Social Constraints of Political Change* (London: Methuen, 1979), for a synthesis of monographic research.

On the last years of the Napoleonic period, R.S. Alexander, *Bonapartism and Revolutionary Tradition in France: The Fédérés of 1815* (Cambridge: Cambridge University Press, 1991) is a valuable contribution.

Index